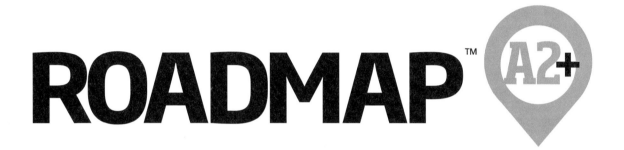

ROADMAP™ A2+

Teacher's Book
with digital resources and assessment package

Damian Williams, Hayley Crawford

CONTENTS

Introduction

Teacher's notes

Resource bank

Contents

3

Contents

5

7

Roadmap is a new, flexible eight-level general English course for adults. Recognising that every class is different and every learner is unique, *Roadmap* provides a dual track approach that allows all learners to develop confidence in speaking while taking a more tailored approach to skills development. It does this by providing smooth syllabus progression based on the *Global Scale of English*, by putting clear and achievable speaking goals at the heart of every lesson, and by providing in-depth skills development lessons for teachers to choose from at the back of the Students' Book. Multiple opportunities are provided for learners to practise outside the classroom in print, online and using the mobile app.

Map your own route through the course

It can be challenging for institutions and teachers to deal with the different needs, interests and abilities of each student, especially if they have a wide mix of learners in the same class. The unique dual track approach of *Roadmap* helps you solve this problem.

- The **fast track route** concentrates on developing learners' speaking skills as well as giving them the grammar, vocabulary and functional language they need to achieve their goals.

- The **extended route** gives learners valuable practice in reading, writing and listening as well as specific training and strategies for developing these skills.

Fast track route:
10 core units featuring grammar, vocabulary and pronunciation with each lesson leading to a final GSE-related speaking activity.

Extended route:
10 core units plus additional skills-based lessons (reading, writing and listening) linked to the content of each lesson.

This unique approach also allows you to adapt material to suit different course lengths. Whatever the number of hours in your course and whatever the interests of your learners, the flexible organisation of *Roadmap* makes it easy for you to choose the best route for your students' success.

Build your students' confidence

Learners need to know what they are aiming for and why. This is key to building confidence, increasing motivation and helping learners make rapid, tangible progress.

- *Global Scale of English* learning objectives provide students with clear goals for every lesson (the goals have been selected to be useful and relevant to students in real-life situations).

- Grammar and vocabulary has been specifically selected according to how useful it is in terms of helping learners reach specific goals.

- Carefully structured tasks with 'models' and opportunities to review performance, *Check and reflect* activities and regular progress tests allow learners to see how well they are doing and highlight the areas they need to improve.

Make the most of your skills as a teacher

Roadmap is designed to be as supportive and easy to use as possible, whatever your level of experience, with:

- 'pick-up-and-go' lessons with clear aims and outcomes that are guaranteed to work.

- clear instructions on how to exploit each lesson, including help with tricky language points, ideas for warmers, fillers, extension and homework activities.

- a huge range of additional support materials, including video, photocopiable games and activities, online and mobile app practice activities, are provided to add variety to your lessons.

The front of class presentation tool makes it easy to access all the support material in one place and enhances your performance as a teacher.

COURSE COMPONENTS

FOR LEARNERS

STUDENTS' BOOK WITH DIGITAL RESOURCES AND MOBILE APP

- Ten units with three main input lessons linked to three *Develop your skills* lessons at the back of the book.
- Each lesson includes grammar, vocabulary and pronunciation and leads to a final speaking task based on *Global Scale of English* learning objectives.
- Key language presented and cross-referenced to a *Grammar bank* at the back of the book.
- A *Vocabulary bank* extends some of the key lexical sets in each unit and focuses on important areas such as word-building and collocation.
- An *English in action* lesson in each unit covers key functional language.
- *Check and reflect* pages at the end of each unit show learners how their confidence and mastery of spoken language has improved.
- Light-hearted video clips and worksheets (available online) extend and consolidate key language covered in the unit.
- Extra grammar and vocabulary exercises, available on the mobile app (the *Pearson Practice English* app), consolidate language points covered in the Students' Book.
- *Develop your skills* lessons at the back of the book expose learners to different genres and give them strategies for developing skills.
- *Communication games* at the back of the book enable learners to practise key language in a fun, communicative way.
- Audio/video scripts and word lists available online.

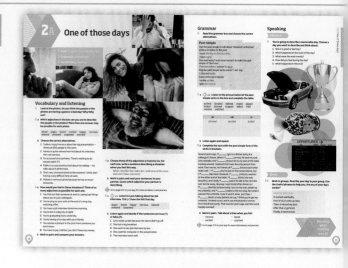

STUDENTS' BOOK WITH ONLINE PRACTICE, DIGITAL RESOURCES AND MOBILE APP

- Provides online practice for students, class management for teachers and a gradebook to review performance.
- Includes all the Students' Book material plus a digital version of the exercises and activities from the Workbook and Tests.
- Includes tools for managing and assigning self-study and practice activities to students, with automatic marking to save time.
- Includes a gradebook for reviewing performance of individual students and classes.

WORKBOOK WITH KEY AND ONLINE AUDIO

- Ten units provide additional practice of material covered in the Students' Book.
- Additional grammar, vocabulary and functional language practice activities.
- Additional reading, writing and listening practice activities.
- Answer key at the back of the book allows learners to check their answers.
- Audio available online.

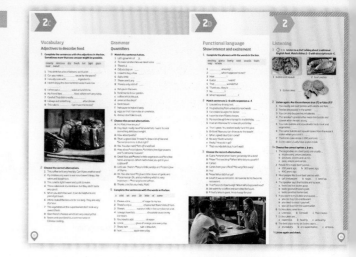

OR TEACHERS

TEACHER'S BOOK

The Teacher's Book features a host of support materials to help teachers get the most out of the course.

- Teacher's notes for every unit with warmers, fillers, alternative suggestions, advice on dealing with tricky language items, culture notes etc.
- Teaching tips on useful areas such as dealing with mixed abilities, teaching grammar, vocabulary and pronunciation.
- Grammar and vocabulary photocopiable worksheets for every unit, including accompanying teacher's notes and answer keys.
- Class audio scripts and answer keys.
- Photocopiable worksheets for each Students' Book unit accompanied by teaching notes and answer key.

TEACHER'S DIGITAL RESOURCES

Additional resources can be accessed on the *Pearson English Portal* using the access code in the Teacher's Book.

- Class audio.
- Video and video worksheets.
- Audio and video scripts.
- Word lists.
- Students' Book answer key.
- Assessment package with a range of tests including unit tests (grammar, vocabulary and functional language), achievement and mid and end of course tests (grammar, vocabulary, functional language and skills), with accompanying audio.
- Workbook audio.

VIDEO

- Ten videos – one for each unit – designed to consolidate key language and illustrate some of the quirkier aspects of real life.
- Each video features a roving reporter who goes out on location to visit interesting places, meet interesting people and/or try new experiences.
- Video clips are 2–3 minutes in length and are designed to entertain learners and provide a bit of light relief.
- Video worksheets (to exploit the language in the videos) are available online.

PRESENTATION TOOL

- Interactive version of the Students' Book with integrated audio and video is available on the *Pearson English Portal*.
- Planning mode (includes teacher's notes) and teaching mode.
- Easy navigation via book page and lesson flow.
- Answers to exercises at the touch of a button.
- Integrated audio.
- Integrated video, with timed-coded video scripts.
- A host of useful classroom tools.

The **Students' Book** has ten units featuring three double-page main lessons containing approximately 90 minutes of teaching material. Each lesson features grammar, vocabulary and pronunciation activities which lead up to a final speaking task. Each lesson links to a *Develop your skills* lesson and other material at the back of the book including a *Grammar bank*, *Vocabulary bank*, *Communication bank* and *Communication games*.

1. Clearly defined *Global Scale of English* objectives at the start of each lesson.
2. Different topics for each lesson to maintain interest and motivation.
3. Striking images provoke interest in the topic and provide a vehicle for teaching vocabulary.
4. Key vocabulary is presented in context and practised through personalised activities.
5. Short reading and/or listening texts featuring real-life information are used to present grammar and/or vocabulary.
6. Grammar rules are clearly highlighted and target language practised through form-based and communicative practice activities.
7. Additional practice is provided on the mobile app and in the *Grammar bank* at the back of the book.
8. Pronunciation is highlighted and practised in each lesson.
9. Carefully staged speaking tasks with 'models' and time to prepare build learners' confidence.
10. Relevant, meaningful tasks engage learners and prepare them for real life.
11. *English in action* pages focus on functional language.
12. Each unit ends with a *Check and reflect* page that consolidates key grammar and vocabulary.

ROADMAP™ A2+

STUDENTS' BOOK
with digital resources and mobile app

Lindsay Warwick and Damian Williams

P Pearson

Pearson Practice English App   GSE

2A One of those days

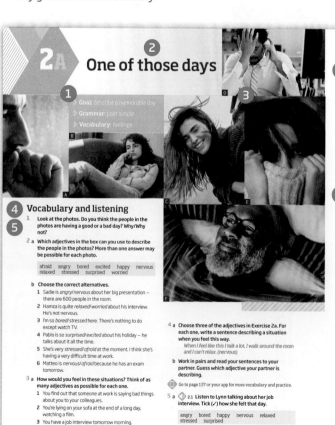

Vocabulary and listening

1 Look at the photos. Do you think the people in the photos are having a good or a bad day? Why/Why not?

2 a Which adjectives in the box can you use to describe the people in the photos? More than one answer may be possible for each photo.

afraid   angry   bored   excited   happy   nervous
relaxed   stressed   surprised   worried

b Choose the correct alternatives.
1 Sadie is *angry/nervous* about her big presentation – there are 600 people in the room.
2 Hamza is quite *relaxed/worried* about his interview. He's not nervous.
3 I'm so *bored/stressed* here. There's nothing to do except watch TV.
4 Pablo is so *surprised/excited* about his holiday – he talks about it all the time.
5 She's very *stressed/afraid* at the moment. I think she's having a very difficult time at work.
6 Matteo is *nervous/afraid* because he has an exam tomorrow.

3 a How would you feel in these situations? Think of as many adjectives as possible for each one.
1 You find out that someone at work is saying bad things about you to your colleagues.
2 You're lying on your sofa at the end of a long day, watching a film.
3 You have a job interview tomorrow morning.
4 You're lost in a big city at night.
5 You're graduating from university.
6 You're having a fun day with your friends.
7 You receive a present in the post from someone you don't know.
8 You have to pay a bill but you don't have any money.
b Work in pairs and compare your answers.

4 a Choose three of the adjectives in Exercise 2a. For each one, write a sentence describing a situation when you feel this way.
When I feel like this I talk a lot, I walk around the room and I can't relax. (nervous)

b Work in pairs and read your sentences to your partner. Guess which adjective your partner is describing.
Go to page 137 or your app for more vocabulary and practice.

5 a 2.1 Listen to Lynn talking about her job interview. Tick (✓) how she felt that day.

angry   bored   happy   nervous   relaxed
stressed   surprised

b Listen again and decide if the sentences are true (T) or false (F).
1 Lynn woke up late because her alarm didn't go off.
2 She had a big breakfast.
3 She went to her job interview by bus.
4 She used her computer in the presentation.
5 The interview went well.

Grammar

6 Read the grammar box and choose the correct alternatives.

Past simple
Use the past simple to talk about [1] *finished/unfinished* actions or states in the past.
I took the bus to the interview.
I was angry.
Use was/wasn't and were/weren't to make the past simple of [2] *be/have*.
The interviewers weren't happy.
Regular past simple verbs end in [3] *-ed/-ing*.
It started badly.
Some verbs are irregular.
I woke up late.
I got into my car.

7 a 2.2 Listen to the pronunciation of the past simple verbs in the box and complete the table.

arrived   decided   deleted   ended   played
looked   showed   stopped   talked   tried
wanted   watched

/d/	/ɪd/	/t/
showed	decided	looked

b Listen again and repeat.

8 a Complete the text with the past simple form of the verbs in brackets.

Several years ago, I [1]_____ (go) to a dinner party at a colleague's house. When I [2]_____ (arrive), he took my coat and umbrella, and [3]_____ (show) me to my seat at the table. Looking around, I realised that I was the only person from work. Even worse, his friends all [4]_____ (know) each other really well – I [5]_____ (try) to join in the conversations, but it [6]_____ (be) hard. However, I [7]_____ (notice) a woman at the other end of the table. I [8]_____ (think) she was beautiful, and I really [9]_____ (want) to talk to her, but she was too far away. Anyway, I was bored after dinner so I [10]_____ (decide) to leave early. I put on my coat, picked up my umbrella, and [11]_____ (walk) to the bus stop. But when I opened the umbrella, I saw it wasn't mine. Just then, I [12]_____ (hear) a voice behind me say, 'I think you've got my umbrella.' I looked round, and it was the beautiful woman from the dinner party. That was ten years ago, and now we're happily married!

b Work in pairs. Talk about a time when you felt:
• nervous   • bored
• excited   • surprised

7 Go to page 118 or your app for more information and practice.

Speaking

PREPARE

9 You're going to describe a memorable day. Choose a day you want to describe and think about:
1 Was it a good or bad day?
2 What happened at the start of the day?
3 What were the main events?
4 How did you feel during the day?
5 What happened in the end?

DEPARTURES ✈

LOS ANGELES
CHICAGO
PHILADELPHIA
NEW YORK
DALLAS
MIAMI
WASHINGTON
LAS VEGAS
ATLANTA
TORONTO

SPEAK

10 Work in groups. Describe your day to your group. Use the Useful phrases to help you. Are any of your days similar?

Useful phrases
It started well/badly.
First of all, (I woke up late).
Then, (I missed my bus).
After that, (I got lost).
Finally, (I went home).

Develop your reading
page 89

2B You're never too old

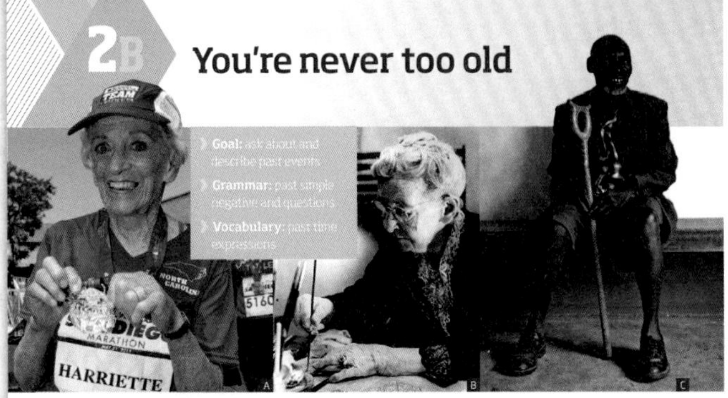

Goal: ask about and describe past events
Grammar: past simple negative and questions
Vocabulary: past time expressions

YOU DON'T HAVE TO BE YOUNG TO DO AMAZING THINGS

This week we're looking at three people who did something amazing later in their lives. Who were they? What did they do? Why did they do it?

1 Kimani Maruge
Kimani Maruge was born in Kenya. When he was a child, people in his country had to pay to go to school, so he didn't learn to read and write. Then, in 2003, primary schools became free so he decided to get an education. He started school for the first time at 84 years old. Learning wasn't easy for him but he worked hard. This experience completely changed his life. In fact, in 2005, he travelled to New York to talk to people at the United Nations about free education.

2 Harriette Thompson
Harriette Thompson was born in 1923 in the US. She worked as a piano player for most of her life. On 23 May 1999, one of Harriette's friends decided to walk the San Diego marathon for charity. Harriette joined her but she didn't walk – she ran. She was 76 years old. She ran the marathon every year between 1999 and 2015, except for one year when she was very ill. When she was 94 years old, she became the oldest woman to complete a marathon. It took her 7 hours, 24 minutes and 36 seconds and she collected more than $100,000 for charity.

3 Laila Denmark
Laila Denmark was born in 1898 in Atlanta, USA. She wanted to become a doctor so she could help children. Studying medicine wasn't usual for women at the time. In fact, she was the only woman in a class of 52 students. Most people stop working when they're about 65, but Dr Denmark didn't retire until she was 103 years old! She lived for 11 more years.

Reading and vocabulary

1 **Look at the photos. What amazing thing do you think you each person did?**

2 a **Read the article. Match descriptions 1–3 to photos A–C and answer the questions in the introduction.**

b **Read the article again and answer the questions.**
1 When did Kimani Maruge start school?
2 When did he travel to the US?
3 When did Harriette first run a marathon?
4 When did she become the oldest woman to run a marathon?
5 When did Laila Denmark retire?
6 How old was she when she died?

c **Work in pairs. Who do you think did the most amazing thing? Why?**

3 a **Put the time expressions in order from the most recent (1) to the oldest (6).**

in 2018 last month *1* on 23 May 2017
six weeks ago until 2015 when I was five

b **Complete the expressions with the words in the box.**

ago in last on until when

1 ______ I was a child
2 ______ week
3 A few years ______
4 ______ my 10th birthday
5 ______ last year
6 ______ 2015

c **Write six sentences using each expression.**
When I was a child, I loved playing outside.

d **Work in pairs. Tell each other your sentences. Give more information.**
When I was a child, I loved playing outside. I always played football in the park with my brother.

Go to your app for more practice.

Grammar

4 **Read the grammar box and choose the correct alternatives.**

Past simple negative and questions

Use [1]*didn't/doesn't* + infinitive to make past simple negative sentences.
*She **didn't walk** – she ran.*
*Dr Denmark **didn't retire** until 2001.*
Use [2]*isn't and aren't/wasn't and weren't* with the verb *be*.
*Schools **weren't** free.*
*Learning **wasn't** easy for him.*
Use [3]*do/did* + infinitive to make past simple questions.
*What **did** they do?*
*Why **did** they do it?*
Use [4]*did/was and were* in past simple questions with *be*.
*Who **were** they?*

5 a 2.3 **Listen to the conversations. Notice the pronunciation of *did/didn't* and *was/wasn't*.**
1 **A:** Did you learn to sing at school?
B: Yes, I did.
2 **A:** Did she finish the marathon?
B: No, she didn't.
3 **A:** How old were you?
B: I wasn't very old, actually.
4 **A:** Was he from Italy?
B: No, he wasn't?

b **Work in pairs. Listen again and repeat.**

6 a **Use the prompts to make questions with *did, was* or *were*.**
1 How / you / learn to play the piano?
How did you learn to play the piano?
2 it / difficult to get into your university?
3 When / you / get your driving licence?
4 you / happy with your exam results?
5 you / enjoy water skiing?
6 he / win the race?

b **Complete each answer with *didn't, wasn't* or *weren't*.**
a When I was 35. I ______ have lessons until I was in my 30s.
b It was really hard. Maths ______ an easy exam.
c I taught myself. I ______ have a teacher.
d No, we ______.
e I loved it. It ______ scary at all.
f No, he ______. He came second.

c **Work in pairs. Take it in turns to ask a question in Exercise 6a and answer with a response from 6b.**

Go to page 118 or your app for more information and practice.

Speaking

PREPARE

7 a 2.4 **You're going to talk about something special you did in the past. First, listen to Dan and Megan. What did Megan do?**

b **Write three questions Dan could ask Megan to find out more information.**

c 2.5 **Listen to the rest of their conversation. Did Dan ask any of your questions? What other things did you learn about Megan?**

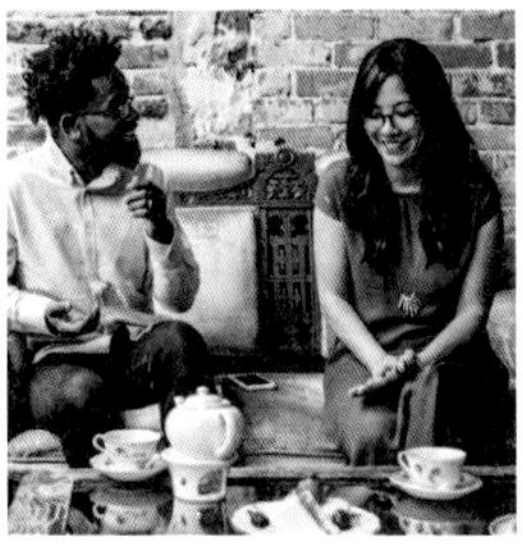

8 **Think of something special that you did in the past, for example: an event, learning something new or doing something for the first time. Answer the questions below.**
- What did you do?
- When did you do it?
- Where did you do it?
- Who did you do it with?
- Why did you do it?

SPEAK

9 a **Work in pairs. Tell each other about what you did. Ask each other questions to find out as much information as possible.**

b **Work in different pairs. Tell each other what you learnt about your first partner.**

Develop your writing page 90

2D 11 English in action

Goal: show interest and excitement

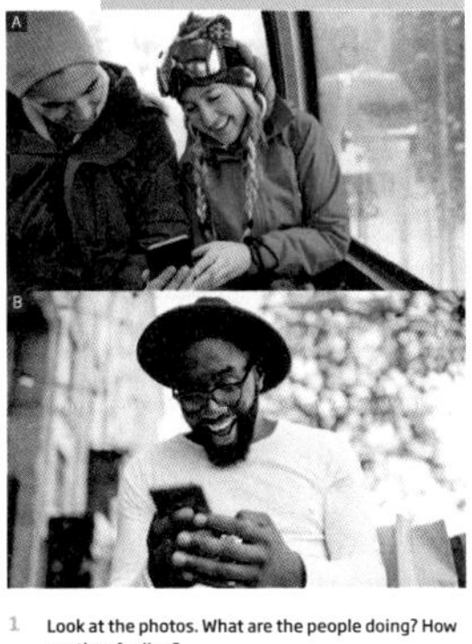

1 **Look at the photos. What are the people doing? How are they feeling?**

2 a 2.14 **Listen to four conversations and answer the questions.**
1 Why is Ali happy?
2 How did Marco help Fran?
3 What time is Ricky's party?
4 What did Simone win?

b **Choose the correct alternatives to complete the extracts from the conversations.**
1 80 percent? *That's/What's* brilliant!
2 *It's/They're* lovely. Thanks!
3 That *looks/sounds* great!
4 I love your curries. They're *really/so* good.
5 No way! That's *amazing!/great!*

c **Listen to the conversations again and check your answers.**

3 a 2.15 **Listen to the sentences. Does speaker 1 or speaker 2 show interest/excitement in each one?**
1 That sounds fantastic!
2 Amazing!
3 How exciting!
4 What a great idea!
5 That sounds really interesting!

b 2.16 **Listen to the speakers showing interest/ excitement again and repeat.**

4 a **Complete the conversations with an appropriate response. Use the Useful phrases to help you. More than one answer might be possible.**
1 **A:** I'm going to run a marathon next month.
B: Really? That ______ exciting! And difficult!
2 **A:** We were in Mexico this time last week.
B: ______! ______ you have a good time?
3 **A:** I've just got my dream job!
B: Really? That's ______!
4 **A:** I'm making your favourite pasta for dinner.
B: ______!
5 **A:** We went to that new Italian restaurant last night.
B: Really? What ______ you think of it?
A: It was ______!

Useful phrases

Creating interest
Guess what (happened to me)!?
Guess what I did/where I went?

Responding to information
Great!/Brilliant!/Fantastic!/Amazing!
It's/They're (delicious/lovely).
That's (amazing/great).
How (exciting/amazing/fantastic)!
What a (good idea).
That sounds (lovely/wonderful)!
No way!

Asking follow-up questions
What happened (exciting/next/after that)?
How did that/it go?
Who did you go with?

b **Work in pairs. Practise the conversations with the appropriate intonation.**

Speaking

PREPARE

5 a **Work in pairs. You're going to share some exciting news. It can be real or imagined. Student A go to page 151 and Student B go to page 152.**

SPEAK

b **Share your news with each other. Show interest and excitement when appropriate. Use the Useful phrases to help you.**

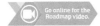

Go online for the Roadmap video.

12 Check and reflect

1 a **Complete the sentences with the correct form of the verbs in the box.**

be get up go have meet play take watch

1 I ______ a really good film last month.
2 My family and I ______ on holiday last summer.
3 I ______ a great meal last night.
4 My sister ______ a train to Moscow two weeks ago.
5 I ______ some video games last night.
6 My friend and I ______ at a coffee shop last week.
7 I ______ late yesterday, after 10am.
8 I ______ bored yesterday.

b **Work in pairs. Which sentences are true for you? Give more information about them.**

2 a **Complete each sentence with an adjective of feeling. The first and last letter of each word are given.**
1 I've got so much work to do. I'm really s______d.
2 Our holiday starts tomorrow. I'm so e______d!
3 I'm a______d of spiders. I hate them.
4 Jon never gets stressed. He's always r______d.
5 When Sam dropped Abi's phone, she got really a______y with him.
6 I've got my driving test tomorrow and I'm really n______s.
7 Billy just won a competition. He's really h______y.
8 Everyone was s______d when they heard the news.

b **Work in pairs. Choose five of the adjectives and talk about when you last felt like that.**
I was angry last week when I lost my keys.

3 a **Make each sentence negative.**
1 We went to the gym last night.
2 Sara was happy yesterday.
3 I went to bed late last night.
4 They were very busy last week.
5 We played cards yesterday.
6 Jimmy lived in San Diego when he was a child.

b **Work in pairs. Tell each other three things you wanted to do yesterday but didn't do.**
I wanted to go to the gym but I didn't have time.

4 a **Put the words in the correct order to make questions.**
1 last night / you / did / do / what / ?
2 you / who / chat to / yesterday / did / ?
3 were / last weekend / you / where / ?
4 did / go / what time / last night / to bed / you / ?
5 have for dinner / what / yesterday / you / did / ?
6 was / your / what colour / first car / ?
7 TV / last / you / did / night / watch / ?
8 this English course / decide / why / you / did / do / to / ?

b **Work in pairs. Take turns to ask and answer the questions.**

5 a **Match the sentence halves.**
1 I didn't learn to swim until I was
2 Cara was born on
3 We first met each other last
4 Liam started a new job a few weeks
5 I moved to Rome in
6 I didn't study English when

a year.
b 17 April 1999.
c ten years old.
d I was at school.
e ago.
f 2017.

b **Work in pairs. Tell each other some things you did in the past using some past time expressions.**
I went to France last week.

6 a **Choose the correct alternatives.**

This is a meal that I cook for friends. It's simple but delicious and they love it!

I make pasta with a tomato sauce. I cook [1]*some/a few* spaghetti and then I fry half [2]*an/some* onion in [3]*a little/a few* oil. Then I add [4]*a few/any* herbs and [5]*a few/a little* garlic but not too much. Finally, I mix the spaghetti and sauce together. I then put [6]*a/a lot of* parmesan cheese on top because I love it so much. There isn't [7]*any/a little* meat in this dish because I'm vegetarian but you can put [8]*an/some* in if you like.

b **Work in pairs. Describe your favourite meal. What is it? What's in it?**

7 a **Put the letters in italics in the correct order to make adjectives.**
1 This orange juice is really *etswe*.
2 This sandwich doesn't taste of anything. It's very *ialpn*.
3 I love this chocolate cake. It's *coleusidi*.
4 Let's eat something *thigl* like a salad.
5 Aargh! This lemon juice is really *orus*!
6 Is this milk *shref* or old?
7 I can't eat this cake. It's too *meaycr*.

b **Work in pairs. Think of other food that you can describe with each adjective in Exercise 7a.**

c **Tell each other three foods you think are delicious and three foods you think are plain. Do you agree?**

Reflect

How confident do you feel about the statements below? Write 1–5 (1 = not very confident, 5 = very confident).
- I can describe a memorable day.
- I can ask about and describe past events.
- I can describe a special dish.
- I can show interest and excitement.

Want more practice? Go to your Workbook or app.

STUDENTS' BOOK

The **Students' Book** also features *Develop your skills* lessons at the back of the book. These lessons are based on GSE learning objectives and are thematically linked to the main lessons. They focus on developing specific strategies for improving reading, writing and listening and expose learners to a wide variety of different text types/genres. The *Develop your skills* lessons can either be done in class following the main lessons they are linked to, or they can be used for homework.

1. *Develop your reading* lessons provide practice of specific genres such as stories, articles, reviews, factual texts, reports, social media and blog posts.
2. *Develop your listening* lessons provide practice in different types of listening such as short talks and monologues, conversations, radio interviews and discussions.
3. *Develop your writing* lessons provide practice of specific genres such as stories, formal and informal emails, blog posts, descriptions, invitations and reviews.
4. Each *Develop your skills* lesson has a clearly defined genre-related goal and a focus which teaches a sub-skill related to the genre.
5. Special *Focus boxes* highlight reading, listening and writing sub-skills such as identifying the main ideas in a text, guessing the meaning of words from context, identifying positive and negative attitudes, organising ideas, using paragraphs, explaining reasons and results, using time expressions and linkers etc.
6. Practice exercises are provided to ensure learners can recognise and use the sub-skills in focus.
7. Follow-up questions round-up the lesson and provide opportunities for further discussion.

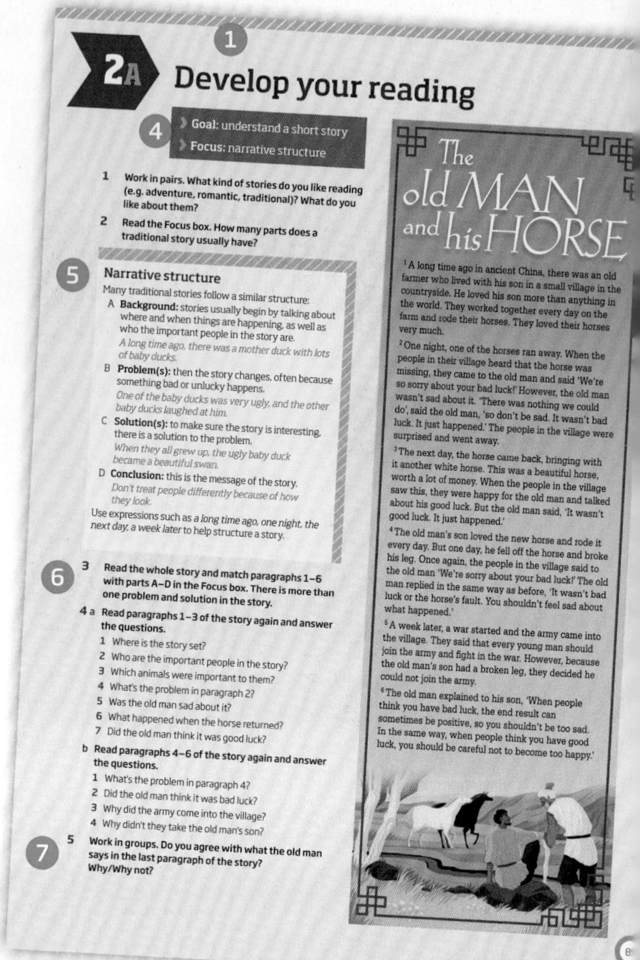

1

2A Develop your reading

4 Goal: understand a short story
Focus: narrative structure

1 Work in pairs. What kind of stories do you like reading (e.g. adventure, romantic, traditional)? What do you like about them?

2 Read the Focus box. How many parts does a traditional story usually have?

5 **Narrative structure**
Many traditional stories follow a similar structure:
A **Background:** stories usually begin by talking about where and when things are happening, as well as who the important people in the story are.
A long time ago, there was a mother duck with lots of baby ducks.
B **Problem(s):** then the story changes, often because something bad or unlucky happens.
One of the baby ducks was very ugly, and the other baby ducks laughed at him.
C **Solution(s):** to make sure the story is interesting, there is a solution to the problem.
When they all grew up, the ugly baby duck became a beautiful swan.
D **Conclusion:** this is the message of the story.
Don't treat people differently because of how they look.
Use expressions such as *a long time ago, one night, the next day, a week later* to help structure a story.

6 3 Read the whole story and match paragraphs 1–6 with parts A–D in the Focus box. There is more than one problem and solution in the story.

4 a Read paragraphs 1–3 of the story again and answer the questions.
1 Where is the story set?
2 Who are the important people in the story?
3 Which animals were important to them?
4 What's the problem in paragraph 2?
5 Was the old man sad about it?
6 What happened when the horse returned?
7 Did the old man think it was good luck?

b Read paragraphs 4–6 of the story again and answer the questions.
1 What's the problem in paragraph 4?
2 Did the old man think it was bad luck?
3 Why did the army come into the village?
4 Why didn't they take the old man's son?

7 5 Work in groups. Do you agree with what the old man says in the last paragraph of the story? Why/Why not?

The old MAN and his HORSE

[1] A long time ago in ancient China, there was an old farmer who lived with his son in a small village in the countryside. He loved his son more than anything in the world. They worked together every day on the farm and rode their horses. They loved their horses very much.

[2] One night, one of the horses ran away. When the people in their village heard that the horse was missing, they came to the old man and said 'We're so sorry about your bad luck!' However, the old man wasn't sad about it. 'There was nothing we could do', said the old man, 'so don't be sad. It wasn't bad luck. It just happened.' The people in the village were surprised and went away.

[3] The next day, the horse came back, bringing with it another white horse. This was a beautiful horse, worth a lot of money. When the people in the village saw this, they were happy for the old man and talked about his good luck. But the old man said, 'It wasn't good luck. It just happened.'

[4] The old man's son loved the new horse and rode it every day. But one day, he fell off the horse and broke his leg. Once again, the people in the village said to the old man 'We're sorry about your bad luck!' The old man replied in the same way as before, 'It wasn't bad luck or the horse's fault. You shouldn't feel sad about what happened.'

[5] A week later, a war started and the army came into the village. They said that every young man should join the army and fight in the war. However, because the old man's son had a broken leg, they decided he could not join the army.

[6] The old man explained to his son, 'When people think you have bad luck, the end result can sometimes be positive, so you shouldn't be too sad. In the same way, when people think you have good luck, you should be careful not to become too happy.'

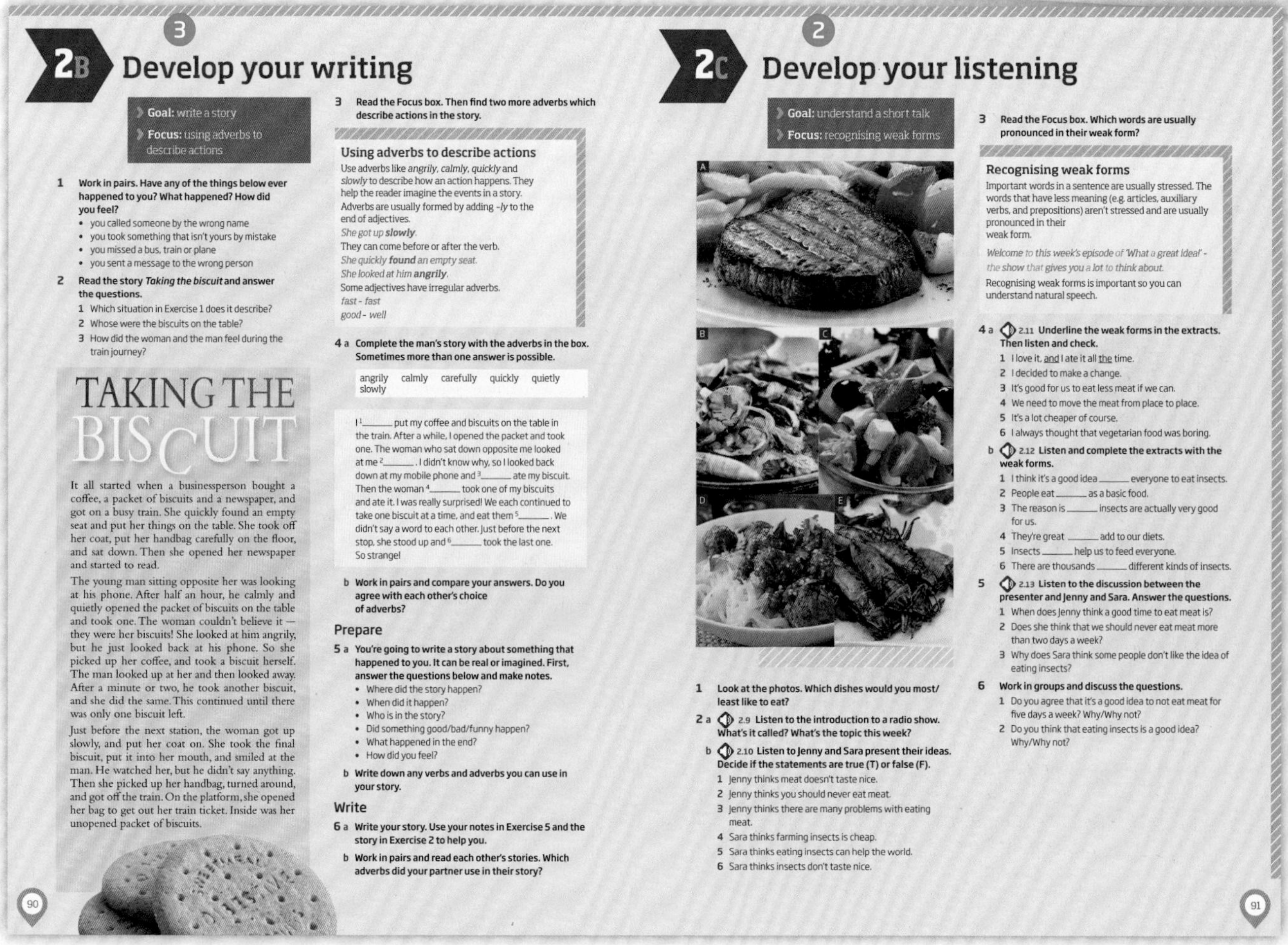

3

2B Develop your writing

Goal: write a story
Focus: using adverbs to describe actions

1 Work in pairs. Have any of the things below ever happened to you? What happened? How did you feel?
- you called someone by the wrong name
- you took something that isn't yours by mistake
- you missed a bus, train or plane
- you sent a message to the wrong person

2 Read the story *Taking the biscuit* and answer the questions.
1 Which situation in Exercise 1 does it describe?
2 Whose were the biscuits on the table?
3 How did the woman and the man feel during the train journey?

TAKING THE BISCUIT

It all started when a businessperson bought a coffee, a packet of biscuits and a newspaper, and got on a busy train. She quickly found an empty seat and put her things on the table. She took off her coat, put her handbag carefully on the floor, and sat down. Then she opened her newspaper and started to read.

The young man sitting opposite her was looking at his phone. After half an hour, he calmly and quietly opened the packet of biscuits on the table and took one. The woman couldn't believe it – they were her biscuits! She looked at him angrily, but he just looked back at his phone. So she picked up her coffee, and took a biscuit herself. The man looked up at her and then looked away. After a minute or two, he took another biscuit, and she did the same. This continued until there was only one biscuit left.

Just before the next station, the woman got up slowly, and put her coat on. She took the final biscuit, put it into her mouth, and smiled at the man. He watched her, but he didn't say anything. Then she picked up her handbag, turned around, and got off the train. On the platform, she opened her bag to get out her train ticket. Inside was her unopened packet of biscuits.

3 Read the Focus box. Then find two more adverbs which describe actions in the story.

Using adverbs to describe actions
Use adverbs like *angrily, calmly, quickly* and *slowly* to describe how an action happens. They help the reader imagine the events in a story.
Adverbs are usually formed by adding *-ly* to the end of adjectives.
*She got up **slowly**.*
They can come before or after the verb.
*She quickly **found** an empty seat.*
*She looked at him **angrily**.*
Some adjectives have irregular adverbs.
fast – fast
good – well

4 a Complete the man's story with the adverbs in the box. Sometimes more than one answer is possible.

angrily calmly carefully quickly quietly slowly

I [1]_____ put my coffee and biscuits on the table in the train. After a while, I opened the packet and took one. The woman who sat down opposite me looked at me [2]_____. I didn't know why, so I looked back down at my mobile phone and [3]_____ ate my biscuit. Then the woman [4]_____ took one of my biscuits and ate it. I was really surprised! We each continued to take one biscuit at a time, and eat them [5]_____. We didn't say a word to each other. Just before the next stop, she stood up and [6]_____ took the last one. So strange!

b Work in pairs and compare your answers. Do you agree with each other's choice of adverbs?

Prepare

5 a You're going to write a story about something that happened to you. It can be real or imagined. First, answer the questions below and make notes.
- Where did the story happen?
- When did it happen?
- Who is in the story?
- Did something good/bad/funny happen?
- What happened in the end?
- How did you feel?

b Write down any verbs and adverbs you can use in your story.

Write

6 a Write your story. Use your notes in Exercise 5 and the story in Exercise 2 to help you.

b Work in pairs and read each other's stories. Which adverbs did your partner use in their story?

90

2

2C Develop your listening

Goal: understand a short talk
Focus: recognising weak forms

A B C D E

1 Look at the photos. Which dishes would you most/least like to eat?

2 a 2.9 Listen to the introduction to a radio show. What's it called? What's the topic this week?

b 2.10 Listen to Jenny and Sara present their ideas. Decide if the statements are true (T) or false (F).
1 Jenny thinks meat doesn't taste nice.
2 Jenny thinks you should never eat meat.
3 Jenny thinks there are many problems with eating meat.
4 Sara thinks farming insects is cheap.
5 Sara thinks eating insects can help the world.
6 Sara thinks insects don't taste nice.

3 Read the Focus box. Which words are usually pronounced in their weak form?

Recognising weak forms
Important words in a sentence are usually stressed. The words that have less meaning (e.g. articles, auxiliary verbs, and prepositions) aren't stressed and are usually pronounced in their weak form.
Welcome to this week's episode of 'What a great idea!' – the show that gives you a lot to think about.
Recognising weak forms is important so you can understand natural speech.

4 a 2.11 Underline the weak forms in the extracts. Then listen and check.
1 I love it, and I ate it all the time.
2 I decided to make a change.
3 It's good for us to eat less meat if we can.
4 We need to move the meat from place to place.
5 It's a lot cheaper of course.
6 I always thought that vegetarian food was boring.

b 2.12 Listen and complete the extracts with the weak forms.
1 I think it's a good idea _____ everyone to eat insects.
2 People eat _____ as a basic food.
3 The reason is _____ insects are actually very good for us.
4 They're great _____ add to our diets.
5 Insects _____ help us to feed everyone.
6 There are thousands _____ different kinds of insects.

5 2.13 Listen to the discussion between the presenter and Jenny and Sara. Answer the questions.
1 When does Jenny think a good time to eat meat is?
2 Does she think that we should never eat meat more than two days a week?
3 Why does Sara think some people don't like the idea of eating insects?

6 Work in groups and discuss the questions.
1 Do you agree that it's a good idea to not eat meat for five days a week? Why/Why not?
2 Do you think that eating insects is a good idea? Why/Why not?

91

The **Students' Book** also has extensive back of book material including a *Grammar bank*, a *Vocabulary bank, Communication games* and a *Communication bank.*

Vocabulary bank

1C Everyday activities

1 Match the everyday activities 1–14 with photos A–N.
1 get the bus to work/school
2 chat to your friends
3 bake a cake/bread/biscuits
4 make a meal/breakfast/lunch/dinner
5 go to the gym
6 have a rest
7 do the housework
8 iron your clothes
9 order pizza/a takeaway
10 go online
11 get ready for work/to go out
12 brush your hair
13 ...

2 Complete the sentences with one missing word.
1 I usually get the bus _____ work.
2 I go _____ the gym early every morning before work.
3 Sally's tired so she's having _____ rest.
4 You need to do your homework, don't just chat _____ your friends online.
5 It's your turn to wash _____ dishes!
6 This weekend I'm making _____ meal for my friends.
7 I really tired. I just want to stay _____ in tonight.
8 It's 7 a.m. - I need to get ready _____ for work.

3 Describe a typical day for you. Use as many of the phrases in Exercise 1 as possible.
I get up at around 7 a.m. I have a sho...

2A Feelings

1 Choose the correct alternatives.

1 exhausted/cheerful   2 annoyed/calm   3 upset/annoyed   4 frightened/calm

5 annoyed/miserable   6 cheerful/worried   7 upset/confident   8 annoyed/worried

2 a Choose five of the adjectives in Exercise 1. Think about the last time you felt this way and why.

b Work in pairs. Share your ideas with your partner.
I felt exhausted yesterday because I had too much work.

2C Food

1 Match the food and drink 1–15 with photos A–O.
1 burger
2 butter
3 cereal
4 chilli
5 crisps
6 fish
7 fizzy drinks
8 grapes
9 juice
10 lamb
11 mango
12 mushrooms
13 salad
14 steak
15 yoghurt

2 Work in pairs and discuss the questions.
1 Which of the food and drink in the photos do you like/dislike? Why?
2 Which do you think are healthy/unhealthy?

Communication games

Four in a row (Units 1–2 review)

Play in two teams. Take turns to choose a square and answer the question. If you answer correctly you win the square. The first team to win four squares in a row (down, across or diagonally) wins!

How does a person feel when there's nothing to do?	What's the past simple form of feel, laugh, hear?	Read the answer. What's the question? *I listen to classical music.*	Say three countable nouns.	Say three things you have a few of.
Correct the mistake in this sentence. *I go often to the park.*	Say three past simple sentences with time expressions.	Correct the mistake in this sentence. *I read a good book at the moment.*	Complete B's reply and sound excited: A: I want to join a gym. B: That ...	Say four adjectives that describe the taste of food.
What two questions could you ask after someone tells you this? *I found some money yesterday.*	What's the missing word? *The first thing people often do in the morning is c_____ their messages.*	Look at the answer. What's the question? *I go to the supermarket about twice a week.*	What's the missing word? *I'll pay for dinner. I've got _____ of money.*	Say three things that you have a lot of.
Make this sentence negative. *Marc said hello.*	What's the missing word? *I went to the cinema _____ night.*	Say three sentences about what your family or friends are doing now.	How do you pronounce the past simple tense of need, stay and watch?	Read the answer. What's the question? *I usually get here at about six.*
What's the missing word? *I started my English course four weeks _____*	What's the missing adjective? *I always feel r_____d before interviews. They don't make me nervous.*	Complete the sentence. *To be successful, it's important to have clear g_____*	Does a countable or uncountable noun come after a few?	Say two things you have a little of.
Say three things you did last week using the past simple.	Say one thing you often do, one thing you hardly ever do and one thing you never do.	How does a person usually feel when something unexpected happens?	Say two nouns that can go with the verb spend.	Say two nouns that go with the verb take.

146

Communication bank

Lesson 1D
6

Student A
1 Ask Student B for the information below. Check the details they give you.
1 what time the concert tonight starts
What time does the concert start?
2 what the homework for tonight is
3 when the shop is open

2 Answer Student B's questions with the information below and check they understand.
1 The film starts at 6:30 p.m., but everybody is meeting at Café Central at 5 p.m.
2 You'd like some pasta, tomatoes, bread, some salt and a newspaper.
3 You have to go onto the company website, search for the job and then complete the online form.

Lesson 2D
5a

Student A
1 You recently did something exciting (e.g. went to a sports event, went skydiving, passed an exam). Get ready to tell Student B:
* what it was
* where you were
* why you did it
* what happened
* how you felt

2 Student B is going tell you about something exciting that happened to him/her recently. Get ready to ask questions about what, where, why, etc.

Lesson 5D
6

Student A
You and Student B went to another country for a language course. You stayed with different families. You'd like to buy the family you stayed with some gifts. Read the information about your family below.
Gail: 50, doctor, likes running
Martin: 52, businessman, likes golf
Gail's mum: 80, likes reading
Gail's dad: 80, likes films
Now go back to page 44 and ask Student B to help you think of ideas. Give some suggestions for his/her family.

Lesson 10B
2c
Quiz results
1 20 billion
2 minute
3 Jacob Davis. Levi Strauss was his business partner.
4 2,500
5 3,500
6 a Danish king who helped people communicate better.
7 Humphry Davy.
8 more

151

15

SUPPORT COMPONENTS

WORKBOOK WITH ONLINE AUDIO

The *Roadmap* **Workbook** contains a wide variety of grammar, vocabulary and functional language exercises that review all the areas covered in the Students' Book. It also features additional listening, reading and writing practice.

- Extensive practice of grammar, vocabulary and functional language covered in the Students' Book.
- Additional listening, reading and writing practice to further develop learners' knowledge and mastery of skills.
- Full answer keys and audio scripts are provided at the back of the book.

Roadmap Workbook audio is available online for students and teachers in the *Pearson English Portal*.

MOBILE APP

Extra grammar and vocabulary exercises, available on the mobile app (the *Pearson Practice English* app), consolidate language points covered in the Students' Book.

- On-the-go, bite-sized practice which can be done anywhere, any time.
- Instant feedback provided to students.
- Progressive levels of challenge.

ROADMAP A2+
WORKBOOK
with key and online audio
Katy Kelly, Michael Turner

Pearson

GSE

2A

Vocabulary

Feelings

1 Complete the sentences with the adjectives in the box.

afraid angry bored excited
~~happy~~ nervous relaxed stressed
surprised worried

1 My sister was very __happy__ when she finished her exams.
2 Children are often _____ of the dark.
3 Jen is _____ about her interview tomorrow.
4 Susan is feeling _____ and needs a holiday!
5 Betty is really _____ about her birthday party on Saturday.
6 I'm really _____ that Jim isn't helping me cook dinner.
7 I'm _____ in my job, so I want to find a new one.
8 I enjoy spending time with Philip because he's a very _____ person.
9 Kim is _____ about the project because there are some problems.
10 My sister was _____ to see me at the airport.

2 Choose the correct alternatives.

1 A: What's wrong? You look really *relaxed/angry!*
   B: Yes, I am. My boss said she isn't *happy/bored* with my work.
2 A: Are you *worried/bored* about your interview tomorrow?
   B: No, not really. I feel quite *relaxed/afraid* because I know a lot about the job.
3 A: I'm not going to tonight's yoga class. I'm a bit *surprised/bored* with it.
   B: Really? Yoga really helps me when I'm feeling *excited/stressed.*
4 A: I'm so *excited/afraid* about going to Italy this summer.
   B: Aren't you *bored/nervous* about going on your own?
5 A: I'm really *bored/excited,* there's nothing to do here.
   B: I'm *surprised/angry* to hear that. I think it's great!

Grammar

Past simple

3 Complete the sentences with the past simple form of the verbs in brackets.

1 Sebastian _____ (go) to visit his family in Hong Kong.
2 We _____ (decide) to visit the nature park and not the zoo.
3 Ruth _____ (try) to help her sister with her homework.
4 They _____ (show) us around their beautiful new home.
5 Hugo _____ (feel) really tired and went home early.
6 We _____ (talk) about which present to buy Carly.
7 They _____ (go) to Cape Town this morning.
8 Phil and Ben _____ (be) happy to help me fix my car.
9 Robin _____ (watch) the football match with his friends.
10 I _____ (be) surprised to see some new students in the class.

4 Choose the correct alternatives.

1 Hilda *walk/walked* to the swimming pool with her daughter.
2 James *crying/cried* at the end of the film because it was very sad.
3 We *was/were* really cold on the train because there was no heating.
4 Before I *had/have* a baby, I had more time to read books.
5 The waiter *write/wrote* down the order in his notebook.
6 Rachel *flying/flew* to Japan yesterday.
7 I *see/saw* my old teacher in town on Saturday.
8 Georgia *was/were* very lucky to get the job.

5 Complete the text with the past simple form of the verbs in the box.

arrive be (x2) decide feel fly look show talk try
visit watch

In my job I don't get many holidays. I'm always too busy with work! So this year, I ¹_____ to take a holiday in the sun with my family. We ²_____ very excited and ³_____ at the airport early. We had to check in for the flight and hand in our luggage. As we queued, we ⁴_____ about all the things we wanted to do on holiday. When it was our turn to check in, I ⁵_____ at the tickets. I realised that I had booked the wrong holiday. Our tickets were for two weeks' holiday in Manchester, not Morocco! We ⁶_____ to change the tickets, but it wasn't possible. I ⁷_____ my hotel booking to the travel company, but they couldn't change it. In the end, we ⁸_____ to Manchester. The holiday ⁹_____ a lot of fun. I ¹⁰_____ relaxed and happy. We ¹¹_____ films and ¹²_____ great museums. We were surprised to have such a good holiday so close to home!

<small>10</small>

2B

Vocabulary

Past time expressions

1 Choose the correct alternatives.

1 We visited China *at/in* 2014 and saw the Great Wall.
2 Did you go to Brian's 30th birthday party *last/until* August?
3 *When/As* I was ten, I went to live with my aunt in Switzerland.
4 Pete came to visit us two weeks *until/ago.*
5 We moved house *on/at* 17th March.
6 Bob stayed in the job *until/when* 2017 and then started his own business.

2 Match the sentence halves.

1 We didn't know each other until last __d__
2 They had a summer holiday in Cuba in
3 We met my brother's new girlfriend at a party three weeks
4 Sally learnt German when she was
5 Gemma didn't have her own car until
6 We got married on

a seven years old.
b 2016.
c this year.
d February.
e 17th August.
f ago.

3 Complete the sentences with the words in the box.

ago (x2) in last on (x2) until
when

1 I started playing tennis _____ I was about 12 years old.
2 I saw that new film at the cinema a week _____.
3 We met _____ January this year on a skiing holiday.
4 _____ year, three new hotels opened in our town.
5 Daniel lived in France _____ last year, when he moved to Germany.
6 We went to Paris _____ my birthday.
7 I always meet Claire for coffee _____ Saturdays.
8 I met my best friend 15 years _____.

Grammar

Past simple negative and questions

4 Choose the correct alternatives.

1 Last week I *don't/didn't* go out so that I could study.
2 We *weren't/wasn't* surprised that the flight was delayed.
3 Why *did/was* Susan so stressed yesterday evening?
4 Liv *wasn't/didn't* know how to use the new computer system at work.
5 I *wasn't/didn't* excited about the project.
6 I tried to help her, but she *didn't/wasn't* listen to me.
7 Greg *wasn't/weren't* good at sports at school.
8 What *did/was* you say to him?

5 Complete the text with the past simple form of the verbs in brackets.

When I ¹_____ (be) 18 years old, I ²_____ (go) backpacking across Europe with all my friends from school. We ³_____ (not have) a lot of money, but we ⁴_____ (have) a wonderful time. We ⁵_____ (try) to plan the trip well, but there ⁶_____ (be) a few surprises! We ⁷_____ (not find) many cheap places to stay, and in the second week of our trip, my friend Becky ⁸_____ (fall over) and hurt her knee. But it was fun. We ⁹_____ (eat) a lot of great food and ¹⁰_____ (laugh) a lot, too!

6 Put the words in the correct order to make questions.

1 Jim / this / When / morning / did / arrive?
   _____
2 buy / your / you / Where / bike / did?
   _____
3 at / Who / party / Shona's / was?
   _____
4 you / on / go / Where / holiday / did?
   _____
5 late / was / this / Why / Billy / morning?
   _____
6 finish / What / they / did / work / time?
   _____
7 Why / she / to / travel / Italy / did?
   _____
8 see / Which / at / you / did / cinema / film / the?
   _____

<small>11</small>

Reading

1 Read the article about stories from the past. Which parts of the world do these come from?
1 fables _____
2 hula _____
3 griots _____
4 cave art _____

2 Read the article again. Choose the correct alternatives.
1 A long time ago, fables *were/weren't* written in books.
2 These days, people *read/don't read* fables.
3 *Men/Women* usually danced the hula.
4 The dancers *chanted/played* drums.
5 A griot *has/doesn't have* a good memory.
6 A griot *has to/doesn't have to* learn how to play a kora.
7 Sixty thousand years ago in Spain, people *used/didn't use* caves to tell stories.
8 *A few/A lot* of the paintings show animals.

3 Read the article again and answer the questions.
1 Why did Greek people listen to fables?
_____
2 Who was a famous Greek storyteller?
_____
3 What colour were the hula clothes?
_____
4 Why were hula stories important?
_____
5 What does a griot do?
_____
6 Why does it take many years to become a griot?
_____
7 In Spain, where can we find the paintings in the caves?
_____
8 When did people make the cave paintings?
_____

4 Match the words in bold in the article with meanings 1–5.
1 more important than usual things _____
2 a hole under the ground _____
3 very old _____
4 almost the same as something else _____
5 things people do wrong _____

Stories from the past

Stories are very important to us. We all love stories. Today, we tell stories in books, music, photos, art and films, but in the past we told stories in a different way. This article looks at four ways of telling stories that are older than books!

Fables: a spoken story

Long before we wrote stories on paper and in books, people told each other stories and they remembered the stories. The stories were called fables and were popular in Greece a long time ago. Fables were traditional stories that taught lessons about things people should do. They helped people live good lives. People listened to the stories and learnt lessons from other people's **mistakes**. One of the most famous storytellers was called Aesop. People still read and tell his stories today.

Hula: a dance story

The people who lived in Hawaii a long time ago did not write. They danced to share their stories. The dance was called 'hula' and was usually performed by men. People played drums and the men danced hula and chanted. The dancers wore dark green clothes made from plants and trees. The hula stories were **special** because they told the history of the Hawaiian people.

Griots: a song story

In West Africa, there are special storytellers called 'griots'. A griot tells the story of their village. Griots have very good memories. They remember the name of everyone who lives and dies in the village. They sing their stories to music and they play a kora. A kora is **similar** to a guitar. It takes many years to become a griot. This is because a griot has to learn a lot of information.

Cave art: a painted story

People told stories to one another before we spoke languages! In Spain, there are **ancient** paintings on the walls of caves. These paintings are 60,000 years old! We don't know the meaning of these cave paintings, but many of them show animals. Some people believe that a long time ago the paintings helped people to share important information with one another. These **cave** paintings could be the oldest stories in the world!

Writing

1 Read the blog post. What's it about?
a a difficult journey
b a difficult day at the office
c a difficult presentation

What a day!

Have you had a really good day or a really bad day? Tell us here!

A month ago, I had a very bad day. It was the morning of my big presentation at work and I really wanted it to be successful.

The day started well. I woke up early, took a shower and had a good breakfast. I carefully checked my presentation one last time. I was happy with it, so I put my notes in my bag and calmly left the house. I felt great!

On my way to the bus stop, I looked for my wallet, but it wasn't there. I quickly looked in my pockets. Nothing! I went back to my house and then realised that I didn't have my house keys either. 'No!' I shouted angrily, but it was too late. My wallet and my keys were inside the house!

Disaster! I had no money for the bus and my presentation was at 9 a.m. What to do? I found my bicycle at the side of the house, so I cycled fast to get to work. It took me nearly an hour and halfway there it started to rain.

When I arrived at work, I was tired and wet, and I felt terrible. I walked slowly up the stairs and into the office. My boss laughed loudly when he saw me. 'What happened to you?' he asked.

'It's a long story,' I answered.

'I hope you look better tomorrow when you have your big presentation,' he said!

2 Read the blog post again. Put events a–j in the correct order.
a get bike ____ f can't find keys ____
b get to work ____ g have breakfast ____
c look in pockets ____ h leave house ____
d can't find wallet ____ i check presentation ____
e get wet ____ j take a shower __1__

3a Read the Focus box. Then underline the adverbs in the blog post.

Using adverbs to describe actions

Use adverbs like *angrily*, *calmly*, *quickly* and *slowly* to describe how an action happens. They help the reader imagine the events in a story more clearly.

Adverbs are usually formed by adding -*ly* to the end of adjectives.
I quickly looked in my pockets.
They can come before or after the verb.
I carefully checked my presentation.
I walked slowly up the stairs.
Some adjectives have irregular adverbs.
fast (adjective) – *fast* (adverb)
good (adjective) – *well* (adverb)

b Complete the sentences with the adverbs in the box.

badly   carefully   easily   happily   quickly   quietly   slowly   well

1 I _carefully_ picked up the baby.
2 The day started _____ and then got even worse!
3 I _____ ate my food and ran out of the house.
4 The children laughed _____ in the garden.
5 I _____ closed the door because I didn't want to wake my parents up.
6 I was prepared, so I passed the test _____.
7 I walked _____ because I was really tired.
8 We played _____ and won the match.

Prepare

4a You're going to write a blog post about a good or bad day. It can be real or imaginary. First, make notes about the questions below.
• When did it happen?
• Where did it happen?
• Who was there?
• What happened before?
• What happened in the end?
• Why was it good/bad?
• How did you feel?
• How did other people feel?

b Write down any verbs and adverbs you can use in your story.

Write

5 Write your blog post. Use your notes in Exercise 4 and the blog post in Exercise 1 to help you.

ONLINE PRACTICE

Roadmap **Online practice** provides a blended and personalised learning environment with materials that can be assigned at the touch of a button.

• Interactive Workbook exercises with instant feedback and automatic grade book.
• Common errors report that highlights mistakes learners are making.
• Tips and feedback that direct learners to reference materials and encourage them to work out answers themselves.
• Unit, achievement, mid and end of course tests.

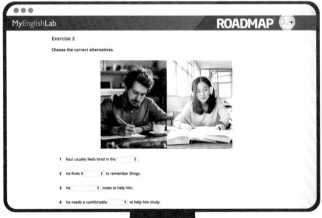

SUPPORT COMPONENTS

TEACHER'S BOOK

The *Roadmap* **Teacher's Book** provides step-by-step instructions on how to exploit the material.

- Teacher's notes for every unit with warmers, fillers, alternative suggestions, culture notes and answer keys.
- Generic teaching tips on useful areas such as grammar, lexis, pronunciation etc.
- Photocopiable grammar and vocabulary worksheets for every unit.
- Class audio scripts.

TEACHER'S DIGITAL RESOURCES

The *Roadmap* digital resources area (accessed via the *Pearson English Portal*) provides a host of support materials to help teachers get the most out of the course.

- Photocopiable grammar and vocabulary worksheets for every unit, with teacher's notes and answer keys.
- Class audio and scripts.
- Workbook audio and scripts.
- Word lists.
- Students' Book answer key.
- Video, video scripts and video worksheets.
- Unit, achievement, mid and end of course tests.
- Tests audio, audio scripts and answer keys.

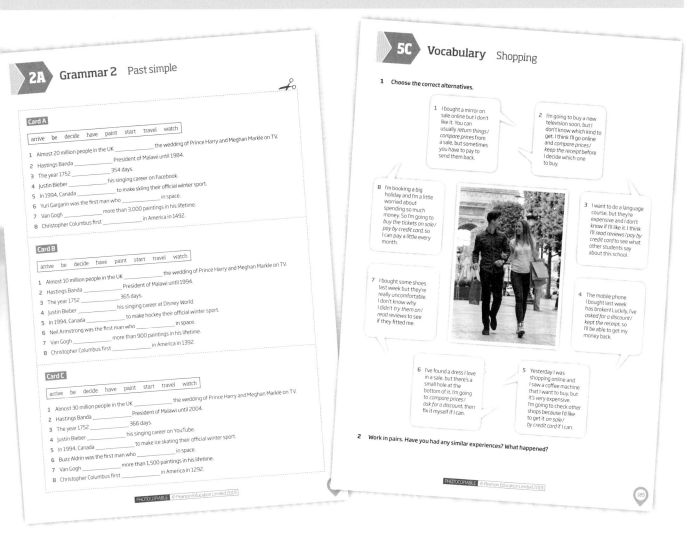

The *Roadmap* **Presentation tool** contains everything you need to make the course come alive. It includes integrated whiteboard software that allows you to add notes, embed files, save your work and reduce preparation time.

Presentation tool:

- Fully interactive version of the Students' Book.
- Planning mode (includes teacher's notes) and teaching mode.
- Easy navigation via book page and lesson flow.
- Answers to exercises at the touch of a button.
- Integrated audio.
- Integrated video, with time-coded video scripts.
- A host of useful classroom tools.

Resources area:

- PDFs of the *Grammar bank* materials.
- Video worksheets.
- Photocopiable activities with teacher's notes.
- Audioscripts.
- Assessment package containing all the course tests.

Syllabus

The *Roadmap* syllabus is built on *Global Scale of English* language learning objectives (see below) but there is a strong focus on the key grammar, functional language, vocabulary and pronunciation needed to perform those objectives in each of the main lessons. Language items have been selected according to their level of difficulty and how useful they are in helping learners to achieve the communicative goal which is at the heart of each lesson. As a result, learners never feel that they are studying grammar, functional language, vocabulary or pronunciation for its own sake and can immediately see the relevance of what they are learning.

- Syllabus built on *Global Scale of English* learning objectives so learners can immediately see the relevance of what they are learning.

- Strong focus on the grammar, vocabulary, functional language and pronunciation needed to achieve the speaking objective at the heart of every lesson.

The Global Scale of English

The **Global Scale of English** (**GSE**) is a standardised, granular scale that measures English language proficiency. Using the GSE students and teachers can now answer three questions accurately: Exactly how good is my English? What progress have I made towards my learning goal? What do I need to do next if I want to improve?

The GSE identifies what a learner can do at each point on a scale from 10 to 90, across all four skills (listening, reading, speaking, and writing), as well as the enabling skills of grammar and vocabulary. This allows learners and teachers to understand a learner's exact level of proficiency, what progress they have made and what they need to learn next.

The GSE is designed to motivate learners by making it easier to demonstrate granular progress in their language ability. Teachers can use their knowledge of their students' GSE levels to choose course materials that are precisely matched to ability and learning goals. The GSE serves as a standard against which English language courses and assessments can be benchmarked, offering a truly global and shared understanding of language proficiency levels.

Teacher Mapping Booklet and GSE Toolkit

You will find the GSE Teacher Mapping Booklet for *Roadmap* online on english.com/roadmap. This booklet provides an overview of all the learning objectives covered in each unit of *Roadmap*, lesson by lesson.

These GSE learning objectives are only a selection from the larger collection contained within the GSE. To explore additional resources to support students, there is an online GSE Teacher Toolkit. This searchable online database gives you quick and easy access to the learning objectives and grammar and vocabulary resources. It also gives you access to GSE job profiles: 250 job skills mapped to GSE learning objectives, enabling you to pinpoint the specific language skills required for professional learners.

For more information please go to english.com/gse.

Topics

Maintaining learners' interest is a vital part of the teacher's role. Research suggests that learners get bored if they stay on the same topic for too long so each lesson in *Roadmap* introduces a fresh theme, although there is always a coherent link in terms of language items covered from one lesson to the next. There is also a topic link with the *Develop your skills* lessons which are an extension of the main lesson. Fresh angles on familiar topics have been used wherever possible and reading and listening texts have been designed to be as authentic as possible. The texts are based on real-world sources and although they have been graded, especially at the lower levels, to make them accessible for students, the 'tone' of the texts is as realistic as possible. Every unit contains a variety of rich and authentic input material including specially filmed video clips.

- New topics are introduced in every lesson so learners never get bored.

- Fresh angles on familiar topics have been introduced wherever possible.

- Reading and listening texts are designed to be as authentic as possible and are based on real-world sources.

Grammar

Successful communication is dependent on an ability to recognise and use grammatical structures. Learners can often manage to make themselves understood with a limited repertoire of words and phrases but as their level progresses, they increasingly need grammar to navigate more complex situations and communicate more sophisticated ideas and opinions. Students also need a knowledge of grammar to understand sentence formation when reading and listening and to be able to produce accurate grammar in professional and exam situations. Grammar is a core feature of learning a language and *Roadmap* recognises this by giving it a central role in each of the main lessons:

- Grammar is introduced in context through short listening/reading texts so that learners can see the language in action, and understand how and when it is used.

- Grammar items are then presented and practised using a 'guided-discovery' approach. Learners study the patterns of a grammar point and are often asked to identify aspects of meaning or form by completing simple exercises and/or rules and tables.

- Language items are presented in a concise form in a Grammar box in the main lesson and a fuller explanation of each grammar point is provided in the *Grammar bank* at the back of the book.

- Each grammar point has one or two controlled practice exercises plus a freer personalised activity which is designed to be genuinely communicative and to offer students the opportunity to say something about themselves or the topic. Learners are also encouraged to use the language they have learned in the final speaking task.

- The *Grammar bank* in the Students' Book, the Workbook and mobile app have additional grammar practice exercises. There are also further photocopiable grammar activities in the Teacher's Book.

Vocabulary

Developing a wide range of vocabulary is also key to developing communicative competence. A good knowledge of vocabulary helps learners to improve their reading and listening skills and is also important for writing. A knowledge of high-frequency collocations and fixed and semi-fixed phrases is also an effective way to increase spoken fluency. Vocabulary is an important feature of every lesson in *Roadmap*. Vocabulary items have been selected a) according to the topic of the lesson and b) according to how useful they are for the final speaking task. Vocabulary is always presented in context through photos or texts and practised through controlled and freer practice activities. Vocabulary is also constantly recycled throughout the course and learners are actively encouraged to use the new vocabulary they have learned to give their personal opinions on the topics in focus and to talk about their own lives and experiences.

- Vocabulary is an important feature of every lesson. It is usually presented in context through quotes and/or short reading texts or illustrated with photos and/or cartoons so that learners can understand how and when an item is used.

- The emphasis throughout is on high-frequency, useful vocabulary. At lower levels, the focus is on presenting lexical sets and at higher levels there is an increased focus on word-building, collocation and useful fixed phrases.

- Vocabulary is practised in a variety of ways with one or two controlled practice activities for each vocabulary section. Learners are often asked to relate the vocabulary they have learned to their own lives making it more memorable.

- Vocabulary is constantly recycled throughout the course and further practice is provided in the *Check and reflect* pages, on the mobile app, in the Workbook and photocopiable activities in the Teacher's Book.

- The *Vocabulary bank* at the back of the Students' Book further extends some of the key vocabulary areas covered in the main lessons.

Functional Language

Learners need to manage communication in a wide variety of different situations and they need to be able to recognise and use phrases and expressions that are appropriate for each situation. These include transactional exchanges, where the focus is on getting something done or interactional exchanges where the focus is on socialising with others.

Roadmap recognises the importance of functional language and each unit has an *English in action* page which focus on useful areas such as giving directions, asking for information, clarifying information etc. Each *English in action* lesson has a communicative outcome based on a GSE learning objective and key functional language items are highlighted in a *Useful phrases* box.

- *English in action* lessons focus on useful functional areas such as giving directions, clarifying information etc.

- Each *English in action* lesson has a communicative outcome based on a GSE learning objective.

- Key functional language items are highlighted in a *Useful phrases* box.

Pronunciation

Teachers often have mixed attitudes towards teaching pronunciation in their lessons. Some consider that it is relatively unimportant, especially if their learners can generally make themselves understood, but others place great importance on developing pronunciation that is more than just intelligible. They consider that a systematic focus on pronunciation in a lesson, however brief, can have a significant impact on developing learners' communicative competence.

In *Roadmap*, we have taken a practical, integrated approach to developing students' pronunciation by highlighting features that often cause problems in conjunction with the areas of grammar, vocabulary or functional language in focus. Where relevant to the level, a grammatical or functional language focus is followed by practice of a feature of pronunciation, for example, the weak forms of auxiliary verbs or connected speech in certain functional exponents. Students are given the opportunity to listen to models of the pronunciation, notice the key features and then practise it.

- Pronunciation is a prominent feature of the syllabus, and practice is generally linked to the main grammar, vocabulary and functional language in focus.

- *Listen and repeat* activities reinforce pronunciation of new language. As and when appropriate, there is an emphasis on areas of pronunciation that affect communication, for example, sentence stress/intonation.

Skills development

Roadmap recognises that effective communication involves receptive as well as productive skills. Although speaking is the main skills focus in each of the main lessons, short reading and listening texts are used to present and practise new language and introduce topics for discussion. These cover a variety of different genres – blogs, articles, fact files etc. – but are never very long as research indicates that teachers want to maximise speaking practice during class time. *Roadmap* also recognises the importance of writing and suggestions for writing extension activities are suggested in the teacher's notes for each of the main lessons.

In addition to the reading, writing and listening material in the main lessons, there is a *Develop your skills* section at the back of the book for learners who want to improve their reading, writing or listening skills. There are three *Develop your skills* lessons for each unit. Each lesson is built around a GSE learning objective and concentrates on a specific skill – reading, listening or writing. They are linked thematically to one of the main lessons and can be done at home or in class. The *Develop your skills* lessons expose learners to different text genres of reading (articles, blogs etc.), writing (emails, reports, essays etc.) and listening (radio broadcasts, conversations etc.) and focus on different strategies or sub-skills to improve general competence in each skill. These strategies are particularly useful for exam training.

Speaking

Most learners, whatever their age and whatever specific goals or reasons they might have for learning English, want to improve their speaking skills. Many learners lack opportunities to practise in the real world so they need to make the most of opportunities to speak English in the classroom. *Roadmap* recognises the importance of speaking and there are many opportunities throughout the course for learners to participate in a wide variety of different speaking activities. For example, learners might be asked to discuss a series of questions, respond to photos or cartoons, give their opinions about the content of a reading or listening text or take part in conversations, discussions and role-plays. Speaking is a fundamental part of each lesson and learners are frequently asked to work together in pairs or groups to maximise opportunities to speak in class.

Many learners are reluctant or unable to speak because they have nothing to say or lack the language they need to say what they want to say. *Roadmap* helps learners to overcome these problems and one of the key aims of the course is to increase learners' confidence and fluency. Each of the four core lessons in each unit are built around a *Global Scale of English* speaking objective and all the grammar, functional language, vocabulary and pronunciation is geared towards helping learners achieve that objective. Learners develop fluency when they are motivated to speak and for this to happen, engaging topics and relevant, carefully-staged speaking tasks are essential. In each lesson of *Roadmap* there is a logical sequence of linked activities that have been carefully constructed and staged to help learners perform the final speaking task to the best of their ability. Learners are given time to prepare their ideas and think about the language they need for the final speaking task in a structured way. Giving learners time to rehearse is crucial in terms of building their confidence and this in turn leads to more motivation and greater accuracy and fluency. As learners' confidence increases, their willingness to experiment with the language also increases. Speaking is systematically developed in *Roadmap* through the following activities:

- Lead in questions and/or striking images engage learners' interest and activate passive knowledge of vocabulary related to the topic.

- Grammar and vocabulary relevant for the final speaking activities are presented and practised.

- Personalised practice activities encourage learners to give their own opinions on the topic and talk about their own lives and experiences

- Learners are given 'models' and time to prepare their ideas for the final speaking task.

- Useful phrases give learners ideas and provide prompts to help them get started.

- Learners perform the speaking task in pairs or groups and are invited to reflect on their performance through a whole class round up activity.

Listening

Listening is an important skill for all users of English and one which learners often find quite challenging. Many learners complain that they can understand their teacher but find it difficult to understand people speaking English outside the classroom, especially if speakers do not make any concessions to their audience in terms of their speed of delivery. Learners with poor listening skills are unlikely to be competent communicators or users of the language so listening features almost as prominently as speaking in the main lessons in *Roadmap*. It is important to expose learners to real language in use as well as different varieties of English. Listening material, particularly at lower levels, is scripted but aims to reflect the patterns of natural speech and is designed to be as authentic-sounding as possible whilst bearing in mind the need to make it accessible for the level. Listening texts are often used to present new grammar or vocabulary and can act as a springboard to stimulate discussion in class. In addition, there is a listening 'model' for each of the speaking tasks in which one or

more speakers perform whole or part of the task. Learners listen to this and try to replicate what they have heard when they come to perform the task themselves.

Listening is a prominent feature in the main lessons but more in-depth practice of different genres, for example, short talks and monologues, conversations, radio interviews and discussions etc. is provided in the *Develop your listening* lessons at the back of the book. The *Develop your listening* lessons also provide invaluable training in listening sub-skills, for example, predicting information, recognising discourse markers and weak forms, identifying examples and sequencing words. Each *Develop your listening* lesson provides an example of the genre as well as highlighting a sub-skill which is outlined in a special *Focus box* and practised in the lesson. As mentioned in the introduction to the Teacher's Book, the *Develop your listening* lessons are optional and can be selected according to the needs of individual learners or classes. They can be used in conjunction with the main lessons to form the extended route through the course or they can be used individually and/or given to learners to do for homework.

- Listening is a prominent feature of the main lessons and is often used to present new grammar or vocabulary or act as a springboard to stimulate discussion.

- Listening 'models' are provided to build learners' confidence.

- Listening material is designed to be as authentic-sounding as possible whilst bearing in mind the need to make it accessible for the level.

- More in-depth practice of different listening genres – short talks and monologues, conversations, radio interviews and discussions – is provided in the *Develop your listening* lessons at the back of the book.

- *Develop your listening* lessons provide an example of the genre as well as highlighting different sub-skills needed to develop mastery of the skill.

- Listening sub-skills are outlined in a special *Focus box* and practised in the lesson.

- *Develop your listening* lessons are optional and can be selected according to the needs of individual learners or classes. They can be used individually and/or given for homework.

Reading

Reading is important for many students, particularly if they need it for their work or studies. The learner who develops confidence in reading both in and outside the classroom will undoubtedly make faster progress. We now have access to a very wide range of English language reading material and it is a good idea to encourage learners to read as much as possible outside the classroom. *Roadmap* provides ample opportunities for learners to practise their reading skills, both in the main lessons and in the *Develop your reading* sections at the back of the book.

Short reading texts are included in the main lessons to contextualise new grammar or vocabulary and they also often serve as a springboard for discussion. As with the listening material, there is an emphasis on authenticity, and although reading texts have been adapted or graded for the level, there is an attempt to maintain authenticity by remaining faithful to the text type in terms of content and style. Texts are relevant and up-to-date, and are designed to stimulate interest and motivate learners to read. The texts represent a variety of genres and mirror the text types that learners will probably encounter in their everyday lives. Texts are generally not exploited in any great depth in the main lessons (as in-depth work on reading is provided in the *Develop your reading* section) but learners are always given a reason to read along with basic comprehension exercises.

More in-depth practice of different genres is provided in the *Develop your reading* lessons at the back of the book. The *Develop your reading* lessons also provide invaluable training in reading sub-skills such as identifying the main ideas in a text, guessing the meaning of words from context, identifying positive and negative attitudes, understanding pronouns, missing words etc. Each *Develop your reading* lesson provides an example of the genre as well as highlighting a sub-skill which is outlined in a special *Focus box* and practised in the lesson. As mentioned in the introduction to the Teacher's Book, the *Develop your reading* lessons are optional and can be selected according to the needs of individual learners or classes. They can be used in conjunction with the main lessons to form the extended route through the course or they can be used individually and/or given to learners to do for homework.

- Reading is a prominent feature of the main lessons and is often used to present new grammar or vocabulary or act as a springboard to stimulate discussion.

- Reading material is designed to be as authentic as possible whilst bearing in mind the need to make it accessible for the level. Text types mirror those learners will encounter in their everyday lives, for example, blogs, social media posts etc.

- More in-depth practice of different reading genres – stories, articles, reviews, factual texts, reports, social media and blog posts etc. – is provided in the *Develop your reading* lessons at the back of the book.

- *Develop your reading* lessons provide an example of the genre as well as highlighting different sub-skills needed to develop mastery of the skill.

- Reading sub-skills are outlined in a special *Focus box* and practised in the lesson.

- *Develop your reading* lessons are optional and can be selected according to the needs of individual learners or classes. They can be used individually and/or given for homework.

Writing

In recent years the growth of email and the internet means that people worldwide are writing more than ever before – for business, for their studies and for personal communication. Learners need effective writing skills for professional and academic purposes but people also use writing – email, text messages, social media posts etc. – as an informal means of communication far more than they used to. The latter isn't simply speech written down and there are all sorts of conventions for both informal and formal writing. It is therefore important to focus on a range of genres, from formal text types such as essays, letters and reports to informal genres such as blog entries and personal messages. *Roadmap* provides extensive training in all these types of writing.

Writing is not a prominent feature of the main lessons in *Roadmap* although learners are frequently asked to make notes as preparation for the speaking task. There are also suggestions in the teacher's notes on ways to extend the tasks with follow-up written work. However, in-depth practice of different genres of writing is provided in the *Develop your writing* lessons at the back of the book. The *Develop your writing* lessons also provide invaluable training in writing sub-skills such as organising ideas, using paragraphs, explaining reasons and results, using time expressions and linkers, constructing narratives etc.

Each *Develop your writing* lesson provides an example of the genre as well as highlighting a sub-skill which is outlined in a special *Focus box* and practised in the lesson. As mentioned in the introduction to the Teacher's Book, the *Develop your writing* lessons are optional and can be selected according to the needs of individual learners or classes. They can be used in conjunction with the main lessons to form the extended route through the course or they can be used individually and/or given to learners to do for homework. Each *Develop your writing* lesson follows a similar format:

- Some writing practice is provided in the main lessons and in-depth work on different genres of writing as well as writing sub-skills is provided in the *Develop your writing* section at the back of the book.

- Each *Develop your writing* lesson starts with a few discussion questions designed to activate learners' vocabulary and get them thinking about ideas related to the topic.

- Each *Develop your writing* lesson provides a model of the genre in focus. These are designed to be as authentic as possible whilst bearing in mind the need to make them accessible for the level. Types of writing mirror those that learners will encounter in their everyday lives, for example, stories, formal and informal emails, blog posts, descriptions, invitations, reviews etc.

- *Develop your writing* lessons provide examples of the genre as well as highlighting different sub-skills needed to develop mastery of it, for example, organising ideas, using paragraphs, explaining reasons and results, using time expressions and linkers, constructing narratives etc.

- Writing sub-skills are outlined in a special *Focus box* and practised in the lesson.

- Learners prepare and then write their own example of the genre in focus and are encouraged to use the sub-skills they have practised in the lesson.

- *Develop your writing* lessons are optional and can be selected according to the needs of individual learners or classes. They can be used individually and/or given for homework.

Review and consolidation

Language items are constantly recycled in each lesson of *Roadmap*. At end of each unit, there is a *Check and reflect* page which is designed to review all the language points covered and give learners an opportunity to reflect on how their confidence and mastery of the language has improved. In addition, each unit is accompanied by a short video – the *Roadmap report* – that can be used to provide a break from the routine of the Students' Book as well as revise and consolidate language in a fun, light-hearted way. Each *Roadmap report* features a 'roving reporter' who goes out on location to visit interesting people and places and has a variety of new experiences. The videos are designed to illustrate some of the quirkier aspects of real life as well as show language items covered in the unit in realistic contexts.

- Video clips and extension activities consolidate key language covered in each unit and illustrate some of the quirkier aspects of real life.

- Video clips are 2–3 minutes in length and are designed to entertain learners and provide a bit of light relief.

- Video worksheets (to exploit the language in the videos) are available online.

OVERVIEW

1A Getting to know you

Introduction

The goal of this lesson is for Ss to get to know each other by asking and answering questions. To help them achieve this, they will learn question words, and word order in questions, in the context of social media posts.

Warm-up

Before the class starts, write on the board, in a random order, some basic information about yourself which you don't mind sharing with the class, e.g. where you live, what you do, the time you start work, your birthday, your favourite singer, etc. Elicit a question by pointing at one of the pieces of information, drawing a question mark on the board and pointing from the class to yourself. Put Ss in pairs to write the rest of the questions, e.g. *Where do you live? What do you do? Who's your favourite singer?*, etc. While they are working, monitor and check how well they are forming questions. When they have finished, elicit the questions and write them on the board (or invite Ss to come up and write them on the board). Ss then ask and answer the questions in their pairs.

Reading and vocabulary

Question words

1 Go through the questions with the class and check Ss understand them. Put Ss in pairs and give them a few minutes to discuss the questions. Monitor and help with new vocabulary where necessary. When they have finished, ask a few students to Ss their ideas with the class.

2a With **weaker classes**, you may want to pre-teach/check: *trainers* (= sports shoes). You could draw or show pictures. Focus attention on the social media post and its title. Ask Ss if they ever see/post things like this on social media and where they see them. Next, focus attention on the photos at the top of the page. Put Ss in pairs to discuss the topics they think Magda mentions in her post. Make sure Ss don't read the text at this stage, just use the photos. When they have finished, elicit Ss' ideas and write them on the board.

b Ss read the text alone, then answer the questions in pairs. Check answers with the whole class. Elicit what Magda said about each one, too.

Answers:
1 2, 5, 6, 10
2 at home
3 No. She has only met her once.
4 How many pairs of shoes she has. (*I always wear the same pair of trainers. My family and friends think they're my only shoes.*)

3a Ss work alone, then check answers. In feedback, check answers with the whole class.

Answers: 1g 2d 3e 4b 5c 6a 7i 8f 9k 10h 11j

Grammar checkpoint

We use *what* when there are many possible answers. We use *which* when there are only a few/a restricted number of possible answers. We usually say *What kinds of* before a plural noun, e.g. *What kinds of vegetables do you like?* and *What kind of* before a singular or uncountable noun, e.g. *What kind of music do you listen to?*

b Explain that these are Diego's answers to the same questions in the social media post. Elicit the first answer as an example with the whole class. Ss match the rest of the answers alone, then check in pairs. In feedback, check answers with the whole class.

Answers: a 9 b 5 c 2 d 6 e 3 f 1 g 10 h 7 i 4 j 8

c Give Ss a minute to choose which six questions they want to ask. Ss discuss their chosen questions in pairs. In feedback, ask a few Ss to share any interesting information they found out about their partner with the class.

Further practice

Photocopiable activities: 1A Vocabulary, p148

Grammar

Word order in questions

4a Books closed. Write on the board: *How ___ ___ ___ to work?* Underneath, write: *you, travel, do.* Elicit which of the three words goes in each gap. Ss open their books again, read the Grammar box and choose the correct verb forms alone, then check in pairs. Don't check answers with the class yet.

b Focus attention on the example questions in the Grammar box and explain that these all come from the social media post in Ex 2. Ask Ss to find them and check their answers to Ex 4a. Then check answers with the whole class. Be prepared to clarify any points Ss aren't sure about, using examples.

Answers: 1 does 2 Do 3 is 4 Are

GRAMMAR BANK 1A   pp.116–117

Stronger classes could read the notes at home. Otherwise, check the notes with Ss. In each exercise, elicit the first answer as an example. Ss work alone to complete the exercises, then check their answers in pairs. In feedback, elicit Ss' answers and drill the questions. Ss can refer to the notes to help them.

Answers: 1A

1 1 ~~are~~ is   2 ~~this is~~ is this   3 ~~lives~~ live   4 ~~it is~~ is it
   5 ~~costs this shirt~~ does this shirt cost
   6 ~~drives he~~ does he drive   7 ~~You want~~ Do you want
   8 ~~How many do you have children?~~ How many children do you have?
   9 Does he speak French?   10 Does she like Italian food?
2 1 How many brothers or sisters does he have?
   2 How do you go/get to work?
   3 Where do you buy your clothes from?
   4 What time does the lesson start?
   5 What do you do at the weekends/on Saturdays and Sundays?
   6 How often do you check your messages?
   7 Why is your sister happy?
   8 Which language do they speak?

5a 🔊 1.1 Ss listen to the questions and decide if the speaker's voice goes up or down at the end of each question. Elicit the answers from the whole class and model them further if necessary.

Answer: The speakers' voices usually go down at the end of the question.

b Ss listen again and repeat each question after they hear it.

Pronunciation checkpoint

It is often taught that our intonation goes down with open questions and up with *yes/no* questions. However, recent research shows that the difference is not so clear, especially with *yes/no* questions. At this stage, it's best to focus on how the voice falls naturally at the end of open questions.

6a Elicit the first answer from the class as an example and write it on the board. If necessary, refer back to the information in the Grammar box on word order in questions. Ss write the rest of the questions alone, then check in pairs. Check answers with the whole class.

Answers:
1 How many hours do you spend online each day?
2 Who do you talk to online?
3 Whose photos do you look at online?
4 What kind of websites do you like?
5 Are you from this area?
6 How long is your normal working day?

Optional alternative activity

Stronger classes might enjoy a further challenge here. Books closed. Put Ss in small teams and ask each team to think of a team name. Write team names on the board. Read out the jumbled words for each question. Ss listen to the words and the first team to say the question correctly gets a point (write a mark on the board next to their team name). The team with the most points at the end wins.

b Write on the board: *people you live with?* and elicit possible questions, e.g. *Who do you live with? Do you live with your family? Which people do you live with?*, etc. Go through the example with the class and let Ss know that more than one question might be possible. Ss write their questions alone. While they're writing, monitor and help where necessary.

Answers: (Answers may vary)
1 When's your birthday?
2 What's/Which is your favourite TV show at the moment?
3 What (kind of) films do you like?
4 How many/Which languages do you speak?
5 Where do you go at weekends?
6 When does this lesson finish?

c Put Ss in pairs. Explain that they should choose three questions from each exercise (6a and 6b) to ask their partner. Remind Ss that our voice usually goes down at the end of the question. Ss ask and answer the questions. When they've finished, choose a few students to share something they learnt about their partner with the class.

Further practice

Photocopiable activities: 1A Grammar 1, p146;
1A Grammar 2, p147

Speaking

Prepare

7a 🔊 **1.2** The aim of the listening activity is to provide a model for the final speaking task in Ex 9. Go through the questions with the class and make sure Ss know what to listen for. Ss listen and answer the questions, then check answers in pairs. Check answers with the whole class.

> **Answers:** 1 Three 2 Because Josh watches a lot of films (almost one a day/six or seven films a week).

b Write on the board: *... like films?* Ask if Ss can remember the first question in the audio. (*Do you like films?*) Ask if Ss can remember the other questions Becky asked, but don't give any answers yet. Play the audio again for students to check, then check answers with the whole class.

> **Answers:** Do you like films? What kind of films do you like? Which films do you recommend? Is that online? How many do you watch a week?

Optional alternative activity

With **weaker classes**, write the following on the board:
... kind of films do you like?
... films do you recommend?
... that online?
... do you watch a week?

Ss listen and complete the questions with the missing words.

Audioscript 1.2

Becky: So, Josh, do you like films?
Josh: Oh yeah, I love films.
Becky: Great! What kind of films do you like?
Josh: Oh, er, all kinds, really. I watch a lot.
Becky: Really? Lucky you ... I don't watch any these days. I'm always too busy, but I do have some free time tonight. Which films do you recommend?
Josh: Well, there's *Kicks*, about football players at an American high school. If you like sports films, you'll like this one. And, er ... there's a film about the police that I saw last week. I sort of enjoyed that, but I can't remember what it's called. Maybe not that one ... Then there's a comedy called *Surf Brothers*. I saw that last night, really funny!
Becky: Oh good, I like comedies. Is that online?
Josh: No, it's in the cinema at the moment.
Becky: Oh, right, OK ... Wow, you really do watch a lot of films. How many do you watch a week?
Josh: Six or seven.
Becky: That's almost one a day!
Josh: I know. I told you. I watch a lot of films!

8 Refer Ss back to the questions Becky asked in Ex 7 as examples and read them with the class. Ss write their questions alone. Monitor and help with ideas where necessary, and check they're forming questions correctly.

Teaching tip

Speaking activities are almost always more productive when Ss are adequately prepared for them. This doesn't just give them ideas of what to speak about, but also means they start the activity feeling more confident about what they have to say. During the preparation stage, give Ss as much support and encouragement as you can to help them prepare for the final speaking activity.

Speak

9a Go through the Useful phrases with the class. Explain that they are useful ways of responding when listening to someone. *Really?* shows surprise and *Me too!* shows we agree. Read the examples with the class and use the first question (*Do you like sport?*) as an example to elicit possible follow-up questions, e.g. *Which is your favourite sport? How often do you play it? What's the best/worst thing about it?*, etc. Put Ss in small groups to ask and answer their questions. While they are speaking, monitor and make notes on their use of language for later feedback, paying particular attention to their use of questions.

b When they have finished, choose a Ss from each group to share interesting information with the class.

Reflection on learning

Write the following questions on the board:
How easy was it to think of questions to ask other students?
When do you think you would use these questions in the future?
What did you do well in this lesson?

Put Ss in pairs to discuss the questions. When they have finished, ask if anyone wants to share their ideas with the class, but don't force them to if they'd rather not.

Homework ideas

Ex 9a: Ss write a description of their partner based on their discussion.
Grammar bank: 1A Ex 1–2, pp.116–117
Workbook: Ex 1–6, p4
App: grammar and vocabulary practice

Fast route: continue to Lesson 1B
Extended route: go to p106 for Develop your listening

1B Successful people

Introduction

The goal of this lesson is for Ss to describe the habits and routines of a successful person they admire. To help them achieve this, Ss will learn adverbs of frequency and phrases related to success.

Warm-up

Before the class starts, write the following statements on the board:

Success only comes from hard work.
Some people can never be successful.
Only lucky people are successful.

Put Ss in small groups. Ask them to discuss which of the statements they agree/disagree with and briefly say why (they don't need to go into lengthy explanations). Ask them to think of real examples of people if they can. When they have finished, ask Ss to share their ideas with the class and have a brief class discussion.

Listening and vocabulary

Success

1 Focus attention on the photos and elicit who the people are, referring to the information in the Culture notes below. Ss work in pairs and discuss the questions. When they have finished, ask a few Ss to share their ideas with the class.

Culture notes

Roger Federer is a professional tennis player from Switzerland. He has won more Grand Slam titles than any other male player, as well as numerous other competitions.

Meryl Streep is an American actor. She has appeared in the theatre, as well as films and TV. She has won an Oscar three times and, up to 2018, had been nominated 21 times, and has won several other awards for her acting.

Stephen Hawking was a scientist who published books about his scientific theories. He suffered from motor neurone disease from his 20s and in his later life was only able to move his eye, which he used to control a computer that provided his voice. He died on 14th March 2018, aged 76.

Natalia Petrovna Osipova is a Russian ballet dancer. She is a principal dancer at The Royal Ballet in London and the Mikhailovsky Theatre Ballet in St. Petersburg.

2a 1.7 Ss listen to the podcast and tick any ideas they wrote down in Ex 1 about what habits Ss think successful people have. Elicit answers from the whole class.

Optional alternative activity

After Ss have discussed their ideas in Ex 1, invite them to write them on the board. After they listen in Ex 2a, go through the ideas on the board and tick off the ones they heard.

b Ask Ss to read through the list of tips and highlight any phrases they don't understand, then give them an opportunity to ask you for explanations/examples. As Ss if they agree with any of the tips. Ss listen again and order the tips, then check answers in pairs. Check answers with the whole class and ask if they agree with the podcast.

Answers: 1 have clear goals 2 try new things
3 ask a lot of questions 4 listen carefully
5 plan your time well 6 take care of yourself 7 take time off
8 start again

Audioscript 1.7

Welcome to podcast 32 – *Success*. Do you want to be better at your job? How often do you think, 'I want to be more successful, but I'm not sure how'? We talked to some successful people to try and find out about their habits. Here are eight tips for you to be more like them:

1 Have clear goals. Successful people always know what they want in life and they work hard to get it.

2 Try new things. Successful people are rarely bored and they always look for new and exciting experiences.

3 Ask a lot of questions. Successful people always want to know more. In fact, they want to know everything about everything.

4 Listen carefully. Successful people are often good listeners and don't do all the talking in conversations.

5 Plan your time well. Successful people don't usually do lots of things at the same time. They check their emails every three or four hours. They sometimes check their messages only once a day.

6 Take care of yourself. Successful people usually have busy and stressful lives, so try to sleep well, eat well and do regular exercise.

7 Take time off – it's important! Successful people hardly ever work at weekends, so make sure you spend time with friends and family, too.

8 And finally, eight – if things don't work, just start again! Successful people never stop trying.

3a Books closed. Write the first gapped item on the board (*Do you _____ , or do lots of things at the same time?*) and elicit the answer (*plan your time well*). Ss open their books and complete the questions, using the phrases from Ex 2b. Monitor and help where necessary. When they have finished, Ss check answers in pairs, before checking with the whole class.

Answers: 1 plan your time well 2 try new things
3 start again 4 listen carefully 5 ask a lot of questions
6 have clear goals 7 take care of yourself 8 take time off

Teaching tip

After listening activities, it's a good idea for Ss to check answers in pairs before going through them with the whole class. This allows Ss to share information their partners might not have picked up during the lesson and means they'll be more confident sharing ideas with the class.

b Put Ss in pairs to discuss the questions and compare their own habits. Monitor and make notes on Ss' language for later feedback. When they have finished, choose a few Ss to share their ideas with the class.

Further practice

Photocopiable activities: 1B Vocabulary, p151

Grammar

Adverbs of frequency

4a 🔊 **1.7** Ss listen again and choose the correct alternatives, then check answers in pairs. Check answers with the whole class.

> **Answers:** 1 always 2 rarely 3 often 4 don't usually
> 5 sometimes 6 usually 7 hardly ever 8 never

Optional alternative activity

Stronger classes could attempt the exercise first from memory, then listen and check.

b Focus attention on the adverbs and ask which ones Ss already know. Ss complete the activity alone, then check answers in pairs. Check answers with the whole class by writing the adverbs on the board and eliciting answers.

> **Answers:** 1 always 2 often 3 usually 4 sometimes
> 5 hardly ever/rarely 6 never

5a Give Ss plenty of time to read the Grammar box and choose the correct alternatives, before checking in pairs. Check answers with the class and be prepared to give further explanations/examples where necessary.

> **Answers:** 1 how often 2 after 3 before 4 after
> 5 at the end

GRAMMAR BANK 1B   pp.116–117

Stronger classes could read the notes at home. Otherwise, check the notes with Ss. In each exercise, elicit the first answer as an example. Ss work alone to complete the exercises, then check their answers in pairs. In feedback, check answers with the whole class. Ss can refer to the notes to help them.

> **Answers: 1B**
> 1 1 always 2 Sometimes 3 hardly ever 4 every
>   5 always 6 once 7 always 8 usually
> 2 1 They go on holiday to France once a year.
>   2 She is rarely late.
>   3 I usually play tennis on Friday.
>   4 We hardly ever watch TV.
>   5 They don't often go to the beach.
>   6 We aren't usually free at the weekend.
>   7 He doesn't normally drive to work.
>   8 I don't have breakfast every day.
>   9 Do you sometimes work at the weekend?
>   10 Is he always late?

b 🔊 **1.8** Focus attention on the letters in bold in the sentences. Play the audio for Ss to listen to how they're connected. If you think it's useful, explain the information in the Pronunciation checkpoint box below, using the examples given.

Pronunciation checkpoint

We often connect words when we say them quickly. When a word ends with a consonant sound (e.g. *doesn't*) and the next word begins with a vowel sound (e.g. *often*), the words may be linked (e.g. *sometimes asks*) or the consonant sound might be omitted, especially with 't' and 'd', or if a glottal stop is used. With *doesn't often*, the 't' links to the 'o' in *often*. In sentence 5, the 'y' at the end of *hardly ever* and the 'r' at the end of *ever* are pronounced because they come before a vowel sound. Before a consonant sound, they're not usually pronounced in British English.

c Ss listen again and repeat, paying attention to the linking. Drill both chorally and individually if necessary.

6a Go through the example with the class. Ss complete the sentences alone, then check in pairs. Check answers with the whole class.

> **Answers:**
> 1 Ben **always** does one activity at a time.
> 2 Ana tries a new activity **once a month**.
> 3 I'm **hardly ever** successful in exams.
> 4 We don't **often** have a clear goal.
> 5 I **sometimes** take time off in June.
> 6 Jon works hard **all the time**.
> 7 They're not **usually** busy in the morning.
> 8 I **rarely** check my work emails at weekends.

b Go through the example with the class and elicit one or two further examples of questions they could ask. Put Ss in pairs to ask and answer questions. Monitor and help where necessary, paying attention to the correct use of adverbs. When they have finished, ask a few Ss to share what they found out about their partner with the class.

Optional extra activity

With *weaker classes*, you could revise word order in questions from lesson 1A before starting this exercise. Choose two or three items from the box (include an example with *be* as the main verb), elicit the questions and write them on the board.

Further practice

Photocopiable activities: 1B Grammar 1, p149; 1B Grammar 2, p150

Speaking

Prepare

7a 🔊 **1.9** Explain that Ss are going to describe a successful person they admire, but first they'll listen to someone else doing the same. Go through the questions and make sure Ss know what to listen out for. Ss listen and answer the questions, then compare with a partner. Check answers with the whole class, feeding in information from the answers below where necessary.

> **Answers:**
> 1 His grandma Elizabeth.
> 2 She is 85.
> 3 She is happy. She is 85 and very active. She looks after her great-grandchildren once a week.

b Go through the activities with the class and elicit what Ss can remember, but don't give any answers yet. Ss listen and write their answers, then check with a partner. Check answers with the whole class.

> **Answers:** 1 always 2 usually 3 hardly ever
> 4 every Wednesday

Audioscript 1.9

Alex: Actually, a person who I think is really successful is my grandma, Elizabeth. My mum's mum.

Marian: That's lovely! Why's that, then?

Alex: Well, she's not famous or rich, but she's a really nice and happy person. She's retired now, but she's still very active – even at 85! She always gets up between five and six in the morning and cleans the house. After breakfast, she usually goes out for a long walk. She walks everywhere, actually – she hardly ever uses public transport.

Marian: She sounds great! Tell me more …

Alex: OK, so, every Wednesday she looks after my kids (her great grandchildren!) all day. They're three and four – and very energetic! She was a teacher in a primary school, so she's very good with children. She plays with them all the time.

Marian: Wow! To be like that at 85, that's amazing! OK, so a person who I think is successful is …

c Give Ss a few minutes to make notes. Explain that it can be someone they know or a famous person. Monitor and help with vocabulary where necessary and encourage Ss to think about which adverbs of frequency they can use.

Optional extra activity

If you have time, Ss could rehearse their descriptions and record them onto an audio recorder app on their mobile devices. They can then listen back to them and reflect on the content of their descriptions and their use of adverbs of frequency. Ss then think about what to improve before they work in groups and describe the person to others.

Speak

8 Put Ss in small groups to take it in turns to describe their successful person. Monitor and take notes on their language use for later feedback and encourage Ss to ask follow-up questions to find out more information. Go through the Useful phrases with the class and explain that we use *Tell me/us more* and *What else does he/she do?* to elicit more information and the other two to respond to information. When Ss have finished, ask a member of each group to report back to the class on anything interesting they found out. Go over any common errors you heard and/or examples of good language use with the whole class.

Reflection on learning

Write the following questions on the board:

How far do you think you achieved today's lesson goal?
How can you improve?

Put Ss in pairs to discuss the questions. When they have finished, ask if anyone wants to share their ideas with the class, but don't force them to if they'd rather not.

Homework ideas

Ex 8a: Ss write a description of the successful person they described.

Grammar bank: 1B Ex 1–2, pp.116–117

Workbook: Ex 1–6, p5

App: grammar and vocabulary practice

Fast route: continue to Lesson 1C
Extended route: go to p87 for Develop your writing

1c ▶ A new lifestyle

Introduction

The goal of this lesson is for Ss to describe everyday activities in the context of trying a new lifestyle for a month. To help them achieve this, they will learn the present simple and present continuous with time expressions.

Warm-up

Ask Ss to imagine that they are going to live on a remote island for a month, with no communication with the outside world. Give them a few minutes to think of and write down five objects they'd take with them (no computers or mobile phones allowed). They must include one book and one type of food. When they are ready, put Ss in small groups to share their ideas and say why they chose them. When they have finished, nominate a student from each group to share their ideas with the class.

Reading

1a Focus attention on the photos and ask Ss what kind of things they think Marek and Kim do. When they have finished, nominate Ss to share their ideas with the class and write them on the board.

b Give Ss a few minutes to read the blog post quickly and check their ideas in Ex 1a. Explain that they will have a chance to read the blog post again more carefully later, so they shouldn't worry if they don't understand every word. Check answers with the class and tick off any of the ideas from Ex1a on the board which were mentioned.

Teaching tip

Rather than set a time limit for a first gist reading, you could have Ss do it as a race. Ss cover the text until you say *Go!* and the first person to find the answers wins. This ensures they only read quickly the first time for general understanding.

2a With **weaker classes**, you may want to pre-teach/check: *library*. Ss read the post again and answer the questions alone, then check in pairs. Check answers with the whole class.

Answers: 1 once a week   2 in a shop   3 at 5.30 a.m.
4 play cards; read; sit in the garden   5 around 9 p.m.

b Ss work in pairs and discuss the questions. Monitor and make notes on their language use for later feedback. In feedback, choose two or three Ss to share their ideas with the class and have a class discussion.

Grammar

Present simple and present continuous

3a Write on the board: *1 We get up at 5.30 a.m. every day.* and *2 Kim and I are trying a new lifestyle.* next to each other. Review how we form each tense by writing (preferably in a different colour) the form under each sentence (*1 I/you/we/they get up; he/she/it gets up; 2 be + verb -ing*). Ss read the Grammar box and choose the correct alternatives, using the examples to help them, then check in pairs. Check answers with the whole class and be prepared to give further explanations/examples where necessary.

Answers: 1 present simple   2 present continuous
3 temporary

b Focus attention back on the text in Ex 1 and ask Ss which tense in the Grammar box the sentence *Kim and I are trying a new lifestyle* is an example of (present continuous to describe a temporary situation). Ss continue alone, then compare answers in pairs. Check answers with the whole class.

Answers:
present simple: *We usually live in the big city,; we come into town once a week; we always walk here; We get up at 5.30 a.m. every day.; We have a simple breakfast; We pick vegetables in the garden and we collect wood in the forest; We finish work at about 6 p.m.; we play cards, read or just sit in the garden; We go to bed early, too,*
present continuous: *Kim and I are trying a new lifestyle; we're living in a forest without electricity; So, how am I writing this blog?; I'm using the computer; Kim's looking for some blankets; We're living in a really simple house; We're not missing TV at all; we're really enjoying it so far*

GRAMMAR BANK 1C pp.116–117
Stronger classes could read the notes at home. Otherwise, check the notes with Ss, especially the description of state/active verbs. In each exercise, elicit the first answer as an example. Ss work alone to complete the exercises, then check their answers in pairs. In feedback, check answers with the whole class. Ss can refer to the notes to help them.

Answers: 1C
1 1 get 2 play 3 'm watching 4 go 5 checks
6 is cleaning 7 read 8 's studying
2 1 eat 2 'm trying 3 have 4 go 5 buy 6 'm eating
7 'm learning 8 cook 9 make 10 loves 11 don't like
12 know

4a 🔊 **1.10** Ss listen and choose the answers alone, then check in pairs. Check answers with the whole class. Be prepared to give further examples and drill the contractions chorally and individually.

Answers: 1 We're 2 She is 3 I'm 4 They are

Pronunciation checkpoint
If Ss find it difficult to hear the contractions, then model each pair of sentences, with and without the contractions, for Ss to hear the difference. You can make it even clearer by using your fingers. For example, say *we are having* and point to each of your fingers in turn. Then put two of your fingers together and say *we're having*. Repeat for the other sentences.

b 🔊 **1.11** Ss listen again to the sentences in Ex 4a and repeat, paying attention to the contractions.
5 Explain that it's now a week later from Marek's first post and he's just posted a new update. Ss complete the text alone, then check in pairs. Check answers with the whole class.

Answers: 1 don't have 2 'm sitting 3 work 4 feel
5 want 6 are 7 am thinking

6a As an example, tell Ss how you would complete each of the prompts with information about yourself. You can also write your answers on the board. Give Ss a few minutes to complete the sentences for themselves. Monitor and help with vocabulary/ideas where necessary.

Optional extra activity
Fast finishers can write two more sentences: one about a temporary situation and one about something they never do.

b Go through the example, modelling with one of the **stronger Ss** and ask follow-up questions to find out more information. Put Ss in pairs to share their ideas and encourage them to ask follow-up questions. In feedback, nominate Ss to share interesting information about their partners with the class.

Optional alternative activity
In Ex 6a, ask Ss to complete three of the prompts with true information and the other two with false information. In Ex 6b, Ss share their information and guess which is true/false.

Further practice
Photocopiable activities: 1C Grammar 1, p152; 1C Grammar 2, p153

Vocabulary
Everyday activities
7a Read the example with the class. Ss complete the phrases alone, then check in pairs. Check answers with the class and drill the phrases chorally and individually.

Answers: 1 take 2 play 3 watch 4 have 5 start/finish
6 get 7 check 8 spend

b Ss add the words alone, then check in pairs. Check answers with the whole class.

Answers: have a good time; start/finish a language course; watch a show; take a taxi; get home; spend money; check the answers; play the piano

Teaching tip
You may want to encourage Ss to keep a vocabulary notebook, so they can refer back to it. There are different ways of recording new vocabulary, e.g. by topic or keyword. Ask Ss to share how they like to record vocabulary and encourage them to try different ways until they find one which works for them.

c Read an example to the class from Ex 7a, e.g. 'watch' and 'TV'. Ss practise in pairs. In feedback, ask different Ss to practise in open pairs.

VOCABULARY BANK 1C p136
Everyday activities
This is an optional extension to the vocabulary section, extending the lexical set and providing further practice. If you're short of time, this can be done for homework.
1 Elicit the first answer as an example. Ss match the words and photos alone, then check in pairs. Check answers with the whole class.

Answers: 1 C 2 I 3 H 4 D 5 F 6 B 7 A 8 L 9 K
10 N 11 E 12 M 13 G 14 J

2 Ss complete the sentences and check answers in pairs.

Answers: 1 to 2 to 3 a 4 with 5 the 6 a 7 in 8 for

3 Read the example with the class. Ss practise in pairs. In feedback, ask different Ss to practise in open pairs.

Speaking

Prepare

8a 1.12 Explain that Ss are going to imagine a change in their lifestyle, then describe it to someone else. First, Ss will listen to an example of someone else doing the same. Go through the lifestyle changes in the list and check understanding. Ss listen and choose which lifestyle Stephanie is trying. Check answers with the whole class.

Answer: trying a new diet

b Ss listen again and answer the questions, then check in pairs. Check answers with the whole class.

Answers:
1 cooking (a stir fry)
2 She has some fruit on her morning break. She walks to work.
3 a lot better

Audioscript 1.12

P: Hey Stephanie, how's it going?
S: OK thanks. Guess what? I'm trying a no-sugar diet for a month.
P: What?! But you love chocolate and sweets. You always have something for dessert. You can't live without sugar! So, how's it going?
S: OK, so far. I'm trying lots of new types of food and drink. I miss chocolate, though. I usually have some for a snack, but now I just have some fruit instead – an apple, or something.
P: And what about exercise?
S: Well, I'm not doing any sport at the moment, but I walk to work every day. It's great actually, I feel a lot better!
P: Well, seriously, that's brilliant, Stephanie. Well done!

9 Explain that Ss can choose one of the topics in Ex 8a, or think of their own if they prefer. While they're making their notes, monitor and check which lifestyle Ss have chosen and help with ideas/vocabulary where necessary.

Speak

10 Go through/drill the Useful phrases. Ss describe their change in lifestyles in pairs. Monitor and make notes on their language use for later feedback. When they have finished, ask a few Ss to describe their partner's lifestyle to the class and ask which they think sounds the most interesting. Go over any common errors and/or examples of good language use from the lesson with the class on the board.

Reflection on learning

Write the following questions on the board:
How could the language you learnt in today's lesson help you in your everyday life?
What question(s) would you like to ask about the language in today's lesson?
Put Ss in pairs to discuss the questions. When they have finished, ask if anyone wants to share their ideas with the class, but don't force them to if they'd rather not.

Fast route: continue to Lesson 1D
Extended route: go to p88 for Develop your reading

1D English in action

Introduction

The goal of this lesson is for Ss to practice asking for and checking information. To help them achieve this, they will learn a range of phrases for asking for and checking information in a variety of contexts.

Warm-up

Write the following on the board:
language courses in your local area
medical information
how to cook a dish
travel information
Put Ss in pairs and ask them to discuss where they usually go to find out information on each of these things, e.g. someone they know, a website/app, etc. When they have finished, elicit ideas from a few Ss and find out if anyone said the same things.

1 Focus attention on the pictures and elicit what's happening in each one. Put Ss in small groups to work in pairs and discuss what kind of help each person needs. Encourage Ss to ask follow-up questions to find out more information. When they have finished, choose one Ss from each group to share their ideas with the class.

2a 1.13 Ss listen and match the conversations to the pictures in Ex 1. Check answers with the whole class.

Answers: 1 B 2 C 3 D

b Ss listen again and answer the questions, then check in pairs. Check answers with the whole class.

Answers: 1 Manchester 2 325 3 5

Audioscript 1.13

Conversation 1
A: Excuse me, can you help me?
B: Of course, what's the problem?
A: I'm trying to buy a ticket to Manchester, but I don't know how to use this machine.
B: Ah, no problem. You need to choose your ticket on the main screen there.
A: OK. Right ... Like this?
B: That's right. Then put your card in here to pay and your ticket will come out here.
A: Oh, thank you.
B: You're welcome!

Conversation 2

A: Good afternoon.

B: Hi there, I'm looking for somewhere to stay for a couple of nights.

A: No problem – we have lots of options. What sort of thing are you looking for?

B: Well, I'd like somewhere in the centre and not too expensive.

A: Well, there's the Ramblers Inn over on Queen Street, which is very nice. Lots of young people there and it's also the cheapest place to stay in the centre.

B: That sounds lovely. What's the quickest way to get there? I'm quite tired after the train journey here.

A: Take the number 325 bus from the stop of the High Street, in front of the bank. It'll get you there in about ten minutes and costs one pound. Is that clear?

B: Um, sorry, can you repeat that, please?

A: Yes, of course. Go to the High Street and find the bus stop.

B: Right.

A: It's in front of the bank. Take bus number 325.

B: Thanks!

Conversation 3

T: … and then check your answers with the person next to you.

S1: Did you get that?

S2: Um … no. Sorry, I didn't hear what she said, I'm not feeling well today. What do I need to do?

S1: Answer the questions then we compare our answers.

S2: OK. Which exercise is it?

S1: Exercise 5. It's this one here.

S2: Oh great. Thanks for your help.

3a ◆ 1.14 Focus attention on the box with the functional phrases and give Ss a minute or two to read through them. Ss listen and tick which ones they hear, then check in pairs. Check answers with the whole class.

> **Answers:** Can you help me?; It's this one here.; Which one is it?; Can you repeat that, please?

b Play the audio again for Ss to listen and repeat. If necessary, be prepared to drill any problematic phrases further.

4 Ss complete the conversations with the missing words. Encourage them not to look at the Useful phrases box while they do this, but they can if they need to. Check answers with the whole class.

> **Answers:** 1 **A:** help, **B:** need 2 **A:** that, **B:** repeat 3 **A:** do, **B:** It's

5 Ss work in pairs (A and B) and practise the conversation.

Speak

6 Ss have conversations in pairs, swapping roles each time they start a new conversation. Monitor and make notes on their language use for later feedback. When they have finished, nominate two or three pairs to perform a conversation for the class. Go through any common errors and/or examples of good language use with the class.

> **Reflection on learning**
>
> Write the following questions on the board:
>
> *How confident did you feel asking for and checking information? When can you use the phrases you learnt today?*
>
> Put Ss in pairs to discuss the questions. When they have finished, ask if anyone wants to share their ideas with the class, but don't force them to if they'd rather not.

Homework ideas

Reflection on learning: Write your answers.

Workbook: Ex 1–3, p7

App: grammar and vocabulary practice

1 Check and reflect

Introduction

Ss revise and practise the language of Unit 1. The notes below provide some ideas for exploiting the activities in class, but you may want to set the first exercise in each section for homework or use them as a diagnostic or progress test. For each grammar or vocabulary point, the first activity reviews the language and the second is more communicative, involving pairwork.

1 Books closed. Write on the board: *What time you get up in the morning?* and elicit where to put *do*. Ss add the missing word to each sentence, then check in pairs. Check answers with the class.

> **Answers:**
> 1 What time **do** you get up in the morning?
> 2 What**'s** your favourite food?
> 3 Whose pen **is** this?
> 4 **How** long is the lesson?
> 5 Which film do **you/they/we/I** want to watch?
> 6 How **many** brothers and sisters have you got?

2a Elicit examples of questions Ss could write for one or two of the topics and write them on the board. Give Ss plenty of time to write their questions, and monitor and help where necessary.

b Demonstrate with a **stronger Ss**, and ask follow-up questions. Ss discuss their questions in pairs. While Ss are speaking, monitor and note down any common errors, and examples of good language use for later feedback. When they have finished, ask one or two Ss to share any interesting information they found out about their partner with the class.

3a Ss choose the correct alternative alone, then check in pairs. Check answers with the whole class.

> **Answers:** 1 Who's 2 How long 3 Whose 4 How many 5 How

b Ss work in pairs and discuss the questions from Ex 3a. Monitor and encourage Ss to ask follow-up questions to find out more information. When they have finished, ask one or two Ss to share any interesting information they found out about their partner with the class.

4a Demonstrate the activity by telling the class one or two of the sentences about yourself. Give Ss plenty of time to complete the sentences and monitor to check they're adding the adverbs of frequency in the correct position.

b Arrange Ss in groups to share their phrases from Ex 5a and find out if others agree. In feedback, nominate a student from each group to share the things people in their group have in common.

5a Elicit the first answer with the class as an example. Tell Ss that in most cases, more than one answer is possible. Ss match the verbs and endings alone, then check in pairs. Check answers with the whole class.

> **Answers:** 1 c/d/f 2 h 3 a 4 g 5 c/e/g 6 f 7 c/e 8 b/c/d/g

b Give one or two examples of your own to demonstrate, e.g. *I plan my time well when I'm studying for an exam. I ask a lot of questions when I'm in class.* Ss write sentences alone. Monitor and help with new vocabulary where necessary. When they have finished, you could put Ss in pairs to compare their sentences.

6 Ss choose the correct alternatives alone, then check in pairs. In feedback, ask a pair to read out the conversation for the class to check.

Answers: 1 are you doing   2 'm just watching   3 have
4 'm not doing   5 is doing   6 usually plays

7a With **weaker classes**, elicit the first answer as an example. Ss complete the questions alone, then check in pairs. Check answers with the whole class.

Answers: 1 do you usually go   2 are you studying
3 are you doing   4 do you listen   5 are you wearing

b Ss work in pairs and discuss the questions. Monitor and encourage them to ask follow-up questions to find out more information. In feedback, ask Ss to share any interesting information they found out about their partner with the class.
8a Ss complete the sentences alone, then check in pairs. **Weaker classes** can refer back to lesson 1C to help. Check answers with the whole class.

Answers: 1 check   2 start   3 spend   4 get   5 play
6 have   7 take   8 watch

b Give one or two of your own examples to demonstrate. Ss change the sentences alone, so they're true for them.
c Ss work in pairs and compare their sentences. In feedback, ask if any Ss have anything in common.

Reflect

Ask Ss to rate each statement alone, then compare in pairs. Encourage them to ask any questions they still have about any of the areas covered in Unit 1.

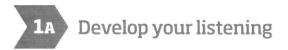

1A   Develop your listening

Introduction

Ss develop their listening skill of understanding the main points in a short talk. Ss learn to understand the main idea in the context of a radio programme about greetings around the world.

Warm-up

Write on the board:
How many languages can you say 'hello' in?
Ss discuss in pairs and say the word for hello in each language they know. In feedback, elicit all the ways to say hello in different languages the class knows and write them on the board.

1a Start by reviewing vocabulary for parts of the body. Make sure you include the following items: *arm, cheek, chest, finger, hand, head, mouth, nose* and *tongue*. Focus attention on the photos and elicit what parts of the body Ss can see. Ss work in pairs and identify which greetings they can see in the photos (three greetings are not shown). Check answers with the whole class and be prepared to offer further explanations or mime the greetings if necessary.

Answers: shake hands (A)   bow your head (B)
press your noses together (C)   kiss someone on the cheek (D)
put your hands together (E)   hug someone (F)

b Elicit ideas from the class, but don't give any answers yet.
c 🔊 1.3 Ss listen and identify which of the greetings are mentioned, then check in pairs. Check answers with the whole class.

Answers: shake hands; kiss someone on the cheek

Audioscript 1.3

Presenter:

Hello! Welcome to this week's Culture Show with me, Anna Taylor. Today we are talking about greetings. What to say or do in that first moment when you meet someone?

It can be difficult, can't it? You meet someone new and you decide to shake hands, but the other person decides to give you a kiss on the cheek. Has anything like this ever happened to you? This kind of thing happens all the time, because there are so many different greetings from all over the world. How we greet someone for the first time is important because we want people to like us. So let's take a look at some different ways of greeting, so that next time you do it the right way!

2 Ss read the Focus box and answer the question. Go through anything that isn't clear, giving further explanations/examples where necessary.

Answer: Key words are usually stressed.

3a Ss mark the key words alone, then check in pairs. While they're working, write the statement on the board. In feedback, invite a student to come to the board and underline the key words, then ask if the rest of the class agrees.
b 🔊 1.4 Ss listen and check. Check answers with the class.

Suggested answers: How, greet, first time, important, want, like

Audioscript 1.4

Presenter:

How we greet someone for the first time is important because we want people to like us.

4 🔊 1.5 Ss listen and choose the correct alternatives, then check in pairs. Check answers with the class.

Answers: 1 shake hands 2 hug 3 shake hands
4 sometimes 5 put their right hand on their chest
6 press their noses together

Audioscript 1.5

Presenter:

In the US, most people shake hands when they meet new people. Women often kiss both their male and female friends on the cheek or hug them. Men often do the same with their female friends, but they usually shake hands with their male friends.

In Brazil, people shake hands when they meet someone new. With friends and family, men still shake hands, but women usually kiss each other on the cheek. It's sometimes difficult to know how many times to kiss. In some areas they kiss once, in some they kiss twice, and in other areas, they kiss three times!

In Qatar, people usually shake hands when they meet for the first time. However, when men and women meet, they don't usually do this. They put their right hand on their chest. When female friends meet, they kiss each other on the cheek, or touch each other's hands. When male friends meet, they shake hands or press their noses together twice – a traditional greeting in Qatar.

5 🔊 1.6 Give Ss a minute to read the notes and think about what type of information they need to listen for. Ss listen and complete the notes, then check in pairs. Check answers with the whole class.

Answers: 1 heads 2 bow 3 low 4 hands 5 chest
6 high 7 tongue

Audioscript 1.6

Presenter:

In South Korea, the traditional greeting is to bow. With friends, men and women bow their head. However, in important meetings, business people bow with the top half of their body. Younger people bow low when they're with someone older. They can only stand up after the older person stands up.

In Thailand, people put their hands together in front of them when they meet new people. Then they bow their head. When they meet friends, their hands are low, in front of their chest. But when they meet someone older or more important, their hands are high and their fingers are near the top of their head.

And finally, in Tibet, the greeting is a little unusual. In many countries, showing your tongue to another person is not polite, but in Tibet it's a traditional way of saying hello. People put their hands together in front of them and then show their tongue but only for a very short time.

So, if you ever go to South Korea, Thailand or Tibet, now you can greet people in the right way.

6 Ss work in pairs and discuss the questions. In feedback, elicit their ideas and have a class discussion to round off the lesson.

Homework ideas

Workbook: Ex 1–4, p7

1B Develop your writing

Introduction

Ss develop their writing skill of completing a questionnaire. Ss learn how to give reasons in the context of language learning preferences.

Warm-up

Write on the board: *quelch* and explain that this is a word in a language they don't know (decide what it means, e.g. *hospital*, but don't tell Ss). Explain that they need to ask you questions to find out what it means, e.g. *Is it a thing or a person? Can you drive a quelch? Is it big or small?*, etc. Have Ss from around the class ask you questions until they guess what it is.

1a Ss work in pairs and discuss the questions. In feedback, elicit answers from the class and have a class discussion. Write any useful strategies Ss mention on the board.

b The aim of this lesson, as well as developing students' writing skills, is to act as a needs analysis for your class, providing you, as the teacher, with useful information about your learners' language-learning preferences. Focus attention on the questionnaire and ask if Ss have ever completed something like this when starting a new course. With **weaker classes**, you may want to pre-teach/check: *look up* and *hardest*. Ss read the answers and match the questions alone, then check in pairs. Check answers with the whole class.

Answers: A5 B6 C3 D1 E2 F4

2 Ss read and decide if the sentences are true or false alone, then check in pairs. Check answers with the whole class.

Answers: 1 F 2 T 3 T 4 T 5 T

3 Give Ss a few minutes to read the Focus box and ask about anything they're not sure of. Then ask Ss to underline examples in Miguel's answers in Ex 1. Check answers with the class.

Answers:

<u>That's why</u> I'm studying English. I like having conversations in class, <u>because</u> I can't practise speaking English at home. But I also like reading interesting articles, <u>because</u> I can learn new things. Pronunciation is the hardest thing for me <u>because of</u> all the different sounds in English.

4 With **weaker classes**, elicit the first answer as an example. Otherwise, Ss match the sentences halves, then check in pairs. Check answers with the whole class.

Answers: 1 b 2 d 3 a 4 c

5 Ss choose the correct alternatives alone, then check in pairs. Check answers with the whole class.

Answers: 1 so that 2 because 3 because of 4 That's why
5 so that

Prepare

6 Give Ss plenty of time to think about their own answers to the questions and make notes. Monitor and help with ideas/new vocabulary where necessary.

Write

7 Because this activity is also meant as a needs analysis, you might want to ask Ss to write their answers on a separate piece of paper, so that you can collect them in at the end and refer to them when planning future lessons. Focus Ss attention on the Useful phrases. While Ss are writing, monitor and help where necessary. Ss can also use the Focus box to help them. When they have finished, ask Ss to check their writing and think about whether they have used the language for giving reasons correctly.

Homework ideas

Workbook: Ex 1–5, p9

1c Develop your reading

Introduction

Ss develop their reading skill of understanding short texts. Ss learn how to read for specific information in the context of an article about a man who records his life.

Warm-up

Write on the board:
How often do you take photos?
What do you take photos of?
Do you like taking photos with your phone or with a real camera?
Ss work in small groups and discuss the questions. When they are ready, nominate a student from each group to share their ideas with the class.

1 Ask Ss to read the title and introduction to the news article. Ask if any Ss have heard of this person. Make sure they don't read any further at this stage. Ss discuss the question in pairs. Check answers with the class.

Answers: He's taken photos and made lots of notes.

2 Give Ss time to read the Focus box, then discuss the question in pairs. Explain that reading for specific information is something we do subconsciously in our first language and is a good strategy to use when learning a new language to help us understand specific information.

Suggested answers: dates and names

3a With **weaker classes**, you may want to pre-teach/check: *look back*. Ss read the text and find the answers to the questions, then check in pairs. Check answers with the whole class.

Answers: 1 1,200 2 2010 3 4.36 p.m. 4 Villarroel 5 every 30 seconds

b Ss work in pairs and discuss the questions. In feedback, elicit their ideas and have a class discussion.

4 Ask Ss to read the title and introduction. Ask if any Ss have heard of this film. Make sure they don't read any further at this stage. Ss discuss the question in pairs. In feedback, elicit their ideas and have a class discussion.

b Ss find the information alone, then check in pairs. Check answers with the whole class.

Answers: 1 Ridley Scott 2 24th July 2010 3 80,000 4 YouTube 5 94 minutes and 53 seconds

Optional extra activity

Suggest Ss watch the film at home, then choose their favourite clip. In the next class they can share their favourite clips, saying why they like them.

5 Ss work in pairs and describe their typical day. When they have finished, ask a few Ss to share any interesting information they found out about their partners with the class.

Homework ideas

Workbook: Ex 1–4, p8

2 OVERVIEW

2A One of those days
Goal | describe events in the past
Grammar | past simple
Vocabulary | feelings
GSE learning objective
Can describe very basic events in the past using simple linking words (e.g. 'then', 'next')

2B You're never too old
Goal | ask and answer questions about the past
Grammar | past simple negative and questions
Vocabulary | past time expressions
GSE learning objective
Can ask and answer questions about past times and past activities

2C Unusual tastes
Goal | describe a popular dish
Grammar | quantifiers
Vocabulary | adjectives to describe food
GSE learning objective
Can give straightforward descriptions on a variety of familiar subjects

2D English in action
Goal | show interest and excitement
GSE learning objective
Can express enthusiasm and excitement in a limited way

Check and reflect
(a) I can describe a memorable day.
(b) I can ask about and describe past events.

VOCABULARY BANK

DEVELOP YOUR SKILLS

2A Develop your reading
Goal | understand a short narrative text
Focus | narrative structure
GSE learning objective
Can understand short, simple narrative texts

2B Develop your writing
Goal | write a story
Focus | using adverbs to describe actions
GSE learning objective
Can write short basic descriptions of past events and activities

2C Develop your listening
Goal | understand a short talk
Focus | recognising weak forms
GSE learning objective
Can identify the main points in short talks on familiar topics, if delivered slowly and clearly

---

2A One of those days

Introduction

The goal of this lesson is for Ss to talk about events in the past by describing a memorable day in their lives. To help them achieve this, Ss will learn/revise the past simple and vocabulary to describe feelings.

Warm-up

Write on the board:
A good day is when … A bad day is when …
Elicit an example of each, e.g. *A good day is when I get home early from work. A bad day is when I miss my bus.* Ss complete the sentences alone. Encourage them to complete each one with a few ideas. Monitor and help with vocabulary where necessary, writing any new words/phrases on the board. When they are ready, put Ss in small groups to share their ideas, then choose the best for each sentence. Nominate a student from each group to share their best ideas with the class.

Vocabulary and listening

Feelings

> **Teaching tip**
>
> At the start of the class, create a vocabulary section on your board for writing up new words/phrases and leave it up for the rest of the class. At the end of the lesson, take a photo of this section, or write down the words/phrases, and keep the record safe. You can then spend the first and last few minutes of each section reviewing/recycling the words/phrases by asking, e.g. *Who can remember a word which means very bad?* (terrible).

1 Focus attention on the photos and elicit what kind of day the people are having in one or two of them with the whole class. Ss look at the other photos, and work in pairs and discuss the questions. When they have finished, nominate one or two Ss to share their ideas with the whole class.

2a Demonstrate the activity by choosing a photo and eliciting which adjective(s) could describe the person in it. With **weaker classes**, go through the meanings of the adjectives first, checking understanding and giving examples of each one. Ss match the adjectives and photos in pairs. Monitor and help with the meanings of the adjectives where necessary. Check answers with the whole class, eliciting Ss' ideas. Be prepared to give further explanations and examples for each of the adjectives, and drill the adjectives with the class chorally and individually.

> **Vocabulary checkpoint**
>
> Nervous is a 'false friend' in many languages. A similar word exists, but it has a meaning more similar to *angry* or *irritated*. In English, it's meaning is more similar to *worried* or *anxious*.

> **Pronunciation checkpoint**
>
> When drilling the vocabulary, pay attention to the following adjectives and their pronunciation: *bored* /bɔːd/, *stressed* /strest/, *nervous* /ˈnɜːvəs/ and *relaxed* /rɪˈlækst/.

Suggested answers: A afraid/worried B bored C happy
D stressed E nervous/worried F relaxed/happy

b Elicit the first answer as an example with the class. Ss choose the correct alternatives alone, then check in pairs. Check answers with the whole class.

Answers: 1 nervous 2 relaxed 3 bored 4 excited
5 stressed 6 afraid

3a Read the first situation with the class and elicit how Ss might feel, and write the adjectives they come up with on the board. Ss work alone to write adjectives for how they might feel in each situation. Tell Ss that they can use adjectives which are not in Ex 2a if they know any. Monitor and encourage Ss to write as many adjectives as they can for each situation.

b Put Ss in pairs to compare their answers. In feedback, nominate a different pair for each situation and elicit what they wrote.

Suggested answers: 1 angry, surprised 2 happy, relaxed
3 nervous, stressed 4 afraid, nervous, worried
5 excited, happy 6 excited, happy
7 surprised, happy, excited, (maybe nervous!)
8 worried, stressed, angry

4a Read the example with the class. Give Ss a few minutes to choose their three adjectives and write their sentences. **Fast finishers** can write one or two more sentences. Monitor and help with vocabulary where necessary.

b Ss work in pairs and read their sentences for their partners to guess which adjective they are describing. When they have finished, ask one or two Ss to read their sentences for the class to guess.

VOCABULARY BANK 2A p137
Feelings

This is an optional extension activity in the vocabulary section, extending the lexical set and providing further practice. If you're short of time, this can be done for homework.

1 Elicit the first answer as an example. Ss choose the correct alternatives alone, then check in pairs. Check answers with the whole class and be prepared to give further explanations/examples where necessary.

Answers: 1 exhausted 2 calm 3 upset 4 frightened
5 miserable 6 cheerful 7 confident 8 annoyed

2a Give an example about yourself to demonstrate with the class. Ss work alone to choose their adjectives and think of the situation. Tell them they can make notes if they want. Monitor and help with vocabulary where necessary.

b Ss share their ideas in pairs. When they have finished, ask a few pairs to share their ideas with the class.

Optional alternative activity

Stronger classes can complete Ex 1 and 2a at home, then discuss Ex 2b in the next class.

Further practice

Photocopiable activities: 2A Vocabulary, p152

5a ◁) **2.1** You may want to pre-teach/check: *(car) battery, broke down, soaking wet* and *spilt*. Explain that Ss are going to listen to Lynn describing a job interview and elicit which adjectives might be appropriate. Ss listen and tick the adjectives, then check in pairs. Check answers with the whole class and elicit why she felt that way for each adjective.

Answers: angry (she woke up late and she didn't have time for breakfast); nervous (she spilt water on her laptop and about the rest of the interview): happy (the day ended): relaxed (about the presentation at the interview): stressed (the car battery was flat and she had to take the bus but it broke down)

b Give Ss a minute to read through the sentences and guess which ones are true or false, then play the recording again for them to check. Ss check answers in pairs, then play the recording again if necessary. Check answers with the whole class.

Answers: 1 T 2 F 3 T 4 F 5 F

Teaching tip

Be careful about playing a recording too many times in class, as this isn't something Ss can do when they listen in real life. It's a good idea to train Ss to get as much information as they can from listening just one or two times. You can do this by giving them opportunities to compare answers with other Ss after they listen and before feedback. Not only will this help them get any answers they missed, but it will also make them more confident about the answers they have.

Audioscript 2.1

T: So, how did your job interview go the other day, Lynn?
L: Oh, it was terrible!
T: Oh, no! What happened?
L: Well, it was just one of those days, you know? It started badly and just got worse. First of all, my alarm didn't go off. When I woke up, my clock was on the floor. I think the cat played with it during the night and broke it.
T: Oh, no!
L: Oh, yes! I got up late and didn't have time for breakfast. So, I started the day angry and hungry!
T: Oh dear.
L: Then I got into my car and – I couldn't believe it – the battery was dead! So, I had to take the bus. Well, you can imagine that at this point, I was really stressed.
T: Let me guess – you missed the bus?
L: Ha, no. I caught it, but half way there, it broke down!
T: So, what did you do?
L: Well, we had to wait for the next bus, but then it started raining really heavily and, of course, I didn't have an umbrella. When I arrived for the interview, I was soaking wet.
T: Oh, Lynn.
L: It got worse, though. I had to give a presentation as part of the interview. I felt quite relaxed about it, actually. But just before I started, I spilt a glass of water all over my laptop. I tried to turn it on, but it didn't work.
T: Oh, no!
L: Yeah, so by now I was really nervous, and my presentation was terrible. I even forgot to say some important things … the interviewers weren't happy.
T: Oh, I'm sorry to hear that, Lynn.
L: I know, thanks, Tony. I was so happy when that day ended! I've got another interview next week, though. I'll just make sure the cat sleeps in another room!
T: Ha, good idea!

Grammar

Past simple

6 Books closed. Write on the board: *I ___ the bus to the interview. (take) I ___ angry. (be)* Elicit the past forms and write them on the board. Point to the sentences and ask *past, present or future?* (past). Ss then open their books and look at the Grammar box. Give Ss a few minutes to choose the correct alternatives, using the examples in the box to help them. Monitor and help where necessary. When they have finished, check answers with the whole class and be prepared to give further explanations/examples where necessary.

Answers: 1 finished   2 be   3 -ed

GRAMMAR BANK 2A   pp.118–119

Stronger classes could read the notes at home. Otherwise, check the notes with Ss, especially the irregular past simple verb endings. In each exercise, elicit the first answer as an example. Ss work alone to complete the exercises, then check their answers in pairs. In feedback, elicit Ss' answers and drill the words. Ss can refer to the notes to help them.

Answers: 2A
1 1 had   2 woke   3 left   4 tried   5 ran   6 waited
   7 weren't   8 read   9 went   10 arrived
2 1 began   2 watched   3 moved   4 ate   5 arrived
   6 taught   7 bought   8 planned

7a 🔊 **2.2** Books closed. Write the three verbs in the table on one side of the board and the phonemes on the other. Say the verbs and ask Ss to match the phonemes and the verbs. Ss open their books again. Focus attention on the table and check answers. Play the recording, pausing after each verb for Ss to write it in the chart. Ss compare answers in pairs, but don't give any answers yet.

b Ss listen again and check their answers. Drill the verbs chorally and individually for further practice if necessary.

Answers:
/d/: arrived, played, tried
/ɪd/: deleted, ended, wanted
/t/: stopped, talked, watched

Optional extra activity

After Ex 7b, write each of the phonemes /d/, /ɪd/ and /t/ on separate pieces of paper. Stick each piece of paper to a different wall in the classroom and ask the whole class to stand up. Call out the verbs in Ex 7a randomly. Each time you call one out, Ss run to the correct wall which matches the phoneme of the past simple ending of the verb.

Alternatively, if you don't have much classroom space, put the class in three groups and assign one of the phonemes to each group. Take turns to call out each verb. When a group thinks it has their phoneme, they either stand up or raise their hands.

8a Elicit the first answer as an example. Ss complete the text with the verbs in the past simple alone, then check in pairs. Check answers with the whole class.

Answers: 1 went   2 arrived   3 showed   4 knew   5 tried
6 was   7 noticed   8 thought   9 wanted   10 decided
11 walked   12 heard

Optional extra activity

With *weaker classes*, ask these questions to check comprehension of the story: *How did the writer feel at the party?* (bored); *Who did he see there?* (a beautiful woman); *How did he meet the woman?* (He took her umbrella by mistake.)

---

b Describe a time when you felt one of the adjectives yourself as an example. Give Ss a few minutes to think of their ideas and help with vocabulary where necessary. Ss discuss their experiences in pairs. When they have finished, ask a few Ss to share their experiences with the class, picking a different adjective each time.

Optional alternative activity

When Ss discuss their experiences in Ex 8b, tell them not to say which adjective they are describing. Their partners then listen and guess the adjective.

Further practice

Photocopiable activities: 2A Grammar 1, p153;
2A Grammar 2, p151

Speaking

Prepare

9 Read the instructions with the class. Give Ss plenty of time to think of ideas and make notes. Make sure they don't write full sentences here, just key words and phrases. Monitor and help with vocabulary where necessary.

Speak

10 Arrange Ss in groups and go through the Useful phrases. Ss take turns to describe their days within their groups, and listen to other Ss' stories. While they are speaking, monitor and make notes on any examples of good language use and any common errors for later feedback.

Teaching tip

When Ss are doing a speaking activity like in Ex 10, the focus is on fluency. Because we don't want to interrupt their 'flow', rather than correct errors as we hear them, it's a good idea to make notes on these errors for later feedback. After the activity, write the errors on the board and correct them together as 'class errors', so as not to embarrass the Ss who made them. For examples of good language use, drill these around the class and write them on the board, saying who said them.

Reflection on learning

Write the following questions on the board:
How confident did you feel describing a memorable day?
Was there any vocabulary in today's lesson you found difficult?
What can you do to help you remember/practise it?
Put Ss in pairs to discuss the questions. When they have finished, ask if anyone wants to share their ideas with the class, but don't force them to if they'd rather not.

Homework ideas

Grammar bank: 2A Ex 1–2, pp.118–119
Workbook: Ex 1–5, p10
App: grammar and vocabulary practice

Fast route: continue to Lesson 2B
Extended route: go to p89 for Develop your reading

2B You're never too old

Introduction

The goal of this lesson is for Ss to describe something special they've done in the past. To help them achieve this, Ss will learn/revise past simple negative sentences and questions, and past time expressions in the context of people who have done amazing things.

Warm-up

Bring/Download three photos of people you know or famous people who have done something special or amazing. Show them to the class and describe what they did, giving details. This is an opportunity to recycle the past simple verbs from Lesson 2A, so try to include some here. Give Ss a few minutes to think of three people in their family who have done something special and make notes about what they did. Monitor and help with vocabulary, writing any new words/phrases on the board. When they are ready, Ss share their information in pairs. In feedback, nominate a few Ss to share their partner's information with the class.

Reading and vocabulary

Past time expressions

1 Focus attention on the photos and elicit the answer to the question. Encourage Ss to speculate about who they are, where they are and what amazing thing they could have done.

Answer: They're all achieving things at an older age.

2a You may want to pre-teach/check: *primary school, a marathon* and *retire*. Give Ss a few minutes to read the article quickly, match the people to the photos and answer the questions in the introduction. Tell Ss they'll have a chance to read the article again more carefully afterwards. Ss compare answers in pairs, then check with the whole class.

Answers:
1C **Kimani Maruge:** A man who started school for the first time aged 84, because the law changed in his country to make primary schools free.
2A **Harriette Thompson:** She ran the San Diego marathon aged 76, then ran it almost every year for the next 16 years. She was the oldest woman to run a marathon at 94. She ran marathons to raise money for charity.
3B **Laila Denmark:** An American doctor who worked until she was 103, because she wanted to help children.

b Ss read the text again and answers the questions alone, then check in pairs. Check answers with the whole class.

Answers: 1 In 2003 2 In 2005 3 On 23rd May 1999 4 When she was 94 years old. 5 When she was 103 years old. 6 She was 114 years old.

Optional alternative activity

Stronger classes can try to answer the questions from memory, before they read the text again. Ss then read the text to check.

c Ss work in pairs and discuss the questions. Encourage them to give reasons for their choices. In feedback, elicit their ideas and have a class discussion.

3a Go through the time expressions in the box, elicit the most recent one (last month) and write it on the left-hand side of the board. Ss put the expressions in order alone, from the most recent to the oldest, then check in pairs. Check answers with the whole class and ask Ss to come to the board and write them in a line.

Answers: 1 last month 2 six weeks ago 3 in 2018 4 on 23rd May 2017 5 until 2015 6 when I was five

b With **weaker classes**, elicit the first answer as an example. Ss complete the expressions alone, then check in pairs. Check answers with the whole class.

Answers: 1 when 2 last 3 ago 4 on 5 until 6 in

Optional extra activity

Say *in 2014* and elicit another way of saying this with the time expressions (*a few years ago*). Ss work in pairs and take turns to say a time expression for their partner to rephrase using another expression.

c Read the example with the class and demonstrate by saying one or two sentences about yourself, using different expressions from Ex 3b. Give Ss plenty of time to write their sentences. Monitor and help with vocabulary where necessary. Check Ss are using the past simple and the time expressions correctly.

d Put Ss in pairs to share their sentences. Read the example with the class and refer back to your own example in Ex 3c to give further information. Monitor and encourage Ss to give more information for each sentence. When they have finished, nominate a few Ss to share some of their partners' sentences with the class.

Further practice

Photocopiable activities: 2B Vocabulary, p155

Grammar

Past simple negative and questions

4 Books closed. Write on the board: *She walked.* + *Schools were free.* + Then erase the plus signs and write negative signs. Elicit the negative forms of the verbs and write them on the board (*didn't walk, weren't*). Ss read the Grammar box and choose the correct alternatives alone, then check in pairs. Encourage Ss to use the examples to help. When they have finished, check answers with the whole class. Be prepared to give further explanations/examples where necessary.

Answers: 1 didn't 2 wasn't and weren't 3 did 4 were

Pronunciation checkpoint

The form of past simple negatives and questions is very similar to that of the present simple, e.g. *Where do you work?* (present), *Where did you work?* (past). You may want to point this out to Ss as you look at the past simple.

GRAMMAR BANK 2B pp.118–119

Stronger classes could read the notes at home. Otherwise, check the notes with Ss, especially the different form of questions with *be*. In each exercise, elicit the first answer as an example. Ss work alone to complete the exercises, then check their answers in pairs. In feedback, elicit Ss' answers and drill the questions. Ss can refer to the notes to help them.

Answers: 2B

1 1 didn't start   2 didn't meet   3 wasn't   4 weren't
   5 wasn't   6 didn't have   7 didn't know   8 didn't say

2 1 What did you do yesterday?
   2 How long was your journey to school today?
   3 Who did you see last weekend?
   4 Where did you go last night?
   5 How did you feel yesterday?
   6 Where were you at six o'clock yesterday?
   7 What time did you get up this morning?
   8 What was your favourite game when you were a child?
   9 When did you start your English course?
   10 What were your favourite programmes when you were young?

5a 🔊 **2.3** Ss listen and answer the question about the pronunciation alone, then check in pairs. Make sure they only focus on the questions, i.e. what speaker A says. Check answers with the whole class.

> **Answer:** They're usually unstressed: /wəz/ and /wə/.

b Ss listen again, this time focusing on the answers (speaker B) to elicit what they notice about the pronunciation. Elicit the answer from the class. If necessary, provide further practice by drilling chorally and individually.

> **Answer:** They're usually stressed.

Optional extra activity

Ss work in pairs and practise the conversations in Ex 5a. When they have finished, Ss swap roles and repeat.

6a Write the prompts in the first question on the board and elicit the question, and write it on the board as an example. Ss then use the prompts to write the questions alone. Encourage them to look back at the rules and examples in the Grammar box if they get stuck. Check answers with the whole class.

> **Answers:**
> 1 How **did** you learn to play the piano?
> 2 **Was** it difficult to get into your university?
> 3 **When** did you get your driving licence?
> 4 **Were** you happy with your exam results?
> 5 **Did** you enjoy water skiing?
> 6 **Did** he win the race?

b Ss complete the sentences alone, then check in pairs. Check answers with the whole class.

> **Answers:** a didn't   b wasn't   c didn't   d weren't   e wasn't
> f didn't

c With *weaker classes*, demonstrate the activity by asking a question from Ex 6a and eliciting the answer from Ex 6b. Ss ask and answer in pairs. When they have finished, ask a pair to read out the first question/answer for the class, then a different pair for each subsequent question/answer. Check that they are

stressing the auxiliaries correctly. Ask if any of the answers are true for anyone in the class.

> **Answers:** 1 c   2 b   3 a   4 d   5 e   6 f

Further practice

Photocopiable activities: 2B Grammar 1, p153;
2B Grammar 2, p154

Speaking

Prepare

7a 🔊 **2.4** Ss listen and answer the question alone, then check in pairs. Check answers with the whole class.

> **Answer:** She taught herself to play the guitar.

Audioscript 2.4

Dan: You're so good at the guitar, Megan. Where did you learn?
Megan: Well, I taught myself actually.
Dan: Really. That's amazing!
Megan: Yeah, I'm really proud of it.
Dan: I'm not surprised!

b Give Ss time to think of and write their questions. Monitor and help with vocabulary where necessary, writing any new words/phrases on the board.

Optional extra activity

If Ss are having difficulty thinking of ideas, give them a few prompts on the board, e.g. *When/start?*; *difficult?*; *Why/decide/learn the guitar?*

c 🔊 **2.5** Ss listen and answer their questions from Ex 7b (if possible). Elicit what Ss found out about Megan with the whole class.

Audioscript 2.5

Dan: How did you teach yourself?
Megan: My parents bought me a guitar when I was about 13, I bought myself some books and then learnt from those.
Dan: Did you teach yourself to read music, too?
Megan: No, I could already do that. I had some piano lessons when I was younger.
Dan: Oh right. How long did it take you to learn?
Megan: I could play quite well after about two years, I think.
Dan: How often did you practise?
Megan: Every day, sometimes for about two hours.
Dan: That's quite a lot.
Megan: I know! I really wanted to learn. I wanted to be a musician and write my own music.
Dan: Did you write your own music?
Megan: Yes and I still do sometimes.
Dan: I didn't know that! Can I hear some of it?
Megan: Sure, I've got a YouTube channel. You can hear some of it on there. Look, I'll show you …

8 Demonstrate by briefly talking about something special you did in the past, using the questions as prompts. Explain that Ss can speak about something small, e.g. an event, learning something new or doing something for the first time, etc. It doesn't have to be anything big like those in the reading texts in Ex 2. Give Ss time to think about their answers to the questions and make notes.

Speak

9a Ss talk about what they did in pairs. Encourage them to use their notes from Ex 8 to find out as much information as possible. Monitor and make notes on any common errors, or examples of good language use, for later feedback.

b Rearrange Ss so that they work with another partner. Ss tell their new partner as much as they can remember about their previous partner. Monitor and make notes as before.

> **Teaching tip**
>
> When rearranging students into new pairs, make sure you ask the class to stand up before telling them where to go. This will ensure they pay attention and don't end up in the wrong place.

> **Reflection on learning**
>
> Write the following questions on the board:
> *Which did you find most difficult, describing your special thing or describing your partner's? Why?*
> *Which three expressions from this lesson do you think you'll use again in the future?*
>
> Put Ss in pairs to discuss the questions. When they have finished, ask if anyone wants to share their ideas with the class, but don't force them to if they'd rather not.

Homework ideas

Ex 9: Ss write a description of their special day.
Grammar bank: 2B Ex 1–2, pp.118–119
Workbook: Ex 1–6, p11
App: grammar and vocabulary practice

Fast route: continue to Lesson 2C
Extended route: go to p90 for Develop your writing

 2c Unusual tastes

Introduction

The goal of this lesson is for students to describe a dish they know well. To help them achieve this, they will learn/revise countable and uncountable nouns, and quantifiers. Ss will learn adjectives to describe food in the context of a range of popular dishes from around the world.

Warm-up

Before class, write the following questions on the board:
What's your favourite food?
What types of food don't you like?
What types of food is your country famous for?
Think of three or four countries: what famous dishes do you know from them?

Ss work in pairs and discuss the questions. Monitor and help with vocabulary where necessary. When they have finished, ask a few Ss to share their ideas with the class and have a brief class discussion.

Listening and vocabulary

Adjectives to describe food

1 Divide up the board into three sections and write the food categories listed at the top of each one. Elicit a type of food for each category as an example and write them on the board. Give Ss a few minutes to think of as many types of food for each category as they can. In feedback, elicit the food and write it in each category, checking understanding as you go along.

Optional alternative activity

After a few minutes, nominate a Ss to come to the board and give them a pen, but make sure they don't bring any notes with them. Ask the other Ss to call out examples of food to the Ss at the board, who writes them in the correct category. When they have finished, check the spelling and give further explanations if necessary.

2a Focus attention on the photos and ask Ss to discuss the questions. Be open to all their ideas at this stage.

b Ask Ss to read the descriptions and match them to the photos. Ask Ss to underline any new words as they read the descriptions and match them to the photos. Ss check answers in pairs and ask if their partner knows any of the new words they underlined. Check answers with the class and explain any new words, giving examples where possible. Refer back to their ideas in Ex 2a and ask if anyone guessed correctly. Also, elicit whether Ss think the dishes sound nice.

Answers: 1 B   2 E   3 A   4 D   5 C

3 ◁ 2.6 Ss listen and answer the questions for each speaker, then check answers in pairs. Check answers with the whole class.

Answers: 1 Brigadeiro; yes   2 Nasi Lemak; no
3 Ahi Poke; yes

4a Go through the adjectives in the box with the class, reading them aloud, so Ss can hear what they sound like. Check the pronunciation of *delicious* /dɪˈlɪʃəs/. Ss listen and write the number of the conversation next to each adjective as they hear it, then check their answers in pairs. Check answers with the whole class.

Answers: 1 sweet, creamy, delicious   2 plain, dry, hot, sour
3 light, fresh

Audioscript 2.6

1
A: This is a very popular cake where I come from, Kara. Would you like to try it?
B: Yes, please! … mmm, it tastes just fantastic! But it's very, very sweet – is there a lot of sugar in it?
A: Actually, there isn't any sugar in it. I mean, we don't add any when we make it. But there's a lot of chocolate and milk, and that's what makes it taste so sweet.
B: … and creamy! Well, I love it, it's absolutely delicious. Um … could I have another one?
A: Of course!

2
W: Here you are, sir.
C1: Oh, I love that dish, great choice.
C2: Mm, I don't know – it looks a bit plain. Rice, egg and cucumber.
C1: Go on, try a bit. I'm sure you'll like it.
C2: … um … well, it is a bit dry.
C1: Have some sauce with it, it's amazing.
C2: OK, that might help … Oh! Wow!
C1: What's wrong?
C2: Oh, it's hot! Really hot!
C1: Ha! Yes, it's got lots of chilli in it. Do you like it?
C2: Well, not really. Sorry! It's quite sour, too. I think I'll order something different. Excuse me, I'd like …

3

A: What's that you're eating, Manu?
B: It's a salad from my part of the world. Would you like to try it?
A: Yes, please. I'll give it a go. Mmm, it's light and fresh.
B: Yes, all the ingredients are fresh and it's got a little oil in it. It's pretty healthy.
A: Mmm, lots of different flavours, too. I really like that!
B: Yes, there are a few herbs and spices to give it more flavour. I usually have a bit of bread with it, too. I'll give you the recipe later if you like.
A: Yes, please! That would be great!

b Ss answer the question in pairs. Encourage them to use dictionaries or their mobile devices to look up any new words. In feedback, check answers with the class and be prepared to give further explanations/examples where necessary.

Answers:
Positive: sweet, creamy, delicious, light, fresh
Negative: plain, dry, hot, sour (hot and sour often negative, but can be positive)
Neutral: typical

Vocabulary checkpoint

Point out that *hot* can mean the opposite of *cold*, but that here it means *spicy*.

c Demonstrate with an example, e.g. fresh: *fish* and *vegetables*. Put Ss in pairs to think of two dishes or types of food for each adjective. In feedback, elicit Ss' answers from the class.

VOCABULARY BANK 2C p137
Food

This is an optional extension to the vocabulary section, extending the lexical set and providing further practice. If you're short of time, this can be done for homework.

1 Ss match the food and drink (1–15) with the photos (A–O) alone, then check in pairs. Check answers with the whole class.

Answers: A steak B lamb C fizzy drinks D juice
E mushrooms F fish G burger H cereal I salad J grapes
K chilli L butter M mango N crisps O yoghurt

2 Ss work in pairs and discuss the questions. In feedback, elicit Ss' ideas and have a brief class discussion.

Optional alternative activity

Ss think of two dishes or types of food for each adjective alone and write them down. Monitor and help with vocabulary where necessary. When they have finished, put Ss in pairs. They then take it in turns to read out their dishes/types of food in random order for their partner to guess the adjective.

Further practice

Photocopiable activities: 2C Vocabulary, p155

Grammar

Quantifiers

5 2.7 Ss listen to the extracts and choose the correct alternatives, then check in pairs. Check answers with the whole class.

Answers: 1 any 2 a lot of 3 some 4 lots of 5 a
6 little 7 a few 8 a bit of

Optional alternative activity

Stronger classes could do the exercise first, then listen to the extracts and check their answers.

Optional extra activity

Quickly revise countable/uncountable nouns by calling out the words below in random order and asking Ss to tell you if they're countable or uncountable:
Countable: *potato, onion, egg, banana, mango*
Uncountable: *herbs and spices, fish, milk, oil, bread, meat, butter*

6 Ss choose the correct alternatives in the Grammar box alone, then check in pairs. Encourage them to use the extracts in Ex 5 and the examples in the box to help. In feedback, check answers with the whole class and be prepared to give further explanations/ examples where necessary.

Answers: 1 singular countable 2 plural countable
3 uncountable 4 small 5 big

GRAMMAR BANK 2C pp.118–119
Stronger classes could read the notes at home. Otherwise, check the notes with Ss and be prepared to give further explanations/examples where necessary. In each exercise, elicit the first answer as an example. Ss work alone to complete the exercises, then check their answers in pairs. In feedback, elicit Ss' answers and drill the questions. Ss can refer to the notes to help them.

Answers: 2C
1 1 There's 2 onion 3 bread 4 wine 5 there are
  6 potatoes 7 are 8 sugar
2 1 there isn't ~~no~~ **any** OR there's no 2 a lot **of** sugar
  3 **a** bit 4 There are a few ~~of~~ blueberries
  5 I always eat ~~any~~ **cheese** at the weekend.
  6 There~~'s~~ are no good cooks OR There aren't any good cooks

7a 2.8 Focus attention on the letters in bold in the sentences. Play the audio for Ss to listen to how they're connected. If you think it's useful, explain the information in the *Pronunciation checkpoint* box below using the examples given.

Answer: The sounds link together.

Pronunciation checkpoint

This type of linking occurs when the final consonant sound of a word joins with the initial vowel sound of the next word, so that they link together smoothly and sound like one word. You can show this to Ss by using your fingers. Point to each finger on one hand when saying each word in the sentence, then push the two fingers together to illustrate the words which link together smoothly.

b Play the recording again for Ss to repeat each sentence after they hear it. If necessary, drill the sentences chorally and individually for further practice.

8 Write on the board: *White pizza* and elicit what Ss think it is, but don't give any answers yet. Give Ss one minute to read the text quickly (without completing the gaps) and check their ideas. Ss then complete the text alone, then check in pairs. Check answers with the whole class and ask if Ss like the sound of this dish. You could also elicit which adjectives in Ex 4 they'd use to describe it.

Answers: 1 a lot of 2 any 3 any 4 lots 5 few 6 little

9a Give an example or two about yourself first to demonstrate the activity. Ss complete the sentences with their own ideas, working alone. Monitor and help with vocabulary where necessary, writing any new words on the board.

> **Teaching tip**
>
> When Ss need vocabulary they don't know for an activity, this can be an opportunity for real learning. Help supply them with the new words or phrases they need, but then make a note of them or write them on the board. At the end of the activity, teach the new words/phrases to the class. If Ss have a real need for this emerging language, it's highly likely that they'll learn and remember it.

b Ss work in pairs and share their ideas and find out if they have anything in common with each other. When they have finished, nominate a few Ss to share their ideas with the class.

Further practice

Photocopiable activities: 2C Grammar 1, p156; 2C Grammar 2, p160

Speaking

Prepare

10 Go through the list of options with the class and give them time to decide on a dish they'd like to describe. Ss make notes on their dish, using the adjectives from Ex4a and the Useful phrases to help. Monitor and help with new vocabulary where necessary, writing any new words/phrases on the board.

Speak

11a Arrange Ss in user groups to describe their dishes to their group. Monitor and encourage them to ask follow-up questions to find out more information.

b When they have finished, ask each group to choose the one they'd most like to try, then share their description of this dish with the class.

Optional extra activity

When they have chosen the best dish in each group, Ss write a description and add a photo, then post it on a class blog or website.

> **Reflection on learning**
>
> Write the following questions on the board:
> *How easy was it to describe your dish?*
> *Are there any adjectives or quantifiers you're still not sure about? What can you do to study them more?*
>
> Put Ss in pairs to discuss the questions. When they have finished, ask if anyone wants to share their ideas with the class, but don't force them to if they'd rather not.

Homework ideas

Ex 10b: Ss write a description of their dish.
Ex 10b: Ss film/record themselves giving a description of their dish, then add it to their GSE portfolio.
Grammar bank: 2C Ex 1–2, pp.118–119
Workbook: Ex 1–5, p12
App: grammar and vocabulary practice

Fast route: continue to Lesson 2D
Extended route: go to p91 for Develop your listening

2D English in action

Introduction

The goal of this lesson is for Ss to practice showing interest and excitement. To help them achieve this, they will learn a range of phrases for creating interest, responding to information and asking follow-up questions in a variety of contexts.

Warm-up

Write the following things on the board in random order:
you won something, you had some good news, someone you know got married, you met someone interesting, you found something
Ask Ss to think of the last time each of these things happened to them. When they are ready, put Ss in pairs to share their experiences. Encourage them to use the past simple and ask follow-up questions to find out more information. When they have finished, nominate a few Ss to share their experiences with the class and ask how they reacted.

1 Focus attention on the photos. Put Ss in pairs to discuss what they think the people in the photos are doing and how they are feeling. Monitor and help with vocabulary where necessary, writing any new words/phrases on the board.

2a ◁ **2.14** Tell Ss not to worry if they don't understand every word at this stage, they just need to listen for the general meaning and will have a chance to listen again afterwards. Ss listen and check in pairs, then check answers with the whole class. Ask Ss which person was most excited and why they think that, and who is the least interested/excited, but is being polite.

Answers: **1** He got a good result in his exam.
2 He fixed her shower. **3** at 8 o'clock
4 two tickets to a music festival

Audioscript 2.14

1
Ali: Hey, Kate. I got 80 percent in my history exam. Can you believe it?
Kate: 80 percent!? That's brilliant! You always do well, Ali! ... I got my chemistry results back, too.
Ali: Oh! And?
Kate: ... I got 51 percent.
Ali: Ah ... Hey, that's not that bad, and it's only the first year!

2
Fran: Hi Marco, this is for you, for fixing my shower last week.
Marco: Oh, thanks, but I was happy to help, you know.
Fran: I know, but I wanted to buy you a thank you gift. Go on, open it.
Marco: Oh er ... socks ... with cats on them. They're ... They're ... er ... lovely. Thanks.
Fran: They're a bit silly, but you know me. I always like being different.
Marco: Well, thank you. It's really nice of you, Fran.
Fran: No problem. Glad you like them!

3
Ricky: Hey, Helena, I'm having a party at mine on Saturday. Just a few friends. Do you want to come?
Helena: Yeah, that sounds great! What time?
Ricky: Any time from 8 o'clock.
Helena: OK. Do I need to bring anything?
Ricky: Well, I'm asking people to bring drinks, but don't worry about food. I'm going to make a big curry.
Helena: Oh, great! I love your curries. They're so good!

4
Simone: Hey, Ray, guess what?
Ray: You sound excited. Tell me ...
Simone: Do you remember that competition I entered on the local radio station?

Ray: Oh yeah, how did that go?
Simone: I won it!
Ray: Brilliant Simone! How exciting! What did you win?
Simone: Two tickets to the music festival next week.
Ray: No way! That's amazing! Who are you going with, then?
Simone: You, of course!
Ray: Me? Really?
Simone: Yeah.

b Ss choose the correct alternatives alone.

c Play the recording again for Ss to check their answers, then check answers with the whole class.

Answers: 1 That's 2 They're 3 sounds 4 so 5 amazing!

3a 🔊 **2.16** Ss listen to the speakers and decide who shows no interest or excitement, then check in pairs. Check answers with the whole class and ask how they know.

Answers: Speakers 2 and 5 – their intonation is flat.

Optional alternative activity

With **weaker classes**, pause the recording after each speaker and elicit whether they sound interested/excited or not.

b 🔊 **2.16** Play the recording for Ss to repeat each phrase. Encourage them to copy the intonation to sound interested/excited, but make sure they don't exaggerate it too much.

4a Focus attention on the Useful phrases. Go through each phrase, and drill chorally and individually. Ss complete the conversations alone, then check in pairs. Direct them to the different adjectives in the box to create a variety of expressions. When they have finished, elicit Ss ideas with the class.

Suggested answers:
1 sounds
2 fantastic, wonderful, brilliant; Did
3 exciting, amazing, wonderful, fantastic, brilliant, great
4 Brilliant, Wonderful, Fantastic, Great, Delicious
5 did; amazing, fantastic, great

b Ss practise their conversations in pairs. Encourage them to use intonation to show interest/excitement. When they have finished, Ss swap roles and practise the conversations again. Encourage them to use a variety of adjectives and expressions. In feedback, nominate a different pair to perform each conversation to the class

Speaking

5a Put Ss in new pairs and direct them to their instructions. Give them time to read what they need to do and answer any questions they have. Give Ss plenty of time to prepare, and make sure they don't write full sentences, just key words and phrases. Monitor and help with vocabulary/ideas where necessary.

b Remind Ss of the Useful phrases and encourage Ss to use them where possible. Ss practise their conversations in pairs. While they are speaking, monitor and make notes on any common errors and examples of good language use for later feedback. When they have finished, nominate a few pairs to perform their conversations in front of the class. Correct any common errors you noted on the board with the class and drill any examples of good language use.

Optional extra activity

Ss film/record themselves having their conversations, then add this to their GSE portfolio.

Reflection on learning

Write the following questions on the board:
How well do you think you achieved the lesson goal (show interest and excitement) from 1–5? (1=not well, 5=very well) What could you do to improve?
What other situations in your life can you show interest and excitement in?
Put Ss in pairs to discuss the questions. When they have finished, ask if anyone wants to share their ideas with the class, but don't force them to if they'd rather not.

Homework ideas

Reflection on learning: Write your answers.
Workbook: Ex 1–3, p13
App: grammar and vocabulary practice

2 Check and reflect

Introduction

Ss revise and practise the language of Unit 2. The notes below provide some ideas for exploiting the activities in class, but you may want to set the first exercise in each section for homework, or use them as a diagnostic or progress test. For each grammar or vocabulary point, the first activity reviews the language and the second is more communicative, involving pairwork.

1a Ss complete the sentences alone, then check in pairs. In feedback, invite Ss to come and write their answers on the board, so that you can check for correct spelling of the past simple forms of the verbs.

Answers: 1 watched 2 went 3 had 4 took 5 played
6 met up 7 got up 8 was

b Ss work in pairs and discuss which sentences from Ex 1a are true for them. For the sentences which aren't true, ask Ss to change them, so they are true. Encourage Ss to ask follow-up questions to find out more information.

2a Ss complete the sentences alone, then check in pairs. Check answers with the whole class.

Answers: 1 stressed 2 excited 3 afraid 4 relaxed
5 angry 6 nervous 7 happy 8 sad

b Read the example with the class. Ss choose five adjectives from Ex 2a and think about when they last felt that way. When they are ready, Ss work in pairs and share their experiences. Encourage them to ask follow-up questions to find out more information.

3a With **weaker classes**, do the first one together as an example. Ss make the sentences negative alone, then check in pairs. Check answers with the whole class.

Answers:
1 We didn't go to the gym last night.
2 Sara wasn't happy yesterday.
3 I didn't go to bed late last night.
4 They weren't very busy last week.
5 We didn't play cards yesterday.
6 Jimmy didn't live in San Diego when he was a child.

b Read the example with the class. Explain that Ss can use the ideas in Ex 3a or their own ideas. Ss share their ideas in pairs. In feedback, nominate Ss to share their ideas with the class.

4a Ss order the questions alone, then check in pairs. Check answers with the whole class.

Answers:
1 What did you do last night?
2 Who did you chat to yesterday?
3 Where were you last weekend?
4 What time did you go to bed last night?
5 What did you have for dinner yesterday?
6 What colour was your first car?
7 Did you watch TV last night?
8 Why did you decide to do this English course?

b Ss work in pairs and discuss the questions from Ex 4a. When they have finished, nominate one or two Ss to share any interesting information with the class.

5a Ss match the sentence halves alone, then check in pairs. Check answers with the whole class.

Answers: 1c 2b 3a 4e 5f 6d

b Read the example with the class. Ss work in pairs and discuss the things they did. When they have finished, ask a few Ss to share any interesting information they found out about their partner.

6a Ss choose the correct alternatives alone, then check in pairs. Check answers with the whole class.

Answers: 1 some 2 an 3 a little 4 a few 5 a little 6 a lot of 7 any 8 some

b Ss work in pairs and describe their favourite meal. Monitor and help with vocabulary where necessary, writing any new words/ phrases on the board. In feedback, ask one or two Ss to describe their partner's favourite meal to the class.

7a Ss rearrange the letters to create adjectives alone, then check in pairs. Check answers with the whole class.

Answers: 1 sweet 2 plain 3 delicious 4 light 5 sour 6 fresh 7 creamy

b Give one or two of your own examples to demonstrate. Ss work in pairs to think of other foods for each adjective from Ex 7a. In feedback, elicit Ss' ideas and write them on the board.

c Ss work in pairs and discuss their choice of foods and the question. When they have finished, ask a few Ss to share their ideas with the class and find out if other Ss agree.

Reflect

Ask Ss to rate each statement alone, then compare in pairs. Encourage them to ask any questions they still have about any of the areas covered in Unit 2.

2 Four in a row (Units 1–2 review)

Introduction

Ss revise and practise the language of Units 1 and 2. Put Ss into two teams. Teams take it in turns to choose a square and answer the question in that square. If they answer correctly, they win the square. The aim is to get a row of four squares in a line (down, across or diagonally). The first team to do this, wins. While Ss are playing the game, monitor and check answers where necessary. Make a note of any common areas of weakness for further practice.

Optional alternative activity

Instead of aiming to get a row of four squares, teams can keep playing until all the squares on the board are 'taken'. The team with the most squares wins. Alternatively, **fast finishers** could aim to get as many squares as possible after the first team has got a row of four.

Answers:
1 lonely
2 felt, laughed, heard
3 What kind of music do you like/listen to?
4 e.g. book, table, teacher
5 e.g. a few coats, a few friends, a few pens
6 I often go to the park.
7 e.g. last month I went on holiday, six weeks ago we went to the coast, I learnt to ride my bike when I was five
8 I'm reading a good book at the moment.
9 That sounds good/That's fantastic!
10 e.g. creamy, sweet, delicious or tasty/horrible
11 e.g. Where did you find it? How much did you find?
12 check
13 How often do you go shopping/to the supermarket?
14 lots/a lot
15 e.g. enthusiasm, books, clothes
16 Marc didn't say hello.
17 last
18 e.g. My dad's sitting at home; My mum's shopping; My friend Carla is working.
19 needed /ɪd/ stayed /d/ watched /t/
20 e.g. What time do you normally arrive?
21 ago
22 relaxed
23 goals
24 countable noun
25 e.g. money, time
26 e.g. I went to the cinema., I took the bus to school., I woke up late for my interview.
27 Students' own answer
28 e.g. surprised/shocked/excited
29 e.g. money, time
30 e.g. take a break, take a taxi

2A Develop your reading

Introduction

Ss develop their reading skill of understanding short narrative texts by learning about narrative structure.

Warm-up

Write on the board:

Has anything amazing ever happened to you?
Did it happen because of luck?
Have you had any good luck recently? What happened?

Ss work in pairs and discuss the questions. In feedback, ask if anyone has any interesting experiences to share.

1 Ask Ss what kind of stories they like reading and what they like about them. Share ideas with the class.

2 Ss read through the Focus box and the examples alone, or read the box as a class. Elicit the answer to the question *How many parts does a traditional story usually have?*.

> **Answer:** Four

3 Ss read the story, and match the parts and paragraphs alone, then check in pairs. Check answers with the whole class.

> **Answers:** 1 A 2 B 3 C 4 B 5 C 6 D

4a Ss read paragraphs 1–3 again, then work in pairs and answer the questions. Check answers with the whole class.

> **Answers:**
> 1 ancient China
> 2 an old farmer, his son, the people in the village
> 3 their horses
> 4 One of the horses ran away.
> 5 No, he wasn't sad. He said it wasn't bad luck, it just happened.
> 6 It brought a beautiful white horse with it.
> 7 No, he didn't. He said it wasn't good luck, it just happened.

b Ss read paragraphs 4–6 again, then work in pairs and answer the questions. Check answers with the whole class.

> **Answers:**
> 1 The son fell off the white horse and broke his leg.
> 2 No, he said it wasn't bad luck or the horses's fault.
> 3 They were taking young men to fight in the war.
> 4 He had a broken leg.

5 Ss work in groups and discuss the questions. When they have finished, nominate a student from in group to share their ideas with the class.

Homework ideas

Workbook: Ex 1–4, p14

2B Develop your writing

Introduction

Ss develop their skill of writing a story by learning how to use adverbs to describe actions.

Warm-up

Revise the adjectives to describe feelings from Lesson 2A (afraid, angry, bored, excited, happy, nervous, relaxed, stressed, surprised, worried) by thinking of a situation for each one, e.g. *bored: how I feel when I wait in a long queue*, telling the class the situation and eliciting the adjectives onto the board. Give Ss a few minutes to choose three of the adjectives and think of a situation where they felt each one and make notes. Put Ss in pairs to describe their situations for their partner to guess the adjectives.

1 You could introduce the topic by describing when one (or more) of the things in Ex 1 happened to you. Ss work in pairs and discuss the situations. In feedback, ask if anyone wants to share their experiences with the class.

2 You may want to elicit/check: *biscuit* (show a picture or realia). Give Ss plenty of time to read the story alone, then answer the questions. Ss check in pairs, then check answers with the whole class.

> **Answers:** 1 taken something that isn't yours by mistake
> 2 the man's 3 He was calm and she was angry.

3 Give Ss time to read the Focus box or go through it together. You could explain adverbs further by writing on the board: *He's a nice man. He behaves nicely.* Explain that in the first sentence, *nice* is an adjective and describes the noun *man*. In the second sentence, *nicely* is an adverb and describes how he behaves (the verb). Ss find two more adverbs of manner in the story. Check answers with the class.

> **Answers:** From: quickly, quietly, calmly, angrily, slowly

4a Explain that this is a story told by the man in the story in Ex 2. Emphasise that more than one adverb is possible in each gap. Ss complete the story alone, but don't check any answers yet.

b Put Ss in pairs to compare their answers. Check answers with the whole class.

> **Answers:** 1 carefully 2 angrily
> 3 slowly/quickly/quietly/calmly 4 slowly/quickly 5 silently
> 6 slowly/quickly/silently

Prepare

5a Make sure Ss understand that it doesn't have to be a spectacular story, just something simple that has happened to them. Give Ss plenty of time to answer the questions. Monitor and help with vocabulary where necessary, writing any new words/phrases on the board.

b Remind Ss of the adverbs in Ex 3. Give Ss a few minutes to think of, and note down, any they can use in their story.

Write

6a Ss write their story alone. Monitor and check Ss are using the adverbs correctly and be on hand to help where necessary.

b Ss share their stories in pairs. In feedback, ask a few Ss to share their stories with the class.

Homework ideas

Workbook: Ex 1–5, p15

2c Develop your listening

Introduction

Ss develop their listening skill of identifying the main points in a short talk by learning how to recognise weak forms.

Warm-up

Write on the board:

Do you like to experiment with new kinds of foods, or just eat what you like?
What's the strangest thing you've ever eaten?

Ss work in small groups and discuss the questions. When they have finished, elicit a few Ss' answers and have a brief class discussion.

1 Focus attention on the photos and elicit what Ss can see. Write any new words on the board, and drill chorally and individually. In groups, Ss discuss which dishes they would most/least like to eat. When Ss have finished, go through each dish, and find out who would like to eat it and who wouldn't. Ask a few Ss why (not), too.

2a ◁) **2.9** Ss listen to the introduction and answer the questions. Check answers with the whole class.

Answers: It's called *What a great idea!*.
Guests present unusual ideas. This week's topic is food.

Audioscript 2.9

Presenter:

Hello and welcome to *What a great idea!* – the show that gives you a lot to think about. The topic this week is food, and we have two guests who are going to present their ideas. Firstly, Professor Jenny Hattie will argue that eating meat five days or more a week isn't good for you. Then chef Sara Caligan will argue that we should all eat ... er ... insects. Hmm. Before we discuss these ideas, each guest will have sixty seconds to present their idea.

b ◁) **2.10** Go through the list of things with the class, so they know what to listen for. Ss listen, decide if the statements are true or false, then check in pairs. Check answers with the whole class.

Answers: 1 F 2 F 3 T 4 T 5 T 6 F

Audioscript 2.10

Presenter: So, let's start with Jenny. Jenny, your time starts ... now.
Jenny: Thanks Rob. Right, well, I'd like to talk about meat. I love it, and I ate it all the time until last year, when I decided to make a change. I started to eat vegetarian dishes five days a week and meat only on two days. I think it's a good idea for everyone to do the same, and here's why. First, in general, it's good for us to eat less meat if we can. I certainly feel healthier these days.
I also think it's better for the world around us. Producing meat uses a lot of water and energy. And we need to move the meat from place to place. It's really not very good for the environment. Also, it's a lot cheaper of course. Actually, I always thought that vegetarian food was boring, but you know what? There are lots of really great vegetarian dishes. So why not give some a try?
Presenter: Thanks, Jenny! OK, so now it's Sara's turn. Sara, you have just sixty seconds to present your idea. Go!
Sara: Well, I think it's a good idea for everyone to eat insects. You know, in many parts of the world, people eat them as a basic food. The reason is that insects are actually very good for us. They have important, healthy, things in them so they're great to add to our diets. Insects are also good for the environment because they're small, so they don't cost much

to produce. The possibility to produce lots of healthy food cheaply is really important. This is because there are around seven billion people in the world today, and the number is growing all the time. Insects can help us to feed everyone. Many people don't like the idea, but actually, there are thousands of different kinds of insects, all with a different delicious taste.
Presenter: Very interesting! Thanks, Sara.

3 Ss read through the Focus box and examples alone, or read the box as a class. Check the answer with the class.

Answer: articles, auxiliary verbs, prepositions

4a ◁) **2.11** Write the first sentence on the board and play it for Ss to hear. Elicit the weak forms and underline them. Ss listen to the rest of the sentences and underline the weak forms alone, then check in pairs. Check answers with the whole class.

Answers: 1 and, the 2 to, a 3 for, to 4 to, the, from, to
5 a, of 6 that, was

b ◁) **2.12** Ss listen and complete the sentences alone, then check in pairs. Check answers with the whole class.

Answers: 1 for 2 them 3 that 4 to 5 can 6 of

5 ◁) **2.13** By now Ss should be able to put what they've learnt into practice. Ss listen and answer the questions alone, then check in pairs. Check answers with the whole class.

Answers:
1 on only two days every week 2 no
3 Some people are afraid of insects and we didn't eat them when we were children.

Audioscript 2.13

Presenter: Well, thanks to both of you for your interesting ideas. Jenny, let's start with yours. You say that we should all become vegetarian for five days a week. Does it need to be five days?
Jenny: Well, we usually work or study for five days and so that's a good time to change something. Then, at the weekends, when you go out and meet friends, you don't need to worry. You can eat what you want.
Sara: But how about being vegetarian for just one or two days a week?
Jenny: Yeah, that's good, too. It doesn't need to be five days, it can be one, two or three days if that's easier for you. The important thing is to eat less meat, I think.
Sara: And maybe we can eat insects instead!
Jenny: Yes, of course!
Presenter: I must say, Sara, I don't really like the idea of eating insects. Vegetarian food OK, there are some good dishes, but insects, well, I can't imagine a good insect dish.
Sarah: I know, insect dishes don't sound very tasty, do they? It's an unusual idea for most people.
Presenter: It sure is!
Sara: Well, OK, a lot of us are afraid of insects, but only because we didn't eat them when we were children ... , so it seems very strange to us. But if we prepare meals with insects for the children of today, they won't think it's strange in future.
Presenter: That's a good point Sara, thank you. Now, tell us about some of these lovely insect dishes you cook ...

6 Ss work in groups and discuss the questions. In feedback, elicit Ss' ideas and have a brief class discussion.

Homework ideas

Workbook: Ex 1–3, p13

3 OVERVIEW

 **Urban escapes**

Introduction

The goal of this lesson is for Ss to describe and compare different places in a city in the context of making a list of their favourite places to visit. To help them achieve this, they will learn/revise comparatives and adjectives to describe places in a city.

Warm-up

Before class, write the following questions on the board:
What's your favourite place in your town or city?
What can you do there?
How often do you go there?
Why do you like it?
Tell the class about your favourite place as an example, then put Ss in pairs to discuss the questions. When they have finished, nominate Ss to share their ideas with the class and find out if anyone has places in common.

Vocabulary and reading

Adjectives to describe places

1 Focus attention on the photos and elicit what Ss can see. Ss work in pairs and discuss the questions. In feedback, nominate different Ss to share their ideas with the class, but don't say where the places are yet.

2a Look at the example with the class and read out the adjectives for Ss to hear how they sound. Ss work alone and decide if the adjectives are positive or negative. Encourage them to use dictionaries or their mobile devices to check the meaning of any new words. Don't check any answers yet.

b Ss compare answers in pairs, then check with the whole class. Be prepared to give further explanations/examples where necessary.

> **Vocabulary checkpoint**
> Note that *touristy* in English is generally negative, meaning that a place has been overdeveloped.

> **Answers:**
> **Positive:** beautiful, cheap, clean, exciting, interesting, lively, modern, (old), peaceful, popular
> **Negative:** crowded, dirty, noisy, (old), touristy

3a Ss complete the sentences alone, then check in pairs. Check answers with the whole class.

> **Answers:**   1 popular   2 beautiful   3 dirty   4 crowded
> 5 modern

b Focus attention on the first photo and elicit which adjectives used in Ex 2a could describe it. Ss answer the questions in pairs. In feedback, elicit Ss' ideas and ask what other adjectives they could use to describe the places in the photos, writing any new words on the board.

VOCABULARY BANK 3A   p138

Places in a town

This is an optional extension to the vocabulary section, extending the lexical set and providing further practice. If you're short of time, this can be done for homework.

1 Elicit the first answer as an example. Ss choose the correct alternatives alone, then check in pairs. Check answers with the whole class and be prepared to give further explanations/examples where necessary.

Answers: 1 F   2 C   3 A   4 E   5 J   6 H   7 B   8 I   9 G
10 D

2 Read the examples with the class. Ss compare the places alone, then check in pairs. In feedback, elicit Ss' ideas and find out if the rest of the class agrees.

Further practice

Photocopiable activities: 3A Vocabulary, p161

4a Look at the travel forum posts, and ask if anyone uses these kinds of forums and what for exactly. Set a time limit of one minute for Ss to read and match with two of the photos. Explain that Ss will have a chance to read them more carefully afterwards. Check answers with the class. If you asked Ss to guess where the places were in Ex 1, check answers with them now.

Answers: 1 C   2 A

Teaching tip

When we want Ss to read a text quickly for gist, we can set a time limit. It's important we stick to this limit though, in order to give them a real reason to read quickly. Another way of doing this is to do it as a reading race. Ss cover the texts, while you set it up, then start reading when you say *Go!*. The first Ss to find the correct answer(s) wins.

---

b Ss read the posts again and decide if the statements are true or false alone, then check in pairs. Check answers with the whole class, eliciting why each statement is true or false.

Answers:
1 F (It can get very crowded.)
2 T (It's a really lively area.)
3 F (It's a bit further away.)
4 T (It's livelier than other beaches.)
5 T (They're a few kilometres out of Rio.)

c Ss work in pairs and discuss the question. In feedback, ask a few Ss to share their ideas with the class and have a brief class discussion.

Grammar

Comparatives

5a Books closed. Write on the board: *The market is ___ ___ ___ the park. (popular)*. Elicit the comparative form (*more popular than*) and write it on the board. Ss read the box and choose the correct alternatives alone, then check in pairs. Check answers with the class, going through the examples. Be prepared to give further explanations where necessary.

Answers: 1 short   2 long   3 irregular

Optional alternative activity

With **weaker classes**, read through the box and choose the alternatives together, giving further explanations/examples as you go along.

---

b Ss find one further example of each comparative in the forum posts alone, then check in pairs. Check answers with the whole class.

Answers:
Rebecca: a bit <u>further</u> away.; it's <u>not as noisy as</u> Camden Market.; I think it's <u>cheaper</u> and <u>quieter</u>, too!
Pedro: It's <u>longer than</u> the other beaches; It's <u>livelier than</u> other beaches, too
Patrizio: They're <u>cleaner than</u> the city beaches, too, which are <u>noisier</u> and <u>more crowded</u>.
Bethany: Prainha and Grumari are <u>better</u>; They're <u>less noisy</u> and <u>more beautiful</u>,

GRAMMAR BANK 3A   pp.120–121

Stronger classes could read the notes at home. Otherwise, check the notes with Ss, especially the spelling of comparative adjectives. In each exercise, elicit the first answer as an example. Ss work alone to complete the exercises, then check their answers in pairs. In feedback, elicit Ss' answers and drill the questions. Ss can refer to the notes to help them.

Answers: 3A
1 1 ~~beautifuler~~ more beautiful   2 correct
    3 is ~~more~~ richer   4 ~~dirter~~ dirtier   5 correct
    6 ~~farer~~ further   7 is ~~the~~ more expensive   8 ~~then~~ than
2 1 The park is quieter than the main square.
    2 Museums are much more interesting than shopping centres.
    3 The beach is dirtier than the countryside.
    4 The centre is more modern than the rest of the city.
    5 Cafés in Green Street are less expensive than cafés in the High Street.
    6 Oak End is (a) poorer (area) than Greenfields.

6a 🔊 **3.1** Play the recording for Ss to listen to how the weak forms are pronounced. You may wish to explain the information in the *Pronunciation checkpoint* below.

Answer: /ə/

Pronunciation checkpoint

The schwa /ə/ is the most common sound in English, and it's always unstressed, coming from the centre of the mouth. It's a good idea to practise its pronunciation, because it helps Ss' spoken English sound more natural and also helps identify weak forms when listening.

---

b Play the recording again for Ss to repeat the sentences. If necessary, drill them chorally and individually, too.

7 Explain that the text describes one of the places in the photos in Ex 1 which wasn't mentioned in the forum posts. Ss complete the text alone, then check in pairs. Check answers with the whole class.

Answers: 1 quieter   2 as cheap   3 more peaceful
4 not as dirty   5 bigger

Invite a student to the board to conduct feedback, eliciting answers from the class and writing them on the board. If you have a projector, show the text on the board so that you can complete it together.

8a Books closed. Write the prompts for sentence 1 on the board. Elicit a sentence with one of the adjectives in Ex 2a and write it on the board underneath the prompts. Ask Ss to open their books again and compare the sentence on the board with the example. Ss complete the remaining sentences alone. Monitor and help with ideas and vocabulary, writing any new words/phrases on the board.

b Arrange Ss in pairs to compare their ideas. In feedback, nominate a student from each pair to share their ideas with the class and find out if other Ss agree.

Books closed. In Ex 8a, arrange Ss into teams. Each take turns to call out the two things to be compared (e.g. *Rio de Janeiro/Madrid*). The first team to produce a correct comparative sentence wins a point and writes it on the board. The team with the most points at the end wins. Afterwards, Ss work in the same teams and discuss if they agree with the statements on the board.

Photocopiable activities: 3A Grammar 1, p159; 3A Grammar 2, p163

Speaking

Prepare

9a 🔊 **3.2** The aim of this listening is to provide Ss with a model for the final speaking activity. First, play the recording for Ss to answer the question. Tell Ss not to worry if they don't catch every word as they'll have a chance to listen again.

> **Answer:** The British Museum and Prague Castle.

b Ss listen again and answer the questions alone, then check in pairs. Check answers with the whole class.

> **Answers:**
> 1 She thinks they're too popular.
> 2 It's more modern.
> 3 It's modern and popular, but not as crowded as Mark's choices.

Audioscript 3.2

Mark: Right, so we need to write this article on the top ten places to visit by tomorrow. There are five categories and we have to write about two places for each one. Let's choose the places we want to write about first. How about we start with 'famous buildings'? My favourite buildings are the Louvre in Paris and the Colosseum in Rome.

Sandra: Oh really? I'm not sure, they're very famous places and everyone knows about them. I think we should choose somewhere less popular. What about Prague Castle? It's quieter and more peaceful than those two.

Mark: OK, but I don't think we should just pick places because they're less popular. The Louvre is nice because it's more modern than Prague Castle, but it can get very crowded in the summer.

Sandra: Yes, I see what you mean. OK, let's choose the Louvre. What about the British Museum for the other one? It's a lovely building. It's popular, but not as crowded as the Colosseum.

Mark: Good idea – it's much cheaper, too. In fact, it's free!

Sandra: That's true! OK, great, next category, street markets …

10a Ss make their lists alone. Monitor and help with ideas and vocabulary where necessary.

b Refer Ss back to the adjectives in Ex 2a and encourage them to ask you for any other adjectives they might need.

Speak

11a Before they start, elicit/teach a few phrases for agreeing and disagreeing and write them on the board, e.g.:

Agreeing: *That's a good idea. I agree. Yes, let's do that.*
Disagreeing: *I'm not sure about that. I don't think so. I don't think that's the best.*

Put Ss in pairs and read the example together. Make sure Ss are clear about what to do, and monitor while they make their lists, noting down any common errors and examples of good language use for later feedback.

b Groups take it in turns to share their lists with the class and find out if any others made similar choices. When they have finished, give Ss feedback on their speaking, using any notes you made in Ex 11a.

Ss carry out a survey of the choices made in Ex 11b with the whole class, then present a class 'Top 10'.

Write the following questions on the board:
Did you agree on places to include in your list?
How confident do you feel about using comparatives?
What things could you do to improve your knowledge of comparatives?

Put Ss in pairs to discuss the questions. When they have finished, ask if anyone wants to share their ideas with the class, but don't force them to if they'd rather not.

Grammar bank: 3A Ex 1–2, pp.120–121
Workbook: Ex 1–4, p16
App: grammar and vocabulary practice

Fast route: continue to Lesson 3B
Extended route: go to p92 for Develop your reading

3B A place to stay

Introduction

The goal of this lesson is for Ss to plan a class trip by comparing places to stay. To help them achieve this, they will learn/revise superlatives and vocabulary related to hotels and places to stay.

Warm-up

Revise the adjectives from the previous lesson with a backwards dictation. Arrange Ss in small teams and explain that in each turn you will read out the letters of an adjective backwards, e.g. for *old*, you'll say *D–L–O*. As soon as Ss guess the adjective, they shout it out (they don't need to wait until you've finished) and score a point for their team. Write the adjective on the board when it's guessed.

The team with the most points at the end wins. If you have time after the game, Ss describe different parts of their town or city in pairs, using the adjectives on the board.

Vocabulary and reading

Hotels and places to stay

1 Demonstrate the activity by getting the Ss to ask you the questions and sharing your answers with the class first. Ss then work in small groups and discuss the questions. When they have finished, nominate a student from each group to share their ideas with the class.

2a Ss match the words alone, then check in pairs. Check answers with the whole class, and ask questions to check understanding, e.g. *When does a 24-hour reception close? What do you order from room service?* Be prepared to give further explanations/examples where necessary.

Answers: 1 g 2 e 3 h 4 j 5 b 6 a 7 i 8 c 9 f 10 d

Vocabulary checkpoint

When it's a verb, *check out* is two words, e.g. *I'd like to check out, please.* When it's a noun, *checkout* is one word, e.g. *What time is checkout?*

b Ss complete the sentences alone, then check in pairs. Check answers with the whole class.

Answers: 1 airport transfer 2 checkout
3 breakfast included 4 sea-view 5 room service
6 24-hour reception 7 organised tour 8 double room

3a Introduce the activity by telling Ss about the last time you stayed in a hotel, answering questions about the services included. Give Ss plenty of time to make notes and ensure they don't write whole sentences at this stage. Monitor and help with vocabulary, writing any new words/phrases on the board.

b Read the examples with the class. Ss work in pairs and share their ideas. Encourage them to ask follow-up questions and make sure they're using the vocabulary correctly. In feedback, ask a few Ss to share any interesting information they found out from their partners.

VOCABULARY BANK 3B p138

Places to stay

This is an optional extension to the vocabulary section, extending the lexical set and providing further practice. If you're short of time, this can be done for homework.

1 Ss match the places and photos alone, then check in pairs. Check answers with the whole class.

Answers: 1 C 2 E 3 D 4 G 5 B 6 A 7 H 8 F

2 Ss complete the sentences and check their answers in pairs.

Answers: 1 campsite 2 an apartment 3 holiday cottage
4 resort 5 caravan

3 Ss work in pairs and discuss the questions. In feedback, find out which places are most popular.

Further practice

Photocopiable activities: 3B Vocabulary, p161

4a Focus attention on the photos in the article. Ss work in pairs and discuss the question. Make sure they don't read the article yet. When they are ready, elicit Ss' ideas and write them on the board.

b Ss read the article and check their ideas. Check answers with the whole class and tick off any ideas on the board that they mentioned.

Answers:
Bela Vista Hostel: enjoy the views; relax with a cold drink; go on a tour of the local forest
Matahari Village: learn about traditional cooking; meet local people; stay in a wooden house
The Princess Margarita Resort: see tropical fish

Optional alternative activity

Put the class in three large groups, and ask each group to read about one of the hotels. When they have finished, arrange Ss in groups of three, with one person from each of the previous groups. Ss share what they've read and check their ideas in Ex 4b.

5a Read the example with the class. Ss read the article again and match the descriptions alone, then check in pairs. Check answers with the whole class.

Answers:
1 *Bela Vista Hostel*
2 *Matahari Village*
3 *The Princess Margarita Resort*
4 *The Princess Margarita Resort*
5 *Bela Vista Hostel*
6 *Matahari Village*

b Ss work in pairs and discuss the questions. In feedback, elicit answers and have a brief class discussion.

Grammar

Superlatives

6a Write on the board: *1 Hostels are cheaper than hotels.*
2 Hostels are the cheapest places to stay. Ask: *(1) Which sentence compares more than two things? (2) How do we usually form the superlative?*
(Use *the + adjective + -est*). Ss read the box and choose the correct alternatives alone, then check in pairs. Check answers with the class, going through the examples. Be prepared to give further explanations where necessary.

Answers: 1 short 2 long

b Ss find further examples in the article alone, then check in pairs. Check answers with the whole class.

Answers:
Bela Vista Hostel: It had some of <u>the best</u> views; you can see the <u>furthest</u> from it; it's <u>the biggest</u> room; the best thing is – it's <u>the least expensive</u> place
Matahari Village: it was <u>the nicest</u> place we stayed in; it was <u>the most comfortable</u> place we stayed in
The Princess Margarita Resort: It's <u>the most beautiful</u> view ever; Fish are <u>the quietest</u> neighbours in the world!

Optional extra activity

Number the statements in the Grammar box 1–4. Ask Ss to match the underlined examples in Ex 6b to the statements in the Grammar box. Check answers with the class.

Answers: *Bela Vista Hostel:* It had some of <u>the best</u> views (4); you can see the <u>furthest</u> from it (4); it's <u>the biggest</u> room (2); the best thing is (4); it's <u>the least expensive</u> place (3); *Matahari Village:* it was <u>the nicest</u> place we stayed in (2); it was <u>the most comfortable</u> place we stayed in (3); *The Princess Margarita Resort:* It's <u>the most beautiful</u> view ever (3); Fish are <u>the quietest</u> neighbours in the world! (2)

GRAMMAR BANK 3B pp.120–121
Stronger classes could read the notes at home. Otherwise, check the notes with Ss, especially the spelling of superlative adjectives. In each exercise, elicit the first answer as an example. Ss work alone to complete the exercises, then check their answers in pairs. In feedback, elicit Ss' answers and drill the questions. Ss can refer to the notes to help them.

Answers: 3B
1 1 best 2 biggest 3 most beautiful 4 most expensive 5 richest 6 the quietest 7 nicest
2 Student's own answers

7a 3.3 Play the recording for Ss to listen to how the superlatives are pronounced. You may want to explain the information in the Pronunciation checkpoint below.

Answer: It is pronounced in two different ways.

Pronunciation checkpoint
Before consonant sounds, *the* is pronounced as its weak form /ðə/. Before a vowel sound, *the* is pronounced /ðiː/. It also links to the next vowel sound with /j/. So, for example, *the easiest* is pronounced /ðiːˈjiːziːjɪst/.

b Play the recording again for Ss to repeat the sentences. If necessary, drill them chorally and individually, too.

8 With ***weaker classes***, elicit the first answer as an example and write it on the board. Ss complete the sentences alone then check in pairs. In feedback, for each sentence ask a different student to come up and write it on the board and check spelling.

Answers: 1 the smallest 2 the most modern 3 the best 4 the least expensive 5 the prettiest 6 most amazing

9a Ss complete the questions alone, then check in pairs. Check answers with the whole class.

Answers: 1 the most expensive 2 the cheapest 3 the best 4 the nicest 5 the easiest 6 the most difficult 7 the most interesting 8 the furthest

b Ss work in pairs and discuss the questions about the hotels in the magazine article in Ex 9a. In feedback, elicit Ss' answers and find out if the rest of the class agrees.

Further practice

Photocopiable activities: 3B Grammar 1, p159; 3B Grammar 2, p163

Speaking
Prepare
10 3.4 The aim of this listening is to provide Ss with a model for the final speaking activity. Before they listen, write on the board: *Casa Tranquila, The Mantra Resort* and *The Happy Campers Village.* Ss listen and answer the questions alone, then check in pairs. Check answers with the whole class.

Answers: 1 *The Mantra Resort* 2 *Casa Tranquila* 3 *Happy Campers Village*

Audioscript 3.4
Pat: So where do you think we should stay, ladies? I'd like to do something different and exciting.
Andrea: Yes, well, I had a stressful year at work – I really just want to relax in a five star hotel. I love the look of this place, *The Mantra Resort.* Look at the colour of that sea! It looks like the most beautiful place in the world.
Shannon: Yeah, but it's the most expensive! Look at those prices!
Andrea: Yes, I suppose so, it is a bit pricey …
Shannon: I really like the look of *Casa Tranquila.* It looks really quiet and peaceful, and it's the cheapest option. And look at those views!
Pat: But you know I hate heights, Shannon!
Andrea: Ha! This is going to be difficult …
Pat: And it's the furthest place from the airport. It would take a really long time to get there. I don't want to spend the whole time travelling!
Andrea: You're right and we don't have much time, only a week.
Pat: What about the *Happy Campers Village*? It's out in the countryside.
Andrea: Hmm, yes, actually I think it looks like the most interesting place to stay. I like the idea of staying in the countryside.
Shannon: Me too. And the food looks great, too, cooked on an open fire – yum!
Pat: OK, let's go there. I'll book it now.

11a Introduce the activity by telling Ss what's important for you, referring to the things in the list. Ss rank each thing alone.
b Ss read the descriptions on p152 and choose where they want to stay using the information in Ex 11a.

Speak
12 Read the examples with the class. Arrange Ss in small groups to discuss their choices and agree on a place to stay. Encourage Ss to use the Useful phrases. While they're speaking, monitor and make notes on their use of language. When they have finished, nominate a student from each group to share their choice and say why they chose it. Give Ss feedback on their language use as a class.

Reflection on learning
Write the following questions on the board:
What were the three most useful words/phrases you learnt in this lesson?
How will you use them in the future?
Put Ss in pairs to discuss the questions. When they have finished, ask if anyone wants to share their ideas with the class, but don't force them to if they'd rather not.

Homework ideas
Grammar bank: 3B Ex 1–2, pp.120–121
Workbook: Ex 1–5, p17
App: grammar and vocabulary practice

Fast route: continue to Lesson 3C
Extended route: go to p93 for Develop your writing

3c ▶ Never ever

Introduction

The goal of this lesson is for Ss to describe personal past experiences in the context of a game. To help them achieve this, they will learn the present perfect with *ever* and *never* for past experiences, and verb phrases to describe common activities.

Warm-up

Start the lesson with a visualisation. Ask Ss to close their eyes and relax, then read out the following:

You're lying in bed and it's Monday morning. You've just woken up and you can see the light coming through the window. It's five minutes before your alarm goes off and you're thinking about the rest of the day. After a few minutes you get up.

Then ask Ss to open their eyes and write down the first five things they do after waking up. Ask them to try and do it without thinking too much about it. When they are ready, arrange Ss in small groups to compare what they've written and find out if they have anything in common.

Vocabulary

Verb phrases

1a You may want to pre-teach or check: *chopsticks*. Demonstrate the activity by eliciting which word/phrase goes with *be*. Ss match the verbs and words/phrases alone, then check in pairs. Check answers with the whole class, eliciting which activities can be seen in the photos.

> **Answers:** be on TV, break a bone, cook a meal, drive a sports car, eat a meal/with chopsticks, fall asleep in public, go skiing, learn to swim, ride a bike, share a meal/a photo online, visit an art gallery, watch a football match

b Focus attention on the photos and elicit what Ss can see.

> **Answers:** break a bone, go skiing, watch a football match, cook a meal, eat a meal, ride a bike

2a Look at the first example in Ex 1a (*be on TV*) and ask if most people do this in their lives (probably not). Ss discuss the others in pairs. When they have finished, nominate a few Ss to share their ideas with the class and have a brief class discussion.

> **Suggested answers:**
> **Most people:** cook/eat a meal, eat with chopsticks (if they live in Asia), fall asleep in public (like babies), learn to swim, ride a bike, share a photo online, visit an art gallery, watch a football match.
> **Most people don't usually:** appear on TV, drive a sports car, eat with chopsticks (if they live outside Asia), break a bone.

b With **weaker classes**, demonstrate the activity by writing one or two sentences about yourself on the board first, using the prompts. Ss complete the sentences alone. Monitor and help with ideas where necessary.

c Read the example with the class to show how they can give more information. Ss work in pairs and share their ideas. When they have finished, ask a few Ss to share their partner's ideas with the class and find out if they have any answers in common with other people in the class.

Further practice

Photocopiable activities: 3C Vocabulary, p167

Listening

3a 🔊 **3.5** If possible, introduce the topic of the recording by describing a common activity that you've never done. Go through the activities and reasons with the class, and explain that Ss will hear four people describing things they've never done and why. Ask Ss to cover the conversations in Ex 3b before they listen. Ss listen and write the activities/reasons alone, then check in pairs. Check answers with the whole class.

> **Answers:**
> 1 learn how to swim, no lessons
> 2 ride a bike, a bad family experience (her brother fell off his)
> 3 watch a football match at a stadium, prefers something else
> 4 cook a meal, doesn't need to (parents do it)

Optional alternative activity

With **weaker classes**, play the recording twice. The first time Ss listen for the activity and the second time they listen for the reason.

b Ss choose the correct alternatives alone, then check in pairs. Play the recording again for Ss to check their answers, then check answers with the whole class.

> **Answers:** 1 learnt 2 swum 3 ridden 4 saw 5 watched
> 6 tried 7 ever 8 never

> **Teaching tip**
> When doing a listening activity like this, it's a good idea for Ss to go through the possible options/answers first, to avoid coming to the listening 'cold'. One way of doing this is to ask Ss to predict the answers, even if they have no chance of knowing them at that point. This helps them become familiar with the words and know what type of information to listen for.

Audioscript 3.5

Presenter:	So, today we're asking you about common activities that you've never done in your life. Let's talk to our first caller. Val, are you there?
Val:	Yes, Jon, I'm here. Um, well … I've never learnt to swim.
Presenter:	Oh, OK. Can you tell us why?
Val:	Well, I've never had the opportunity. I've never had lessons and I don't really like the seaside.
Presenter:	Have you ever tried?
Val:	Yes, I have. I went to a pool when I was in Spain once, but I've never swum in the sea.
Presenter:	Well, Val, it's never too late to learn, you know.
Val:	Oh, I'm not sure about that. I think I'm too old now!
Presenter:	I'm sure that's not true. OK, nice talking to you, Val. Let's speak to our next caller, Kate. Hi, Kate!
Kate:	Hi! Well, Jon, most people laugh when I tell them this, but I've never ridden a bike.
Presenter:	Really? Surely you've tried it at least once?
Kate:	Well, when I was a child, I saw my brother fall off his bike and he broke his arm. He cried so much! So, when my parents bought me a bike, I was really scared and I didn't want to ride it.
Presenter:	Are you still scared?
Kate:	Er, I don't think so. Maybe one day I'll learn. Who knows?!
Presenter:	Thanks Kate. Now let's speak to Eddie. Hi, Eddie!
Eddie:	Hi Jon! I'm not calling about me, actually, I'm calling about my friend Jim. He's never watched a football match in his life. Can you believe it?
Presenter:	Never? Not even on TV?

Eddie:	Well, sure, I think he's seen a match on TV. I meant that he's never been to the stadium. We talk about football all the time, we go to the matches, but he's just not interested.
Presenter:	Have you ever tried to take him to a match?
Eddie:	Yes, we all have – my friends and I, that is. Many times. But he just won't come!
Presenter:	Well, thanks Eddie. I guess he just doesn't like football. Right, let's talk to one more caller before the news. Andy, are you there?
Andy:	Hi, yeah, I'm here. I … er … I've never cooked a meal.
Presenter:	Wow. How old are you?
Andy:	I'm 22.
Presenter:	How do you eat, then?
Andy:	Well, I still live at home, so my parents cook for me.
Presenter:	Right. I see … er … Have you ever boiled an egg?
Andy:	Er … no, I haven't. I've made sandwiches and toast, and I've put things in the microwave, but I've never used a cooker.
Presenter:	Wow! That is unusual.
Andy:	I've ordered pizza lots of times though!
Presenter:	I'm sure you have, Andy. Now, it's time to …

Grammar

Present perfect with *ever* and *never*

4 Write the first example in the Grammar box on the board. Ask: *Do we know when he saw the tennis matches?* (No) *Is it important?* (No). Ss read the box and choose the correct alternatives alone, then check in pairs. Check answers with the class and highlight the position of *ever* and *never* between the auxiliary and the past participle. You can also direct Ss to the list of irregular verbs on p160.

Answers: 1 don't   2 past participle   3 past simple
4 statement   5 question

GRAMMAR BANK 3C   pp.120–121

Stronger classes could read the notes at home. Otherwise, check the notes with Ss, especially the irregular verbs. In each exercise, elicit the first answer as an example. Ss work alone to complete the exercises, then check their answers in pairs. In feedback, elicit Ss' answers and drill the questions. Ss can refer to the notes to help them.

Answers: 3C
1   1 've done   2 've travelled   3 cycled   4 were
     5 've seen   6 saw   7 were   8 've dived   9 've never
     10 visited   11 stayed   12 swam   13 drove   14 took
2   1 Have you ever ridden a motorbike?
     2 Have you ever been to a music festival?
     3 Have you ever fallen over in the street?
     4 Has you ever baked bread?
     5 Have you ever slept outside?
     6 Have you ever sung in public?
     7 Have you ever climbed a mountain?
     8 Have you ever written a story?
     9 Have you ever run a marathon?
     10 Have you ever broken a bone?

5a 3.6 Play the recording for Ss and ask them what they notice about the pronunciation of *has/have* and *have/haven't*. Check answers with the whole class.

Answers: *Has* and *have* are stressed in short answers. *Hasn't* and *haven't* are always stressed.

Pronunciation checkpoint

Has/Have are contracted in statements. *Has/Have* in questions are pronounced with a schwa in their weak forms /həz/ or /həv/. In negative statements and in short answers, *hasn't/haven't* are stressed.

b Ss work in pairs and listen to the recording again. One student takes the role of A, the other student takes the role B to practice pronunciation of *has/hasn't* and *have/haven't*.

6a Elicit the first answer with the class as an example, making sure Ss put *never* in the correct position and write it on the board. Ss complete the sentences alone, then check in pairs. Monitor and help where necessary. Check answers with the whole class, checking spelling of the past participles.

Answers: 1 've/have never shared   2 have never learnt
3 've/have never ridden   4 've/have never driven
5 have never watched   6 've/have never met
7 has never visited   8 've/have never eaten

b Ss work in pairs and discuss in Ex 6a the sentences. In feedback, elicit a few answers and find out how many people each sentence is true for.

Optional alternative activity

Do Ex 6b as a mingle activity. Ss stand up and walk around, discussing sentence 1 with as many Ss as possible. After a while, call out *sentence 2!* and Ss continue mingling and discussing sentence 2. Repeat for all sentences until they've finished, then ask a few Ss to share what they learnt with the class.

7a Read the example with the class, then elicit a few more ideas. Write *Have you ever … ?* on the board, e.g. *rode a motorbike, cooked a meal*, etc. Ss write their three questions alone. Monitor and help with vocabulary, writing any new words/phrases on the board. If Ss are struggling to think of ideas, refer them back to the verb phrases in Ex 1a to help.

b Ss work in pairs and discuss their questions, including the follow up questions if possible. When they have finished, nominate one or two Ss to share their partner's answers with the class.

Further practice

Photocopiable activities: 3C Grammar 1 p165; 3C Grammar 2, p166

Speaking

Prepare

8a 3.7 Play the recording for Ss to listen and find out how the game works, then check understanding by asking: *What does Player 1 do first?* (asks a question) *What must Player 2 do?* (answer the question) *How does Player 1 find out if it's the truth or a lie?* (by asking questions). If necessary, you may also want to demonstrate it with a ***stronger Ss***. Find out if anyone has ever played this before.

b ***Stronger classes*** could attempt this from memory first before listening to check. Otherwise, Ss listen and put the questions in order alone, then check in pairs. Check answers with the whole class.

Answers: 1 d   2 b   3 a   4 c   5 e

Audioscript 3.7

Rob: Shall I start?
Amy: OK.
Rob: I've been on TV.
Amy: When was that?
Rob: Er ... it was maybe two years ago.
Amy: What happened?
Rob: Well, it's a funny story, actually. I had a job interview at a local TV station. I arrived and waited in reception.
Amy: What was the job?
Rob: Oh ... er ... it ... it was in the IT department. Anyway, after a few minutes someone took me into this room where there were some cameras and a woman in a suit.
Amy: Why were there cameras in the IT department?
Rob: Well, this is the funny bit – suddenly, the lights came on and the woman started talking to the camera. She was a news reporter talking about a news story and, suddenly, I was on TV.
Amy: Really? What did you do?
Rob: Well, I was really surprised. The woman started asking me lots of questions.
Amy: And what did you say?
Rob: I tried to answer them, but I couldn't, and I told her I was the wrong person.
Amy: What did she do?
Rob: She said sorry and started talking to the camera again, and someone quickly took me out of the room.
Amy: How did they make that mistake?
Rob: Apparently, the real person had the same name as me.
Amy: What about the job? Did you get it?
Rob: Job? Oh ... er ... no, I didn't. So, am I telling the truth or a lie?
Amy: Hmm, I'm not sure ...

c Ss work in pairs and discuss the question, giving reasons for their answers. Elicit Ss' ideas and keep a tally on the board, but don't give the answer yet.

d ◊ 3.8 Ss listen to the end of the game and check their ideas. Then check with the whole class.

> **Answer:** Rob says that the story is true, but it happened to someone else, not him.

Audioscript 3.8

Amy: Hmm, I'm not sure. It's a crazy story, but you gave me a lot of information so I think ... er ... I think you're telling me the truth. Am I right?
Rob: No, sorry. The story's true – I read about it in a newspaper – but it didn't happen to me. I've never been on TV.
Amy: Oh! One point to you then.

> **Culture notes**
> This is a real story, which happened to a man called Guy Coma on the BBC in 2006. You can find video clips of the interview online.

9 Using the example ideas, Ss prepare their experiences alone, then show them to their partner, so they can prepare. Monitor and help with vocabulary, writing any new words/phrases on the board.

Speak

10a Go through the Useful phrases. Ss work in pairs and play the game. Monitor and make notes on Ss' language use for later feedback, especially forming the present perfect and word order.

b When they are ready, rearrange Ss so they can play again with a different partner. Monitor Ss' language use as they do so.

> **Teaching tip**
> There are lots of ways of rearranging Ss, for example:
> * If Ss are sitting in a semi-circle, ask one student at the end to move to the other end, then arrange Ss in pairs.
> * Give each student half a phrase on a piece of paper (phrases you've recently been studying) and ask them to find their partner.
> * Use a question frame which practises language Ss have recently learnt, e.g. *Have you ever ... ?*, and Ss mingle until they find someone who gives the same answer, and sit down with them.

c Discuss the question as a class, nominating Ss to share their partner's true/false stories. Go over any common errors or examples of good language use with the class.

> **Reflection on learning**
> Write the following questions on the board:
> *Was it easy or difficult to use the present perfect in the game? Why?*
> *Which three phrases from the lesson will you use most in the future? Why?*
> Put Ss in pairs to discuss the questions. When they have finished, ask if anyone wants to share their ideas with the class, but don't force them to if they'd rather not.

Homework ideas

Grammar bank: 3C Ex 1–2, pp.121–122
Workbook: Ex 1–5, p18
App: grammar and vocabulary practice

Fast route: continue to Lesson 3D
Extended route: go to p94 for Develop your listening

3D English in action

Introduction

The goal of this lesson is for Ss to practice giving and responding to personal news. To help them achieve this, they will learn a range of phrases for giving, asking for and responding to news.

Warm-up

Play *good news, bad news*. Start by telling the class: *The good news was I found some money. The bad news was it was a different currency. The good news was I gave it to charity. The bad news was ...* and nominate a student to finish the sentence. They then say *The good news was ...* and nominate another student to finish the sentence, and so on. Try to keep the story going as long as possible.

1 Focus attention on the photo and elicit what Ss can see. Go over the topics in the box and the example, then Ss work in pairs and discuss the question. Make sure Ss understand that by *news* we mean something that's happened to them, not something in the news. In feedback, elicit answers and have a brief class discussion.

Suggested answers:
family: marriage, birth, holiday, day out
friends: marriage, birth, new job, new home, something funny or annoying
holidays: location, when, who with
home: new kitchen, neighbours, problem with the electricity
interests: new hobby, day out, film they saw, sport
technology: new phone/computer, new website they found
travel: a holiday, a day out, a visitor
work: new job, new activities in job/promotion, things that annoy you, colleagues

2a 🔊 **3.13** You may want to pre-teach/check: *kids, bedtime* and *smartwatch*. Ss listen and tick the topics in Ex 1 the people speak about. Play the recording once and explain that they'll have a chance to listen again afterwards. Ss check in pairs, then check answers with the whole class.

Answers:
conversation 1: family (marriage)
conversation 2: travel (a holiday)
conversation 3: technology

b Go through the Useful phrases with the class, checking understanding where necessary. Ss listen again and write the conversation numbers next to the correct phrases in the box, then check in pairs. Play the recording again if necessary, then check answers with the whole class.

Answers:
conversation 1: Have you heard about? How are things? That's fantastic news! That's not good.
conversation 2: How have you been? Lucky you! What a shame.
conversation 3: Guess what! That's great. Sorry to hear that. Sounds fantastic.

Audioscript 3.13

1
Angie: Jack! Is that you?
Jack: Oh, hi, Angie.
Angie: Hi! I haven't seen you in ages! How are things?
Jack: Great. Alex and I finally got married in the summer.
Angie: Did you? Oh, that's fantastic news. Congratulations!
Jack: Thanks. Yes, we live in Dayton now.
Angie: Oh, right. I've never been there. What's it like?
Jack: Well, it's quieter than here, but we like it. The area's really nice. What about things here?
Angie: Hmm, have you heard about the park on Green Street?
Jack: No. What?
Angie: They want to build lots of news houses on it.
Jack: Oh no, that's not good. That's where all the kids play soccer. I loved it there when I was young.

2
Charlie: Hello. Hello? Hi.
Rose: Hi! I can't see you. Oh, now I can.
Charlie: How are you?
Rose: I'm great, thanks. What time is it there? It must be late.
Charlie: Yeah, it's eleven o'clock. Nearly bedtime! So, how have you been?
Rose: OK, thanks. I'm really busy at work, but I had two weeks off last month. I went to Vancouver, actually.
Charlie: Oh, lucky you! How was it? We talked about going there when we were at university. Do you remember?
Rose: Yes, I do, of course. It was great! We went camping and did some water sports.
Charlie: That's brilliant!
Rose: Didn't you go on holiday recently, too?

Charlie: Yeah, but it wasn't much fun. We had a problem with the apartment – no hot water for three days! Then I got ill, so we had to come home early.
Rose: Oh, what a shame. Were you very ill?
Charlie: Yes, kind of – I was in bed for a week. I felt awful.
Rose: Oh, well, hopefully you can have another holiday later in the year.
Charlie: Yeah, hopefully. But tell me a bit more about Vancouver …

3
Dylan: Hi, Mara.
Mara: Oh, hey, Dylan. How are you?
Dylan: Fine. Guess what!
Mara: What?
Dylan: I got this yesterday. See?
Mara: Oh, a watch.
Dylan: It's not just a watch, Mara. It's the best smartwatch you can have.
Mara: Really? What does it do, then?
Dylan: I can make calls, send messages, pay for things with it. I can listen to music and …
Mara: Wow, OK, so it's pretty good, then.
Dylan: Yeah, it's amazing! It's got running apps, maps, things like that.
Mara: Sounds amazing. My news is not so great – I lost my phone last week. I can't find it anywhere.
Dylan: Oh, no. Really sorry to hear that. Have you bought a new one?
Mara: No, I haven't got enough money. But it's OK – I don't have to check my messages every few minutes!

3a 🔊 **3.14** Explain that Ss will hear each response twice and they must choose which sounds most appropriate. Ss listen and decide alone, then check in pairs. Check answers with the whole class.

Answers: 1 speaker 1 2 speaker 2 3 speaker 1 4 speaker 1 5 speaker 2

b 🔊 **3.15** Ss listen and repeat. Check how they are pronouncing the phrases and, if necessary, drill them chorally and individually for further practice.

Pronunciation checkpoint
It can be difficult to work on intonation in class, because when we isolate phrases it's easy to exaggerate the intonation. Try to keep it as natural-sounding as possible by saying the phrases at natural speed when you drill with the class.

4a Go through the sentences and check understanding where necessary, especially *missing*. Ss think of responses alone. Monitor and help where necessary, using ideas from the *Suggested answers* box.

Suggested answers: 1 Lucky you! 2 Oh no. 3 Oh, that's a shame. 4 Oh, that's terrible! 5 OK, thanks. 6 Sorry to hear that. 7 That's fantastic! 8 Really?

b When they're ready, put Ss in pairs to practise their conversations. Encourage Ss to take turns to read a sentence and respond. Monitor and check Ss are using appropriate responses with natural intonation. In feedback, ask a few pairs to read out the sentences and responses to the class.

Teaching tip
When conducting feedback from pairwork activities, it's useful to use open pairs. Nominate a student to read the sentence, then ask (or get that student to nominate) a different student from the class to respond. Repeat this for all the sentences. This will provide Ss with further practice and they should feel more confident responding in front of the class having practised in pairs during the activity.

Speaking

Prepare

5 Give Ss plenty of time to think of their news, and monitor and help with vocabulary where necessary, writing any new words/ phrases on the board.

Ss work in pairs to think of their news ideas, then work with different partners in Ex 6.

Speak

6a Ss work in pairs and practice their conversations using the Useful phrases to help them. While Ss are speaking, monitor and make notes on their language use for later feedback.

b Ss repeat the conversation with a different partner. When they have finished, ask one or two Ss to perform their conversation for the class using open pairs.

Ss film/record themselves having their conversations, then add this to their GSE portfolio.

Reflection on learning

Write the following questions on the board:

How confident do you feel using the phrases from this lesson? What can you do to practise this language further?

Put Ss in pairs to discuss the questions. When they have finished, ask if anyone wants to share their ideas with the class, but don't force them to if they'd rather not.

Reflection on learning: Write your answers.
Workbook: Ex 1–2, p19
App: grammar and vocabulary practice

 3 Check and reflect

Ss revise and practise the language of Unit 3. The notes below provide some ideas for exploiting the activities in class, but you may want to set the first exercise in each section for homework, or use them as a diagnostic or progress test. For each grammar or vocabulary point, the first activity reviews the language and the second is more communicative, involving pairwork.

1a Ss complete the sentences alone, then check in pairs. Check answers with the whole class, checking understanding of the meaning of each adjective if necessary.

Answers: 1 dirty 2 interesting 3 lively 4 modern
5 peaceful 6 noisy

b Ss work in pairs and describe the area. In feedback, elicit Ss' ideas and find out if everyone agrees.

2a With **weaker classes**, quickly revise the different comparative forms on the board before starting this activity. Ss complete the text alone, then check in pairs. Check answers with the whole class by inviting Ss to write them on the board, so that you can check the spelling of the different comparative forms.

Answers: 1 smaller 2 busier 3 noisier 4 more interesting
5 more exciting 6 fresher 7 as crowded 8 better
9 less busy

b Ss work in pairs and discuss their places in pairs. Monitor and check Ss are using comparatives correctly, noting down any common errors for later feedback. When they have finished, elicit a few comparisons from the class and find out if other Ss agree.

3a With **weaker classes**, elicit the first answer as an example. Ss complete the sentences alone. Monitor and check Ss are forming the superlatives correctly, and help with ideas where necessary.

Answers: 1 best 2 nicest 3 quietest 4 most delicious

b Ss compare their sentences and try to persuade each other to change their mind if they can. In feedback, ask a few Ss what they agreed on for each sentence.

4a Ss complete the text alone, then check in pairs. Check answers with the whole class.

Answers: 1 five-star 2 24-hour reception 3 sea view
4 breakfast included 5 room service 6 free parking
7 airport transfer 8 organised tours

b Ss work in pairs and discuss their dream hotel. Encourage them to use the words in Ex 4a to help them with ideas. When they have finished, ask each pair to share their ideas with the class, then ask the class to vote for their favourite one.

5a Remind Ss that we use the past simple when it's clear when something happened in the past, and elicit the first answer as an example. Ss choose the correct words alone, then check in pairs. Check answers with the whole class.

Answers: 1 has 2 ever 3 seen 4 went 5 I never
6 Have 7 has 8 spoke

b Go through the example conversation with the class. Ss practise asking and answering questions in pairs. When they have finished, nominate a few Ss to share any interesting information about their partners with the class.

6a Ss complete the sentences alone, then check in pairs. Check answers with the whole class.

Answers: 1 appeared/been 2 learnt 3 fell
4 ridden/been on 5 drove 6 had

b Give Ss plenty of time to write their lists alone. Monitor and help with ideas and vocabulary, writing any new words/phrases on the board.

c When they are ready, Ss work in pairs and discuss which they've done. In feedback, ask each pair how many answers they have in common.

Reflect

Ask Ss to rate each statement alone, then compare in pairs. Encourage them to ask any questions they still have about any of the areas covered in Unit 3.

3A ▶ Develop your reading

Introduction

Ss develop their reading skill of understanding factual texts by learning how to guess the meaning of words.

Warm-up

Write on the board:
How often do you go to a park?
What do you do there?
What's the most important thing for a park to have, in your opinion?

Ss work in pairs and discuss the questions. When they have finished, elicit their ideas and have a brief class discussion.

1 Give Ss a few minutes to read the text and answer the question. Explain that they'll have a chance to read the text again more carefully afterwards, so they shouldn't worry if they don't understand every word.

Answer: three parts

2 Ss read the text again and answer the questions, then check in pairs. Check answers with the whole class.

Answers:
1 Answers may vary depending on the date – it opened in June 2012.
2 Copenhagen
3 from all over the world
4 Black Market
5 It's completely green.

3 Give Ss a few minutes to read the information in the Focus box or read it together with the class. Ss work in pairs and answer the question, then check the answer with the whole class.

Answer: Use the information around it and the context.

4 Encourage Ss to use the advice in the Focus box for each word before they choose the best meaning. Monitor and help where necessary. Check answers with the whole class.

Answers: 1 people's family … 2 things you find …
3 things to sit on 4 a type of path 5 a thing with …

5 Before Ss read, ask if anyone in the class has heard of Metropol Parasol or been there. Ss read the text quickly and look for things you can do there, then check in pairs. Check answers with the whole class.

Answers: visit a museum, go to the street market, meet people, go to a restaurant, go for a walk and enjoy the views of the city

6a Remind Ss of the Focus box and the process for guessing new words described there. Ss find the words and write definitions alone.

b Ss work in pairs and compare their definitions. In feedback, elicit Ss' ideas and then allow them to check in dictionaries.

Answers:
obstacle: something that makes it difficult to achieve something
ruins: what's left of old or damaged buildings
shade: dark area where the sun is blocked out
stunning: very beautiful
inspired (by): given the idea from something
unique: the only one of its kind

7 Ss work in small groups and discuss the question. In feedback, elicit Ss' ideas and have a brief class discussion.

Homework ideas

Workbook: Ex 1–4, p20

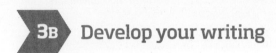

3B ▶ Develop your writing

Introduction

Ss develop their skill of writing a hotel review by learning how to organise ideas.

Warm-up

Write the following questions on the board:
Do you read reviews of hotels before you book them?
What kinds of things do you look for?
Have you ever written a review of a hotel?
Was it good or bad? Why?

Ss work in small groups and discuss the questions. In feedback, ask a student from each group to share their ideas with the class.

1 Ss work in pairs and discuss the questions. When they have finished, elicit their ideas and have a brief class discussion.

2a Give Ss a few minutes to read the review and answer the question. Check answers with the whole class.

Answer: a hotel

b Ss read the review again and answer the questions, then check in pairs. Check answers with the whole class.

Answers:
1 **food:** + good for the price. – little choice for vegetarians
sports facilities: + good. – small
the area: + beautiful, walks, peaceful. – near a noisy road
the room: + comfortable and a good size – cleaners only came in twice during our stay, noisy road outside
the wifi: + worked well most days – didn't work well all the time
transport: – you need a car to get around
2 Ask for a room on the quieter south side; ask yourself two questions before you decide to go.
3 **paragraph 1:** the area
paragraph 2: the hotel
paragraph 3: the transport/main problems
paragraph 4: recommendation

3 Ss read through the Focus box and examples alone, or read the box as a class. Elicit the answer.

Answer: So that the reader can understand our ideas clearly.

4 Go through the notes and check Ss understand the words and phrases used. Ss match the notes to the categories in the Focus box alone, then check in pairs. Check answers with the whole class.

Answers:
1 stayed for two weeks in summer; went on sailing holiday to France with family
2 friendly staff; hotel in excellent sailing area; big, comfortable rooms; great restaurant
3 beach really busy in the morning
4 best hotel – everyone should go there

Prepare

5a Give Ss plenty of time to make notes, and make sure they don't write full sentences at this stage. Monitor and help with vocabulary, writing any new words/phrases on the board.

b Ss choose two things to write about for each topic alone.

c Remind Ss of the categories in the Focus box, and give them a few minutes to think about how to organise their ideas.

Write

6 Go through the Useful phrases with the class. Ss write their reviews alone. Monitor and check Ss' work, and help where necessary.

Homework ideas

Workbook: Ex 1–5, p21

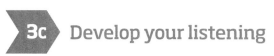

3c Develop your listening

Introduction

Ss develop their listening skill of understanding an interview by learning how to predict information.

Warm-up

Write on the board: *My bucket list* and explain what it is, i.e. a list of things you'd like to do before you die. Tell Ss some of the things that are on your bucket list. Give Ss a few minutes to think about what to put on theirs and write it down. Monitor and help with vocabulary, writing any new words/phrases on the board. When they have finished, put Ss in small groups to share their ideas and find out if they have anything in common.

1a Focus attention on the photos and elicit what Ss can see. Ss work in pairs and match the activities to the photos. Check answers with the whole class.

Answers: A walk along the Great Wall of China   B learn to fly
C climb Mount Kilimanjaro   D go on a safari holiday
E ride a snowmobile/see The Northern Lights

Culture notes

Mount Kilimanjaro is the highest mountain in Africa and is located in Tanzania. It's 4,900 m from the base. While it's challenging for non-climbers to climb, many do so with some training as it's more of a trek than a climb. The lack of oxygen can make it challenging, however, and it can also be quite windy.

The Northern Lights (Aurora Borealis) are coloured lights that appear in and dance around the sky in most northern countries in the world.

b Ss work in pairs and discuss the questions. In feedback, ask a few Ss to share their ideas with the class.

2 3.9 Ss listen to the introduction and answer the question. Check the answer with the whole class.

Answer: To do a different, amazing and life-changing experience each year for the next twenty years.

Audioscript 3.9

Presenter:
I'm here today with Karen Jackson. Karen's trying to have one amazing, life-changing experience every year. She made a list of twenty things she'd like to do over twenty years, and she's already done five of them. Karen, tell us why you're doing this.

3 Ss read the Focus box alone, then work in pairs and answer the question. Check answers with the whole class.

Answer: knowledge of the topic, the situation and the speaker

4 3.10 Elicit a possible reason first as an example, e.g. Karen wants to learn new things. Ss think of their own predictions alone, then check in pairs. When they are ready, play the recording for Ss to check their predictions and then check answers with the whole class.

Answers: Karen wants to look back when she's older and feel like she had done lots of exciting things. She wants to set goals and achieve them to give her confidence. She plans to do things, see things and go to places.

Audioscript 3.10

Karen: Well, there are two reasons, really. Firstly, when I'm old, I want to look back and feel like I've done lots of exciting things in my life. And secondly, it's great to have goals in life. It makes you feel good.
Presenter: OK, so tell me. What kinds of activities are on your list?
Karen: Well, things I'd like to do, things I'd like to see, and places I'd like to visit.

5a Read the example with the class. Ss write some ideas alone, then compare ideas in pairs. Elicit Ss' ideas as a class and write them on the board.

b 3.11 Ss listen and check their ideas. In feedback, tick off the ideas on the board that Ss came up with that she mentions.

Suggested answers:
The Great Wall of China: long, amazing views, quiet and relaxing
Iceland: Northern Lights, very cold, bright moon, storm, whales
Mount Kilimanjaro: difficult, felt sick, difficult to breathe, amazing sunrise

Audioscript 3.11

Presenter: And what places have you visited so far?
Karen: Well, I've been to the Great Wall of China and Iceland.
Presenter: Did you walk along the Great Wall?
Karen: Yes and no. I wanted to walk along it from start to finish, but it's really long – over 20,000 kilometres! I only walked about 200 kilometres in the end, but I was happy with that. The views were amazing, and in some places it was just so quiet and relaxing.
Presenter: And why did you go to Iceland?
Karen: I wanted to see the Northern Lights. For three nights, my friend and I sat outside – but unfortunately we didn't see them, and it was very, very cold!
Presenter: Why didn't you see them?
Karen: Well, unfortunately it was very cloudy.
Presenter: Oh dear, sorry to hear that!
Karen: Yeah, but we'll try again! There were lots of great things to do in Iceland during the day. We went on a great boat trip. That was really fun, actually. Oh, and I've climbed Mount Kilimanjaro, too.
Presenter: You have? Wow! Tell us about that.
Karen: Well, everybody says it's really difficult so I wanted to try it. You definitely need to be very fit and healthy. I felt sick quite a lot of the time because it's difficult to breathe up there, but when I finally got to the top, well, the view was fantastic.

c Go through the questions so that Ss know what to listen for. Ss listen again and answer the questions alone then check in pairs. Check answers with the whole class.

Answers:
1 She walked 200 km.
2 Amazing, calm and relaxing.
3 It was very cloudy.
4 Went on a boat trip.
5 People say it's really difficult to climb, so she wanted to try it.
6 She felt sick because it is difficult to breathe.

6a Write the three activities on the board and draw a circle round each one. Elicit a prediction for *learning to fly* as an example and write it on the board, drawing a line to connect it to the relevant circle, e.g. to see the world from up high. Ss work in pairs and make predictions and write them down. Monitor and help with ideas and vocabulary where necessary.

b 🔊 **3.12** Ss listen and check their predictions. In feedback, elicit any predictions made correctly.

c Ss listen again and answer the questions alone, then check in pairs. Check answers with the whole class.

Answers:
1 Because she is afraid of flying.
2 She thinks learning to fly a plane will help her get over her fear of flying.
3 Africa – maybe Kenya or Tanzania.
4 Lions and elephants.
5 It's not the same when you see animals in a zoo.

Audioscript 3.12

Presenter: And what activities have you planned for the future?
Karen: Right, so next year I'd like to learn to fly, but it isn't going to be easy.
Presenter: Really? So why do you want to do it then?
Karen: Because I'm afraid of flying and I think learning how to fly a plane will help me.
Presenter: OK, well the best of luck with that! What else?
Karen: I'd like to go on a safari holiday somewhere in Africa – maybe northern Kenya or Tanzania.
Presenter: Why's that?
Karen: I'd really like to see lots of wild animals like lions and elephants. It's not the same when you see them in the zoo.
Presenter: It all sounds great, Karen. Thank you very much for sharing your plans with us today. And lots of luck for the future.
Karen: Thanks.

7 Ss work in groups and discuss the questions. In feedback, elicit Ss' ideas and have a brief class discussion.

Homework ideas

Workbook: Ex 1–3, p19

4 OVERVIEW

4A Special days

Speaking | talk about plans for a special day
Grammar | *be going to*, *want* and *would like*
Vocabulary | celebrations

GSE learning objectives
Can ask and answer questions about basic plans and intentions; can describe plans and arrangements

4B Organising events

Speaking | make offers
Grammar | *will/won't* + infinitive for offers and decisions
Vocabulary | organising events

GSE learning objective
Can make and accept offers

4C Rules of the race

Speaking | talk about rules
Grammar | *can* and *have to*
Vocabulary | *-ed* and *-ing* adjectives

GSE learning objective
Can explain the rules of a familiar game or sport using simple language

4D English in action

Goal | make invitations and plans to meet

GSE learning objectives
Can discuss what to do and where to go, and make arrangements to meet

Check and reflect

(b) I can organise an event.
(c) I can present an idea for an event.
(d) I can make plans to meet.

VOCABULARY BANK

4C Sport

DEVELOP YOUR SKILLS

4A Develop your writing

Goal | write and respond to an invitation
Focus | inviting and responding

GSE learning objectives
Can write a basic informal email/letter of invitation with simple, key details; can write a basic email/letter accepting or declining an invitation

4B Develop your listening

Goal | understand instructions
Focus | sequencing words

GSE learning objective
Can understand instructions delivered at normal speed and accompanied by visual support

4C Develop your reading

Goal | understand a review
Focus | understanding pronouns

GSE learning objective
Can make basic inferences from simple information in a short text

4A Special days

Introduction

The goal of this lesson is for Ss to describe a celebration. To help them achieve this, they will learn/revise phrases to describe future plans and intentions, and words/phrases to describe celebrations.

Warm-up

Before class, write on the board:
My favourite way to celebrate my birthday is …

Give Ss a minute or two to complete the sentence however they want to. Monitor and help with new vocabulary where necessary, writing any new words/phrases on the board. When they are ready, arrange Ss in small groups to share their ideas. In feedback, ask a student from each group to share their ideas with the class.

Reading and vocabulary

Celebrations

1 Focus attention on the photos, and ask Ss to work in pairs and discuss the questions. When Ss have finished, elicit their ideas and write them on the board, but don't give any answers yet.

2a You may want to pre-teach/elicit: *poet*, *supper* and *haggis*. Ss read the text quickly and check their ideas in Ex 1 alone, then check in pairs. Check answers with the whole class and tick off any of the ideas on the board that were mentioned.

> **Answers:** A Moon Festival   B Burn's Night   C Friend's Day

b Ss read the text again and answer the questions alone, then check in pairs. Check answers with the whole class. If your Ss are interested, you may wish to tell them more information from the Culture notes below.

Answers:
1 Friend's Day: 20th July in Argentina; Moon Festival: each autumn, but on different days in China; Burn's Night: 25th January in Scotland
2 Friend's Day: meet up with friends and go out for a meal; Moon Festival: celebrate at home, go out to look at the moon, eat traditional mooncakes; Burn's Night: have dinner parties, eat traditional food, read poems
3 the Moon festival

> **Culture notes**
>
> **Mooncakes** are round pastries with a thick filling made from red bean or lotus seed paste. Sometimes they also have the yolks from salted duck eggs. They're usually eaten with tea during the festival.
>
> **Haggis** is traditionally made from a sheep's stomach, filled with its heart, liver, lungs, oats, onion and spices.

3a Draw Ss' attention to the words in the box. Encourage them to use dictionaries or their mobile devices to help with meanings. Ss complete the questions alone, then check in pairs. Check answers with the whole class and be prepared to give further explanations/examples where necessary.

Answers: 1 get together   2 contact old friends
3 have dinner parties   4 public holiday   5 go out for a meal
6 give gifts   7 festivals   8 celebrate   9 traditional
10 have fun

Vocabulary checkpoint

In British English, *holiday* can mean a day when you don't go to work or a time when you travel for pleasure. In US English, *holiday* is a day when you don't work and *vacation* is when you travel.

b Ss work in pairs and take turns to ask and answer the questions from Ex3a. When they have finished, ask a few Ss to share any interesting information about their partner with the class.

Further practice

Photocopiable activities: 4A Vocabulary, p170

Grammar

4a 🔊 **4.1** You may want to pre-teach/elicit: *try my best* and *dessert*. Ss listen and answer the question then check in pairs. Check answers with the whole class.

Answers: Jane is going to invite her neighbours to her house and cook a meal. Ben is going to go to his parent's house for a family meal.

b Ss listen again and complete the sentences, then check in pairs. Check answers with the whole class.

Answers: 1 going   2 going to   3 like   4 not going
5 want to   6 are you going to

Audioscript 4.1

Ben: Hey Jane. What are your plans for Burn's Night?
Jane: Well, I'm going to invite my neighbours to my house for dinner. What about you?
Ben: I'm going to be at my parent's house. My mum's going to cook for the whole family.
Jane: How many people is that?
Ben: I don't know, maybe fourteen.
Jane: Fourteen?!
Ben: Yeah. It's a bit crazy, but we always have fun. What are you going to cook?
Jane: Well I'd like to make a traditional meal, but I'm not a very good cook. I'm going to try my best though.
Ben: Good for you.
Jane: I'm not going to cook haggis though!
Ben: Are you crazy!? You have to cook haggis on Burns Night!
Jane: Alright, alright, haggis it is then ... I want to ask my neighbours to bring a dessert. Do you think that's OK?
Ben: Yes, I'm sure that'll be fine. What poems are you going to read?
Jane: I don't know. I'm going to sit down and plan everything next week.
Ben: Next week? My mum started planning everything a month ago!

be going to, *want* and *would like*

5 Write the first example in the Grammar box on the board (*I'm going to invite my neighbours for dinner*) and ask *When did I decide this: now or in the past?* (in the past) *Does this sentence talk about the present or future?* (the future). Ss read the box and choose the correct alternatives alone, then check in pairs. Check answers with the class, going through the examples and be prepared to give further explanations where necessary.

Answers: 1 infinitive   2 infinitive

Grammar checkpoint

Note that *be going to* can also be used for predictions based on something we already know or based on evidence, e.g. *It's going to be cold tomorrow. We're going to beat you in the game!* This lesson just looks at future plans and intentions, so only mention this if a student brings it up.

GRAMMAR BANK 4A   pp.122–123

Stronger classes could read the notes at home. Otherwise, check the notes with Ss. In each exercise, elicit the first answer as an example. Ss work alone to complete the exercises, then check their answers in pairs. In feedback, elicit Ss' answers and drill the questions. Ss can refer to the notes to help them.

Answers: 4A
1 1 ~~want do~~ want to do
  2 ~~I like~~ I'd/would like
  3 ~~go to do~~ going to do
  4 ~~wants not~~ doesn't want
  5 ~~Would like you~~ Would you like
  6 ~~I going~~ I'm/am going
  7 ~~would like get~~ would like to get
  8 ~~going seeing~~ going to see
2 1 I'm going to play golf
  2 Where are you going to do that?
  3 we want to enter it
  4 Lee and I are going to see a band
  5 How are you going to get there?
  6 he's going to drive
  7 I'd/would like to get

6a 🔊 **4.2** Play the recording for Ss to listen to the weak form of *to*, then elicit how it's pronounced. You may wish to explain the information in the Pronunciation checkpoint below.

Answer: /tə/ (weak form)

Pronunciation checkpoint

Going to in fast, natural speech is sometimes shortened to *gonna* (/ˈɡənə/). While Ss don't need to use this pronunciation, it can be useful to point it out so that they can recognise it when they hear it.

b Ss listen again and repeat. If necessary, drill chorally and individually for further practice.

7a Read the example with the class. Ss complete the conversation alone, then check in pairs. Don't give any answers yet.

Answers: 1 are   2 going to celebrate   3 'm going to meet up
4 're going to have   5 'd like to go   6 are [you]   7 going to do
8 want to find

b Ss practise the conversation in pairs. In feedback, nominate two Ss to perform it for the class in an open pair.

Optional extra activity

With ***stronger classes***, ask Ss to change some of the key details and practise the conversation again, e.g. *Have you had any idea's for Burn's Night? I'm going to have a dinner party*, etc.

8a Draw a long horizontal line on the board. Elicit the nearest and furthest time expressions from the class, and write them on opposite ends of the line. Ss order the expressions alone, then check in pairs. In feedback, ask different Ss to come to the board and write their answers on the line.

> **Answers:** 1 in an hour 2 at two o'clock tomorrow
> 3 the day after tomorrow 4 this Saturday
> 5 in two months' time 6 next April 7 the year after next
> 8 in 2060

b Demonstrate by giving a few examples which are true for you, then read the example with the class. Ss complete the sentences on their own. Moniter, and help with ideas and vocabulary, writing any new words/phrases on the board.

c Read the example with the class and encourage them to ask follow-up questions. Ss compare their ideas in pairs. Monitor and check they're using the grammar correctly. When they have finished, nominate a few Ss to share any interesting information about their partners with the class.

Further practice

Photocopiable activities: 4A Grammar 1, p168; 4A Grammar 2, p169

Speaking

Optional extra activity

Introduce the activity and provide a model by talking about a celebration you know. Make sure you answer all the questions in Ex 8 and ask Ss to make notes while you describe it. After listening, Ss work in pairs and compare their notes, then check answers to the questions with the whole class.

Prepare

9 Ss work alone to plan what they're going to say. Monitor and help with vocabulary, writing any new words/phrases on the board.

Speak

10a Go through the Useful phrases with the class. Arrange Ss in small groups to share their celebrations. Monitor and make notes on Ss' language use for later feedback.

Teaching tip

When monitoring a speaking activity, it's important not to interrupt the Ss so they can practise fluency. However, you don't need to be too strict about this. If an opportunity comes up for you to respond to what a student says, or ask follow-up questions, then do so.

b Give Ss a minute to decide, then ask each group to share their most interesting celebration with the class.

Reflection on learning

Write the following questions on the board:
Did you use any of the vocabulary from the lesson when describing your celebration?
How confident do you feel giving a description?
What things could you do to improve?

Put Ss in pairs to discuss the questions. When they have finished, ask if anyone wants to share their ideas with the class, but don't force them to if they'd rather not.

Homework ideas

Ex9a: Ss write a description of their celebration.
Grammar bank: 4A Ex 1–2, p122
Workbook: Ex 1–5, p22
App: grammar and vocabulary practice

Fast route: continue to Lesson 4B
Extended route: go to p95 for Develop your writing

4B Organising events

Introduction

The goal of this lesson is for Ss to organise an event. To help them achieve this, they will learn/revise *will/won't* for offers and decisions, and vocabulary related to organising an event.

Warm-up

Before class, write on the board:
This week I'm going to …
I'm not going to …
This year I'm going to …
Next year I'm not going to …

Give Ss a minute or two to complete the sentences with their plans. Monitor and help with new vocabulary where necessary, writing any new words/phrases on the board. When they have finished, ask Ss to stand up, walk around and share their plans with other Ss. In feedback, find out if any Ss have plans in common.

Reading

1 Go through the events with the class and check understanding. Ss work in pairs and discuss which they've done. In feedback, elicit answers and have a brief class discussion.

2a Ss work in pairs to discuss how organised they are and to give themselves a score from 1–30. For example, if they are always on time, but occasionally are late, Ss award themselves a mark of about 25. If they are always late, but occasionally on time, they award themselves a mark of about 5.

b Ss work in pairs and answer the questions, noting down their answers. When they are ready, Ss turn to p153 and add up their partner's score, then read the results to them. In feedback, ask a few Ss if they agree with their scores and why (not).

Optional extra activity

Have a class discussion based on the quiz results. By a show of hands, find out how many Ss gave different responses to each question in the quiz. Ask Ss to share any answers they disagreed with and say why.

3 Ss work in pairs and discuss the questions. When they have finished, nominate a student from each group to share their ideas with the class.

Grammar

will/won't for decisions and offers

4 Ss choose the correct alternative alone, then check in pairs. Encourage them to look back at the examples in the quiz to help. Check answers with the class and be prepared to give further explanations/examples where necessary.

Answers: 1 without to

Grammar checkpoint

You can contrast the use of *will* here with the use of *be going to* in Lesson 4A, by explaining that with *will* we make the decision at, or just before, the time of speaking, while *be going to* describes something we previously planned/decided.

GRAMMAR BANK 4B pp.122–123

Stronger classes could read the notes at home. Otherwise, check the notes with Ss, especially the other uses of *will* described here. In each exercise, elicit the first answer as an example. Ss work alone to complete the exercises, then check their answers in pairs. In feedback, elicit Ss' answers and drill the questions. Ss can refer to the notes to help them.

Answers: 4B
1 1 'll check   2 'll do   3 'll meet   4 'll look after
   5 'll play   6 'll save
2 1 I'll give you a lift.
   2 I'll lend you some money.
   3 I'll carry some of those for you.
   4 I'll help you move.
   5 I'll bake a cake.

5a ◀) **4.3** Ss listen and choose the correct alternative alone, then check in pairs. Check answers with the whole class.

Answers: 1 I drive to work.   2 We'll help them clean.
3 I call Ella in the evening.   4 We'll play on Sunday.

Pronunciation checkpoint

We almost always contract this use of *will* when speaking, so it's a good idea to ensure your Ss get a feel for the contraction by listening and repeating it through practice.

b Ss listen again and repeat. If necessary, drill chorally and individually for further practice.

6 Elicit the first answer as an example. Ss complete the conversation alone, then check in pairs. Check answers with the whole class. Ss work in pairs and practise the conversation, then swap roles and repeat. In feedback, ask different Ss to practise the conversations in open pairs.

Answers: 1 'll carry   2 'll come   3 'll make   4 'll do   5 'll clean

Further practice

Photocopiable activities: 4B Grammar 1, p171;
4B Grammar 2, p172

Vocabulary

Organising events

7a Books closed. Contextualise this activity by saying that you're organising a surprise party for your friend, but you've never done it before, so you need some help. Elicit one or two things you need to do and write them on the board. Ask Ss to open their books to Ex 7a then put them in pairs to make lists. Monitor and help with vocabulary where necessary, writing any new words/phrases on the board. Elicit answers from the class and build a list on the board.

Optional alternative activity

When Ss have written their lists in pairs, give out two or three board pens, and ask Ss to come up to the board and add one thing to the class list. They then give their pen to someone else who adds one further thing, until you've built up a class list with everyone's ideas. Ss then work in pairs to put the things on the board in the order they think they need doing. When they have finished, ask a few pairs to share their order with the class and find out if other Ss agree.

b Focus attention on the 'to do' list and explain that the verbs are missing. Ss complete the list alone, then check in pairs. Check answers with the whole class and be prepared to offer further explanations/examples where necessary.

Answers: 1 set   2 choose   3 book   4 send   5 bake
6 make   7 plan   5 remind

c Revisit the class list you made in Ex 7a and tick any that are mentioned in Ex 7b. Ask Ss if there's anything else they can add to the list and write their ideas on the board.

8 Ss complete the conversation alone, then check in pairs. Don't give any answers yet.

Answers: 1 set   2 book   3 choose   4 send   5 bake
6 make   7 plan   8 remind

Further practice

Photocopiable activities: 4B Vocabulary, p173

Speaking

Prepare

9a Go through the list of ideas with the class and arrange them in groups to decide. Monitor and encourage different groups to plan different types of events.

b Ask each group to choose a 'writer' who will note down their ideas and make the list. Ss create their lists in groups. Encourage Ss to use the vocabulary in Ex 7 and help with any other vocabulary they need.

Speak

10 Go through the Useful phrases with the class and demonstrate the activity with a ***stronger Ss*** if necessary. Ss decide who will do which task and when. Monitor and make notes on Ss' language use for later feedback.

11 Ss present their group's ideas to the class. When they have finished, give Ss feedback on their use of language during the speaking task.

Optional alternative activity

When Ss have finished planning their events, ask each group to say who is doing what, but without saying what type of event it is. Ss listen and guess the type of event.

Homework ideas

Grammar bank: 4B Ex 1–2, pp.122–123
Workbook: Ex 1–5, p23
App: grammar and vocabulary practice

Fast route: continue to Lesson 4C
Extended route: go to p96 for Develop your listening

 4c Rules of the race

Introduction

The goal of this lesson is for Ss to design and present a race. To help them achieve this, they will learn/revise *can, can't, have to* and *don't have to* to describe rules and *-ed, -ing* adjectives.

Warm-up

Arrange Ss in pairs. Give them a few minutes to brainstorm and write all the sports they can think of in English and make a list. When they have finished, combine pairs into small groups and find how many sports they all wrote. In feedback, nominate a student from each group to come to the board without their written answers, and ask the groups to call out the sports for them to write on the board. Check spelling on the board.

Listening

1a Discuss the questions as a class, eliciting whether Ss have ever taken part in any kind of race (not necessarily an extreme one as in the photos) and, if so, what kind of race it was. If anyone has taken part in a race, encourage Ss to ask them further questions to find out more details.

b You may want to elicit/check *muddy*, i.e. full of mud (wet earth) and *climb*, i.e. move up using your hands and feet – you could mime this. Focus attention on the photos and elicit what type of races they show. Ss read the description then work in pairs and answer the questions. Check answers with the class and elicit Ss' ideas.

Answers: Photos: swim through muddy water; jump over fire
Possible answers: They want to challenge themselves; they want to do something exciting; they want to be successful in something; they want to do more exercise.

2 4.7 You may want to pre-teach/check: *fit, jump, climb,* and *picnic*. Go through the items in the box with the class. Ss listen and answer the questions, then check in pairs. Check answers with the whole class.

Answers: 1 breaks, health, teams, visitors, what to wear   2 Yes

3a *Stronger classes* can do the exercise from memory, then listen again and check. Otherwise, Ss listen again and tick the true statements, then check in pairs. Check answers with the whole class.

Answers: 1 True   2 No, but it's a good idea.   3 True   4 No
5 True   6 True   7 True   8 No

Audioscript 4.7

Felicity: Lucas, you ran the Massive Mud Run last year, didn't you?
Lucas: Yeah, why?
Felicity: I'm interested in doing it myself, but I'm not sure.
Lucas: Well I really enjoyed it. It's an interesting course.
Felicity: I've never done anything like it before. Do I have to be very fit?
Lucas: Yes, you do. It's not easy. In fact, it's really tiring. Do you run regularly?
Felicity: Yeah, I do. I run 10 kilometres three times a week.
Lucas: Then, with some training, you'll be fine. You don't have to see a doctor before you do it, but it's a good idea. It might make you feel better if you're worried.
Felicity: Good idea, thanks.
Lucas: And take a look at a map of the course. Make sure you can jump and climb and do everything necessary. Runners have to do everything on the course. You can't miss anything. That includes jumping over the fire!
Felicity: Oh right, OK. Well, I guess that's fair. What kind of clothes do you suggest?
Lucas: You don't have to wear any special clothes. You can wear what you want. But remember that there's a lot of mud and water on the course.
Felicity: Yes, I've seen the photos! Can people come and watch?
Lucas: Yeah, all my family came last year!
Felicity: Nice! Is there somewhere for them to eat? Can people bring their own food?
Lucas: Sure. Lots of people had their own picnics last year. You can also buy food on site, and runners can buy food and drinks in the rest area.
Felicity: Oh, can I have a rest during the race?
Lucas: Yes, the race lasts 12 hours, so you'll be tired. You'll need to take some breaks.
Felicity: Oh, right.
Lucas: But if you don't want to run on your own, you can run in a team.
Felicity: Can you? How does that work?
Lucas: Well, only one person in the team runs at one time, so the others have more time to rest.
Felicity: Oh, I didn't know that. That's probably better for me. Where can I find a team?
Lucas: Try the race website, there's loads of information there.
Felicity: Oh great. I'll have a look tonight. I'm really excited about it now!
Lucas: Good. It's exhausting, but really good fun, too. You have to be sure you want to run though – because after you pay, you can't get your money back.
Felicity: OK, thanks, good tip.
Lucas: And one last thing – take a lot of clean clothes with you. You'll need them!

b 4.8 *Stronger classes* can complete the sentences, then listen and check. Otherwise, Ss listen and complete the sentences, then check in pairs. Play the recording again if necessary, then check answers with the whole class.

Answers: 1 have   2 to   3 have   4 don't   5 Can   6 Can
7 can   8 can't

c Ss work in pairs and discuss the questions. When they have finished, nominate a few Ss to share their ideas and have a brief class discussion.

Grammar

can and *have to*

4 Ss complete the rules alone, then check in pairs. Encourage Ss to look at the examples in Ex 3b to help. Check answers with the whole class and be prepared to give further explanations/examples where necessary.

> **Answers:** 1 have to 2 don't have to 3 can 4 can't

GRAMMAR BANK 4C pp.122–123

Stronger classes could read the notes at home. Otherwise, check the notes with Ss. In each exercise, elicit the first answer as an example. Ss complete the exercises alone, then check their answers in pairs. In feedback, elicit Ss' answers and drill the questions. Ss can refer to the notes to help them.

Answers: 4C
1 1 can/can't 2 have to/can't/don't have to
   3 can't/have to/have to 4 don't have to/have to
2 1 can 2 have to 3 can't 4 can 5 can't
   6 don't have to 7 have to 8 can

5a 🔊 4.9 Ss listen and answer the questions alone, then check in pairs. Check answers with the whole class.

> **Answer:** *Can* is stressed in a short answer, but not in a question or statement. *Can't* is stressed in statements and short answers.

b Ss listen again and repeat. If necessary, drill chorally and individually for further practice.

6a You may want to pre-teach/check: *donkey, accident* and *neighbour*. Elicit the first answer as an example. Ss complete the text alone, then check in pairs. Check answers with the whole class.

> **Answers:** 1 have to try 2 can't be 3 has to take
> 4 can push 5 have to carry 6 can't run 7 doesn't have to be

b Ss work in pairs and discuss the question, then compare Ss' answers as a whole class.

Optional extra activity

If Ss have taken part in a competition (a race, game, contest, etc.) before, ask them to describe the rules in pairs, using *can, can't, have to* and *don't have to*. Otherwise, they could describe a competition they know about.

7a Demonstrate the activity first by sharing your own sentences with the class. Encourage Ss to ask you follow-up questions to find out more information. Give Ss plenty of time to complete the sentences. Monitor and help with ideas and vocabulary where necessary.

b Read the example with the class. Ss work in pairs and share their information. When they have finished, ask a few Ss to share any interesting information they found out about their partners.

Further practice

Photocopiable activities: 4C Grammar 1, p174; 4C Grammar 2, p175

Vocabulary

-ed/-ing adjectives

8a Focus attention on the sentences and ask Ss to answer the questions in pairs. Check answers with the whole class, giving further examples if necessary.

> **Answers:** 1 a feeling 2 a thing 3 a thing 4 a feeling

b Ss choose the correct alternatives alone, then check in pairs. Check answers with the whole class.

> **Answers:** 1 boring 2 relaxed 3 excited 4 interesting
> 5 worried 6 tiring 7 exciting 8 surprising

c Ss work in pairs and take turns to ask and answer the questions in Ex 8b. Monitor and check they're using the correct forms of the adjectives. In feedback, ask a few Ss to share their ideas with the class.

Optional alternative activity

Ss can do Ex 8c as a class survey. Arrange Ss in pairs and allocate a question to each pair. They then ask their question to all the other Ss in the class, also asking follow-up questions, e.g. *Why do you feel like that? What happened?* to find out more information. When they have finished, each pair takes it in turns to present their results to the class.

VOCABULARY BANK 4C p139

Sport

This is an optional extension to the vocabulary section, extending the lexical set and providing further practice. If you're short of time, this can be done for homework. However, it's useful to do this activity before the final speaking task in Exs 9–11 as the vocabulary will help when describing sports.

1 Ss match the words and photos, using dictionaries or mobile devices to help. Check answers with the class, giving further explanations/examples where necessary.

> **Answers:** 1 K 2 A 3 I 4 D 5 C 6 F 7 H 8 J 9 B
> 10 L 11 E 12 M 13 N 14 G

2 Ss match the sentence halves and check their answers in pairs.

> **Answers:** 1 c 2 g 3 a 4 e 5 b 6 f 7 h 8 d

3 Ss work in pairs and using the vocabulary from Ex 1 take turns to say what each photo shows.

Further practice

Photocopiable activities: 4C Vocabulary, p176

Speaking

Prepare

9a 🔊 4.10 Ss listen and answer the question. Check the answer with the class.

> **Answer:** It's a race for dog owners and their dogs.

b Go through the questions and elicit the answers Ss can remember, but don't give any answers yet. Ss listen and answer the questions alone, then check in pairs. Check answers with the whole class.

Answers:
1 Silver Sands Beach
2 It's a team race – the runners run with their dogs.
3 The dogs wear a number around their neck and humans wear a number on their back.
4 Each person has to pay £10 to enter. You have to run the race with your dog. The dogs have to run all the way.
5 The winners get a free meal (for the runners) and special dog chocolate (for the dogs).

Audioscript 4.10

Marco: We'd like to tell you about the Dog and Bone Race on Silver Sands Beach. It's a team race. In each team, there's one dog and one person. People with big dogs have to run two kilometres along the beach. People with small dogs have to run one kilometre. Dogs have to wear a number around their neck. The people have to wear a number on their back.

Lei: The rules of the race are simple. You have to run the race with your dog from start to finish. The dogs have to run all the way – you can't carry them if they get tired. And the dogs can't carry you either! You can carry water and food for your dogs if you want, but you don't have to – there'll be dishes of water for the dogs on the beach.

Maria: The winning team in each group wins prizes – for you, a free meal at a restaurant, and for the dogs some special dog chocolate. We think this is an exciting event because dogs and people can enjoy the race together. They can take their usual walk but do an amazing event at the same time. Families can come and watch the race, too. It'll be a great day out for everyone.

10 Arrange Ss in groups for them to plan their race. Encourage Ss to use the questions in Ex 9b to help with ideas. Monitor and help with vocabulary where necessary, writing any new words/phrases on the board. If Ss are having trouble thinking of ideas, suggest some of these and have Ss invent the details: *a water race, a skateboard race, a litter-picking race, an underground race, a stairs race*. Ss prepare their presentations and decide who will say what and make sure that everyone is involved.

Speak

11a Go through the Useful phrases with the class. Ss take turns to present their races to the class. Encourage other Ss to ask questions to find out more information. Monitor and make notes on the Ss' language use for later feedback.

b Hold a class vote for the best race, making sure Ss don't vote for their own race. Afterwards, give Ss feedback on their use of language as a class.

> **Reflection on learning**
>
> Write the following questions on the board:
> *What new vocabulary did you use most during the speaking task? How can you practise the other vocabulary from this lesson?*
> Put Ss in pairs to discuss the questions. When they have finished, ask if anyone wants to share their ideas with the class, but don't force them to if they'd rather not.

Homework ideas

Ex 11: Ss write a description of their race and add it to their GSE portfolio.
Grammar bank: 4C Ex 1–2, pp.122–123
Workbook: Ex 1–5, p24
App: grammar and vocabulary practice

Fast route: continue to Lesson 4D
Extended route: go to p97 for Develop your reading

4D English in action

Introduction

The goal of this lesson is for Ss to practise making invitations and plans to meet. To help them achieve this, they will learn a range of phrases for inviting people, responding to invitations, making arrangements and responding to suggestions.

Warm-up

Before class, draw a pie chart on the board showing the approximate amount of time you spend doing different free-time activities, e.g. watching TV, relaxing, sleeping, meeting friends, etc. Explain the different sections to the class and encourage them to ask you follow-up questions to find out more detail. Give Ss a few minutes to draw their own diagrams. Monitor and help with vocabulary where necessary. When they are ready, Ss work in pairs and share/explain their diagrams. In feedback, ask a few Ss to share anything interesting they found out about their partners.

Listening

1 Focus attention on the photos and elicit what Ss can see. Ss work and discuss the questions. When they have finished, ask a few Ss to share their ideas and have a brief class discussion.

2a ◁ 4.11 You may want to pre-teach/check: *picnic* and *ages*. Ss listen and match the conversations to the photos alone, then check in pairs. Check answers with the whole class.

Answers: 1 C   2 A   3 B

b Go through the questions with the class and elicit any answers Ss can remember, but don't give any answers yet. Ss listen again and answer the questions then check in pairs. Check answers with the whole class.

Answers:
1 Because it will be too busy.
2 In front of the bank in Queen Street.
3 Because he's working in Edinburgh.
4 Because he's having a big family dinner.
5 Because it's too expensive.
6 They can share the cost.

Optional alternative activity

With **weaker classes**, arrange Ss in groups of three. In each group, Ss listen out for answers from a different conversation each. They then share answers within the group. Check answers with the class.

---

3 Give Ss a minute or two to read the phrases and ask any questions. Play the recordings again for Ss to listen and number the phrases, then check in pairs. Check answers with the whole class.

Answers:
Inviting people
Would you like to come? 1
Do you want to meet up (this Friday)?
Do you want to join us? 3
Responding to invitations
I'd love to! 1
Yes, that sounds (fun/great). 3
I don't think I can, sorry. 2
I'm sorry I can't, I'm busy. 2

Answers:

Organising when and where to meet

Where/What time shall we meet? 2

Shall we meet (at ten/at the park)? 1

Let's meet (in front of the bank/at five o'clock). 1, 2

Responding to suggestions

That's a good idea. 1

I'm not sure about that. 3

Audioscript 4.11

1

Susan: Hi Lucy! How's it going?

Lucy: Good thanks, Susan! How are you?

Susan: I'm fine, thanks. A few of us are having a picnic on Saturday. Would you like to come?

Lucy: I'd love to! The weather's going to be great!

Susan: Great. Shall we meet at ten, by the entrance to the park?

Lucy: I don't know. It gets really busy there and we might not see each other. Let's meet in front of the bank in Queen Street.

Susan: OK, no problem! I'll let the others know.

Lucy: Good, see you then!

2

Jimmy: Hello?

Chris: Hi Jimmy, Chris here.

Jimmy: Chris! We haven't spoken in ages!

Chris: Exactly! That's why I'm phoning actually. Do you want to meet up this Friday?

Jimmy: Ah, I don't think I can, sorry. I'm working in Edinburgh on Friday. What about Sunday?

Chris: I'm sorry I can't, I'm busy. We're having a big family dinner. Hmm … next week some time? Wednesday?

Jimmy: Wednesday's good for me. Where shall we meet?

Chris: How about Flavio's café in town? We can have lunch together.

Jimmy: That's a good idea. What time?

Chris: One o'clock?

Jimmy: Perfect. One o'clock it is!

3

Paul: Do you have any plans for the weekend, Tanya?

Tanya: Oh yes! I'm going to Pop in the Park with some friends.

Paul: Oh, is that the free concert? I heard about that.

Tanya: That's right. Do you want to join us?

Paul: Yes, that sounds fun. How are you getting there?

Tanya: We're not sure yet. Maybe public transport, but it's going to be really busy.

Paul: Shall we get a taxi together?

Tanya: I'm not sure about that. Taxis are expensive.

Paul: Yes, but if we share one, it'll be cheaper.

Tanya: That's a good point. I'll ask the others and see what they think.

Paul: OK.

4a 🔊 **4.12** Play the first two phrases and elicit the stressed words as an example. Ss listen to the rest and marked the stressed words alone, then check in pairs. Check answers with the class.

Answers:

1 Would you <u>like</u> to <u>come</u>?

2 Do you <u>want</u> to <u>join</u> us?

3 I'd <u>love</u> to.

4 Where shall we <u>meet</u>?

5 <u>Shall</u> we <u>meet</u> at ten?

6 <u>That's</u> a good idea.

b Ss listen and repeat. Check how they are pronouncing the phrases, and if necessary drill them chorally and individually for further practice.

In fast, natural speech, we usually stress content words, i.e. words which carry the most information. For example, in *Do you want to come? want* and *come* carry the message of the question. *Do, you* and *to* join the content words together in a grammatically correct sentence. This is good news for Ss, as they only need to listen out for these stressed words to understand the main meaning of the utterance.

5a Books closed. Write the first set of prompts on the board. Elicit the question, drill it, then write it underneath the prompts. Ss write the remaining questions alone, then check in pairs. Check answers with the class by nominating a different student to come to the board for each question and write it up.

Answers:

1 Would you like to go to the cinema tomorrow?

2 Do you want to play football with us at the weekend?

3 Shall we go to a restaurant?

4 What time shall we meet?

5 Shall we meet at seven o'clock?

b Demonstrate the activity with a ***stronger Ss*** by asking a question for them to respond to. Ss practise in pairs. Monitor and check they're stressing the phrases correctly. In feedback, nominate Ss to ask and respond in open pairs.

Speaking

6 Ss think of their details alone and use the question prompts to help them. Monitor and help with vocabulary where necessary, writing any new words/phrases on the board.

Speak

7a Go through the example with the class. Explain that Ss are going to go around the class and invite people to meet up. The Ss who are invited have to respond to the other people's invitations. Ss walk round inviting people. Monitor and make notes on their language use for later feedback.

b Ss work in pairs and discuss the question. In feedback, nominate Ss to share their answers, then give feedback on their use of language as a class.

Reflection on learning

Write the following questions on the board:

What was most useful in today's lesson?

What do you need to work on? How can you do this?

Put Ss in pairs to discuss the questions. When they have finished, ask if anyone wants to share their ideas with the class, but don't force them to if they'd rather not.

Reflection on learning: Write your answers.

Workbook: Ex 1–2, p25

App: grammar and vocabulary practice

4 Check and reflect

Introduction

Ss revise and practise the language of Unit 4. The notes below provide some ideas for exploiting the activities in class, but you may want to set the exercises for homework, or use them as a diagnostic or progress test.

1a With **weaker classes**, elicit the first answer as an example. Ss correct the mistakes alone, then check in pairs. Check answers with the whole class.

Answers: 1 going **to** move   3 I'm going to   4 want **to** retire
6 I'd like or ~~like~~ **want**   8 my friends **are**

b Demonstrate by changing one or two sentences so they're true for you, then ask Ss to do the same for all the sentences. Monitor and help with vocabulary where necessary, writing any new words/phrases on the board.
2 Ss match the verbs and noun phrases alone, then check in pairs. Check answers with the whole class.

Answers: 1 b   2 d   3 a   4 f   5 g   6 c   7 e

3 Ss work in pairs and discuss the questions. Monitor and check they're using the phrases in Ex 2 correctly. In feedback, nominate a few Ss to share their ideas with the class and find out if anyone has similar answers.
4a Ss choose the correct alternatives alone, then check in pairs. Check answers with the whole class and check Ss are contracting *will* properly.

Answers: 1 carry   2 'll   3 look   4 lend   5 I'll

b Elicit a problem for the first one as an example, e.g. *These bags are heavy.* Ss work in pairs to think about what might have been said before each offer.
5 Ss reorder the sentences alone. Check answers with the whole class.

Answers:
1 I'd like to go to party Sam's.
2 Do you want to go running?
3 This August Mark's going to Ibiza.
4 Are you going to watch the match on Saturday?
5 She'll come home after dinner.
6 I'm not going to stay out late tonight.
7 Kate doesn't want to change her job.
8 Would you like to travel around the world?

6 Ss complete the sentences alone, then check in pairs. Check answers with the whole class.

Answers: 1 plan   2 bake   3 makes   4 send   5 remind   6 set

7 Ss discuss their experiences in pairs. If they haven't organised an event before, ask them to think of an event they've been to and discuss what the organisers did.
8a Ss complete the rules alone, then check in pairs. Check answers with the whole class.

Answers: 1 can, can't   2 don't have to, can   3 have to
4 have to   5 can, can't   6 can, can't   7 have to, can, can

b Ss work in pairs to think of another sport and its rules. Use the rules in Ex 8a as prompts.
9a Ss choose the correct alternatives alone, then check in pairs. Check answers with the whole class.

Answers: 1 worried   2 frightening   3 relaxed   4 surprised
5 exciting   6 interested   7 bored   8 tiring

b Ss work in pairs and change the sentences in Ex 9a so they are true for them. In feedback, elicit answers and have a brief class discussion.

Reflect

Ask Ss to rate each statement alone, then compare in pairs. Encourage them to ask any questions they still have about any of the areas covered in Unit 4.

4 Keep talking (Units 3–4 review)

Introduction

Ss revise and practise the language of Units 3 and 4 in a communicative game. This can be done after the Check and reflect page as a fun way to revise the language of Units 3 and 4.

Put Ss in pairs or groups and explain that Ss in each pair/group should share the speaking role. Each team chooses a topic from the table. Make sure a different person speaks each time and that everyone in each team has a chance to speak. Each team has two minutes to plan what to say. The chosen student then speaks for 30 seconds on that topic to win one or two points. The other pairs/groups listens and then decides how many points to award them, depending on how fluent they were and how much of the topic language they included. Repeat four more times, choosing different topics. Monitor and be ready to adjudicate where necessary. When they have finished, elicit which team won in each group.

4A Develop your writing

Introduction

Ss develop their skills of writing and responding to invitations by learning how to use fixed phrases for invitations.

Warm-up

Write on the board: *social media 'event', email, text message, phone call, letter.* Ss work in pairs and discuss which of these things they use to invite people when they have a party or other event and whether the type of event affects which one they use. When they have finished, ask by a show of hands how many Ss use each thing.

1a Ss read the invitation and answer the question alone, then check in pairs. Check the answer with the whole class.

Answer: a dinner party

b Ss read the invitation again and answer the question. Check the answer with the whole class.

Answer: any time after 6

2 Give Ss a few minutes to read the Focus box or read it together with the class. Ss work in pairs and discuss the question. When they have finished, elicit their ideas and write them on the board.

3a Give Ss one minute to read the replies and say who can come. Check the answer with the whole class.

Answer: Sue and Phil

b Ss read the replies again more carefully and answer the questions alone, then check in pairs. Check answers with the whole class.

Answers:
1 We'd love to come.
2 Could you tell us the best way to get to your house? Do you want us to bring anything?
3 I'm afraid I can't come.
4 He's going to be away on a business trip.

4 Ss read another invitation and the responses, and choose the correct alternatives alone, then check in pairs. Check answers with the whole class.

Answers: 1 love 2 make it 3 I'd 4 unfortunately 5 great 6 we'll

Prepare

5 Go through the things to make notes about and elicit one or two examples for each one, e.g. *event* – a birthday party, a family meal, a sports event, etc. Give Ss plenty of time to make notes. Monitor and help with vocabulary, writing any new words/phrases on the board.

Write

6a Ss write their invitations alone. Make sure they write them on a separate piece of paper, so they can give it to someone else when they've finished. Monitor and help where necessary. Check Ss' writing as you go around.

b Put Ss in pairs to swap invitations and then write a reply below the invitation to accept. Encourage them to use the phrases in the Focus box. Monitor and help where necessary.

c Rearrange Ss into different pairs to swap invitations again. Remind Ss that when rejecting an invitation, they need to give a reason why. When they have finished, Ss return the invitations with the response.

Homework ideas

Workbook: Ex 1–7, p27

4B Develop your listening

Introduction

Ss develop their listening skill of understanding instructions by learning how to understand sequencing words.

Warm-up

Ask Ss to 'invent' an app they think is needed in their own or others' lives. Monitor and help with ideas and vocabulary where necessary. When they have finished, ask each pair to present their app to the class and vote for the best one.

1 Focus attention on the photos and elicit what Ss can see. Ss work in pairs and discuss the questions. When they have finished, elicit their ideas and have a brief class discussion.

2a ◁)) **4.4** Write the names of the apps (Buzz Tree and Evenroot) on the board. Elicit Ss' ideas about what they think the apps are for and write them on the board. Ss listen to the recording and check their predictions. Check answers with the class.

Answers: *Buzz Tree* gives you ideas for things to do. *Eventroots* helps you manage an event and invite people.

b **Stronger Ss** can do the activity from memory then listen again and check their answers. Otherwise, go through the statements with the class, so they know what to listen for. Ss listen again and match the statements to the apps alone, then check in pairs. Check answers with the whole class.

Answers: 1 E 2 B 3 B 4 E 5 E

Audioscript 4.4

Alicia: What are you doing for Sam's birthday, Jake?
Jake: I'm not sure yet. I want to organise a big night out with all our friends, you know? Maybe a meal or something, but I have no idea where to start.
Alicia: Oh, I know a great app you can use! Let me show you on my phone. It's called Buzz Tree and it gives you lots of interesting ideas for things to do.
Jake: Oh really? So how does it work?
Alicia: First, you answer some questions about you. Things like your age, interests, if you want to eat, that kind of thing.
Jake: I see.
Alicia: Next you press 'Go'. And then it gives you ideas for things to do, using the information you put in.
Jake: Thanks, that looks great. So then I just have to call all our friends and invite people?
Alicia: Call people? Seriously? It's not the 90s Jake. Use this app!
Jake: Ha, OK. Tell me about it.
Alicia: It's called Eventroots. It organises everything for you.
Jake: Wow. How does it do that?
Alicia: Well, to start with, you add the details in this box here. You need to add the date, time and location.
Jake: Date, time and location. Right.
Alicia: Next, you invite people by adding their email addresses.
Jake: How do I do that exactly?
Alicia: Just add them from your contacts, or you can type them in here.
Jake: OK.
Alicia: After that, people can reply and say if they can come or not. See?
Jake: Got it.
Alicia: Finally, you can update the event, like if you want people to bring something, or you want to change the time, and so on.
Jake: That's great, Alicia, thanks for your help.
Alicia: You're very welcome. Have a great night! I'm sure Sam will love whatever you organise.
Jake: I hope so!

3 Ss read through the Focus box and examples alone, or read the box as a class. Put Ss in pairs to think of more sequencing words. When they have finished, elicit their ideas and write them on the board.

Suggested answers: First of all, secondly, thirdly, afterwards, then, lastly

4a 🔊 4.5 Ss choose the sequencers alone, then listen and check their answers. Check answers with the whole class.

Answers: 1 First 2 Next 3 then 4 to start with 5 Then
6 After that 7 Finally

b Read the example with the class. Ss complete the chart alone, then check in pairs. Check answers with the whole class.

Answers:

start	middle	end
First, to start with,	*Then After that,*	*finally,*

5a 🔊 4.6 Go through the stages with the class, saying them out loud, so Ss know what to listen for. Ss listen to the instructions and order the stages alone, then check in pairs. Check answers with the whole class.

Answers: 1 b 2 d 3 f 4 c 5 a 6 e

Audioscript 4.6

A: I've found a useful app which I want you to download, OK? It's called Famsafe, and we can use it to see where everyone in the family is. It lets you share your location with me.
B: Famsafe, oh yes, I've got that, but I've never used it. How do I share my location?
A: First, make sure you have GPS turned on, like this.
B: Right.
A: Then find me in your contacts.
B: OK.
A: Next, select 'share my location with this user'.
B: Got it.
A: After that, when I open the app I can see where you are in real time. We can use it when we go to big events, and things like that.
B: OK. Is that it?
A: No. Finally, if you need to call me in an emergency, just say 'call Mum' and your phone will call me.
B: Right – hopefully I'll never need to do that!

b Ss listen again and complete the conversation alone, then check in pairs. Check answers with the whole class.

Answers: 1 First 2 Then 3 Next 4 After that 5 Finally

6 Ss work in pairs and discuss the questions. In feedback, ask a few Ss to share any interesting information they found out about their partners with the class.

Homework ideas

Workbook: Ex 1–3, p25

4c Develop your reading

Introduction

Ss develop their reading skill of understanding an online review by learning how to understand pronouns.

Warm-up

Write on the board:
How do you keep fit?
Do you play any sports?
Have you ever tried any unusual sports or fitness activities?
Did you like them?
Ss work in small groups and discuss the questions. In feedback, ask each group to choose the most interesting answers and share them with the class.

1 Ss read the advertisement. Ss answer the question alone, then check in pairs. Check the answer with the whole class.

Answer: a weekend of exercise and activities to get fit

2 Give Ss a few minutes to read the reviews and match with the headings. Explain that they'll have a chance to read them again more carefully afterwards. Ss check answers in pairs, then check with the whole class.

Answers: 1 B 2 A 3 C

3 Ss read the Focus box alone or read it with the class. Elicit other pronouns and write them on the board.

Suggested answers: he, we, you, him, her, them, these, those

4a Focus attention on the words in bold in review A in Ex 2a. Elicit which word the first pronoun (*It*) refers to from the class. Ss find the other words in bold alone, then check in pairs. Check answers with the whole class.

Answers: 1a the farmhouse
2b guests have to share a bathroom b sharing a bathroom
b go to the bootcamp

b Elicit the first answer as an example. Ss find the pronouns alone, then check in pairs. Check answers with the whole class.

Answers:
1 It (was really loud – review B)
2 They (were building a bigger gym – review B)
3 it (helped me find it – review C)
4 them (I talked more without them – review C)

5 Ss read the reviews again and answer the questions alone, then check in pairs. Check answers with the whole class.

Answers: 1 B 2 A 3 B/C 4 A 5 A/C 6 C 7 B 8 C

6 Ss work in small groups and discuss the questions. When they have finished, elicit a few answers and have a brief class discussion.

Homework ideas

Workbook: Ex 1–4, p26

5 OVERVIEW

5A The right person
Speaking | give information about a job
Grammar | relative clauses with *who*, *which* and *that*
Vocabulary | job skills and preferences
GSE learning objectives
Can give an extended description of everyday topics
(e.g. people, places, experiences)

5B Appearances
Speaking | describe people
Grammar | *look like*, *look* + adjective, *be like*
Vocabulary | appearance
GSE learning objectives
Can use simple language to describe people's appearance;
can use simple language to describe people's personality and
emotions

5C Shopping tips
Speaking | give advice
Grammar | *should, shouldn't* and imperatives
Vocabulary | shopping
GSE learning objective
Can give basic advice using simple language

5D English in action
Goal | make and respond to suggestions
GSE learning objective
Can make and respond to suggestions

Check and reflect
(a) I can describe a job.
(c) I can give advice about shopping.

VOCABULARY BANK

5A Jobs

DEVELOP YOUR SKILLS

5A Develop your reading
Goal | understand an article
Focus | identifying positive and negative points
GSE learning objective
Can understand basic opinions related to familiar topics,
expressed in simple language

5B Develop your listening
Goal | follow a short talk
Focus | understanding linkers
GSE learning objective
Can follow the sequence of events in a short, simple
conversation or narrative

5C Develop your writing
Goal | write a guide
Focus | linking ideas
GSE learning objective
Can write about everyday things (e.g. people, places, job, study)
in linked sentences

5A The right person

Introduction

The goal of this lesson is for Ss to give information about a job.
To help them achieve this, they will learn/revise defining relative
clauses, and pronouns and vocabulary related to job skills and
preferences.

Warm-up

Bring/Download photos of people doing unusual jobs, e.g.
professional queuer, waterslide tester, pet psychologist, chocolate
taster. Show them to the class and elicit ideas about what these
people do. Ss then work in pairs and discuss what they think the
job involves, and what skills you need to do each one. In feedback,
elicit Ss' ideas, and ask the class if they know, or have read about,
any other unusual jobs.

Vocabulary and listening

Job skills and preferences

1a Ss work in pairs and brainstorm jobs. Set a strict time limit of
two minutes, and monitor and help with vocabulary where
necessary. When they have finished, ask a few Ss to come to the
board to write some jobs, then pass the board pen to other Ss to
continue. Check answers and spelling on the board.

Optional alternative activity

With **stronger classes**, write the letters of the alphabet on the
board, and ask Ss to work in pairs, and try and think of a job that
begins with each letter. In feedback, find out how many jobs they
thought of and ask them to write the jobs on the board.

b Ss match the jobs to the photos alone, then check in pairs.
Check answers with the whole class.

Answers: A shop assistant B tour guide C writer
D businessperson E film extra F architect

Teaching tip
With monolingual classes, check understanding of the jobs
quickly and effectively by asking Ss how to say the jobs in their
first language.

VOCABULARY BANK 5A p140

Jobs

This is an optional extension to the vocabulary section, extending the lexical set and providing further practice. If you're short of time, Ex 1 can be done for homework, with the discussion in Ex 2 done in the following class. However, it's useful to do this activity before Ex 2c, so that Ss can discuss a wider range of jobs.

1 Ss match the jobs and photos, using dictionaries or mobile devices to help. Check answers with the class, giving further explanations/examples where necessary.

Answers: 1 F 2 J 3 A 4 M 5 N 6 H 7 C 8 I 9 L
10 O 11 K 12 B 13 E 14 G 15 D

2 Ss work in pairs and discuss the questions. In feedback, elicit Ss' answers and have a brief class discussion.

Answers: 1 accountant 2 hairdresser 3 actor
4 estate agent 5 lawyer 6 computer programmer
7 plumber 8 waiter/waitress

3 Ss discuss the statements in pairs. In feedback, elicit Ss' answers and have a brief class discussion.

2a Before Ss do the questionnaire, either check understanding of the phrases, e.g. *creative*, *good communication skills*, *working long hours*, part-time in the statements, or encourage Ss to use dictionaries while they do the questionnaire. Monitor and help where necessary.

b Ss compare their answers to the questionnaire in pairs to find out how similar their answers are. Encourage Ss to give reasons for and examples of their answers. When they have finished, ask a few Ss to share their findings with the class.

c Refer Ss back to the jobs in Ex 1b. Ss work in pairs and discuss the questions. Check answers with the whole class.

Further practice

Photocopiable activities: 5A Vocabulary, p179

3a 🔊 5.1 Ss listen and answers the questions alone, then check in pairs. Explain that they'll have a chance to listen again for more detail, so not to worry if they don't understand every word. Check answers with the class.

Answer: film extra

b Ss listen again and answer the questions alone, then check in pairs. Check answers with the whole class.

Answers:
1 She doesn't enjoy her job at the moment.
2 She wants a complete change from what she does now – interesting, unusual, creative, enjoyable.
3 **Review writer:** she doesn't have experience of writing and she doesn't want to work on her own.
Shop manager: too similar to what she does now.
4 Because it sounds interesting and fun and is definitely different.

Audioscript 5.1

James: Hi Cheryl, how are you?
Cheryl: James! Nice to see you!
James: What are you up to?
Cheryl: Oh, I'm just looking for a new job.
James: Really? What about the job you have at the moment?
Cheryl: Well, I've had that job for four years now and I really don't enjoy it. It's just doing the same thing every day, you know? I'd like to find a job that's completely different.
James: OK, well maybe I can help? What sort of thing are looking for?
Cheryl: Well, the most important thing is that I want a job which is interesting, and maybe unusual. A complete change from what I do now. I don't need a well-paid job, I just want to enjoy it. Something creative would be nice …
James: Hmm, OK. What about this one? A review writer – all you have to do is try products and write about them. They want someone who enjoys writing. And look, you can work from home. I think you'd like this!
Cheryl: Oh no, I don't have much experience of writing. Plus I don't want to work on my own every day.
James: OK. Well what about this one? Shop manager. You'll manage a team of twenty-five people in the new shop on the high street. Are you a good manager?
Cheryl: No, not really. And that sounds quite similar to the job I have now.
James: Hmm, let me see. Oh, there is this one … it's quite unusual.
Cheryl: Yes?
James: Well, they're looking for someone that can work part-time …
Cheryl: Go on … what is it?
James: A film extra.
Cheryl: A film extra!?
James: Yeah, you know, when they make a film, there are the main actors, and then there are all the people who don't speak or do anything important – you'd be part of the crowd, or in the street, or something.
Cheryl: Yes, I know what a film extra is, thank you James … But you know what, that sounds like something which could be really interesting … and fun! And it's definitely different. Great idea James!
James: You're welcome Cheryl!

4 🔊 5.2 The aim of this activity is to narrow the focus and lead in to the grammar work in Ex 5. Ss listen and choose the correct alternatives alone, then check in pairs. Check answers with the whole class.

Answers: 1 that's 2 which 3 who 4 that

Grammar

Relative clauses with *who*, *which* and *that*

5 Ss choose the correct alternatives alone, then check in pairs. Encourage them to use the extracts in Ex 4 to help. Check answers with the whole class and be prepared to offer further explanations/examples where necessary.

Answers: 1 people 2 things

GRAMMAR BANK 5A pp.124–125
Stronger classes could read the notes at home. Otherwise, check the notes with Ss. In each exercise, elicit the first answer as an example. Ss work alone to complete the exercises, then check their answers in pairs. In feedback, elicit Ss' answers and drill the questions. Ss can refer to the notes to help them.

Answers: 5A
1 1 b 2 d 3 e 4 a 5 f 6 c
2 1 which 2 which 3 who 4 who 5 which 6 who

6a 🔊 5.3 Ss listen to the clauses, paying attention to the pronounciation of *who*, *which* and *that*.

Pronunciation checkpoint

When checking the answer, try not to spend too long saying *that* in isolation, as it's difficult to show how it's unstressed without being part of a phrase. Once you've established the pronunciation, move on to Ex 6b, so that Ss can practise saying *that* as part of a relative clause naturally.

b Ss listen again and repeat. If necessary, drill chorally and individually for further practice.

7 Books closed. Write the first pair of sentences and the relative pronoun on the board. Elicit how they can be combined and write the answer on the board. Ss open their books and combine the sentences alone, then check in pairs. Check answers with the whole class.

> **Answers:** 1 that 2 who 3 that 4 which 5 who 6 that 7 who 8 that

8 Ss complete the sentences, then check in pairs and guess the job. Check answers with the whole class.

> **Answers:** 1 who 2 that 3 who 4 that 5 which 6 who

9 Read the example with the class. Ss work in pairs and practise describing and suggesting jobs. Ss use the phrases from the questionnaire to help. When they have finished, ask Ss to share which jobs their partner suggested with the class.

Further practice

Photocopiable activities: 5A Grammar 1, p177; 5A Grammar 2, p178

Speaking

Prepare

10 Make sure Ss choose a different job from Ex 9. Then, in pairs, Ss complete the sentences. Give Ss plenty of time to complete the sentences. Monitor and help with ideas and vocabulary where necessary. Remind them to look back at the vocabulary from the lesson for ideas, too.

Speak

11a Go through the Useful phrases with the class. Arrange Ss in groups by combining the pairs from Ex 10 to share their descriptions and guess the jobs. Monitor and make notes on Ss' language use for later feedback.

b Ss work in the same groups and discuss the question using the Useful phrases to help them. Encourage Ss to give reasons and ask questions for more information. When they have finished, give Ss feedback on their language use as a class.

Reflection on learning

Write the following questions on the board:
Did you express your ideas clearly?
How do you think you'll use relative clauses in the future?
Put Ss in pairs to discuss the questions. When they have finished, ask if anyone wants to share their ideas with the class, but don't force them to if they'd rather not.

Homework ideas

Grammar bank: 5A Ex 1–2, pp.124–125
Workbook: Ex 1–5, p28
App: grammar and vocabulary practice

Fast route: continue to Lesson 5B
Extended route: go to p98 for Develop your reading

5B Appearances

Introduction

The goal of this lesson is for Ss to describe people. To help them achieve this, they will learn/revise *look like/ look* + adjective, *be like* and vocabulary to describe appearance.

Warm-up

Describe a famous person that you think Ss will know. Describe the person in detail: their appearance, what they do, what they like/dislike, etc., but don't say who it is. Encourage Ss to ask questions to find out more information. When you have finished, ask Ss to guess who it is.

Reading

1 Introduce the activity by telling the class about social media and why people use it (keep in touch, share photos, etc.). Ss work in pairs and discuss the questions. When they have finished, ask a few Ss to share their experiences with the class.

2 You may want to pre-teach/check: *library* and *beard*. Ss read the post and answer the questions, then check in pairs. Check answers with the class.

> **Answers:** 1 a camera with photos on it 2 on Corona Avenue 3 Share the post, so she can find the owner. 4 Eduardo's brother 5 he's really nice

Grammar

look like, look + adjective, *be like*

3 Ss choose the correct alternatives alone, then check in pairs. Encourage them to use the examples to help. Check answers with the whole class and be prepared to offer further explanations/ examples where necessary.

> **Answers:** 1 noun 2 adjective 3 number 4 appearance 5 character

Optional extra activity

Before Ex 3, write the following sentences on the board:
She looks a doctor.
He looks like happy.
What are they look like?
Ask Ss work in pairs and to correct the sentences, but don't give any answers yet. Ss then work through the Grammar box in Ex 3 and come back to their sentences to check their answers.

GRAMMAR BANK 5B pp.124–125

Stronger classes could read the notes at home. Otherwise, check the notes with Ss. In each exercise, elicit the first answer as an example. Ss work alone to complete the exercises, then check their answers in pairs. In feedback, elicit Ss' answers and drill the questions. Ss can refer to the notes to help them.

Answers: 5B
1 1 looks like 2 look 3 look like 4 looks 5 look 6 like 7 looks 8 like
2 1 What's Brian like?
   2 What does Brian look like?
   3 What does the restaurant look like?
   4 What's the restaurant like?
   5 What does your new dog look like?
   6 What's your new dog like?
   7 What's your new jacket like?
   8 What does your new jacket look like?

4a 5.4 Play the recording for Ss to listen and answer the question. Point out that the sounds link together smoothly and demonstrate this by saying a couple of the sentences to the class.
b Ss listen again and repeat. Drill the sentences chorally and individually for further practice if necessary.
5a Elicit the first answer as an example and write it on the board. Ss match the sentence halves alone, then check in pairs. Check answers with the whole class.

Answers: 1 f 2 c 3 e 4 a 5 b 6 d

Optional alternative activity

Ss could do this as pairwork. Student A reads out the first half of the sentences for student B to finish. They then swap roles and repeat the activity.

b Ss complete the questions and answers alone, then check in pairs. Check answers with the whole class.

Answers: 1 looks 2 look like 3 look 4 's 5 look 6 are/'re 7 like 8 looks

Further practice

Photocopiable activities: 5B Grammar 1, p180; Grammar 2, p181

Vocabulary

Appearance

6a Check understanding of the categories in the list by eliciting an example of a word that could go in each one. Ss work in pairs and add the words to the list. Encourage them to use dictionaries or their mobile devices to help, but also monitor and be prepared to explain any new words. Check answers with the class and elicit whether each word is a verb or noun.

Answers:
clothes: casual, smart
body: slim, tall, tattoo
face: beard, moustache
hair: bald, blonde, curly, dark, long, straight

b Ss think of more words for each category alone. Monitor and help with vocabulary where necessary.

c Ss work in pairs and compare their ideas. When they have finished, ask Ss to come to the board to add their words and check spelling.

Suggested answers:
clothes: stylish, trendy
hair: light brown, red, dark brown
face: blue eyes, brown eyes
body: overweight, muscular, tanned

7a 5.5 Ss listen and tick the words they hear alone, then check in pairs. Check answers with the whole class.

Answers: blonde, long, beard, tall, slim

b Write on the board: *mum, dad, Abby, Lily* and *Bradley* and ask Ss to do the same in their notebooks. Elicit what Ss can remember about each person. Ss listen again and make notes on what each person looks like.

Optional alternative activity

Instead of making notes, Ss could draw the people based on what they hear. Stress that the drawings don't need to be elaborate or even good!

c Ss work in pairs compare their notes, then turn to p82 and guess who the people are. Check answers with the whole class.

Answers:
Mum: is 65, but looks younger, blonde hair, fit and active
Dad: had long, fair hair and a beard, but now has short, grey hair, no beard, quiet, but loves films
Wife Abby: has naturally wavy hair, but makes it straight
Children: Lily is nine and Bradley is seven. Both tall, slim and sporty and have the same hair colour. Lily has long hair and looks like her dad. The boy looks like his other grandad and has a round face and very dark eyes.

Audioscript 5.5

Marcus: Alessia, have I ever shown you a photo of my family?
Alessia: No, I don't think you have.
Marcus: Have a look at this. It's us celebrating my mum's 60th birthday last week.
Alessia: Ah, that's lovely. Is that your mum with blonde hair?
Marcus: Yes, that's her.
Alessia: Wow, she doesn't look 60 at all.
Marcus: I know. She looks younger. She's really fit and active. That's my dad on the left. He's quite smart these days – but when he was young he was in a rock band. In fact, he had long, fair hair and a big beard.
Alessia: What's he like?
Marcus: He's usually quiet … until he starts talking about music and then he doesn't stop.
Alessia: I guess that's your wife next to him.
Marcus: Yeah, that's Abby. She looks really different in this picture because her hair is usually curly!
Alessia: Ha! … Your children are lovely! Your daughter looks older. Is that right?
Marcus: Yes, Lily's nine and Bradley's seven. Bradley looks like his other grandad with his really dark eyes. They're both tall and slim though and they're really good at sports. I don't know where they get that from. Neither me nor Abby are very good at sport.
Alessia: Ah, well it's a lovely photo and you all look really happy.

8a Read the example with the class and demonstrate the activity with a ***stronger Ss***. Ss work in pairs to give descriptions. Monitor and check Ss are using the vocabulary correctly.

b Refer Ss back to the Grammar box in Ex 3 and encourage them to use this language when writing their sentences. Ss work in pairs to write their sentences. Monitor and help with vocabulary, writing any new words/phrases on the board.

c Ss read about each person and check their predictions. In feedback, ask what Ss found surprising.

Ask Ss to find some photos of people they know, e.g. friends, family, on their phones/mobile devices and show them to their partner, who makes guesses about each person.

Further practice

Photocopiable activities: 5B Vocabulary, p182

Speaking

Prepare

9 You could introduce the activity by describing someone who is important to you. Go through the prompts with the class, then ask Ss to make notes. Monitor and help with vocabulary, writing any new words/phrases on the board.

Speak

10 Ss work in pairs and take turns to describe their people and answer questions about them. Monitor and make notes on Ss' language use for later feedback. When they have finished, ask a few Ss to share any interesting information they found out with the class. Go over any common errors or examples of good language use with the class.

> **Reflection on learning**
>
> Write the following questions on the board:
> *How confident do you feel describing what people look like? What could you do to improve?*
> *What were the three most useful words you learnt today? Why?*
>
> Put Ss in pairs to discuss the questions. When they have finished, ask if anyone wants to share their ideas with the class, but don't force them to if they'd rather not.

Homework ideas

Ex 11: Ss write a description of one of the people they described.
Grammar bank: 5B Ex 1–2, pp.124–125
Workbook: Ex 1–5, p29
App: grammar and vocabulary practice

Fast route: continue to Lesson 5C
Extended route: go to p99 for Develop your listening

5c Shopping tips

Introduction

The goal of this lesson is for Ss to share their shopping experiences and give advice. To help them achieve this, they will learn/revise *should* and *shouldn't* and imperatives for giving advice, as well as phrases related to shopping.

Warm-up

Bring some things you've bought recently to class. Take each one in turn, show it to the class and tell the Ss where you bought it, why you bought it there and what other things you usually buy there. Ask Ss to work in pairs and choose three objects they have with them today (or that they've bought recently) and do the same.

Vocabulary

Shopping

1 Focus attention on the photos and elicit what Ss can see. Ss work in small groups and discuss the questions. When they have finished, nominate a student from each group to share their ideas with the class.

2 Ss work in pairs and check they understand the meaning of the phrases in bold in the shopping tips. Ask them to underline any they don't both know. When they have finished, join pairs into groups to check the phrases they don't know and circle any that none of them know (if any). At this point Ss can use dictionaries or their mobile devices to check. Go through the unknown phrases with the class, explaining and exemplifying any that they ask about. Give Ss a few more minutes to discuss in their groups whether they agree with the tips and why. In feedback, elicit Ss' ideas and have a brief class discussion.

Optional alternative activity

With **weaker classes**, go through each of the phrases in bold first as a class. Ss work in pairs and then discuss which tips they agree with.

> **Teaching tip**
>
> Where possible use examples, e.g. a *credit card* or a *receipt*, to show Ss what they look like if you have them with you.

> **Vocabulary checkpoint**
>
> You may also want to teach *ask for a discount* (receive a percentage off the usual price). You may also want to point out the difference between *go shopping* (for pleasure) and *do the shopping* (buy groceries).

3a Ss complete the questions alone, then check in pairs. Check answers with the whole class.

> **Answers:** 1 pay by credit card   2 in a sale
> 3 return something   4 ask for a discount   5 keep the receipt
> 6 read reviews   7 compare prices   8 try them on

b Ss work in pairs and discuss the questions. When they have finished, elicit Ss' answers and have a brief class discussion.

Further practice

Photocopiable activities: 5C Vocabulary, p185

Listening

4a Write *a coffee machine* and *a shirt* at the top of the board. Give Ss a few minutes to brainstorm ideas for potential problems with each item. When they are ready, elicit their ideas and write them on the board under each item.

b 🔊 **5.9** Ss listen and compare the problems with their ideas in Ex 4a then check in pairs. In feedback, elicit the problems and tick off any that are on the board. Answer the questions as a class.

Answers:
Jenny: a coffee machine: bought it quickly then saw it cheaper the next day. Also didn't keep the receipt and couldn't get a refund.
Luke: a shirt: didn't try it on and it didn't fit.

c Ss listen and answer the questions alone, then check in pairs. Check answers with the whole class.

Answers:
1 no
2 It was half the price.
3 He got his good shirt dirty.
4 Because he didn't have much time.
5 It was an unusual shape – very small in the middle and the arms were very long.

Audioscript 5.9

Presenter: It's two o'clock and it's time for 'I can't believe it!' – simple things that make you really angry. This week we're talking about shopping and we want to hear about any problems you've had, and any advice you can give. First, I've got Jenny on the phone. So Jenny, what happened?

Jenny: Well, I'll give you some advice first. You should always compare prices. You shouldn't just buy the first thing you see.

Presenter: That's sounds easy, but we all forget sometimes … Tell us more Jenny …

Jenny: Well, I really like my morning cup of coffee and I've wanted a new coffee machine for a long time. So, finally when I had enough money, I went into town and found one I really liked. It was a bit expensive, but I was excited … so I bought it right there and then.

Presenter: Sounds like a good idea. But?

Jenny: Yesterday, I was in another part of town and saw it in a different shop for half the price!

Presenter: Oh no!

Jenny: Right! It was actually fifty per cent cheaper than what I paid. But that's not the end of the problem. I didn't keep the receipt because I really liked it, so I can't return it and get my money back. So my other piece of advice is 'keep the receipt'!

Presenter: Always good advice, thanks Jenny. So over to Luke – Luke, are you there?

Luke: Yes, hello. Well, I also bought something too quickly. Last month I had a job interview and, on the morning of the interview, I got my only good shirt really dirty. I didn't have much time, so I went quickly to the shopping centre, found a shirt my size and bought it.

Presenter: OK, so what was the problem?

Luke: When I got home I tried it on and it was a really unusual shape. I mean really unusual. It was very small in the middle and the arms were very long. Seriously, I looked really strange! The worse thing is that there wasn't enough time to change it – I had to go to the interview like that!

Presenter: That's not good. Oh no.

Luke: Oh yes! So, my advice is: you should always try clothes on in the shop.

Presenter: OK, thank you. Lots of good advice there. We'll be back next week at …

5 Do the activity as a class, eliciting their reasons.

Answers: 1 L 2 J 3 J

6 Ss work in pairs and discuss the questions. In feedback, ask a few Ss to share their experiences with the class.

Grammar

should/shouldn't and imperatives

7 Ss choose the correct alternatives alone, then check in pairs. Encourage them to use the examples to help. Check answers with the whole class and be prepared to offer further explanations/ examples where necessary. Check the position of *always* and *never* for strong advice by writing on the board: *… try … new clothes on before you buy them* and elicit where *always* goes (at the start of the sentence).

Answers: 1 good 2 bad 3 strong 4 without *to*

GRAMMAR BANK 5C pp.124–125
Stronger classes could read the notes at home. Otherwise, check the notes with Ss. In each exercise, elicit the first answer as an example. Ss work alone to complete the exercises, then check their answers in pairs. In feedback, elicit Ss' answers and drill the questions. Ss can refer to the notes to help them.

Answers: 5C
1 1 ~~seeing~~ **see** 2 correct 3 ~~Calls~~ **Call** 4 ~~to~~ 5 ~~kept~~ **keep** 6 ~~don't should~~ **shouldn't** 7 ~~you~~ 8 correct
2 1 should 2 Never/Don't 3 shouldn't 4 should 5 should 6 Never/Don't 7 Always 8 shouldn't

8a 🔊 **5.10** Ss listen for which words are stressed then check in pairs. Check answers with the whole class.

Answer: *Should* is unstressed, *Shouldn't* is stressed.

Pronunciation checkpoint
Negative forms are usually stressed in English. This is true both for modals, e.g. *shouldn't, couldn't, won't*, etc. and other auxiliaries, e.g. *don't, isn't*, etc.

b Ss listen and repeat the phrases. Check they're stressing *shouldn't* as in the recording. Drill chorally and individually for further practice if necessary.

9a Elicit the first answer as an example by writing the prompts on the board and asking Ss to reorder them. Ss reorder the words alone, then check in pairs. Check answers with the whole class.

Answers:
1 Never buy an old car.
2 Don't buy clothes online.
3 You should always try something before you buy it.
4 Always ask for a discount in the supermarket.
5 You shouldn't pay for expensive things in cash.
6 You should buy fresh food from a market.

b Ss work in pairs and discuss which advice they agree with, giving their reasons. In feedback, elicit Ss' answers and have a brief class discussion.

10a Elicit a piece of advice for one of the topics as an example. While Ss are writing their advice, monitor and help with ideas and vocabulary, writing any new words/phrases on the board.

b Arrange Ss in groups to share their tips and guess what each tip is for. Monitor and check Ss are using the grammar correctly, writing down any common errors/examples of good language use for later class feedback. When Ss have finished, nominate a student from each group to share their advice with the class and find out if others agree.

Further practice

Photocopiable activities: 5C Grammar 1, p183; 5C Grammar 2, p184

Speaking

Prepare

11 Go through the questions with the class. Give Ss plenty of time to prepare by answering the questions and making notes without writing full sentences. Monitor, and help, with ideas and vocabulary where necessary.

Speak

12 Ss work in small groups and share their experiences and advice, then agree on the two best pieces of advice. Monitor and make notes on Ss' language use for later feedback.

Optional alternative activity

Arrange Ss in groups of three and ask them to choose one 'presenter'. The other two share their experiences as a TV programme, similar to the listening in Ex 4, while the 'presenter' asks follow-up questions to find out more information. If there's time, each group could present their programme to the class.

Reflection on learning

Write the following questions on the board:
How confident do you feel giving advice in English?
How will you use the language from this lesson in the future?
Put Ss in pairs to discuss the questions. When they have finished, ask if anyone wants to share their ideas with the class, but don't force them to if they'd rather not.

Homework ideas

Grammar bank: 5C Ex 1–2, pp.124–125
Workbook: Ex 1–5, p30
App: grammar and vocabulary practice

Fast route: continue to Lesson 5D
Extended route: go to p100 for Develop your writing

 **5D** English in action

Introduction

The goal of this lesson is for Ss to practice making, and responding to, suggestions in the context of buying a gift for someone. To help them achieve this, they will learn a range of phrases for making and responding to suggestions.

Warm-up

Before class, write on the board: *an 80-year-old woman, a colleague, your boss, a three-year-old girl, a teenager.* Ss work in pairs and discuss appropriate gifts for each of these people. When they have finished, ask Ss to share their ideas with the class and find out if anyone has the same ideas.

Listening

1 Focus attention on the photos and elicit what Ss can see. Ss work in pairs and discuss the questions. When they have finished, ask a few Ss to share any interesting information they found out from their partners.

2a 🔊 **5.11** Ss listen and answer the questions alone, then check in pairs. Check answers with the whole class and write them on the board, so Ss can check spelling.

> **Answers:**
> **Simon:** a thank-you gift for his aunt
> **Tina:** a birthday present for her dad

b Elicit the first answer as an example. Ss match the sentences alone, then check in pairs. Don't give any answers yet.

Teaching tip

After instructions have been given for a new activity, it's a good idea to check Ss have understood what they need to do. The most effective way of doing this is by eliciting the first answer as an example. For longer, more complicated activities, we can demonstrate with a **stronger Ss**. We can also ask questions to check specific details, e.g. *Are you working alone or in pairs? Are you speaking or writing?* It's important not to overdo these types of questions and only use them to check minor details, otherwise they can sound patronising or be too difficult to answer, e.g. *Are you doing this exercise or nothing? What do you have to do?* After Ss have started the activity, it's also a good idea to walk round and monitor to quickly check everyone knows what they're doing.

c Ss listen to the recording again and check their answers. Check answers with the whole class.

> **Answers:** 1 d 2 b 3 a 4 e 5 f 6 c

Audioscript 5.11

Simon: I'd like to buy something for my aunt, but I don't really know what to get her. Do you have any ideas?

Tina: Is it her birthday?

Simon: No, it's a thank you gift. I stay with her a lot when I'm working in Manchester. She always cooks for me and washes my clothes, but she won't take any money for food or rent.

Tina: That's nice of her. Yes, you should buy her something. How about some flowers?

Simon: I think I'd prefer to get her something a bit more special; something that'll last longer.

Tina: Then what about some jewellery? Like a necklace or something.

Simon: Yeah, that's a good idea. Can you help me pick something? I don't know much about jewellery.

Tina: Sure, no problem. Actually, maybe you can help me. It's my dad's birthday soon and I never know what to get him. He's so difficult to buy for.

Simon: He likes gardening, doesn't he?

Tina: Yeah, he loves it.

Simon: Well, you could get him some gardening books.

Tina: Hmm, maybe, but I think he's got quite a lot of those already.

Simon: OK, well you could give him a gift card for the gardening shop. Then he can buy what he wants.

Tina: Unfortunately, I gave him one of those for his birthday last year! I need to think of something different.

Simon: OK ... well ... why don't you get him a nice sun hat? Has he got one?

Tina: No, I don't think he has – nice idea!

Simon: OK, well why don't we go shopping together at the weekend? I'll help you find a hat and you can help me with the jewellery.

Tina: Sounds great. Let's try the department store on West Street first. They might have what we both need.

3a 🔊 **5.12** Ss listen and then discuss which word has the most stress in pairs. Check the answer with the whole class.

Answers: 1 cake 2 book 3 game 4 trainers 5 chocolates (the last word in each phrase is the most stressed)

b Ss listen again and repeat. If necessary, drill chorally and individually for further practice.

4a Go through the Useful phrases, drilling them with the class and checking understanding if necessary. Read the example to the class to check understanding. Ss use the box to complete the conversations on their own, using their own ideas. Monitor and check they're completing them appropriately.

Suggested answers: 2 go to the park 3 get a bus 4 pizza 5 make him something

b Ss work in pairs. Monitor and check they're using the phrases correctly. When they have finished, ask different Ss to perform their conversations in open pairs.

Optional alternative activity

Instead of doing this in pairs, Ss walk round the class eliciting advice from a different student for each sentence. In feedback, ask them to share the best advice they received with the class.

5 Read the example with the class. Ss work in groups and take turns to talk about a person they'd like to buy a gift for. When they have finished, choose a student from each group to share their best suggestions with the class.

Speaking

Prepare

6 You may want to elicit/check: *retiree*. Put Ss in pairs and ask them to choose who is A and B. Direct them to p154 to read their instructions. Give Ss a few minutes to read their information and check anything they're not sure about.

Speak

7 Ss practise the conversations in pairs. Monitor and check they're using the Useful phrases correctly. When they have finished, choose a pair to perform their conversation for the class.

Optional alternative activity

If you think extra practice would be useful, rearrange the Ss and ask them to practise the conversation again, swapping roles.

Reflection on learning

Write the following questions on the board:
How many of the phrases from today's lesson did you use?
Which phrases are most useful for you to remember, do you think?
Put Ss in pairs to discuss the questions. When they have finished, ask if anyone wants to share their ideas with the class, but don't force them to if they'd rather not.

Homework ideas

Reflection on learning: Write your answers.
Workbook: Ex 1–5, p31
App: grammar and vocabulary practice

5 Check and reflect

Introduction

Ss revise and practise the language of Unit 5. The notes below provide some ideas for exploiting the activities in class, but you may want to set the first exercise in each section for homework, or use them as a diagnostic or progress test. For each grammar or vocabulary point, the first activity reviews the language and the second is more communicative, involving pairwork.

1a Elicit the first answer as an example. Ss choose the correct alternatives alone, then compare answers in pairs. When they have finished, check answers with the whole class.

Answers: 1 who 2 that 3 which 4 who 5 which

b Give Ss plenty of time to write their definitions. Monitor and help with vocabulary where necessary, writing any new words/phrases on the board. Check that Ss are forming relative clauses correctly.

c Read the example with the class. Arrange Ss in groups to read out their definitions for others to guess. When they have finished, nominate a student from each group to share a definition with the class for them to guess.

2a Ss match the sentence halves alone, then check in pairs. Check answers with the whole class.

Answers: 1 a 2 c 3 d 4 b 5 e

b Ss works in pairs and think of jobs for each sentence in Ex 2a. Remind Ss of Vocabulary bank 5a to help them think of jobs. When they have finished, elicit Ss' ideas and ask how many thought of the same jobs for each sentence.

3a Ss choose the correct alternatives alone then check in pairs. Check answers with the whole class.

Answers: 1 look like 2 like 3 do 4 were 5 look like

b Ss complete the exercise alone, then check in pairs. Check answers with the whole class.

Answers: 1 c 2 b 3 e 4 a 5 d

c Ss work in pairs and discuss the questions. In feedback, ask a few Ss to share anything interesting they found out about their partners.

4 Ss complete the description alone, then check in pairs. Check answers with the whole class.

Answers: 1 tall 2 blonde 3 curly 4 moustache 5 slim

5a Ss complete the sentences alone, then check in pairs. Check answers with the whole class and ask Ss if they agree with the advice.

Answers: 1 should 2 Tell, Don't 3 shouldn't, should 4 should, make

b Ss work in pairs and think of any additional advice to give Sheila. In feedback, find out which advice is most popular for the whole class.

6a Ss choose the correct alternatives alone, then check in pairs. Check answers with the whole class.

Answers: 1 prices 2 by 3 receipt 4 try 5 discounts 6 return 7 sale

b Ss work in pairs and discuss the sentences, saying which are true for them. When they have finished, elicit their answers and have a brief class discussion.

7a Ss complete the exercise alone, then check in pairs. Check answers with the whole class.

Answers: 1 discount 2 good communication skills 3 bald 4 work part-time 5 casual

b Ss work in pairs. Check their answers with the whole class.

Reflect

Ask Ss to rate each statement alone, then compare in pairs. Encourage them to ask any questions they still have about any of the areas covered in Unit 5.

5A Develop your reading

Introduction

Ss develop their reading skill of understanding an article by learning how to identify positive and negative sides to an argument.

Warm-up

Write on the board:
My ideal job is … It involves …

Ss complete the sentences alone. Monitor and help with vocabulary, writing any new words/phrases on the board. When they are ready, put Ss in small groups to share their ideas and then choose the most interesting one. In feedback, ask each group to share their most interesting ideal job with the class.

1a Ss work in pairs and discuss the questions. In feedback, elicit a few Ss' answers and have a brief class discussion. If your Ss work, ask them if they think technology makes their working lives easier or more difficult, and why.

b Ss read the article and compare their ideas from Ex 1a with those in the article. In feedback, elicit which things mentioned in the article are the same as their ideas in Ex 1a.

2 Go through the headings with the whole class. Ss match them to the paragraphs in the article alone, then check in pairs. Check answers with the whole class.

Answers: 1 In control of our time 2 Too much time at home? 3 Communication problems 4 Faster but busier

3 Give Ss a few minutes to read the Focus box or read it together with the class. Ss underline the phrases in the article alone, then check in pairs. Check answers with the whole class.

Answers: + This has one main advantage − However

4a Write the first item on the board and elicit what the writer says about it. Ss read the article again and make notes alone, then compare in pairs. Check answers with the whole class.

Answers:
1 You can choose the hours you want to work. (+) You're always at work.
2 People spend less time travelling. (+) You don't see your colleagues − positive if you prefer to work in a quiet place, but negative if you don't like spending time alone. Companies save money by having smaller offices. (+)
3 People work in international teams and meet online … people in the company … can work together easily and cheaply. (+) It can be difficult when people speak quietly or at the same time, or if the internet connection is bad. (−)
4 We can work more quickly because we can share information really fast (+) but our inbox is full of messages all the time. (−) We spend most of our working life reading and responding to these messages. (−)

b Give Ss a minute or two to think about their answers and make notes. Monitor and help with vocabulary where necessary, writing any new words/phrases on the board. Ss work in pairs and discuss the questions. In feedback, ask a few Ss to share their ideas with the class and have a brief class discussion.

Homework ideas

Workbook: Ex 1−3, p32

5B Develop your listening

Introduction

Ss develop their listening skill of following a short conversation by learning how to understand spoken linkers.

Warm-up

Tell Ss what your favourite colour is and why. Ask Ss to say what colours they like and dislike and why, and have a brief class discussion.

1 Focus attention on the photos and elicit what Ss can see. Ss work in pairs and discuss the questions. In feedback, elicit answers from a few Ss and find out if other Ss agree.

2a 🔊 **5.6** Ss listen and identify the colours in Ex 1 alone, then check in pairs. Check answers with the whole class.

> **Answers:** **Speaker 1:** green and blue **Speaker 2:** blue
> **Speaker 3:** green

b *Stronger classes* can do the activity from memory, then listen and check. Otherwise, Ss listen again and complete the sentences, then check in pairs. Check answers with the whole class.

> **Answers:** 1 green 2 blue 3 blue 4 green

Audioscript 5.6

Speaker 1: In the US, green often means jealousy. If we think someone is jealous – that is, they want something another person has got, then we say they have the 'green-eyed monster'. Blue has a couple of meanings. It can mean security and peace. That is why banks often use blue in their logos. On the other hand, we can use it to describe someone who's sad, when we say they have 'the blues'.

Speaker 2: India is mostly Hindu and some colours have special meanings in Hinduism. Blue is associated with the god Krishna and it shows strength and being brave. It also shows how everything is connected, because it's the colour of the seas and rivers.

Speaker 3: I love surfing and here in Indonesia we have some great places to surf, especially in the south, like here in Yogyakarta. You should come and visit! Anyway, don't wear green if you go surfing here, because of Nayai Roro Kidul, the Goddess of the Southern Seas. She loves the colour green and she'll pull you under the waves.

3 Give Ss a few minutes to read the Focus box or read it together as a class. Ss work in pairs and think of more linkers in pairs. In feedback, elicit any other linkers they know, but don't give any answers at this stage.

> **Suggested answers:**
> **additional information:** also, as well
> **contrast:** However, despite
> **change of topic:** That reminds me of something else

4 Ss label the linkers alone, then check in pairs. Check answers with the whole class and ask if they mentioned any of these in Ex 3a.

> **Answers:** 1 A 2 T 3 C 4 A

5 🔊 **5.7** Ss listen and complete the sentences alone, then check in pairs. Check answers with the whole class.

> **Answers:** 1 On the other hand 2 and 3 also 4 Anyway

6 Ss complete the sentences alone, then check in pairs. Check answers with the whole class.

> **Answers:** 1 too 2 but 3 though

7a 🔊 **5.8** Ss listen and identify the colours alone. Check answers with the whole class.

> **Answers:** **Speaker 1:** red, yellow **Speaker 2:** orange

b *Stronger Ss* could complete the extracts first, then listen and check. Otherwise, Ss listen again and complete the extracts. Encourage Ss to look at the linkers used first to help them decide what type of information to listen for. Check answers with the class.

> **Answers:** 1 luck 2 give 3 Yellow 4 money 5 danger

Audioscript 5.8

Speaker 1: In China, the colour red means good luck and happiness. This is why you see many red decorations at New Year. We also give money in red envelopes to couples when they get married. Yellow is an important colour, too. It's the most beautiful colour and it's the centre of everything – just like the sun.

Speaker 2: In many Western cultures, orange means something interesting. It can mean fun and creativity, and it's my favourite colour! Anyway, in the Netherlands, it means rich and strong, and it's the national colour. It also means strong and brave in Ukraine. But in the Middle East it can mean danger and loss.

8 Ss work in pairs and discuss the questions. In feedback, elicit Ss' ideas and have a brief class discussion.

Homework ideas

Workbook: Ex 1–3, p31

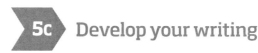

5c Develop your writing

Introduction

Ss develop their writing skill of writing a guide by learning how to link ideas.

Warm-up

Bring/Download photos of different shopping centres around the world (e.g. *GUM* in Moscow, *Galleria Vittorio Emanuele II* in Milan, *Mall of America*). Write on the board:
Where do you think this is?
What do you think you can buy there?
Would you like to go shopping there?
Why (not)?
Ss work in pairs and discuss the questions about each photo. In feedback, elicit answers and have a brief class discussion.

1 Focus attention on the photo and elicit where this is (Tokyo). Ss read the guide and choose the place they'd most like to visit and why. Put Ss in pairs to compare their choices. In feedback, elicit how many people would like to visit each place by show of hands.

2 Give Ss a few minutes to read through the Focus box and examples alone, or read the box as a class. Ss then underline the linkers in the guide alone, then check in pairs. Check answers with the whole class.

> **Answers:**
> **Fashion:** because, but, and
> **Electronics:** so, also
> **Gifts and souvenirs:** or, also, and
> **Shopping and entertainment:** and, That's why, and, too
> **Food:** However, because, and

3 Ss complete the sentences alone, then check in pairs. Check answers with the whole class.

> **Answers:** 1 but   2 or   3 so   4 too   5 That's why
> 6 However

Prepare

4a Ss work in pairs and decide their headings and what to include, using the questions to help.

b Ss plan their guide using the guide in Ex 1 to help them.

Write

5 Ss write their guides. Monitor and correct Ss' work as they go along, and be on hand to help where necessary. Encourage Ss to use the Useful phrases and linkers in the Focus box.

Homework ideas

Workbook: Ex 1–6, p33

6 OVERVIEW

6A Happiness

Introduction

The goal of this lesson is for Ss to make predictions about the future. To help them achieve this, they will learn/revise *will* for predictions and phrases related to happiness.

Warm-up

Write on the board:
Happiness is …
and demonstrate the activity by giving some answers, e.g. *Happiness is spending time with my best friend. Happiness is a beautiful sunset.* Give Ss a few minutes to write their answer. Monitor and help with vocabulary where necessary, writing any new words on the board. When they are ready, Ss walk around the class sharing their ideas with other Ss. When they have finished, elicit Ss' ideas and write them on the board.

Vocabulary and listening

Happiness

1 Focus attention on the photos and elicit what Ss can see. Ss work in pairs, and match the quotes and photos. Encourage them to use dictionaries or mobile devices to check meanings of new words. Check answers with the whole class and be prepared to give further explanations/examples for the phrases in bold if necessary. If you did the warm up, go through the ideas on the board and tick off any which are mentioned in the quotes.

Answers: 1 C   2 G   3 A   4 E   5 F   6 B   7 D

Optional alternative activity

With **weaker classes**, go through the phrases in bold with the whole class first, giving explanations and examples.

Pronunciation checkpoint

Check the pronunciation and stress of *social* /ˈsəʊʃəl/, *humour* /ˈhjuːmə/ and *career* /kəˈrɪə/. Point out that *career* often sounds the same as *Korea*.

2 Elicit the first answer as an example. Explain that Ss are only matching the phrases in bold in Ex 1, not the whole quotes. Ss match the sentences and phrases alone, then check in pairs. Check answers with the whole class.

Answers: 1 a busy social life   2 keep fit
3 earns lots of money   4 a simple life   5 have a lot of interests
6 a sense of humour   7 a good career   8 free time   9 eat well
10 a happy family life

3 Arrange Ss in pairs to discuss the statements in Ex 1. Monitor and help with vocabulary, writing any new words/phrases on the board. When they have finished, nominate a student from each group to share their ideas with the class.

4a 6.1 Ss listen and answer the question for each speaker alone, then check in pairs. Tell Ss they'll have a chance to listen again for more detail, so not to worry if they don't understand every word. Check answers with the whole class.

Answers: **Speaker 1:** yes   **Speaker 2:** no   **Speaker 3:** no
Speaker 4: yes   **Speaker 5:** yes

b Go through the predictions with the class and ask if Ss can remember who said each one. Ss listen again and put the predictions in the order they hear them. Check answers with the whole class.

Answers: 1 4   2 3   3 2   4 1

Audioscript 6.1

Speaker 1: These days, in general, people are much healthier. We know a lot more about the importance of eating well and we try to keep fit, and this makes us happier. In the future, I think we'll be more careful about what we eat. I already go running three times a week – the next thing I should do is eat less chocolate!

Speaker 2: Oh less happy, definitely. People are waiting longer to have children and start a family, usually because their careers come first. I think this will continue in the future and for many people it'll be too late. And I think a happy family life is really important, especially later in life.

Speaker 3: For me, the most important thing to be happy is to have a good career, a job which you really enjoy doing. But I think in the future this won't be easy, because our jobs will be more difficult. People will work harder and I don't think we'll have as much free time, so in general we'll be much less happy than we are now.

Speaker 4: Will we be happier? Definitely. It'll be easier to earn lots of money and that's what's important. More people will have enough money to buy big houses, go on lots of holidays and buy all the nice things that they want.

Speaker 5: Yes, I think so. Look at social media, for example. It's simple to meet people now and it'll be even easier in the future. Having a busy social life makes us happy, and it won't be hard to make friends in the future.

c Ss work in pairs and discuss which predictions they agree/disagree with. When they have finished, elicit a few answers and have a brief class discussion.

Further practice

Photocopiable activities: 6A Vocabulary, p188

Grammar

will for predictions

5 Give Ss time to read the Grammar box and ask any questions they want to. Then, ask Ss to match the statements a–d in the Grammar box with the predictions 1–4 in Ex 4b, then check in pairs. Check answers with the whole class. You could check understanding here by asking *Do we usually make predictions about the past, present or future?* (future) *Do we use will for predictions or plans?* (predictions).

Answers: 1 b   2 a   3 d   4 c

Grammar checkpoint

The use of *I (don't) think + will* for predictions is much more common in spoken English, so it's useful to practise this with Ss at this level.

GRAMMAR BANK 6A   pp.126–127

Stronger classes could read the notes at home. Otherwise, check the notes with Ss. In each exercise, elicit the first answer as an example. Ss work alone to complete the exercises, then check their answers in pairs. In feedback, elicit Ss' answers and drill the questions. Ss can refer to the notes to help them.

Answers: 6A
1 1 I'l   2 be   3 won't   4 we'll   5 probably find   6 think
2 1 ~~using~~ use   2 ~~not will~~ won't   3 ~~won't~~ will
   4 Brazil **will** win   5 ~~to~~   6 ~~I'm~~
   7 She'll **definitely get** the job   8 **Will they** arrive on time?

6a 🔊 **6.2** Ss listen and choose the alternatives they hear, then check in pairs. Check answers with the whole class. Elicit what the difference is (the use of contractions).

Answers: 1 people will   2 won't   3 we'll   4 It'll   5 we'll

b Ss listen again and repeat. Drill chorally and individually for further practice if necessary.

c Read the example with the class. Ss write the predictions alone, then check in pairs. Check answers with the whole class.

Answers:
1 Most people won't have lots of money.
2 Technology will make us happier.
3 I think we'll travel more.
4 I think we won't have (as) much free time.
5 People will have more fun.
6 People won't eat unhealthy food.
7 I don't think people will have simple lives.
8 I think we'll work harder.

Optional extra activity

Fast finishers can write two or three more predictions for the future. You could suggest some topics such as families, animals and exercise.

d Ss work in pairs and discuss the predictions and say why they agree or disagree with them. Monitor and check Ss are using the grammar correctly. In feedback, elicit Ss' answers and have a brief class discussion.

Further practice

Photocopiable activities: 6A Grammar 1, p186; 6A Grammar 2, p187

Speaking

Prepare

7 Refer Ss back to the vocabulary in Ex 1 and the Useful phrases to help with ideas. Give Ss plenty of time to make their predictions, working alone. Monitor and help with vocabulary, writing any new words/phrases on the board. If necessary, help with ideas by asking questions, e.g. *Do you think we'll be healthier or less healthy? Why? Do you think we'll have more or less free time? What will we do in our free time? Do you think families will get bigger or smaller? Why?*

Speak

8a Arrange Ss in groups to share their predictions. Encourage Ss to say if they agree or disagree and why. Monitor and make notes on Ss' language use for later feedback.

Teaching tip

For speaking activities like this, it can be useful to play some soft background music in class while Ss are working. This provides for a natural setting, as most of the places where we speak freely in real life have a fair bit of background noise. It can help to start the activity, as Ss feel less awkward about being the first to speak/make a noise. It can also help to end the activity, as stopping the music indicates that the activity has finished.

b In their groups, give Ss a few minutes to choose which three predictions are the most important, i.e. those which will have the biggest impact on our happiness in the future.

c As a group, Ss the question 'Will we be happier in the future?' When they have finished, give Ss feedback on their language use as a class using the notes you made.

Reflection on learning

Write the following questions on the board:
Which phrases from today's lesson do you remember?
How will you use them in the future?

Put Ss in pairs to discuss the questions. When they have finished, ask if anyone wants to share their ideas with the class, but don't force them to if they'd rather not.

Homework ideas

Ex 9: Write about their predictions, giving reasons for each one.
Grammar bank: 6A Ex 1–2, pp.126–127
Workbook: Ex 1–5, p34
App: grammar and vocabulary practice

Fast route: continue to Lesson 6B
Extended route: go to p101 for Develop your listening

6B A busy week

Introduction

The goal of this lesson is for Ss to make arrangements with their classmates. To help them achieve this, they will learn/revise the present continuous for future arrangements and collocations with *make, do* and *have*.

Warm-up

Write on the board:
A typical week.
Describe your typical week to the class. Give as much detail as possible, describing what you do each day and what you're doing this week. Ss then work in pairs and describe their typical weeks. When they have finished, ask a few Ss to tell the class if their partner has a busy week or not.

Reading and vocabulary

make, do, have

1a Focus attention on the photos and elicit what Ss can see. Ss work in small groups and discuss the questions. In feedback, nominate a student from each group to share their ideas with the class and have a brief class discussion.

b You may want to pre-teach/check: *stressed, nieces, got upset, I feel your pain!* and *fresh air.* Ss read the forum post and answer the questions alone, then check in pairs. Check answers with the whole class and ask if the same is true for them.

Answers:
1 He/she has a really busy week and wants some advice on how to manage this better.
2 Looking after children and meetings at lunchtime.
3 Students' own answers

2a Elicit the first answer as an example. Ss complete the exercise alone, then check in pairs. Check answers with the whole class and explain that *day off* is a noun phrase (a phrase which acts like a noun).

Answers:

do	(some) cooking (some) exercise (some) housework (some) shopping (some) work
make	an appointment (with someone) a cake an excuse a meal
have	a barbecue/picnic a day off a haircut lunch a meeting

Vocabulary checkpoint

It's also possible to say *have an appointment, have a cake, have an excuse* and *have some work.* We can also say *do the shopping/cooking* to refer to specific shopping/cooking, e.g. food or a meal that has already been discussed. *Do some shopping* and *do some cooking* are more general.

b Ss complete the questions alone, then check in pairs. Check answers with the whole class, drilling each question chorally and individually.

Answers: 1 have 2 make 3 make 4 do 5 have 6 do 7 have 8 do

c Read the example with the class and encourage Ss to ask follow-up questions to find out more information, e.g. *What do you usually eat?* Ss work in pairs and discuss the questions. Monitor and check Ss are using the collocations correctly. When they have finished, ask a few Ss to share anything interesting they found out about their partners.

3 Read out situation 1 and elicit Ss' answers. Ss work in pairs and discuss the other situations. In feedback, elicit Ss' answers and find out if the class agrees.

Answers: 1 make an excuse 2 have a meeting 3 have a day off 4 do housework 5 do (some) exercise 6 make an appointment 7 have a haircut 8 have a barbecue/picnic

Further practice

Photocopiable activities: 6B Vocabulary, p191

Grammar

Present continuous for future arrangements

4a Books closed. Write the example from the grammar box on the board and ask *Does this refer to the past, present or future?* (future) *Is this a prediction or an arrangement?* (an arrangement). Ss choose the correct alternatives alone, then check in pairs. Check answers with the whole class and be prepared to give further explanations/examples where necessary.

Answers: 1 arrangements 2 know

Grammar checkpoint

The present continuous and *be going to* are oftenused interchangeably to talk about future plans andarrangements, but we tend not to use the present continuous when talking about plans which do not involve other people.

You can demonstrate this by writing two sentences on the board:

I'm going to see my mother more this year.
I'm meeting my mother on Tuesday for lunch.

Explain that in the first sentence, it's a plan the speaker has decided on (his mother might not know about it yet though). In the second, the plan involves someone else (i.e. my mother knows about it).

b Ss find the examples alone, then check in pairs. Check answers with the whole class.

Answers: I'm making a birthday meal for a friend.; I'm looking after my two nieces.; I'm having dinner with my parents on Wednesday evening.; (my)boss is having a leaving party.

GRAMMAR BANK 6B pp.126–127

Stronger classes should read the notes at home. Otherwise, check the notes with Ss. In each exercise, elicit the first answer as an example. Ss work alone to complete the exercises, then check their answers in pairs. In feedback, elicit Ss' answers and drill the questions. Ss can refer to the notes to help them.

Answers: 6B
1 1 We're having a picnic on Saturday.
   2 Kim's going to a concert tonight.
   3 We're playing a match tomorrow.
   4 Tomasz and I are having dinner later.
   5 He's making lunch for everyone today.
   6 I'm having a day off next week.
   7 Johnny isn't moving to France next year.
   8 My mum and dad are coming for lunch on Sunday.
   9 He's arriving at about six.
   10 They aren't watching the game on Saturday.
2 1 're having 2 'm not meeting 3 's moving 4 are getting
   5 is leaving 6 are going to book 7 is taking
   8 isn't coming

5a 🔊 **6.7** The aim of this activity is to help Ss recognise subject and auxiliary words when they're contracted and unstressed. Ss listen and choose the correct alternative alone, then check in pairs. Check answers with the whole class and elicit whether the main verb is stressed or unstressed.

Answers: 1 're 2 's 3 'm 4 's

b Ss listen again and repeat. Drill chorally and individually for further practice if necessary.

6a With ***weaker classes***, elicit the first answer as an example. Ss complete the sentences alone, then check in pairs. Check answers with the whole class.

Answers: 1 are you doing 2 She's/She is starting
3 my dad's/my dad is going 4 He's/He is doing
5 we're/we are going
6 I'm/I am making, I'm/I am not cooking

b Read the example with the class and tell Ss about some of your own arrangements. Invite them to ask one or two follow-up questions. Ss work in pairs and discuss their arrangements with their partner. Monitor and check Ss are using the present continuous correctly and encourage them to ask follow-up questions to find out more information.

Further practice

Photocopiable activities: 6B Grammar 1, p189; 6B Grammar 2, p190

Speaking

Prepare

7a 🔊 **6.8** The purpose of this activity is to provide Ss with an example of the final speaking task. Ss listen for the time, then check in pairs. Check answers with the whole class.

Answer: 12 p.m.

b Ss listen and order the suggestions, then check in pairs. Check answers with the whole class.

Answers: 4, 2, 1, 3, 5

Audioscript 6.8

Jade: Hey Sam, I'd really like to ask you about that project we have to finish this weekend. Shall we go for a coffee tomorrow?
Sam: Good idea. I'm meeting Professor White at eleven. Can we meet before that?
Jade: Sorry, I can't. I've got a class at ten. How about after your meeting?
Sam: Sure … I can do twelve o'clock?
Jade: Hmm, I'm having lunch with my mum at twelve. Could we do two?
Sam: No, I'm in class all afternoon. What about this evening? I'm free then.
Jade: I don't think I can. Vicky's coming round to my house. I'm making her a meal.
Sam: Maybe Wednesday then?
Jade: I'm busy Wednesday, too. Mmm … OK, let's meet tomorrow at twelve.
Sam: But what about lunch with your mum?
Jade: I'll cancel it. I'm seeing her on Thursday anyway so she won't mind and we need to talk about that project.
Sam: OK, if you're sure.
Jade: Yeah, it's fine, honestly.
Sam: OK, great. Well, I'll see you tomorrow then!

8 Tell Ss to turn to p155, look at the calendar and read the instructions. Focus Ss' attention on the calendar and explain that they can put their eight activities anywhere they want. Monitor and help where necessary.

Speak

9a Elicit some accepting and rejecting phrases, and write them on the board for Ss to refer to, e.g. *Sounds good/great/fun!*; *I'd love to!*; *Sorry, I can't. I'm …*; Demonstrate the activity with a ***stronger Ss***, using thumbs up or down to indicate how they should respond. Ss work in pairs and make an arrangement with their partners.

Optional extra activity

Fast finishers can make two or three arrangements with their partner. Don't let them make any more than this, as they'll need to have enough space left in their diaries for Ex 9b.

b Ss walk round the class making arrangements with other Ss. Monitor and make notes on their language use for later feedback.

c Find out who had the busiest week by asking Ss how many arrangements they made. Use your notes in Ex 9b to give Ss feedback on their language use as a class.

Reflection on learning

Write the following questions on the board:
What's one thing that you've improved in this lesson?
How will you continue to improve it in the future?

Put Ss in pairs to discuss the questions. When they have finished, ask if anyone wants to share their ideas with the class, but don't force them to if they'd rather not.

Homework ideas

Grammar bank: 6A Ex 1–2, pp.126–127
Workbook: Ex 1–5, p35
App: grammar and vocabulary practice

Fast route: continue to Lesson 6C
Extended route: go to p102 for Develop your reading

6c A quiet weekend

Introduction

The goal of this lesson is for Ss to describe their plans and possibilities for next weekend. To help them achieve this, they will learn/revise *may/might* for future possibility, revise the present continuous for future arrangements and *be going to* for future plans, and learn collocations with *do, go* and *play*.

Warm-up

Write four activities that you did last weekend on the board, including one false one. Encourage Ss to ask you questions to find out more information, then guess which one is false. Ss then write four things they did, with one being false. Ss work in pairs to ask questions, then guess which one is false.

Vocabulary and reading

Weekend activities

1 Ss work in pairs and look at the photos and discuss the questions. When they have finished, nominate a few Ss to share any interesting information they found out about their partners with the class.

2 Books closed. Ask Ss to guess what people's top five weekend activities are and write them on the board. Focus attention on the photos, then ask Ss to read the introduction quickly and check their ideas. Ss read the rest of the article, then work in pairs and answer the questions. When they have finished, nominate a few Ss to share with the class any of the activities they have in common with the article.

3a Ss match the nouns in the box with *do, go* or *play*.

b Ss check answers in the article, then with the whole class.

Answers: activities – do; clubbing/dancing – go; cycling – go; gardening – do; golf/tennis/volleyball – play; homework – do; nothing – do; out – go; running/swimming – go; shopping – do; the guitar/in a band – play; video games – play; yoga – do

Vocabulary checkpoint

We usually use *go* with *-ing* forms, e.g. *go swimming*, *play* with ball games, e.g. *play tennis*, and *do* with other activities. However, if we add a quantifier, the verb usually changes to *do*, e.g. *go running*, but *do a lot of running*.

VOCABULARY BANK 6C p141
Weekend activities

It's a good idea to do this with the class before Ex 2, as this will help Ss with vocabulary for speaking about activities, as well as the rest of the lesson.

1 Ss match the activities with *go, play* or *do*. Check answers with the class, giving further explanations/examples where necessary.

Answers: 1 go 2 go 3 play 4 play 5 go 6 do 7 go 8 play 9 go 10 go

2 Ss complete the sentences by choosing the correct alternative. Check answers with the class, giving further explanations/examples where necessary.

Answers: 1 goes 2 went 3 going 4 gone 5 do 6 plays 7 play 8 do

3 Ss complete the sentences. Check answers with the class, giving further explanations/examples where necessary.

Answers: 1 played 2 goes 3 do 4 play 5 going 6 going 7 gone 8 played 9 do 10 go

4 Ss work in pairs and discuss the questions. In feedback, nominate a few Ss to share any interesting information they found out about their partner with the class.

Optional extra activity

Ask **fast finishers** to think of more activities that go with each verb. In feedback, write these on the board.

4 Ss works in pairs and discuss the questions. In feedback, elicit some answers and have a brief class discussion.

Further practice

Photocopiable activities: 6C Vocabulary, p194

Listening

may and *might*

5a 🔊 6.9 Ss listen and answer the questions, then check in pairs. Check answers with the whole class.

Answers:
1 do yoga, play tennis, go shopping, go out, gardening
2 fourteen
3 Ruth

b **Stronger classes** can complete the sentences from memory, then listen again and check. Otherwise, play the recording for Ss to complete the sentences, then check in pairs. Check answers with the whole class. Ask Ss what type of people they think Ruth and Isabel are.

Answers: 1 play 2 do 3 try 4 go 5 sit 6 not

Audioscript 6.9

Ruth: Finally, it's Friday. Are you doing anything this weekend, Isabel?
Isabel: Oh, not much, just a quiet one. I'm doing some yoga with a friend tomorrow morning. Olly and I may play a game of tennis after lunch. Then later on we're going to a friend's house for dinner.
Ruth: That sounds fun.
Isabel: We may not do much on Sunday … But we are cooking lunch for fourteen people. We might make a Turkish dish we like but we haven't decided yet.
Ruth: Wow! Good luck!
Isabel: Yes, so we're going shopping for the food in the morning. That evening, we may go out. There's a concert in town that we're interested in. So, yes, just a quiet weekend for us.
Ruth: Oh, right, just a quiet weekend …
Isabel: What about you? What are you doing?
Ruth: Well … Martin's going out with his brother tomorrow so I'm at home alone. I might sit in the garden and read if it's a nice day. Maybe I'll do some gardening.
Isabel: Oh, er, that'll be nice.
Ruth: Then on Sunday mornings we usually play cards, but we might not this weekend. One of the people we play with isn't feeling very well.
Isabel: Oh dear, that's a shame.
Ruth: It's OK. I enjoy having quiet weekends, too!

Grammar

6 Write the two following sentences on the board: *I'm playing football with my friends on Saturday. I might play football with my friends on Saturday.* Ask *In which sentence are we sure?* (the first) *How do we know?* (It's an arrangement/The speaker uses the present continuous) *Which word in the second sentence means 'maybe'?* (might) Ss read the Grammar box and choose the correct alternatives, then check in pairs. Check answers with the whole class, feeding in the information from the Grammar checkpoint box below if necessary.

Answers: 1 not sure 2 without

Grammar checkpoint

You may want to explain that *may* and *might* in English are similar to *will* + *maybe*. So instead of saying *I'll maybe go out for dinner*, it's more common to say *I might go out for dinner*.

GRAMMAR BANK 6C pp.126–127

Stronger classes could read the notes at home. Otherwise, check the notes with Ss, comparing the different future forms. In each exercise, elicit the first answer as an example. Ss work alone to complete the exercises, then check their answers in pairs. In feedback, elicit Ss' answers and drill the questions. Ss can refer to the notes to help them.

Answers: 6C
1 1 b 2 f 3 c 4 a 5 e 6 d 7 h 8 g
2 1 may/might not like 2 'll/will try 3 'll call
  4 may/might not have 5 'll/will go
  6 may/might see/watch 7 may/might be 8 'll/will see

7a 🔊 6.10 Ss listen to the sentences, focussing on the /t/ sounds in bold. Elicit what happens to it.

Answer: It's dropped before a consonant sound and links to a vowel sound.

Teaching tip

It can be difficult for Ss to notice features of connected speech, when sounds are dropped. The reason it happens is to make it easier to say the words in fast, natural speech. You can help raise awareness of these features by first drilling just the stressed syllables, maintaining a clear, steady rhythm, e.g. *might – club – night*.

Drill this a few times, then keeping the same rhythm, add the unstressed syllables, i.e.

*We **might** go **club**bing to**night**.*

This can help Ss become aware of the features of connected speech by producing them in isolation first.

b Ss listen again and repeat. Drill chorally and individually for further practice if necessary.

8 Ss complete the message alone, then check in pairs. Check answers with the whole class. Ask Ss if they have any of the same plans as in the message.

Answers: 1 may/might go 2 may/might not be
3 may/might see 4 may/might not enjoy
5 may/might choose 6 may/might go

9a Give Ss a few minutes to think of ideas and make notes. Monitor and help with vocabulary, writing any new words on the board. **Fast finishers** can think of two more things.

b Read the example with the class and explain that the second clause supports the use of *might* in the first. Ss work in pairs and share their possible plans. When they have finished, ask a few Ss to share their partners' plans with the class.

Further practice

Photocopiable activities: 6C Grammar 1, p192;
6C Grammar 2, p193

Speaking

Prepare

10 You may want to briefly review the form/use of the present continuous for future arrangements, *be going to* for future plans and *may/might* for future possibility, by writing your own plans on the board reviewing how we use each form, e.g.

I'm having a party on Saturday night.
I'm going to get up late on Saturday.
I might meet some friends for lunch on Sunday, but I'm not sure.

Give Ss plenty of time to make notes, making sure they don't write whole sentences, just note down the activities under each heading. Help with vocabulary where necessary, writing any new words/phrases on the board.

Speak

11a Go through the Useful phrases with the class and read the example with the class, or model the activity with a **stronger Ss**. Arrange Ss in groups to discuss their plans. Monitor and make notes on Ss' use of language for later feedback.

b Ss work in their group and discuss the questions. When they are ready, nominate a student from each group to share their answers with the class. Give Ss feedback on their use of language on the board as a class.

> **Reflection on learning**
>
> Write the following questions on the board:
> *Which part of this lesson was the most useful? Why?*
> *How confident do you feel talking about the future in English?*
> *What future form do you need to work on most?*
>
> Put Ss in pairs to discuss the questions. When they have finished, ask if anyone wants to share their ideas with the class, but don't force them to if they'd rather not.

Homework ideas

Ex 10a: Ss write a message to a friend outlining their plans for the weekend.
Grammar bank: 6C Ex 1–2, pp.126–127
Workbook: Ex 1–5, p36
App: grammar and vocabulary practice

Fast route: continue to Lesson 6D
Extended route: go to p103 for Develop your writing

6D English in action

Introduction

The goal of this lesson is for Ss to practice leaving a phone message for someone. To help them achieve this, they will learn a range of phrases for saying who it is, asking for someone, giving the reason for the message and asking for a reply.

Warm-up

Before class, write on the board:
Ways of communicating.
Elicit one or two ways people communicate these days, e.g. *messaging, voice calls, social media.* Give Ss a few minutes to brainstorm as many ways of communicating these days as they can think of. When they have finished, ask them to come to the board and write their ideas, then check their spelling. Ss then work in pairs and think of an advantage and disadvantage of each way of communicating. When they are ready, elicit Ss' ideas and have a brief class discussion.

Listening

1 Focus attention on the photo and elicit what Ss can see. Ss work in pairs and discuss the questions. When they have finished, elicit a few Ss' answers and have a brief class discussion.

2a 🔊 **6.11** Go through the reasons first and check Ss understand what they're listening for. Ss listen and match the speakers to the reasons alone, then check in pairs. Check answers with the whole class.

Answers: 1 b 2 d 3 a 4 e 5 c

b Ss listen and complete the messages alone, then check in pairs. Don't verify their answers yet.

c Ss check their answers with the Useful phrases box, then check answers with the whole class.

Answers: 1 here; sorry 2 Text 3 message 4 back
5 just calling 6 This 7 get 8 about

Audio script 6.11

Speaker 1: Hi Jamie, it's Chris here. I'm really sorry, but I have to cancel our lunch tomorrow. The area manager is visiting and wants to take us all out. Can we do it next week? Text me to let me know when you're free.

Speaker 2: This is a message for Mr. Williams. I'm calling from Corner Street Dentist's. You have an appointment for 4.30 on Tuesday afternoon, but we now have an earlier one available on Monday at the same time. If you want to change it, then call us back on 0208 4654 7212. Thank you.

Speaker 3: Hello Judith. It's your grandmother here. I'm just calling to remind you about Aunt Claire's birthday. It's next Friday, so don't forget to call her. Hope you're well. Bye.

Speaker 4: Er ... yes, this is Gareth. A few of us are playing tennis on Saturday. It's the usual arrangement, meet at the club in the morning, then lunch after the game. Do you want to join us? Can you call me back when you get this and let me know if you're coming? Cheers.

Speaker 5: Hi Jean, it's Grace here. I'm calling about the meeting on Friday. Give me a call when you have time. Bye.

3 🔊 **6.12** Ss listen again and repeat. Drill chorally and individually for further practice if necessary.

4 Read the example with the class. In pairs, Ss discuss what they'd say for each message. Encourage them to use the Useful phrases. When they have finished, nominate a different pair for each message to share what they'd say with the class and find out if other Ss agree.

Suggested answers:
1 Hi, it's Navid here. I'm calling about the concert tonight.
2 I'm calling to see if you want to come to my party on Saturday evening.
3 I'm calling to remind you to do your homework before you go out.
4 I'm calling to cancel my appointment.
5 Call me back on (07823 664500).
6 Text me if you can come to my party.
7 Can you call me back as soon as you can?

Optional extra activity

After Ex 4, rearrange Ss to work in different pairs. Ss take it in turns to secretly choose a situation and decide what they'd say. The other student listens and says which situation they're responding to.

Speaking

Prepare

5 Refer Ss to page 155. Put Ss in pairs and ask them to choose who is A and B. Give them a few minutes to read their information and check anything they're not sure about with you. Encourage them to make notes on what they'll say.

Speak

6a Refer Ss to the Useful phrases. Ss take it in turns to leave their messages and make notes, making sure they answer the questions. Monitor and make notes on Ss' language use for later feedback.

Optional alternative activity

If it's appropriate in your teaching context, ask Ss to use their mobile devices to send and receive voice messages to each other. Alternatively, each student could record one message on a device. They then go around the class listening to each others' messages and noting down the details.

b When they have finished, Ss show each other their notes and check if they're correct. In feedback, give Ss feedback on their language use as a class.

Reflection on learning

Write the following questions on the board:
How confident did you feel leaving a message in English? Which of the phrases from today's lesson are you most likely to use in the future? Why?
Put Ss in pairs to discuss the questions. When they have finished, ask if anyone wants to share their ideas with the class, but don't force them to if they'd rather not.

Homework ideas

Ex 5: Ss record themselves leaving messages and add it to their GSE portfolio.
Reflection on learning: Write your answers.
Workbook: Ex 1–2, p37
App: grammar and voculary practice

6 Check and reflect

Introduction

Ss revise and practise the language of Unit 6. The notes below provide some ideas for exploiting the activities in class, but you may want to set the first exercise in each section for homework, or use them as a diagnostic or progress test. For each grammar or vocabulary point, the first activity reviews the language and the second is more communicative, involving pairwork.

1a Elicit the first answer as an example. Ss complete the predictions alone, then check in pairs. Check answers with the whole class.

Answers: 1 will improve 2 will have 3 will do 4 won't live
5 will be 6 won't have

b Ss work in pairs and discuss the predictions. Encourage them to give reasons for their opinions. When they have finished, elicit Ss' answers and have a brief class discussion.

2 Ss complete the predictions alone. Monitor and help with vocabulary where necessary, writing any new words/phrases on the board. If you have time, put Ss in pairs to compare their predictions and find out if anyone has the same ideas. In feedback, elicit a few predictions from the class and find out if other Ss agree.

3a Ss choose the correct alternatives alone, then check in pairs. Check answers with the whole class.

Answers: 1 keep 2 have 3 earn, career 4 busy, time
5 humour 6 simple

b Ss work in pairs and discuss which sentences are true for them, changing those that aren't, so they're true. In feedback, elicit answers from a different student for each sentence.

4a Focus attention on the diary and read the example together. Ss write their sentences alone, then check in pairs. Check answers with the whole class.

Answers: She's organising a team meeting on Monday at 10 a.m.; She's going to the dentist on Tuesday at 2 p.m.; She's having lunch with Diana on Thursday at 12.30 p.m.; She's flying to Trieste on Friday at 6 p.m.; She's visiting a museum on Saturday at 10 a.m.; She's catching a train to Bologna on Sunday at 2 p.m.

b Ss work in pairs and discuss their arrangements. In feedback, nominate a few Ss to tell you a few things their partners are doing next week.

5 Ss write sentences alone, then check in pairs. Check answers with the whole class. You could ask different Ss to come to the board to write their answers, then check them with the class.

Answers:
1 Dani isn't travelling to Dallas next month.
2 What time / are you leaving work today?
3 I'm making pizza tonight.
4 She's moving to Frankfurt / in two weeks' time.
5 Are they coming to the party on Friday?
6 We aren't working in London next week.

6a Ss correct the sentences alone, then check in pairs. Check answers with the whole class.

Answers: 1 ~~do~~ **make**   2 ~~made~~ **had**   3 ~~had~~ **do**
4 ~~had~~ **made**   5 ~~do~~ **have**

b Ss work in pairs and discuss the sentences. When they have finished, ask a different student for each sentence to share their ideas with the class and find out if anyone else does the same thing.

7 Ss write sentences alone, then check in pairs. Check answers with the whole class. You could ask different Ss to come to the board to write their answers, then check them with the class.

Answers:
1 I may stay at home this evening.
2 My brother might visit me this weekend.
3 My parents may go on holiday for three weeks this year.
4 I might go running tonight.

8a You could introduce the activity by sharing your answers with the class. Ss complete the sentences about themselves. Monitor and help with new vocabulary where necessary.

b Ss work in pairs and share their sentences. In feedback, find out if they have any answers in common.

9a Ss complete the questions alone, then check in pairs. Check answers with the whole class.

Answers: 1 do   2 went   3 play   4 go   5 go   6 do   7 going
8 doing

b Ss work in pairs and discuss the questions. Encourage them to ask follow-up questions to find out more information. When they have finished, ask a different student from each group a question and find out if the rest of the class agrees.

Reflect

Ask Ss to rate each statement alone, then compare in pairs. Encourage them to ask any questions they still have about any of the areas covered in Unit 6.

6 Roadmap race (Units 5–6 review)

Introduction

Ss revise and practise the language of Units 5 and 6 in a communicative game. This can be done after the Check and reflect page as a fun way to revise the language of Units 5 and 6.

For this game, Ss write numbers 1–6 on small pieces of paper and put them in a bag. All Ss place their counters on the START square. Ss take turns to take out one of the papers and move that number of squares along the board. When they land on a square they must follow the instructions on it. If their answer is incorrect Ss move back to the square they were on before. The first person to reach the FINISH square wins.

While Ss are playing, monitor and be on hand to adjudicate or help where necessary.

Answers:
1   part
2   make
3   Students' own answer
4   I might not go to the show this evening.
5   that
6   Students' own answer
7   Students' own answer
8   My brother looks very happy in this photo.
9   doing
10 Students' own answer
11 humour
12 Students' own answer
13 e.g. I'm really sorry but I have to cancel my appointment.
14 adjective
15 Students' own answer
16 You shouldn't take a taxi. It's expensive.
17 *which* for things, *who* for people
18 Students' own answer
19 going
20 e.g. long hair, short hair
21 Students' own answer
22 Students' own answer
23 Students' own answer
24 fit
25 social
26 like
27 try
28 You should never be late for a job interview.
29 Students' own answer
30 who

6A Develop your listening

Introduction

Ss develop their listening skill of following the main points of a talk by learning how to identify elision in natural speech

Warm-up

Describe the happiest person you know to the class, talking about what they do to be happy and why they're happy. Ss then work in pairs and discuss the happiest person they know.

1 Focus attention on the photos and elicit what Ss can see. In feedback, elicit answers from a few Ss and find out if other Ss agree. Elicit any other ideas they have about living well and write them on the board, and if any of the things they mentioned in the warm up stage came up.

2 6.3 You may want to elicit/check *fix*, i.e. repair things which are broken, and *shy*, i.e. the opposite of confident. Give Ss a few minutes to discuss what they think the speaker will say. Elicit their ideas and write them on the board. Play the recording for Ss to check their ideas and tick off any which are on the board.

Answers: 1 be active 2 learn something new
3 live for the moment 4 be kind to other people
5 connect with other people

Audioscript 6.3

Presenter:

What's the secret to living a good, long life? Well this obviously depends on who you are, but there are some small, simple things we can all do to live well and be happy.

Step one. Be active.
You don't need to go to the gym every day to do regular exercise. You can make small changes to your daily life. For example, when you go shopping, walk to the supermarket instead of driving. If you take the bus to work, get off one stop early and walk. Take the stairs instead of the lift. These small things will make a difference over time, and you'll feel much better because of it.

Step two. Learn something new.
This could be a new skill, like learning how to paint or dance, or learning how to fix things around your house. Or you could do a whole course in a subject that interests you. Many colleges and universities now offer online courses for free.

Step three. Live for the moment.
Don't be afraid of your feelings and emotions. Learn to understand why you feel that way. If you feel sad, remember that tomorrow is a new day and you'll feel better. Don't worry about the past or the future too much.

Step four. Be kind to other people.
Just small things like a smile and saying something nice to the shop assistant when you buy something can make you feel a lot better. Try it today. It can also help you make new friends.

Step five. Connect with other people.
This is the most important point to remember. Don't worry if you're not a sociable person. Call a family member and find out how they are. Bake a cake and take it round to your neighbour. They'll love you for it and will probably do something nice for you in return.

3 6.4 Give Ss a few minutes to read the Focus box, or go through it together as a class. Play the recording for Ss to listen to the examples. If they're having trouble hearing the elided sounds, repeat them for the class to show how the sounds are elided. Answer the question as a class.

Answer: /t/ and /d/ are usually not pronounced when they come before another consonant sound.

4 6.5 Ss listen and repeat the sentences, not pronouncing the underlined letters. Ask a few Ss to say one of the sentences for the class, and drill individually and chorally if necessary.

5a Ss underline the silent letters alone, then check in pairs. Don't give any answers yet.

b 6.6 Play the recording for Ss to check their answers, then check answers with the whole class.

Answers:
1 ... an<u>d</u> you'll feel much better for it.
2 Don'<u>t</u> be afraid of your feelings and emotions.
3 Jus<u>t</u> small things like a smile ...
4 Don'<u>t</u> worry if you're not a sociable person, ...

6 Go through the questions with the class so that Ss know what to listen for. Ss listen again and answer the questions alone, then check in pairs. Check answers with the whole class.

Answers:
1 walk to the supermarket instead of driving; get off the bus one stop early and walk; take the stairs
2 whole courses for free
3 remember that tomorrow is a new day
4 smile; say something nice to a shop assistant
5 it can help you make new friends
6 to connect with other people

7 Put Ss in small groups to discuss the questions. In feedback, elicit Ss' ideas and have a brief class discussion.

Homework ideas

Workbook: Ex 1–3, p37

6B Develop your reading

Introduction

Ss develop their reading skill of understanding the main idea of an article by learning how to use paragraphs to identify main ideas.

Warm-up

Write on the board:
How is work different now from 50 years ago?
and write some categories below this to guide the discussion, e.g. *where we work, hours, colleagues, technology*. Ss work in small groups and discuss the questions. When they have finished, elicit ideas from each group and have a brief class discussion.

1 Focus attention on the photos and elicit what Ss can see (people working alone and people working in a team). Ss work in pairs and discuss the questions. In feedback, write: *Working alone* and *Working in a team* at the top of the board, and ask Ss to come to the board to write their ideas under each heading.

2 Give Ss a few minutes to read the Focus box or read it together with the class. Answer the question as a class.

Answer: by reading the first sentence of each paragraph

3a Set a strict time limit of one minute for this or do it as a race. Ss match the main ideas and paragraphs alone, then check in pairs. Check answers with the whole class.

Answers: 1 c 2 a 3 b

b Ss match the sentences and paragraphs alone, then check in pairs. Check answers with the whole class.

Answers: paragraph 4 = d; paragraph 5 = c; paragraph 6 = b

4 Elicit the first answer as an example. Ss match the sentences to the paragraphs alone, then check in pairs. Check answers with the whole class.

Answers: a 5 b 3 c 1 d 6 e 2 f 4

5 Ss work in pairs and discuss the questions. In feedback, ask a few Ss to share their ideas with the class and have a brief class discussion. Find out which of the activities are most popular with the class.

Homework ideas
Workbook: Ex 1–4, p38

6c Develop your writing

Introduction

Ss develop their skill of writing a description of everyday experiences by learning about paragraphing to organise ideas.

Warm-up

Write on the board:
Where? When? Who with? Activities? Food?
Tell Ss about your last holiday, including information about the question prompts on the board. Give Ss a few minutes to think about their last holiday and make notes answering the question prompts. Monitor and help with vocabulary where necessary, writing any new words/phrases on the board. Ss then work in pairs and share their experiences. When they have finished, ask a few Ss to share any interesting information they learnt from their partners with the class.

1 Ss work in pairs and discuss the questions. When they have finished, elicit a few Ss' answers and find out if other Ss do the same.

2 Books closed. Write on the board *staycation* and ask if Ss know what it is, but don't give any answers yet. Ss open their books and read the blog post to find out. Check the answer with the class.

Answer: It's when you stay at home and relax instead of going away for your holiday.

3 Give Ss a few minutes to read through the Focus box alone or read the box as a class. Answer the question as a class.

Answer: The reader can follow a long text more easily.

4 Ss read the blog post and match the purposes alone, then check in pairs. Check answers with the whole class.

Answers: 1 b 2 a 3 d 4 c

5a With *weaker classes*, elicit where the first paragraph ends together, then ask Ss to divide the other paragraphs. Otherwise, Ss read and divide the information into paragraphs alone.

b Ss work in pairs and compare their answers, then with the whole class.

Suggested answers:
Paragraph 1: Quiet weekends … for the week ahead.
Paragraph 2: Last weekend … great to see him again.
Paragraph 3: Next weekend … on Monday!
Paragraph 4: Relaxing is really important … a perfect weekend!

Prepare

6 Explain that Ss are going to imagine they're on a staycation at the moment. Go through the ideas and elicit one or two ideas for each one, e.g. Paragraph 1: to save money, Paragraph 2: doing jobs round the house, Paragraph 3: do some shopping, Paragraph 4: they're very relaxing, etc.

Write

7 Ss write their blog posts alone. Monitor and check Ss' work while they write and be on hand to offer help where necessary. When Ss have finished, ask them to swap texts with another student to read and think of three things they like about their partner's text.

Homework ideas
Workbook: Ex 1–6, p39

7 OVERVIEW

7A The building project
Speaking | give opinions and reasons
Grammar | *too* and *enough*
Vocabulary | features of city life
GSE learning objective
Can express their opinions on familiar topics using simple language

7B Where I grew up
Speaking | discuss where you grew up
Grammar | *used to*
Vocabulary | natural features
GSE learning objectives
Can describe places using a limited range of phrases

7C A favourite room
Speaking | describe a place
Grammar | articles
Vocabulary | prepositions
GSE learning objective
Can give an extended description of everyday objects (e.g. people, places, experiences)

7D English in action
Goal | make and respond to excuses
GSE learning objectives
Can give a simple excuse for something they have done wrong (e.g. arriving late to class); can respond to excuses using basic fixed expressions

Check and reflect
(a) I can give opinions.
(b) I can talk about where I grew up.

VOCABULARY BANK

7C Rooms and furniture

DEVELOP YOUR SKILLS

7A Develop your listening
Goal | understand a discussion
Focus | agreeing and disagreeing
GSE learning objectives
Can recognise when speakers agree in a conversation conducted slowly and clearly; can recognise when speakers disagree in a conversation conducted slowly and clearly

7B Develop your reading
Goal | understand short articles
Focus | reading for general understanding
GSE learning objective
Can skim a short text to identify its main purpose

7C Develop your writing
Goal | write an informal email
Focus | using informal phrases
GSE learning objective
Can write short, simple notes, emails and messages relating to everyday matters

7A The building project

Introduction

The goal of this lesson is for Ss to have a discussion where they give opinions and reasons using simple language, in the context of a debate about a new housing development. To help them achieve this, they will learn/revise *too* and *enough*, and vocabulary related to features of city life.

Warm-up

Write on the board:
How has your town/city changed in the last ten years?
Are these changes a good or a bad thing?
What changes would you like to see in the next ten years?
Ss work in small groups and discuss the questions. If Ss are from rural areas, they can discuss the town/city nearest to them. When they have finished, nominate a student from each group to share their ideas with the class and have a brief class discussion.

Vocabulary and reading

Features of city life

1 Ss work in pairs and discuss the question. In feedback, elicit their ideas and find out if others agree.

2 Ss read the advert and work in pairs and discuss the questions. Elicit their answers and reasons, and check to see if any of the disadvantages they came up with are mentioned in the advertisement.

3a Ss complete the questions with the words in the box. Encourage them to use the advert and their dictionaries/mobile devices to help with new words, but also be on hand to offer explanations where necessary. Check answers with the class.

Answers: 1 area 2 neighbours 3 location 4 flats 5 public transport 6 cycle paths 7 traffic 8 pollution 9 local 10 night life

Optional alternative activity

With **weaker classes**, go through the words/phrases in the box first, checking understanding and giving explanations/examples where necessary.

b Ss work in pairs and discuss the questions. In feedback, ask different Ss to ask and answer the questions in open pairs.

Further practice

Photocopiable activities: 7A Vocabulary, p197

4 You may want to pre-teach/check: *terrible*, i.e. *very bad*; *to rent*, i.e. *pay each month to live in someone else's home*. Ss read the posts quickly to see what each person thinks, then check in pairs. Check answers with the whole class, but don't ask why each person thinks that yet.

Answers: Max and Nic think it's a good idea. Lisa and Diana think it's a bad idea.

5 Ss read again and answer the questions alone, then check in pairs. Check answers with the whole class.

Answers: 1 Nic 2 Lisa 3 Nic 4 Diana 5 Max

94

Before Ss do Ex 5, ask them to work in pairs and discuss why each person thinks the Horton Fields development is a good or bad idea and write down their reason.

Grammar

too and enough

5 Focus attention on the last social media post in Ex 4 and write this part of the first sentence on the board, underlining these words: they <u>don't have enough money</u> to buy a home and it's <u>too expensive</u> to rent. Point at the first underlined phrase and ask *Do they have the right amount of money?* (no); *Do they have more or less than they need?* (less); *Is it a problem?* (yes). Point to the second underlined phrase and ask *Is the price more or less than they have?* (more); *Is it a problem?* (yes). Ss choose the correct alternatives alone, then check in pairs. Check answers with the class and be prepared to offer further explanations/examples where necessary.

Answers: 1 more 2 right 3 less

Grammar checkpoint

In some languages, the equivalent of *too* + adjective is used as an intensifier, i.e. it just means *very*. Make sure Ss understand that in English *too* means *it's a problem*. You can demonstrate this by writing two sentences on the board:
It's very expensive, but it's nice.
It's too expensive, we can't go there.
Ask Ss which sentence causes a problem (the second).

GRAMMAR BANK 7A pp.128–129

Stronger classes could read the notes at home. Otherwise, check the notes with Ss, especially the word order. In each exercise, elicit the first answer as an example. Ss complete the exercises alone, then check their answers in pairs. In feedback, elicit Ss' answers and drill the questions. Ss can refer to the notes to help them.

Answers: 7A

1 1 don't have enough money   2 too much noise
   3 aren't enough chairs   4 too hot for me
   5 are too many cars   6 isn't big enough
   7 have enough food for everyone   8 's too small for me
2 1 too small   2 'nt/not enough cupboards
   3 'nt/not big enough   4 enough space   5 too much traffic
   6 too noisy   7 too many noisy neighbours
   8 have enough money

7a 7.1 Ss listen and answer the questions. Check answers with the whole class, paying particular attention to the pronunciation of enough /ɪ'nʌf/ since the spelling is so different and the stress is on the second syllable.

Answers: *too* has a long vowel sound; *enough* has two short vowel sounds

Ss listen again and repeat. Drill chorally and individually for further practice if necessary.

8a Ss choose the correct alternatives alone, then check in pairs. Check answers with the whole class.

Answers: 1 enough   2 too many   3 too much   4 too
5 enough   6 big enough

Ss work in pairs and discuss which of the sentences are true for them, then discuss as a class.

b Read the example with the class. With ***weaker classes***, refer Ss back to the words in the box in Ex 3a and elicit which are countable and which are uncountable. Ss complete the sentences alone. Monitor and help with ideas and vocabulary, writing any new words/phrases on the board.

Fast finishers can write two more sentences using *too* and *enough*.

c Read the example with the class. Give Ss a minute or two to think about how they would solve the problems they wrote in Ex 8b. When they are ready, Ss work in pairs and discuss their improvements, also discussing if they agree with each other's suggestions and giving their reasons. When they have finished, ask a few Ss to share their ideas with the class and have a class discussion.

After Ss have shared their ideas in Ex 8b, ask each pair to choose the two most important problems. Arrange pairs in groups to share their ideas, then ask each group to choose the most important problem. When they have finished, elicit each group's most important problem and write them on the board. Have a class discussion, then vote on the most important problem and solution.

Photocopiable activities: 7A Grammar 1, p195;
7A Grammar 2, p196

Speaking

Prepare

9a 7.2 Refer Ss back to the advertisement in Ex 2 and the social media posts in Ex 4. Elicit what Ss can remember about the different opinions and reasons for those opinions on the Horton Fields development. Ss listen to the people discussing the development and answer the question. Check the answer with the class.

Answer: The man thinks the plan is a good idea. The woman doesn't.

b Ss listen again and write who gives the reasons. Ss check in pairs, then check answers with the whole class.

Answers: 1 M   2 C   3 C   4 M

Stronger classes can do the exercise first from memory, then listen again and check.

Audioscript 7.2

Mia: What do you think about this new housing development in Horton Park?
Colin: I think it's quite a good idea – there just aren't enough cheap houses in this area. We need to build homes that young people can buy.
Mia: Yes, that's true, a lot of young people leave the area because they don't have enough money to live here. I can see that.

Colin: Exactly. We need young people to keep the area alive.

Mia: Mm, I agree with that, but what about the location of these homes? It's terrible! Our park is a place where people in the area go for peace and quiet, or to play sport. We all need it to relax and do exercise.

Collin: Yeah, that's true. The park is lovely and it's important to the area.

Mia: So, is it the right place for these homes then? There aren't many parks in town, so I think it's a really bad idea.

Colin: But where else can we build new homes? It seems like the only place possible to me and it's only a small part of the park. There will still be a lot of space for people to use.

Mia: Mm, I don't know – it's a really difficult situation, that's for sure.

10a Go through the first fact as an example and elicit possible good and bad things, e.g. *The project will last three years. Good: it will create jobs. Bad: It will be noisy.* Give Ss plenty of time to think of ideas and make notes alone. Monitor and help with vocabulary, writing any new words/phrases on the board.

b Ss work in pairs and compare their ideas.

Optional alternative activity

In **smaller classes**, As could work together to make notes and Bs could work together to make notes and then pair off As with Bs for the discussion. In **larger classes**, they can make notes in pairs and then have the discussion in groups of four.

Speak

11a Arrange Ss in groups with members of both Group A and Group B. Go through the Useful phrases. Ss discuss the new development, giving reasons as to whether it's a good or bad idea. Monitor and make notes on Ss' language use for later feedback, especially the use of *too* and *enough*.

b Ask Ss if they have changed their mind about the new development after their discussion in Ex 11a. Ask the class to vote whether the development is a good or bad idea. Ask the Ss how many changed their minds and why.

Reflection on learning

Write the following questions on the board:

How confident do you feel using too *and* enough*?*
What could you do to improve?
Did you enjoy having the discussion in Ex 10a? Why (not)?

Put Ss in pairs to discuss the questions. When they have finished, ask if anyone wants to share their ideas with the class, but don't force them to if they'd rather not.

Homework ideas

Grammar bank: 7A Ex 1–2, pp.128–129
Workbook: Ex 1–5, p40
App: grammar and vocabulary practice

Fast route: continue to Lesson 7B
Extended route: go to p104 for Develop your listening

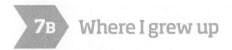

7B Where I grew up

Introduction

The goal of this lesson is for Ss to describe where they grew up. To help them achieve this, they will learn/revise *used to* and vocabulary to describe natural features.

Warm-up

Revise the vocabulary in Lesson 7A with a board race. Arrange Ss in two teams and give each team a board pen. Each turn, give a description of one of the words/phrases from the lesson, e.g. *lots of cars and other vehicles* (traffic). The first team member to write the word correctly on the board wins a point for their team. The team with the most points at the end wins.

Vocabulary and listening

Natural features

1a Focus attention on the photos and elicit what Ss can see. Ss match the words and the photos alone, then check in pairs. Check answers with the whole class.

Answers: **A** river, hill **B** beach, ocean, sea **C** lake, mountain **D** stream, forest, wood **E** hill, wood

b The aim of this activity is for Ss to have a more precise definition of the words by differentiating between similar words. Ss discuss the differences in meanings. Encourage them to use dictionaries or their mobile devices to check words they're not sure of, but also be prepared to help where necessary. Check answers with the whole class.

Answers:
1 An ocean is bigger than a sea.
2 A forest is bigger than a wood.
3 A river is bigger than a stream.
4 A mountain is bigger than a hill.

Optional extra activity

With **monolingual classes**, further check understanding by asking Ss to translate the words into their own language.

2a Go through the questions and elicit what Ss can remember from Ex 1b. Explain that the missing words are words used in Ex 1b. Ss answer the questions, then check in pairs. Check answers with the whole class.

Answers: 1 river 2 mountain 3 ocean 4 wood 5 stream

b Ss work in pairs to compare answers for Ex 2a.
3 Ss work in small groups and discuss the questions. When they have finished, elicit answers from different Ss in the class.

Optional alternative activity

If Ss are all from the same country, they could either discuss question 3 about their country, or discuss different countries they know or have visited.

Further practice

Photocopiable activities: 7B Vocabulary, p200

4a 🔊 **7.5** Ss listen and tick the features alone, then check in pairs. Check answers with the whole class.

Answers: lake, forest, stream, beach, mountains

b Go through the questions and elicit what Ss can remember, but don't give any answers yet. Ss listen again and answer the questions, then check in pairs. Check answers with the whole class.

Answers:
1 Because her parents were hotel managers and had to move every few years.
2 in lots of different countries around the world
3 a lake in the south of Canada
4 a beautiful stream
5 the west coast of Portugal
6 No. She didn't do the things that other kids usually did.
7 no
8 No. She likes where she lives now too much.

Audioscript 7.5

Scott: Is this you in the photos, Natalie?
Natalie: Oh yes – that's me when I was about seven!
Scott: There are lots of different places. Did you use to travel a lot?
Natalie: Um … kind of. My parents worked as hotel managers for a big international hotel company and every two or three years they'd send us somewhere different. We lived all around the world.
Scott: Wow, really? What was that like?
Natalie: Well, it was a lot of fun, mainly. Each new place felt like an adventure and our parents took us to some very interesting places – the kinds of places where people don't usually go.
Scott: Like where?
Natalie: Oh everywhere! I think my favourite place was here in this photo, near a lake in the south of Canada. We used to go walking in the forest nearby every day and one day I remember we found this beautiful little stream. I played in it all day!
Scott: Nice!
Natalie: … this photo is from when we lived on the west coast of Portugal. We used to go camping near this beach. It was a really long beach, with these beautiful mountains in the background.
Scott: It sounds amazing.
Natalie: Yes, it was. But not everything was good. Because we moved all the time, I didn't use to do those things that kids usually do – you know, go to the same places during the holidays, go to the same events, see my grandparents – that kind of thing. Things were always changing.
Scott: I see. But your friends didn't use to travel as much as you, right?
Natalie: That's true. And I've got some wonderful memories.
Scott: Exactly! Do you miss it?
Natalie: Hmm, a bit. But I don't think I could move around that much these days. I like where I live now too much! But as a kid it was a real adventure, definitely. What about you? Did you use to travel much as a child?

---

5 Ss work in pairs and discuss the questions. When they have finished, elicit answers from a few Ss and have a brief class discussion.

Grammar

used to

6 Focus attention on the first example in the Grammar box (*We used to go walking in the forest nearby every day.*) and ask *Is this the past or present?* (past). *Did it happen once or many times?* (many times) *Is it still true now?* (no). Ss choose the correct alternatives alone, then check in pairs. Check answers with the whole class and be prepared to give further explanations/ examples where necessary.

Answers: 1 don't happen anymore   2 use

Grammar checkpoint

Ss sometimes confuse *used to* + infinitive to talk about habits in the past with *be used to* + verb *-ing* to talk about something which is normal in the present. Make sure Ss are clear that *used to* + infinitive only refers to the past. The equivalent to talk about present habits is *usually*, e.g. *We usually go walking in the forest nearby.*

GRAMMAR BANK 7B   pp.128–129

Stronger classes could read the notes at home. Otherwise, check the notes with Ss, especially the negative and question forms. In each exercise, elicit the first answer as an example. Ss work alone to complete the exercises, then check their answers in pairs. In feedback, elicit Ss' answers and drill the questions. Ss can refer to the notes to help them.

Answers: 7B
1   1 used to live   2 used to have   3 used to look
    4 didn't use to like   5 did you use to play
    6 used to watch
2   1 Where did you use to go to school?
    2 I didn't use to like carrots.
    3 We used to go everywhere by bike.
    4 I used to play the piano.
    5 Did you use to drive?
    6 We didn't use to go on holiday much.
    7 They used to live in a flat.
    8 Did she use to study medicine?

7a 🔊 **7.6** The aim of this activity is to highlight the difference between the unvoiced /s/ in *used to* and the voiced /z/ is the verb *use*. Ss listen to the pairs of sentences, then check answers with the whole class.

Answer: different: in *used to*, the s is unvoiced /s/. In *used*, the s is voiced /z/.

b Play the recording again for Ss to repeat the phrases. Drill chorally and individually for further practice if necessary.

Optional extra activity

Before Ss do Ex 7, write on the board:
1 *Where did they grow up?*
2 *Where did they go in the summer?*
3 *Did they like it?*
4 *What did they do?*
Ask Ss to read the text quickly, ignoring the gaps and answer the questions. Ss check in pairs, then check with the whole class (1 in a city; 2 their grandparents' farm; 3 yes; 4 They worked on the farm, played in a forest, learned to drive.)

8 Ss complete the text with *used to* and the verbs then check in pairs. Check answers with the whole class.

> **Answers:** **1** used to stay **2** get up **3** didn't use to work **4** used to play **5** used to climb **6** didn't use to drive

9a Elicit the first answer as an example on the board. Ss write the questions, then check in pairs. Check answers with the whole class.

> **Answers:**
> 1 What games did you use to play?
> 2 Did you use to use the internet a lot?
> 3 Where did you use to live?
> 4 Did you use to travel a lot?
> 5 How did you use to get to school?
> 6 Did you use to stay with your grandparents?
> 7 Where did you use to go on holiday?
> 8 Who did you use to play with?

b Read the example with the class, and/or model the activity with a *stronger Ss* and encourage Ss to ask and answer follow-up questions to find out more information. Ss work in pairs and discuss the questions. In feedback, ask Ss to share what they have in common with the class.

> **Further practice**

Photocopiable activities: 7B Grammar 1, p198; 7B Grammar 2, p199

Prepare

10a 🔊 **7.7** Ss listen and match the speakers to the photos. Check answers with the class.

> **Answers:** A Ian B Teresa

b Ss listen again and answer the questions, then check in pairs. Check answers with the whole class.

> **Answers:** 1 no 2 her brother and sister 3 skiing 4 yes 5 no 6 go fishing in a boat

> **Audioscript 7.7**
>
> **Ian:** Where did you grow up, Teresa?
> **Teresa:** Oh, when I was very young I used to live in a small town in the mountains.
> **Ian:** Really? What was that like?
> **Teresa:** Well, it was very quiet – I didn't use to have many friends. But my brother and sister aren't much older than me, so we spent a lot of time together.
> **Ian:** What kind of things did you use to do?
> **Teresa:** Lots of outdoors stuff. There was a forest nearby where we used to play and in winter there was always a lot of snow to have fun in!
> **Ian:** Nice! Did you use to go skiing?
> **Teresa:** Yeah, we did. Actually, I could ski when I was only four years old.
> **Ian:** Wow!
> **Teresa:** What about you? Where did you use to live when you were a kid?
> **Ian:** I grew up by the sea. My parents used to have a house right on the beach.
> **Teresa:** Cool!
> **Ian:** Yeah, well it was in the summer. I used to make new friends every year and we played on the beach all day. Also, my dad had a boat and he used to take me out fishing. We didn't use to catch much though!
> **Teresa:** Ha, that's nice. What did you use to do in the winter?

> **Ian:** Not much! There didn't use to be many people around, and it got very cold and windy, so we mostly used to just stay inside and play games.
> **Teresa:** Do you miss it?
> **Ian:** Yeah, quite a lot. My parents moved to the city recently, so I don't go back there much.

c Ss can either talk about where they grew up or, if they'd rather not, they can imagine a completely different childhood. Give Ss plenty of time to make notes, and monitor and help with vocabulary, writing any new words/phrases on the board.

Speak

11 Go through the Useful phrases with the class, checking understanding where necessary. Ss share their descriptions in pairs, asking and answering follow-up questions to find out more information. Monitor and make notes on their language use, especially the use of *used to* + infinitive. When they have finished, ask a few Ss to share any interesting information they found out about their partners with the class. Give Ss feedback on their speaking, using the notes you made.

> **Reflection on learning**
>
> Write the following questions on the board:
> *What's one thing that you've improved this lesson?*
> *What's the most difficult thing about using* used to*?*
> *How can you continue to practise this in the future?*
> Put Ss in pairs to discuss the questions. When they have finished, ask if anyone wants to share their ideas with the class, but don't force them to if they'd rather not.

> **Homework ideas**

Ex 10: Ss write a description of where they grew up.
Grammar bank: 7B Ex 1–2, pp.128–129
Workbook: Ex 1–5, p41
App: grammar and vocabulary practice

Fast route: continue to Lesson 7C
Extended route: go to p105 for Develop your reading

7c ▸ A favourite room

Introduction

The goal of this lesson is for Ss to describe a place. To help them achieve this, they will learn/revise prepositions of place and articles.

Warm-up

Divide the board into four sections and label each one *bedroom, living room, kitchen, office*. Arrange Ss in four groups or pairs (depending on the size of your class) and assign a room to each group. Give them a few minutes to brainstorm as many types of furniture commonly found in their room as possible. When they are ready, ask each group to nominate a student to come to the board without any notes. Give each student a board pen and ask the other Ss to call out the names of the furniture for the Ss at the board to write up. When they have finished, check spelling and the meanings of the different words.

Reading and vocabulary

Prepositions

1 Focus attention on the photos and elicit what types of room Ss can see. Ss work in pairs and discuss the questions. In feedback, elicit answers from a few Ss and have a brief class discussion.

VOCABULARY BANK 7C p142
Rooms and furniture
It's a good idea to do this with the class before Ex 2, especially if you didn't do the warmer, as this will help Ss with the vocabulary in the text, as well as the rest of the lesson.
1 Ss answer the questions. Check answers with the class, giving further explanations/examples where necessary.

Answers: 1 kitchen 2 bathroom 3 bedroom
4 living room 5 study 6 garage 7 garden

2 Ss match the words and photos, using dictionaries or mobile devices to help. Check answers with the class, giving further explanations/examples where necessary.

Answers: 1 K 2 N 3 J 4 B 5 F 6 C 7 I 8 H 9 M
10 A 11 L 12 G 13 E 14 D

3 Ss work in pairs and discuss the questions. In feedback, nominate a few Ss to share any interesting information they found out about their partners with the class.

2a If you choose not to do the Vocabulary bank before this activity, use the photos to elicit the names of the different types of furniture in the text and write them on the board. Ss read the description and choose the correct photo. Check the answer with the whole class.

Answer: D

b Ss read the text again and decide if the statements are true or false then check in pairs. Check answers with the whole class.

Answers: 1 F (Because it gets a lot of light.) 2 T
3 F (They're good for you.) 4 T
5 F (It's also a great place to relax and have fun with friends.)

c Write the following extract from the text on the board, with the preposition underlined: *those big windows* <u>behind</u> *the sofa*. Focus attention on photo D and elicit the meaning of *behind* (to the back of something). Ss match the prepositions to the illustrations alone, then check in pairs. Check answers with the whole class.

Answers: opposite *d*; behind *e*; between *g*; n front of *c*;
in the corner of *a*; in the middle of *f*; next to *i*; on *b*; under *h*

Optional extra activity

Put Ss in pairs and ask them to choose a small object they have with them, e.g. a glove, pen, etc. Ss take it in turn to put the object somewhere nearby, for the other student to say where it is, e.g. *It's under the desk. It's between the chairs.*

Further practice

Photocopiable activities: 7C Vocabulary, p203

Grammar

Articles

3 Write on the board: *I have two plants in my room: ___ big one and ___ small one. ___ big one is green and ___ small one is yellow.* Also write: *the, a, nothing.* Elicit the missing articles in the sentences and write them on the board. Ask *Which article do we use with plurals?* (nothing) *Which do we use the first time we mention something?* (a) *Which do we use the second time we mention something?* (the). Ss choose the correct alternatives in the Grammar box alone, then check in pairs. Check answers with the whole class and be prepared to give further explanations/ examples where necessary.

Answers: 1 a or an 2 the 3 no article

GRAMMAR BANK 7C pp.128–129
Stronger classes could read the notes at home. Otherwise, check the notes with Ss, going over each separate use of each article and providing further examples if necessary. In each exercise, elicit the first answer as an example. Ss work alone to complete the exercises, then check their answers in pairs. In feedback, elicit Ss' answers and drill the questions. Ss can refer to the notes to help them.

Answers: 7C
1 1 –, a, a 2 a, a, the, the 3 the, the, the
2 1 a, the 2 – 3 the 4 the 5 a 6 –, – 7 the 8 the

Grammar checkpoint
Articles can be especially difficult for learners at all levels, depending on how (or if) they use them in their first language. Although they're not especially difficult to understand, the number of exceptions makes them difficult to use fluently in conversation. Don't expect too much accuracy from your students in spoken language at this stage. The main thing is that they're intelligible.

4a ◁) 7.8 Ss listen to the sentences, to identify how *a, an* and *the* are pronounced. Check answers with the whole class.

Answer: The same – a weak form: /ə/

b Play the recording again for Ss to repeat the sentences. Drill chorally and individually for further practice if necessary.

5 Ss complete the text alone, then check in pairs. Check answers with the whole class. Ask Ss if they would like a room like this (or if they already have one).

> **Answers:** 1 a 2 – 3 a 4 the 5 a 6 The 7 a 8 the
> 9 – 10 a 11 – 12 The

6 Read the example with the class, building on it if necessary, until the Ss guess which photo it is. Ss take it in turns to describe rooms for their partners to guess. When they have finished, ask one or two Ss to describe a room for the class to guess.

Optional alternative activity

With **weaker classes**, ask Ss to choose a room and write 3–4 sentences about it first. Monitor and make sure Ss are using the grammar and prepositions correctly. When they are ready, put Ss in pairs to read their descriptions for other Ss to guess the room.

Further practice

Photocopiable activities: 7C Grammar 1, p201; 7C Grammar 2, p202

Speaking

Prepare

7 🔊 7.9 Go through the bullet points with the class. Ss listen and put them in the correct order, then check in pairs. Check answers with the whole class.

> **Answers:** 1 how much furniture there is
> 2 the view from the window 3 where he relaxes
> 4 why he likes this room

Audioscript 7.9

Neil: I'm a writer and my favourite room is actually my office! I wanted to keep the room really simple, so I just have enough furniture in there to help me work well. I mainly work at my big desk, which is in front of a window. It gets a lot of light but I don't have a very good view – my neighbour's wall!
In one corner of the room there's a big plant, and in another corner there are some drawers, where I keep all my important notebooks, full of ideas. There's a sofa, too, at one end of the room where I sometimes sit to relax, or if I need to think carefully about something. On the back wall there is a long bookshelf with all my favourite books.
I like this room because it's where I have all my best ideas. I never go in there when I'm not working!!

8 Give Ss plenty of time to make notes. Monitor and help with vocabulary, writing any new words/phrases on the board.

Optional extra activity

Before Ss start making notes, do a visualisation activity. Ask Ss to close their eyes, relax and take deep breaths. Tell them to imagine it's the first day of their holiday. They've just woken up naturally, as they don't have to get up for school or work today. They're in their bedroom and they can see the sunlight coming through the curtains. It's summer and its warm and sunny outside. They're lying there relaxing, thinking about all the things they're going to do today. They look around the room and slowly take in everything that's there. Then ask them to open their eyes and make notes on the room as in Ex 7.

Speak

9a Go through the Useful phrases with the class. Ss take turns to describe their favourite room, asking and answering questions to find out more information. Monitor and make notes on their language use, especially use of articles and prepositions.
b Rearrange Ss so that they're working with a different partner and ask them to discuss the questions.

Reflection on learning

Write the following questions on the board:
Which part of this lesson was the most useful? Why?
How will you continue to work on a) prepositions and b) articles?
Put Ss in pairs to discuss the questions. When they have finished, ask if anyone wants to share their ideas with the class, but don't force them to if they'd rather not.

Homework ideas

Ex 9: Ss write a description of their room and add a photo, then add this to their GSE portfolio.
Grammar bank: 7C Ex 1–2, pp.128–129
Workbook: Ex 1–4, p42
App: grammar and vocabulary practice

Fast route: continue to Lesson 7D
Extended route: go to p106 for Develop your writing

7D English in action

Introduction

The goal of this lesson is for Ss to practice making and responding to excuses in different situations. To help them achieve this, they will learn a range of phrases for making excuses and responding to excuses.

Warm-up

Before class, write on the board:
You're late for class.
You can't come to work today.
You've lost a friend's book.
You broke a glass at a friend's house.
Put Ss in pairs to discuss what they'd do and say in each situation, and if any of the situations have ever happened to them. In feedback, nominate different Ss to share their ideas with the class.

Listening

1a Give Ss a minute or two to look at the cartoon and guess what is happening. When they are ready, nominate Ss to share their ideas with the class.

7.10 Ss listen and check their ideas. Check the answer with the whole class and check the meaning of *excuse*. Point out that excuses can be real or invented, and ask Ss if they think this was a good excuse or not and why.

Answers: The man feels ill so goes to the doctor. The doctor tells him that he needs more vitamin D, so the next day the man calls his manager and tells him he can't come to work because he needs more vitamin D, so is spending the day at the beach.

Audioscript 7.10

Manager: Hello, Olivia Bowen speaking.
Man: Oh hi Olivia. It's Stuart.
Manager: Hi, Stuart, is everything OK?
Man: Well, you know I wasn't feeling well yesterday?
Manager: Yes. How are you feeling today?
Man: A bit better. I went to the doctor's after work and he told me I don't have enough vitamin D. You know, the vitamin we get from sunshine.
Manager: Oh dear, I see, that's not good.
Man: Yeah ... so, I've made a decision ...
Manager: What's that?
Man: I'm not coming in to work today. I'm taking the day off and going to the beach. In fact, I'm at the beach right now!
Manager: Oh! Right ...

2a **7.11** Ss listen and note down the reasons and excuses, then check in pairs. Play the recording again if necessary, then check answers with the whole class.

Answers:
Conversation 1: The student is late to class because of a bus which didn't come.
Conversation 2: Aiden can't go out because he has no clean clothes.
Conversation 3: Frannie can't go for coffee because of a dentist's appointment.
Conversation 4: Toni threw out a shirt she borrowed by mistake.

b Go through the sentences with the class and elicit Ss' ideas, and if they can remember anything from the listening, but don't give any answers yet. Ss listen again and complete the conversations, then check in pairs. Check answers with the whole class.

Answers: 1 sorry, OK 2 can't, problem 3 so, worry 4 afraid, never mind

Audioscript 7.11

1
Professor: Good morning, Mr Young. Or should I say good afternoon?
Student: I'm really sorry I'm late, Professor. I waited for the bus for half an hour, but it still didn't come. Unfortunately, I didn't have enough money for a taxi, so I walked.
Professor: That's OK, but your bus is late every week, Mr Young. Perhaps you need to buy a bike ...

2
Aiden: Hi Tom.
Tom: Hi Aiden. What's up?
Aiden: I'm really sorry Tom, but I can't come out tonight.
Tom: Oh, OK, no problem. What's the matter?
Aiden: Well, you know my mum's away at the moment.
Tom: Yeah.
Aiden: Well, she's not here to wash my clothes, so everything's dirty and I've got nothing to wear. I'll have to stay in.
Tom: I'll explain to the others. See you when your mum's back then!
Aiden: Yeah, will do. See ya.

3
Stephanie: Hey Frannie, do you fancy getting a coffee? There's a place around the corner that makes a great cappuccino and really nice cakes, too.
Frannie: Oh no, sorry, I have a dentist's appointment, so I can't today.
Stephanie: Don't worry about it. Maybe another day?
Frannie: Yeah, absolutely.

4
Toni: Carrie, you know that shirt I borrowed from you?
Carrie: Yeah, what about it?
Toni: Well, I'm afraid I lost it. I washed it but now I can't find it anywhere. I'm so sorry!
Carrie: Oh well, never mind. It's just a shirt.

3 **7.12** Ss work in pairs and listen and answer the question. Check answers with the whole class.

Answers: The speakers who respond in conversations 1 and 3 sound unhappy. The speakers who respond in conversations 2 and 4 sound happy. We know this because of the tone of their voice.

Audioscript 7.12

1
A: I'm sorry I'm late. I didn't hear my alarm clock.
B: Never mind, you're here now.

2
A: I'm really sorry. I've lost your book. I put it on the seat of the train and I forgot to pick it up again.
B: It doesn't matter. I've already read it.

3
A: I'm really sorry I didn't call you last night. I completely forgot!
B: Don't worry. It wasn't important.

4
A: I'm afraid I've lost the report. My computer crashed and it just disappeared.
B: That's OK. These things happen.

4a Ss match the excuses and responses alone, then check in pairs. Check answers with the whole class.

Answers: 1 d 2 c 3 b 4 a

b Ss work in pairs and practise the excuses and responses. Ask one of the Ss to cover the responses in their book and try to remember them when responding. When they have finished, Ss swap roles and repeat. In feedback, ask different Ss to practise the excuses and responses in open pairs.

Optional extra activity

After Ex 4, rearrange Ss to work in different pairs. Ss take it in turns to secretly choose a situation and say what they'd say. The other student listens and says which situation they're responding to.

Speaking

Prepare

5 Split the class into two groups: A and B and refer Ss to page 153 for their instructions. Within in each group, Ss work in pairs to think of excuses in each situation, but make sure both Ss write any notes they make, as they'll need them when they work with someone else afterwards. Monitor and help with ideas and vocabulary, writing any new words/phrases on the board.

Speak

6 Read the example with the class, and/or read with a **stronger student** to model the conversation. Go through the Useful phrases with the class, drilling the phrases chorally and individually. Rearrange Ss in pairs, with one member from each of the groups in Ex 5. Ss take it in turns making and responding to excuses. Monitor and make notes on Ss' use of language for later feedback. When they have finished, ask different Ss to make excuses and respond in open pairs. Give Ss feedback on their language use as a class, using the notes you made while they were speaking.

> **Reflection on learning**
>
> Write the following questions on the board:
> *How confident do you feel making an excuse in English?*
> *In what situations do you think you'll use these phrases outside class?*
> Put Ss in pairs to discuss the questions. When they have finished, ask if anyone wants to share their ideas with the class, but don't force them to if they'd rather not.

Homework ideas

Reflection on learning: Write your answers.
Workbook: Ex 1–4, p43
App: grammar and vocabulary practice

7 ▶ Check and reflect

Introduction

Ss revise and practise the language of Unit 7. The notes below provide some ideas for exploiting the activities in class, but you may want to set exercises for homework, or use them as a diagnostic or progress test. For each grammar or vocabulary point, the first activity reviews the language and the second is more communicative, involving pairwork.

1a Elicit the first answer as an example. Ss make sentences alone, then check in pairs. Check answers with the whole class.

> **Answers:**
> 1 There are too many coffee shops in this area.
> 2 This street is too crowded at the weekend.
> 3 My street isn't wide enough for big cars.
> 4 Theatre tickets here cost too much for most people.
> 5 There isn't enough nightlife around here.
> 6 There are enough car parking spaces for everyone.

b Ss write their sentences alone. Monitor and help with ideas and vocabulary where necessary.

c Ss work in pairs and share their ideas, and ask and answer questions. In feedback, ask a few Ss to compare their replies with the class.

2a Ss complete the text alone, then check in pairs. Check answers with the whole class.

> **Answers:** 1 area 2 location 3 local 4 public transport 5 traffic 6 cycle paths 7 night life

b Give Ss a minute or two to read the text again and make notes on similarities and differences. When they are ready, Ss share their ideas in pairs. Encourage them to give reasons.

3a Elicit the first answer as an example. Remind Ss of the different spelling of *use to* for negatives and questions. Ss complete the sentences alone, then check in pairs. Check answers with the class.

> **Answers:** 1 used to play 2 didn't use to talk 3 use to watch 4 didn't use to eat 5 use to take 6 didn't use to be

b Ss write their sentences alone. Monitor and help with ideas and vocabulary where necessary.

c Ss work in pairs and share their ideas and ask and answer questions. In feedback, ask a few Ss to share any interesting information they found out with the class.

4a Ss complete the sentences alone, then check in pairs. Check answers with the whole class.

> **Answers:** 1 hill 2 wood 3 stream 4 river 5 beach 6 forest

b Give Ss a few minutes to think about their answers and make notes if they want. Ss share their experiences in pairs. When they have finished, ask a few Ss to share their experiences with the class and ask if anyone else chose the same place(s).

5a Ss choose the correct alternatives alone, then check in pairs. Check answers with the whole class.

> **Answers:** 1 of 2 in front of 3 the 4 on 5 in front of 6 between

b Ss work in pairs and describe the room. In feedback, elicit a few descriptions from the class.

6 Ss complete the text alone, then check in pairs. Check answers with the whole class.

> **Answers:** 1 a 2 a 3 the 4 – 5 a 6 a 7 an 8 the

Reflect

Ask Ss to rate each statement alone, then compare in pairs. Encourage them to ask any questions they still have about any of the areas covered in Unit 7.

7A Develop your listening

Introduction

Ss develop their listening skill of understanding a discussion between two people by learning phrases for agreeing and disagreeing.

Warm-up

Explain to Ss that the school has commissioned an artist to create a work of art (painting, sculpture, etc.) to install in the school reception. Ss work in pairs to decide what it will be. It should reflect what happens at the school overall. When they are ready, pairs take it in turns to present their ideas to the class and vote for the best one.

1 Focus attention on the photos and give Ss a minute to read the dictionary definition. Elicit an example of a landmark in the local area to check understanding. Ss work in pairs and discuss the question. In feedback, elicit their ideas.

Culture notes

The Obelisco de Buenos Aires in Argentina stands in the Plaza de la República in Buenos Aires. It was built in 1936 to commemorate 400 years since the birth of the city.

Mount Fuji is Japan's highest mountain. It's actually a volcano, but it hasn't erupted for 300 years. On a clear day you can see Mount Fuji 60 km away in Tokyo.

The Didcot Power station is a large power station in the south of England that can be seen from nearby motorways.

The Palace of Culture and Sport in Warsaw, Poland, was built in 1955 and is now a centre for business and cultural events such as concerts.

2 ◁ 7.3 Ss listen to the conversations and match them to the photos alone, then check in pairs. Check answers with the whole class.

Answers: 1 d 2 c 3 b 4 a

3 Give Ss a few minutes to read the Focus box or go through it together as a class. Answer the question as a class.

Suggested answers:
Disagree: No way; Absolutely not; Not necessarily

4a *Stronger Ss* can complete the conversations from memory, then listen again and check. Otherwise, play the conversations again for Ss to complete, then check in pairs. Check answers with the whole class.

Answers: 1 agree 2 right 3 true 4 right 5 sure
6 neither 7 afraid

Audioscript 7.3

1
Man 1: And you can just see our tallest landmark over the top of the buildings there.
Man 2: Oh yeah, I've seen it before in pictures. It is really tall, isn't it? It's a nice design. Simple, but attractive.
Man 1: I agree. It's in the middle of the main square. Football fans go there to celebrate their wins.
Man 2: Oh, that's great. Every city needs an area like that, so that people can get together.
Man 1: You're right. And with a tall landmark like that in the middle, no-one will get lost trying to find it!

2
Man: Look over there.
Woman: Oh, wow, a volcano.
Man: Yes. It's beautiful, isn't it?
Woman Yeah, it really is.
Man: It looks perfect, doesn't it? Like a painting.
Woman: That's true – it must be popular with tourists.
Man: That's right. It's the country's biggest and most famous landmark. It's very special.
Woman: I can see why.

3
Woman 1: Oh, look there's the power station. Not long now.
Woman 2: Ugh, it's so ugly. It really makes the area look terrible.
Woman 1: Yeah, but I love it.
Woman 2: Do you? Why?
Woman 1: Well, it means we're nearly home. It makes me happy whenever I see it.
Woman 2: Really? Hmm. I'm not sure I feel the same.

4
Man: When I first moved here, I didn't like it at all.
Woman: Me neither. It's too big for the area.
Man: Yes and it's right next to the old part of the city with its small, pretty buildings.
Woman: I agree. The styles are very different.
Man: But I've been here for five years and I actually really like it now. It's a landmark that everyone knows. I know I'm in Warsaw when I see it.
Woman: That's true, but I'm afraid I don't feel the same. It's just not the kind of thing I like.

b Ss listen again and answer the question. If you feel they can answer the question without listening a third time, then ask them to answer the question in pairs. Check answers with the whole class.

Answers: 1 agree 2 agree 3 disagree 4 agree

5a ◁ 7.4 Ss listen and answer the questions alone, then check in pairs. Check answers with the whole class.

Answers:
1 In the city centre 2 around a hundred
3 To attract people to the city centre and raise money for charity.

b Give Ss a minute or two to read the sentences and alternatives, so they know what to listen for. Ss listen again and choose the correct alternatives alone, then check in pairs. Check answers with the whole class.

Answers: 1 b 2 a 3 a 4 b

c Ss listen again and answers the question. If you feel they can answer the questions without listening a third time, then ask them to answer the questions in pairs. Check answers with the whole class.

Answers: 1 disagree 2 agree 3 disagree 4 agree

Audioscript 7.4

Katy: Have you seen the cows?

Matt: No, what cows?

Katy: The painted ones outside the Palace of Culture and Science. Look, I took a photo.

Matt: Oh right. I've read about those. They've been in cities all around the world. They stand next to famous landmarks. I didn't know they were here. That's great!

Katy: Is it? There are about a hundred of them. Why are they here?

Matt: They tell a story.

Katy: What story? There's no reason for them to be here. There aren't any farms here!

Matt: Ha. You're right, but they're still interesting.

Katy: Are they?

Matt: I read that the artists put them in the centre to make people go out of their houses and talk about them. I think it's a good reason to have them.

Katy: That's true, it's good for people to go out. People stay at home too much these days. And there were a lot of people looking at them.

Matt: So it works.

Katy: You can't really call them 'art' though, can you?

Mat: I disagree. Art should get people thinking and talking. We're talking about it now.

Katy: I know but I could paint those cows. And I'm not an artist, so how is it art?

Matt: Hmm, I'm not sure you could paint them. I think it's more difficult than it looks.

Katy: Yeah, you're probably right.

Matt: But, you know, it's not just famous artists that paint them. Local artists paint them, too. I think that anything that gets people interested in art is good.

Katy: Yes, you're right.

Matt: They also collect money for charity, so that's a good thing.

Katy: Oh, I didn't know that. OK, so that's a good thing. Maybe they're OK. And they won't be here for very long, so I won't have to look at them forever!

6 Ss work in pairs and discuss the questions. In feedback, elicit Ss' ideas and have a brief class discussion.

Homework ideas

Workbook: Ex 1–3, p43

7B Develop your reading

Introduction

Ss develop their reading skill of understanding an article on social media by learning how to read for general understanding.

Warm-up

Bring/Download some titles of 'listicles' (short articles online which give a list of things, e.g. *Ten things to do for free in London. Five things you didn't know about oranges*, etc.) and show them to the class. Write on the board:

How often do you read articles like this online? What kinds of topics are they usually about? Would you like to read any of these articles? Why (not)?

Ss work in pairs and discuss the questions, then have a brief class discussion.

1 Ss work in pairs and discuss the questions. In feedback, elicit Ss' ideas and have a brief class discussion.

2 Give Ss a few minutes to read the Focus box or read it together with the class. Answer the question as a class.

Answer: key words

3 Set a strict time limit of one minute for this or do it as a race to ensure Ss only read the article quickly. Check answers with the whole class.

Answers: 1 d 2 a 3 c 4 b

4 Ss read the article again and answer the questions alone, then check in pairs. Check answers with the whole class.

Answers:
1 It was the only way to travel anywhere.
2 because of the noise
3 It wasn't easy to meet other people.
4 There are fewer buses and trains.

5 Encourage Ss to use key words while they do this. Set a strict time limit again or do this as a race. Ss match the headings alone, then check in pairs. Check answers with the whole class.

Answers: 1 b 2 d 3 a 4 e 5 c

6 Ss work in groups and discuss the questions. In feedback, ask a few Ss to share their ideas with the class and have a brief class discussion.

Homework ideas

Workbook: Ex 1–4, p44

7C Develop your writing

Introduction

Ss develop their writing skill of writing an informal email by learning how to use informal phrases.

Warm-up

Write on the board: *How do you usually let people know your news? Phone? Email? Other? When was the last time you shared some important news with people? What was it?* Ss work in pairs and discuss the questions. In feedback, elicit Ss' ideas.

1 Focus attention on the photo. Ss work in pairs and discuss the questions. When they have finished, elicit a few Ss' answers and find out if other Ss agree.

2a Go through the questions first, so Ss know what to read for. Ss read the email and answer the questions alone, then check in pairs. Check answers with the whole class.

Answers:
1 It has a jacuzzi with an amazing view, a huge fridge and a swimming pool.
2 Going for walks, taking photos, visiting local shops and markets. Getting to know the area, spending time at the pool.
3 He wants her to tell everyone that he and Jessie miss them.

Elicit the first answer as an example and write it on the board. Ss order the phrases alone, then check in pairs. Don't give any answers yet.

Ss check their answers with the email. In feedback, ask Ss to come to the board to write the phrases and check answers with the whole class.

Answers:
1 How's everything with you?
2 How was your trip to Lille last month?
3 All's well here in Hong Kong.
4 Anyway, you're welcome here at any time.
5 Let me know what's happening back home.
6 Tell everyone we miss them.

Give Ss a minute or two to read the Focus box or read it together as a class. Ss add the phrases to the box alone, then check in pairs. Check answers with the whole class.

Answers:
Saying how you are: **3**
Responding to an email/Asking how someone is: **1**
Responding to news/Asking about news: **2**, **5**
Ending an email: **4**, **6**

Ss complete the reply alone, then check in pairs. Check answers with the whole class.

Answers:
1 Great to hear from you./Lovely to get your email.
2 It sounds fantastic.
3 Everything's fine here./I'm fine.
4 Take care./Bye for now.

Prepare

Explain that Ss need to imagine what their dream home looks like for this activity. Ss then answer the questions. Encourage them to make notes and help with vocabulary, writing any new words/phrases on the board.

Write

Ss write their emails alone. Monitor and check Ss' work while they write, and be on hand to offer help where necessary.

Homework ideas

Workbook: Ex 1–5, p45

8 OVERVIEW

8A Special photos

Introduction

The goal of this lesson is for Ss to describe a photo that is special to them. To help them achieve this, they will learn/revise the past continuous and verbs of movement.

Warm-up

Write on the board the following questions:
Do you ever take 'selfies'? Why (not)?
When was the last selfie you took?
Did you post it on social media?
Ss discuss in small groups, then have a brief class discussion. If they want to, you could then take a class selfie!

Listening

Past continuous

1 Ss work in pairs and answer the questions. When they have finished, elicit Ss' answers and have a brief class discussion.

Optional extra activity

If Ss are comfortable doing so, you could ask them to choose a few recent photos they took on their phones or mobile devices, and show and describe them to their partner.

2a Focus attention on the photos and elicit what Ss can see in them. Ask Ss to say who they think the people are and what they think happened before the photo was taken. Ss discuss the question in pairs. When they have finished, ask a few Ss to share their ideas with the class, but don't give any answers yet.

b 🔊 **8.1** Go through the questions with the class so that Ss know what to listen for. Ss listen and answer the questions alone, then check in pairs. Check answers with the whole class.

Answers:
1 photo D: It shows a really happy family moment.
2 photo B: He met his old school friend 5,000 miles from home.
3 photo A: Her boyfriend asked her to marry him.
4 photo C: It reminds him of feeling free.

c Ss listen again and match sentences a–h with speakers 1–4. Check answers with the whole class.

Answers: a 4 b 2 c 4 d 1 e 3 f 2 g 1 h 3

Optional alternative activity

Stronger classes can do the exercise first from memory, then listen again to check their answers.

Audioscript 8.1

1
A: I took this photo while we were camping near some woods. It shows a really happy family moment, that's why I like it.
B: It's lovely. Where were you?
A: We were on holiday in Scotland, about five years ago I think.
B: Right.
A: The children were running around playing one afternoon when Sam fell over and hurt herself. She was crying, so I told some funny stories to make her feel better. Everyone was laughing – I'm quite good at telling stories! Sam then decided that we should take a photo. I asked someone who was walking nearby to take it.

: It's lovely. I can see why you like it.

: Yeah, it was such a fun holiday.

: I took this photo a couple of years ago when I was working in Argentina. It's a great story actually.

: What happened?

: Well, I was taking a walk one morning when I went into a busy café. Then I heard someone talking in a loud British accent. So I turned around to see who it was and there was Catherine, a friend of mine from school. The last time I saw her was ten years ago and there she was, five thousand miles away from home!

: No way!

: Yeah, I couldn't believe it! Anyway, we took this photo to put on Instagram to surprise our old school friends.

: Nice.

: Yeah, we see each other quite a lot now. She's a really good friend. Life can be strange sometimes.

: It sure can!

: This is me and my husband on holiday in Thailand last year – we were staying in a small house by the sea.

: Lucky you!

: One afternoon, I was feeling really tired, so I had a sleep. When I got up, Rick told me it was time for dinner. So I got ready and went out. When I opened the door, he was sitting at a table on the beach.

: It looks like it was a really special evening.

: Yes, it was, actually – he asked me to marry him! The lights were really pretty and the food was great. We listened to the sound of the sea while we were eating. It was a lovely evening.

: Wow! Amazing! Were there other people there?

: Just the waiter, but after he brought the food, he only came back to check if we were OK. He also took this photo – I love it!

: My friend Al took this photo while I was sleeping in a train station in Hungary.

: What were you doing in Hungary?

: It was when we were travelling around Europe, the summer before starting university. We were trying to get to Bucharest, but we missed the last train.

: So, you slept at the train station.

: Yeah. I can still remember how tired I was that day. When I lay down on the floor I just went to sleep!

: How was it?

: It wasn't too bad actually. It was a warm evening and I slept for a few hours. I think this photo says a lot about those days. Things like that made us feel really free.

Grammar

Start by eliciting how much Ss know about the past continuous by asking what the difference is between the two types of past actions in each sentence in Ex 2c (one is an action in progress in the past and one is a complete event). Demonstrate the meaning by drawing a timeline on the board showing the two actions in sentence 1 like this:

PAST ————×———~~~~~~~~→ NOW
   Al took this photo   I was sleeping

Ss choose the correct alternatives to complete the Grammar box alone, then check in pairs. Check answers with the class. Delete the labels on the timeline and go through each of the sentences in Ex 2c, pointing to the two actions indicated on the timeline and eliciting which action in each sentence is indicated. Be prepared to offer further explanations/examples where necessary.

Answers: 1 in progress 2 past simple 3 when

GRAMMAR BANK 8A pp.130–131

Stronger classes could read the notes at home. otherwise, check the notes with Ss, especially the use of *when* and *while*. In each exercise, elicit the first answer as an example. Ss complete the exercises alone, then check their answers in pairs. Then check answers with the whole class. Ss can refer to the notes to help them.

Answers: 8A

1 1 were swimming/took   2 was arguing/got
   3 lost/was cycling   4 fell/was leaving
   5 started snowing/were leaving   6 was taking/flew

2 1 I was making lunch when I cut my finger.
   2 Greg fell off his bike while he was cycling to college.
   3 I found a letter while I was reading an old book.
   4 When we were sitting on the beach, we saw an unusual bird.
   5 Fran was practising the piano when I got home.
   6 She told them the news while they were having dinner.
   7 Dan was wearing a really strange coat when I saw him.
   8 Annie fell over while she was running for the ball.

4a ◁ **8.2** Ss listen and answer the question alone, then check in pairs.

Answers: They're unstressed and are pronounced in their weak forms /wəz/ (was) and /wə/ (were).

b Ss listen again and repeat. Drill chorally and individually for further practice if necessary.

5a Read the example with the class. Ss make sentences alone, then check in pairs. Monitor and check they're forming the past simple and past continuous correctly. In feedback, nominate a different student to come to the board and write each sentence. Check spelling of the *-ing* forms.

Answers:

1 or: While I was driving to work yesterday, I had an accident.
2 We saw a snake while we were running this morning. / While we were running this morning, we saw a snake.
3 When I got up this morning it was snowing. / It was snowing when I got up this morning.
4 It started to rain while we were having our picnic. / While we were having our picnic, it started to rain.
5 When I got home, my children were cleaning the house. / My children were cleaning the house when I got home.
6 Dan hurt his back while he was playing with the children. / While he was playing with his children, Dan hurt his back.
7 Leon broke his leg when he was skiing. / When he was skiing, Leon broke his leg.
8 While I was tidying my room, I found 50 euros! / I found 50 euros while I was tidying my room!

b Read the example with the class and give a couple of examples of sentences which are true for you. Ss write their sentences alone. Monitor the class and help with vocabulary where necessary, writing any new words/phrases on the board.

Vocabulary checkpoint

Once here shows that we're not being specific about when it happened, rather than emphasising that it only happened once. It comes just before the past simple verb, e.g. *I once saw a lion when I was travelling in Africa.*

c Read the example with the class. Ss share their sentences from Ex 5b, giving more information where possible. When they have finished, nominate a few Ss to share any interesting information they found out from their partners with the class.

In Ex 5b, ask Ss to write two true sentences and one false. When Ss share their sentences in Ex 5c, encourage them to ask lots of follow-up questions to find out more information, then guess which one is false.

Photocopiable activities: 8A Grammar 1, p204;
8A Grammar 2, p205

Vocabulary

Verbs of movement

6 Ss match the sentence halves alone, then check in pairs. Check Ss understand the meaning of the phrases in bold.

Answers: 1 f 2 e 3 d 4 g 5 h 6 c 7 a 8 b

Ss work in pairs and take it in turns to mime the actions in Ex 6a for their partner to guess the verb.

7a Ss choose the correct alternatives alone, then check in pairs. Check answers with the whole class.

Answers: 1 got up 2 fell over 3 turned round 4 lay down
5 around 6 went into 7 went out, came back

b Read the examples with the class. Give Ss a few minutes to look at the verbs and think about their experiences. Put Ss in pairs to share their experiences. Encourage them to ask follow-up questions to find out more information. In feedback, ask Ss if anyone wants to share their experiences with the class, but don't force them to if they're not comfortable doing so.

Photocopiable activities: 8A Vocabulary, p206

Speaking

Prepare

8a If Ss have phones or mobile devices with them and they want to, you could ask Ss to use a photo they have on it, and look at it while they prepare what they're going to say. Give Ss plenty of time to prepare and make notes, using the questions as prompts.

b Give Ss a few minutes to prepare how they're going to describe the photo. Monitor the class and help with vocabulary, writing any new words/phrases on the board.

Speak

9 Go through the Useful phrases and the example with the class. Arrange Ss in small groups to describe their photos. Encourage them to ask follow-up questions to find out more information, e.g. *How did you feel? Who were you with? What were you doing there?*, etc. While they're speaking, monitor and make notes on Ss' language use (especially the use of the past continuous) for later feedback. When they have finished, nominate a student from each group to share any interesting information with the class. Give students feedback on their use of language as a class.

Write the following questions on the board:
What were the three most useful phrases you learnt this lesson?
How confident do you feel giving a description?
What could you do to improve?
Put Ss in pairs to discuss the questions. When they have finished, ask if anyone wants to share their ideas with the class, but don't force them to if they'd rather not.

Ex 7: Ss write a description of their photo for a social media post.
Grammar bank: 8A Ex 1–2, pp.130–131
Workbook: Ex 1–5, p46
App: grammar and vocabulary practice

Fast route: continue to Lesson 8B
Extended route: go to p107 for Develop your reading

8B Getting around

Introduction

The goal of this lesson is for Ss to describe a journey. To help them achieve this, they will learn/revise the conjunctions *because*, *so* and *to* and vocabulary related to transport.

Warm-up

Put Ss in small groups and give them a few minutes to brainstorm and write down as many types of transport as they can think of. After a few minutes make sure they stop. Give a board pen to someone in each group and ask them to come to the board, but make sure they don't take any notes with them. Members of their group shout out the forms of transport to their group member at the board who writes them on the board. When they have finished, delete any types of transport which have been written by more than one group and award points for each type of transport left to the group that wrote it. The group with the most points wins.

Reading and vocabulary

Transport

1 Focus attention on the photos and elicit what Ss can see. Check answers with the whole class.

Answers: 2 Cable car, bike, train, ferry, tram
Possible answers: car, taxi, minibus, coach, bus, plane, helicopter, boat, monorail, underground/metro, truck/lorry.

2a You may want to elicit/check *memorable*, i.e. something you remember well. Ss read the article and match the journeys to the photos. Explain that they'll have another chance to read the text more carefully, so don't worry if they don't understand every word. Check answers with the class.

Answers: 1 D 2 A 3 B 4 E 5 C

b Explain the difference between *travel for your job*, i.e. take a short trip as part of your work and *work abroad*, i.e. live and have a job in another country. Ss read the article again and answer the questions alone, then check in pairs. Check answers with the whole class.

Answers: 1 Nikki, Holly, Wiktor 2 Dave 3 Nikki, Mo 4 Mo 5 Nikki 6 Holly

c Read the example with the class. Ss complete the phrases alone, then check in pairs. Check answers with the class, and drill the complete phrases chorally and individually.

Answers: 1 park 2 get in, get out of 3 get on, get off 4 rent 5 miss 6 take

VOCABULARY BANK 8B p143

Travel and transport

This can be done before or after the vocabulary work in the main lesson, or for homework with Ex 2 done in the following class.

1a Ss label the pictures alone, then check in pairs. Check answers with the whole class and drill the words/phrases.

Answers: 1 B 2 D 3 J 4 A 5 I 6 F 7 L 8 K 9 E 10 G 11 C 12 H

2 Ss match the sentence halves alone, then check in pairs. In feedback, ask different Ss to start and finish the sentences in open pairs.

Answers: 1 b 2 e 3 a 4 f 5 c 6 d

3 Ss complete the sentences alone, then check in pairs.

Answers: 1 zebra crossing 2 traffic 3 motorway 4 platform 5 timetable 6 passenger

Vocabulary checkpoint

Point out that *petrol* and *petrol station* are British English and *gas* and *gas station* are US English.

d Give Ss a few minutes to think of their answers, then put them in pairs to discuss the questions. Monitor and make sure they're using the verb phrases in Ex 2c correctly. In feedback, nominate a few Ss to share their ideas with the class and compare their experiences with others.

Further practice

Photocopiable activities: 8B Vocabulary, p209

Grammar

because, so and *to*

3a 🔊 8.3 Ss listen and answer the question alone, then check in pairs. Check answers with the class.

Possible answers: Mac caught a big fish, the car broke down, they slept in the car, they rode Harley Davidsons.

> **Culture notes**
> *Harley Davidson* is a luxury motorbike manufacturer, based in the US.

b Go through the sentences with the class and ask Ss to guess the alternatives, but don't give any answers yet. Play the recording again for Ss to check their answers. Check answers with the whole class.

Answers: 1 go fishing 2 they didn't want to walk anywhere 3 went for a walk

Audioscript 8.3

Mac: I've been on a few memorable trips in my life, I'm lucky, but there's one that I remember really well.

Emma: Oh right, what was that?

Mac: I was about 14 and my dad took me to the Blue Ridge Mountains in Virginia. We got in the car early one morning and off we went. That day, when we stopped for lunch, we also walked down to a river to go fishing.

Emma: Did you catch anything?

Mac: Yes, we did actually. It was my first time and I caught a really big fish. My dad couldn't believe it!

Emma: Haha, brilliant!

Mac: Yeah ... but later, when we got back in the car, it didn't start. He tried and tried but nothing. We looked around but there was no-one to help us.

Emma: Oh dear, what did you do?

Mac: Well, we didn't want to walk anywhere because it was getting dark, so we slept in the car until morning.

Emma: Oh no. Were you cold?

Mac: No, it was summer, so it was OK. I got a few hours of sleep, but it wasn't very comfortable. So, I went for a short walk as soon as I woke up.

Emma: Good idea ...

Mac: While I was out walking, two people on motorbikes stopped and asked me if I was OK, so I explained the situation. They offered to help us and gave us a lift on the back of their bikes to the nearest town.

Emma: That was kind of them.

Mac: Yeah, it was. They got us there really quickly because they knew the area well. But do you know the best thing?

Emma: No, what?

Mac: The bikes were big Harley Davidsons! You don't forget getting on a big bike like that when you're just 14.

4 Ss choose the correct alternative alone, then check in pairs. Encourage them to use the examples to help. Check answers with the class and be prepared to give further explanations/examples where necessary. You could check understanding by reading out these sentence starters and asking Ss to finish them:
I went to the library to ... I didn't wear a coat because ... I was lost, so ...

Answers: 1 *to* + infinitive 2 because 3 so

GRAMMAR BANK 8B pp.130–131

Stronger classes could read the notes at home, otherwise, check the notes with Ss, especially the difference between *so* and *so that*. In each exercise, elicit the first answer as an example. Ss complete the exercises alone, then check their answers in pairs. Then check answers with the whole class. Ss can refer to the notes to help them.

Answers: 8B

1 1 so 2 because 3 to 4 so 5 to 6 so 7 Because
  8 so

2 1 I enjoy travelling by train so I do it quite a lot.
  2 My parents are taking an Italian course to have some fun.
  3 We decided not to have a barbecue because it was raining.
  4 Ian wanted to surprise Anne so he planned a weekend away.
  5 Ella took a photo of her new hairstyle to share with her friends.
  6 We went to the cinema because there was a really good film on.
  7 I love the sea so I try and go sailing every few months.
  8 Tony rented a car to pick Helen up from the airport.

5a 🔊 8.4 Read the first sentence to the class and use your finger to indicate the intonation pattern as you say it. Ss listen to the rest of the sentences, paying attention to the pronunciation of *because, so* and *to*.

b Write or show the sentences on the board and trace the intonation patterns over each one. Ss listen again and repeat. While they do this, follow the intonation patterns on the board with your finger. Drill chorally and individually for further practice if necessary.

6a Ss complete the sentences alone, then check in pairs. Check answers with the whole class.

Answers: 1 so 2 because 3 so 4 to 5 because 6 to
7 to 8 so

Optional extra activity

Books closed. Demonstrate the activity by reading out the first half of sentence 1, i.e. *We wanted to go to the beach so …* and elicit any possible response. (Ss don't have to remember the one in the book, they can use their own ideas.) Ss work in pairs, one with their book open and the other with their book closed. One student reads out the sentences and stops after the conjunction to elicit a possible response from their partner. Monitor and help with vocabulary where necessary, writing any new word/phrases on the board. Check that Ss are coming up with logical responses. When they have finished, Ss swap roles and repeat. In feedback, nominate a different pair for each sentence and elicit their responses.

b Read the examples with the class. Give Ss plenty of time to write their sentences. Monitor and help with vocabulary where necessary, writing any new words/phrases on the board.

Optional extra activity

Fast finishers can write two extra sentences.

c Read the examples with the class and demonstrate the activity with a *stronger Ss*, eliciting continued guesses until they guess correctly. Ss read out their sentences for their partner to guess, then swap and repeat when they have finished. When they have finished, ask a few Ss to read out their sentences for the class to guess.

Further practice

Photocopiable activities: 8B Grammar 1, p207; 8B Grammar 2, p208

Speaking

Prepare

7 You could introduce the activity by describing a memorable journey of your own, answering the questions. Give Ss plenty of time to plan what they're going to say. Monitor and help with new vocabulary where necessary, writing any new words/phrases on the board.

Speak

8a Ss work in pairs and share their stories. Encourage them to ask follow-up questions to find out more information and make sure they make notes on their partner's journey, as they'll need these to describe it to someone else after. While they're speaking, monitor and make notes on Ss' language use for later feedback.

b Ss work in different pairs from those in Ex 8a. Ss take it in turns to describe their partner's journey. Their partner can help them with details if they get stuck, but they should try to remember and explain as much of it as they can on their own. When they have finished, nominate a student from each group to share any interesting information with the class and find out if anyone's had the same journey. Give students feedback on their use of language as a class.

Reflection on learning

Write the following questions on the board:
How confident do you feel using because, so and to + infinitive?
What can you do to improve?
Put Ss in pairs to discuss the questions. When they have finished, ask if anyone wants to share their ideas with the class, but don't force them to if they'd rather not.

Homework ideas

Ex 8: Ss write a description of their memorable journey.
Grammar bank: 8B Ex 1–2, pp.130–131
Workbook: Ex 1–5, p47
App: grammar and vocabulary practice

Fast route: continue to Lesson 8C
Extended route: go to p108 for Develop your listening

8c Dream holidays

Introduction

The goal of this lesson is for Ss to plan a special trip and present it to other people. To help them achieve this, they will learn/revise verb patterns and vocabulary related to travel.

Warm-up

Write on the board:

Travel is …

and give a few examples, e.g. *… a way to learn about the world. … the most important thing in my life.* Give Ss about a few minutes to complete the sentence in a way that is true for them. Monitor and help with vocabulary where necessary, writing any new words/phrases on the board. When they are ready, ask Ss to stand up and walk around, sharing their sentences. In feedback, ask a few Ss to share their favourite sentences with the class.

Vocabulary

Travel

1 In pairs, Ss read the quotes and discuss the questions. In feedback, elicit Ss' answers and have a brief class discussion.

Optional alternative activity

If Ss are having trouble thinking of ideas for question 2, write the following topics on the board:

food
accommodation
who you travel with
activities

and ask Ss to discuss their preferences around each topic.

2a Ss complete the phrases alone, then check in pairs. Encourage them to use the quotes in Ex 1 to help. Check answers with the whole class.

Answers: 1 go on 2 pack 3 go 4 try 5 travel 6 plan 7 book

Optional alternative activity

With *stronger classes*, ask them to cover the box and elicit which verbs are missing, but don't give any answers yet. Ss then do the exercise and check their predictions.

b Ss match the phrases and sentences alone, then check in pairs. Check answers with the whole class and elicit the exact phrase in each case.

Answers: a 5 (travel light) b 4 (an organised tour/a cruise) c 7 (book a flight/a hotel) d 3 (go sightseeing) e 6 (plan a trip/holiday) f 1 (try new things) g 2 (pack your bags/suitcase)

c Read the example with the class. Ss work in pairs and discuss. Monitor and check they're using the phrases correctly. When they have finished, ask a few Ss to share any interesting information they found out about their partners.

Further practice

Photocopiable activities: 8C Vocabulary, p212

Listening

3a ◆ 8.7 You may want to elicit/check *campervan* by showing a picture. Ss listen and tick the places Renata and Keith are going then work in pairs and check their answers. Check answers with the whole class.

Answers: Paris, Lisbon, Rio de Janeiro, Buenos Aires

b Give Ss a minute to read through the statements so that they know what to listen for, then play the recording again. Ss work alone, then check in pairs. Check answers with the whole class.

Answers: 1 F 2 F 3 T 4 T 5 F 6 T

Audioscript 8.7

Renata: I can't believe we both hate flying, Keith – it makes planning this trip really difficult. The only place we've decided on is Paris – we're taking the train there on the 19th.

Keith: Yes, it is hard, but I love travelling by land and sea – it's much more exciting. How long are we going to stay in Paris? I'd like to do some sightseeing there.

Renata: Maybe two or three days? That should be enough. Lisa told me that it's easy to get around with the Metro.

Keith: Hmm, I don't mind using the Metro, but we both enjoy walking. If we stay somewhere close to the centre we can walk around.

Renata: OK, sounds good. Right, what next? How about taking the train down to Portugal?

Keith: We could, but look at this. We could rent a campervan in Paris and leave it in Lisbon.

Renata: A campervan? I've never tried that before. Are they comfortable?

Keith: Yeah, they're great. We could drive down to Portugal in one and we wouldn't need to book any hotels. We could stop when and where we want. We could cook our own meals in it. We'd save so much money.

Renata: That sounds like fun. We just need to make sure we arrive in time for the cruise.

Keith: Hmm, right …

Renata: Yes, I know you don't want to do a cruise, but I really think it's the best way. And I'd really like to see a bit of Africa. The cruise stops at a few places on the west coast before crossing the Atlantic.

Keith: I guess so. I just don't want to be on a boat with the same people for such a long time!

Renata: I know, but we'd save a bit of time like this because we stop at each place only for a few hours.

Keith: I guess so. It will make the journey across to South America a bit more comfortable, too. I wouldn't like to be on a normal ship for that long. Did you say the cruise finishes in Colombia? I'd love to see Bogotá.

Renata: No, in Brazil – Rio de Janeiro. I thought we could maybe stay there for a week. There are lots of things to do. You know I enjoy relaxing on the beach and you like hiking in the mountains, so we can do both while we're there.

Keith: Sounds perfect! Then we can get the bus to Buenos Aires.

Renata: Right. It's a long journey, but I don't mind travelling by bus. Then from there we can …

4 ◆ 8.8 The aim of this activity is to provide Ss with examples of the target language before they study it in Ex 5. Ss work in pairs and listen and choose the correct alternative. Check answers with the whole class.

Answers: 1 flying 2 travelling 3 to do 4 using 5 to do 6 to be 7 relaxing 8 hiking

Optional alternative activity

With *stronger classes*, or if you think your Ss already have some knowledge of verb patterns, you could ask them to choose the correct alternative in pairs first, then listen and check.

Grammar

Verb patterns

5 Focus attention on the sentences in Ex 4 and explain that when we have two verbs in a sentence, the form of the second verb often depends on what the first verb in the sentence is. Write sentences 1 and 2 on the board and elicit the two types of verb patterns used (verb + infinitive and verb + -ing). Ss choose the correct alternatives to complete the grammar box alone, then check in pairs. Check answers with the whole class. With **stronger classes** you may want to go through the information in the Grammar checkpoint below, too.

Answers: 1 1, 2, 4, 6, 7, 8   2 3, 5

Grammar checkpoint

With **stronger classes**, you may want to explain the following: with *like*, both forms are often possible, with a subtle difference in meaning. *Like* + -ing expresses our true feelings, e.g. *I don't like getting up early. Like* + infinitive expresses a preference because of a reason, e.g. *On Monday mornings, I like to get up early, so I can plan my work for the week.*

GRAMMAR BANK 8C   pp.130–131

Stronger classes could read the notes at home. Otherwise, check the notes with Ss, especially the types of verbs we use with each pattern. In each exercise, elicit the first answer as an example. Ss work alone to complete the exercises, then check their answers in pairs. Then check answers with the whole class. Ss can refer to the notes to help them.

Answers: 8C
1 1 to take   2 to do   3 travelling   4 meeting   5 to go
  6 going   7 to see   8 flying
2 1 Would you like to visit Antarctica?
  2 Do you like flying?
  3 Why do you hate playing sport?
  4 Do you want to go out this weekend?
  5 Would you like to hike 100 km?
  6 Do you enjoy travelling by bus?
  7 Do you need to get a new passport?
  8 Where did you decide to go on your last holiday?
  9 Did you avoid doing any work at the weekend?
  10 What do you hope to do next weekend?

6a ◁ 8.9 With **weaker classes**, write the first sentence on the board, say it a few times and elicit the stressed words by underlining them on the board. Ss listen and underline the stressed words alone, then check in pairs. Check answers with the whole class.

Answers: 1 I <u>don't mind walking</u>.   2 We'd <u>like</u> to <u>study</u>.
3 She <u>doesn't want</u> to <u>stay</u>.   4 I <u>love cycling</u>.
5 They en<u>joy</u> re<u>lax</u>ing.   6 I <u>hate flying</u>.

b Ss listen again and repeat. Drill chorally and individually for further practice if necessary.

7 Ss complete the conversation alone, then check in pairs. Check answers with the whole class by asking an open pair to read it out.

Answers: 1 to go on   2 to do   3 trying   4 cooking
5 to learn   6 travelling/to stay

8a Introduce the activity by telling the class some of your own answers. Give Ss a few minutes to complete the sentences for themselves. Monitor and help with vocabulary where necessary, writing any new words/phrases on the board.

b Ss work in pairs and share their ideas. In feedback, nominate a few pairs to share some of their sentences and ask if they had any which were the same.

Further practice

Photocopiable activities: 8C Grammar 1, p210; 8C Grammar 2, p211

Speaking

Prepare

9 Give Ss plenty of time to think about their special trip alone and make notes using the questions as prompts. Monitor and help with ideas and vocabulary, writing any new words/phrases on the board.

Speak

10a Read the example with the class. Put Ss in pairs to share their plans and ask questions to find out more information. Monitor and make notes on Ss' use of language (especially verb patterns and the phrases in Ex 7). When they have shared their information, ask them to choose a trip to go on. It could be one of their ideas or a combination of both.

b Ss work in different pairs from those in Ex 10a. Ss take it in turns to describe their partners trip. Encourage them to ask follow-up questions to find out more information. Give students feedback on their use of language as a class.

Reflection on learning

Write the following questions on the board:
What's the most useful thing you learnt this lesson?
How will you use this outside class in the future?
Put Ss in pairs to discuss the questions. When they have finished, ask if anyone wants to share their ideas with the class, but don't force them to if they'd rather not.

Homework ideas

Ex 9: Ss write about their plans for a special trip.
Grammar bank: 8C Ex 1–2, pp.130–131
Workbook: Ex 1–5, p48
App: grammar and vocabulary practice

Fast route: continue to Lesson 8D
Extended route: go to p109 for Develop your writing

8D English in action

Introduction

The goal of this lesson is for Ss to give and follow directions. To help them achieve this, they will learn a range of phrases for giving directions, referring to places and saying where something is.

Supplementary resources

Warm-up: photos of places in a city

Warm-up

Bring/Download some photos of places in a city, e.g. *bank, hospital, supermarket*, etc. Arrange the Ss in teams. Each turn, show a picture to the class quickly. The first team to say the name of the place wins a point. Write the words on the board after each turn. The team with the most points at the end wins.

Listening

1 Introduce the topic by telling the class your own answer to the question. If you have an amusing anecdote about a time you got lost, you could also share this here. Ss work in pairs and discuss the question. When they have finished, ask a few Ss to share their answers with the class and have a brief class discussion.

2 Ss match the phrases and pictures alone, then check in pairs. Check answers with the whole class.

Answers: 1 C 2 B 3 E 4 D 5 A

Vocabulary checkpoint

Use feedback in Ex 2 to elicit/teach any related vocabulary, especially anything relevant to roads in the Ss' countries, e.g. *crossroads, do a U-turn*, etc. Ask Ss if there's anything else related to roads that they'd like to know in English.

3a 8.10 Ss listen to the conversation and answer the question, then check in pairs. Check the answer with the whole class and ask if they think Mike wants to ask someone for directions (no).

Answer: They use satnav, then ask someone for directions.

b Focus attention on the map and find start. Ss listen again and answer the questions. Check answers with the whole class.

Answers: the station, to ask for directions

Audioscript 8.10

Karen: So, you're sure you know how to get to there? Maybe we should ask someone just to be safe?
Mike: No, it's fine. Look, I'll just put the address in my phone … there we are.
Karen: OK …
Satnav: At the roundabout, turn right.
Mike: There we are, turn right …
Satnav: Go straight on. At the traffic lights, go straight on.
Mike: Uh-oh.
Karen: What is it?
Mike: Erm … the road's closed. Hang on, I'll just park in the station for a minute.
Karen: I told you! Look, let me ask that woman over there for directions.
Mike: No, it's fine, I can just …

4a 8.11 Make sure Ss know where they are on the map now. Ss listen and follow the directions, then check the route they take in pairs. Check answers with the whole class.

Answer:

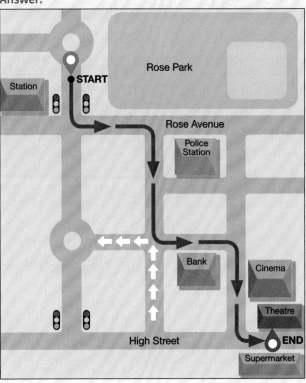

Audioscript 8.11

Karen: Right, that was easier. I said we should just ask someone. It's fine to ask people sometimes you know!
Mike: OK, OK, what did she say?
Karen: OK, so at the traffic lights, turn left into Rose Avenue. Then you'll see a police station on the corner, turn right just before it.
Mike: OK. Wait, let me mark this on the map on my phone.
Karen: If you must …
Mike: Go on then.
Karen: So, turn right at the police station. Then we want to get onto the High Street, but we can't go straight on down there because it's a one-way street.
Mike: OK, got it.
Karen: So, take the second left.
Mike: Yep.
Karen: Then go straight on past the bank and at the end of that street turn right.
Mike: Right … OK.
Karen: Then at the end of that street turn left. Go about 400 metres and it's on the left, opposite the big supermarket.
Mike: Right. Let's go!
Satnav: At the traffic lights, go straight on.
Karen: Oh Mike, turn that thing off!

b 8.12 Ss work in pairs and choose the correct alternative. Encourage them to use the map and point out to each other where each extract shows. When they are ready, play the recording again for Ss to check their answers.

Answers: 1 Turn 2 see 3 Take 4 Go 5 At 6 on, opposite

c Ss listen again and repeat. Drill chorally and individually for further practice if necessary.

When we are listing things, our intonation follows a simple pattern: if there is more information to come, our voice goes up or stays steady. On the last item in the list, our voice goes down and this shows we've finished.

5 Ss follow the directions alone, then check in pairs. Encourage them to draw the route on the map as they read the instructions, using a different colour pen or pencil from the route they drew in Ex 4a. When they have finished, check answers with the whole class.

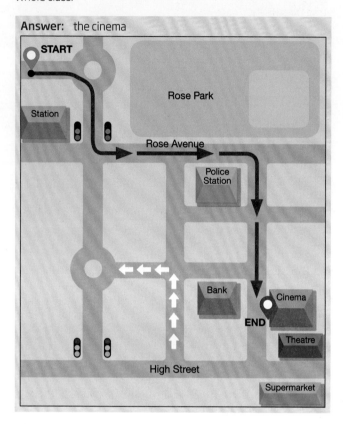

Answer: the cinema

Speaking

Prepare

6 Refer Ss to page 156 for their instructions. Ss work in pairs to think of excuses for each situation. Make sure both Ss write any notes they make, as they'll need them when they work with someone else afterwards. Monitor and help with ideas and vocabulary, writing any new words/phrases on the board.

Speak

7 Ss practise giving directions in pairs. Encourage them to use the map app on their phones if they want to and to use the Useful phrases. Monitor and make notes on Ss' language use for later feedback. When they have finished, give Ss feedback on their language use as a class, using the notes you made earlier.

Reflection on learning

Write the following questions:
How confident do you feel listening to directions in English?
Which phrases will be most useful in the future?
How do you think you'll use them?
Put Ss in pairs to discuss the questions. When they have finished, ask if anyone wants to share their ideas with the class, but don't force them to if they'd rather not.

Workbook: Ex 1–2, p49
App: grammar and vocabulary practice

8 Check and reflect

Introduction

Ss revise and practise the language of Unit 8. The notes below provide some ideas for exploiting the activities in class, but you may want to set exercises for homework, or use them as a diagnostic or progress test. For each grammar or vocabulary point, the first activity reviews the language and the second is more communicative, involving pairwork.

1 Ss correct the sentences alone, then check in pairs. Check answers with the whole class.

Answers: 1 ~~were~~ **was** 2 ~~was going~~ **went**
3 ~~was meeting~~ **met** 4 ~~were stopping~~ **stopped**
5 ~~was turning~~ **turned** 6 ~~while~~ **when**

2 Give Ss a few examples about yourself. Monitor and help Ss with vocabulary while they write their sentences, writing any new words/phrases on the board. When they have finished, put Ss in pairs to share their sentences.

3a Books closed. Write the first item on the board and elicit the answer as an example. Ss reorder the letters alone, then check in pairs. Check answers with the whole class.

Answers: 1 fell over 2 go out 3 lay down 4 get up
5 come back 6 went out

b Ss discuss which sentences are true for them, changing the others while they speak. In feedback, ask a few Ss to share anything interesting they found out about their partner.

4 Ss match the sentence halves alone, then check in pairs. In feedback, ask different Ss to start and finish the sentences in open pairs.

Answers: 1 d 2 c 3 a 4 e 5 b

5 Ss correct the wrong words alone, then check in pairs. Check answers with the whole class.

Answers: 1 ~~in~~ **on** 2 ~~make~~ **take** 3 ~~park~~ **hire** 4 ~~on~~ **in**
5 ~~on~~ **out** 6 ~~lost~~ **missed**

Ss work in pairs and change the sentences in Ex 5 so that they make sense, but without changing the word which is wrong, e.g. 1 *I hate travelling by cable car, so I always get in it slowly.* When they have finished, nominate different pairs to share their ideas with the class.

6 Elicit the first answer as an example. Ss choose the correct alternatives alone, then check in pairs. Check answers with the whole class.

Answers: 1 going 2 pack 3 on 4 booked

7 Elicit the first answer as an example. Ss choose the correct alternatives alone, then check in pairs. Check answers with the whole class.

Answers: 1 to visit 2 driving 3 to come 4 seeing
5 travelling 6 to stay 7 working 8 to leave

8a Go through the prompts with the class. Ask Ss to choose four of them and write a sentence for each.

Optional extra activity

Fast finishers can write two more sentences, or help Ss nearby who haven't finished yet.

b Ss work in pairs and share their sentences. In feedback, nominate a few Ss to share some of their partners' sentences.
9 Ss choose the correct alternatives alone, then check in pairs. Check answers with the whole class.

Answers: 1 journey 2 cruise 3 pack 4 book 5 try
6 light 7 go 8 alone

10a Write on the board: *when, where, who with, how long* and *what happened*. Ss choose two of the activities in the box and make notes about their experiences, using the ideas on the board.
b Ss work in pairs and talk about their experiences. When they have finished, ask a few Ss to share their experiences with the class and find out if anyone else has had similar experiences.

Reflect

Ask Ss to rate each statement alone, then compare in pairs. Encourage them to ask any questions they still have about any of the areas covered in Unit 8.

8 True or false? (Units 7–8 review)

Introduction

Ss revise and practise the language of Units 7 and 8 in a communicative game. This can be done after the Check and reflect page as a fun way to revise the language of Units 7 and 8.

1 Make sure Ss only choose eight of the topics and that they write one true and one false answer for each topic.
2 When they are ready, put Ss in pairs. Ss ask their partner questions and try to guess which answers are true. If they guess correctly they win a point. The person with the most points wins.

8A Develop your reading

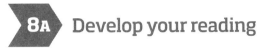

Introduction

Ss develop their reading skill of understanding social media posts by learning how to recognise ellipsis.

Warm-up

This activity revises the verbs of movement from the main lesson. Write these prepositions on the board:
out, up, round, back, into, down, away.
Arrange Ss in small teams. Each turn, call out one of these verbs in random order: *go, get, turn, come, fall, lie.* Each team then writes a sentence containing the verb you say and one of the prepositions on the board, e.g. *come: We had a bad holiday, so we came back early.* The first team to write a correct sentence gets a point. The team with the most points at the end wins.

1 Give Ss a minute or two to read the dictionary definition. Tell the class about a coincidence you've experienced. Ask if anyone's had anything similar happen to them, or if they've experienced other coincidences, and share them with the class.
2 Ss read the social media post and answer the questions alone, then check in pairs. Check answers with the whole class.

Answers: The writer met Steven online and then they found out they lived a few streets away in the same city – Boston. The writer's grandma showed Steven a photo of the writer as a child. Steven saw himself in the background of the photo. They were clearly in the same place at the same time as children.

3 Give Ss a few minutes to read the Focus box, or read it together as a class. Elicit the answer to the question.

Answer: It's clear who or what the writer is talking about and it makes the text easier to read.

4 Elicit the first answer as an example. Ss complete the gaps alone, then check in pairs. Check answers with the whole class.

Answers: 1 we 2 unusual 3 take him 4 we 5 she 6 he

5a Focus attention on the social media posts and elicit the first answer as an example (*they*). Ss complete the gaps alone, then check in pairs. Check answers with the whole class.

Answers: 1 they 2 there 3 I 4 normal
5 have the same birthday 6 I 7 on 8 she

b Ss read the posts in Ex 5a again and answer the questions alone, then check in pairs. Make sure Ss understand that more than one text may answer each question. Check answers with the whole class.

Answers: 1 B, E, H 2 D 3 A, C 4 F, G

Homework ideas

Workbook: Ex 1–4, p50

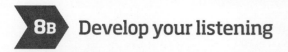

8B Develop your listening

Introduction

Ss develop their listening skill of understanding a short story by learning how to predict events.

Warm-up

Write on the board:

Have you ever helped a tourist or visitor to your town or city?
Why did they need help?
What did you do?

Tell Ss about a time you've done this, answering the questions on the board. Ss work in pairs and discuss the questions on the board. When they have finished, invite a few Ss to share their stories with the class.

1 Focus attention on the photos and elicit what Ss can see. Put Ss in small groups to discuss the questions. In feedback, nominate a student from each group to share their ideas and experiences with the class.

2 ◁ **8.5** Ss listen to the first part of the story and answer the questions alone, then check in pairs. Check answers with the whole class.

Answers:
1 to Malang, a small city about 50 km south of Surabaya
2 his girlfriend
3 by motorbike
4 there was a big storm coming
5 no

3 Give Ss a few minutes to read the focus box, or go through it together as a class. Answer the question as a class.

Answers: by paying attention to the tenses and time expressions.

4 Ss match the sentences 1–5 with a–e. Ss work alone, then check answers in pairs. Check answers with the whole class.

Answers: 1c 2d 3a 4b 5e

Audioscript 8.5

Paul: So this happened when I was living in Surabaya, in Indonesia. I was working out there at the time and one weekend my friends and I decided to visit Malang, a small city about 50 kilometres south of Surabaya. Everyone wanted to go by bus, but I had a motorbike and thought it would be great to ride there with my girlfriend. So we left on Saturday morning and the journey there was really easy. We had a great time when we got there, and on Sunday afternoon we came back. We chose a different route on the way back so we could see the beautiful the countryside. While we were we travelling, we saw a road through the mountains which looked really nice, so we decided to go that way. But what we didn't know was that while we were having fun in Malang the night before, there was an announcement on the radio saying there was a very big storm coming and that people shouldn't drive in the mountains that day. When we were driving up into the mountains the weather was fine and the views were amazing, but as soon as we went over the top of the tallest mountain …

5a ◁ **8.6** Go through the questions with the class so that they know what to listen for. Ss listen and answer the questions, as well as their questions in Ex 3b, then check in pairs. Check answers with the class.

Answers:
1 There was a big storm and they got lost. Their motorbike broke down.
2 They felt frightened

b ***Stronger classes*** can do the exercise from memory, then listen again and check. Otherwise, Ss listen and decide if the statements are true or false alone, then check in pairs. Check answers with the whole class.

Answers: 1 true 2 true 3 false

Audioscript 8.6

Paul: … as soon as we went over the top of the tallest mountain, a huge storm hit us. It was really frightening, we couldn't see very well at all and we had to go slowly. We were really cold and wet and soon we were completely lost. I think we went round in a big circle at least twice. After some time, we came to a village and the road was full of water, it was up to our legs! Suddenly, the motorbike stopped, and I couldn't start it again. By this time, we were starting to get really worried. We felt even more frightened when we saw a big group of people running towards us and shouting. But as they got closer we saw that they were offering to help us. They took our motorbike into their house and gave us hot drinks and food. They were so friendly, and asked us about who we were and what we were doing. They told us about the radio announcement the day before and laughed at us! Two hours later the rain stopped and we were dry and warm again. When his sons fixed the motorbike, we were so happy. Henu, the father of the family, showed us how to get home on a map. We promised to keep in touch with them and invited them to come and visit us in Surabaya in the future. Anyway, a few months later, while we were watching TV at home, we got a phone call. It was Henu! He invited us to a party at his house. We went, but this time we hired a car!

6 Ss work in pairs and discuss the questions. In feedback, elicit Ss' ideas and have a brief class discussion.

Homework ideas

Workbook: Ex 1–3, p49

8c ▷ Develop your writing

Introduction

Ss develop their skill of writing a blog post by learning how to use time expressions.

Warm-up

Write on the board:
Career break.
Tell Ss what you would do if you had a career break, i.e. a year off work. Ss work in pairs and discuss what they would do. In feedback, elicit Ss' ideas.

1 Put Ss in small groups to discuss the questions. They could use their mobile devices to show each other the blogs they read (or write) if they want.

2 Ss read the 'about' page alone, then check in pairs. Check the answers with the whole class.

> **Answers:** Working with children and teaching them lots of different things at school.

3 Focus attention on the photos in the blog post and elicit what Ss can see. Ss read the post and order the things alone, then check in pairs. Check answers with the whole class.

> **Answers:**
> 1 what she did today
> 2 the weather
> 3 what she did last week
> 4 what she's doing next week
> 5 other future plans

4 Give Ss a few minutes to read the Focus box or read it together as a class. Elicit the answer to the question.

> **Answer:** any time

5a Read the example with the class and change it so that it's true for now. Ss rewrite the days and times alone.

b Ss work in pairs and compare their answers. In feedback, invite Ss to the board to write the answers and check them as a class.

> **Answers:** 1 this afternoon   2 the day before yesterday
> 3 in two week's time   4 next month   5 this morning
> 6 last month   7 this Saturday   8 tomorrow

Prepare

6 Give Ss plenty of time to decide what they're doing on their career break and make notes. Monitor and help with vocabulary, writing any new words/phrases on the board.

Write

7 Ss write their blog posts alone. Monitor and check Ss' work while they write, and be on hand to offer help where necessary.

Homework ideas

Workbook: Ex 1–6, p51

OVERVIEW

9A   Good friends

Introduction

The goal of this lesson is for Ss to ask about and describe a friendship. To help them achieve this, they will learn/revise the present perfect with *for* and *since* and vocabulary related to relationships.

Warm-up

Draw a word web on the board with *People I know* in the middle and two labels coming out with *friends* and *family* on each one. Ask Ss to copy the word web into their notebooks. Put Ss in small groups to brainstorm other words for people they know and add them to their word webs, e.g. *colleague*, *boss*, *teacher*, etc. When they have finished, invite Ss to come to the board to add their ideas to the word web. Check meanings and spelling. At this point you could do Vocabulary bank 9A or leave it for homework to recycle the vocabulary.

Listening and vocabulary

Describe a friendship

1 Focus attention on the photos and elicit the activities Ss can see. Ask Ss if they do any of these activities with their friends and how often. Ss work in pairs and discuss the questions. When they have finished, elicit answers from a few Ss and have a brief class discussion.

2 ◁)) **9.1** Read the questions with the class so that they know what to listen for. Ss listen and answer the questions, then check in pairs. Check answers with the whole class.

Answers:
1 at school
2 She always listens to her, she's funny and she's her oldest and closest friend.
3 They have similar interests.
4 They have a meal.
5 Justin
6 They both like the same football team – Tottenham.

Audioscript 9.1

Presenter: Today we're talking about close friends. How did you meet them and why are they important? Fran, Nick and Lewis are here to share their stories. Fran, let's start with you. Tell us about your closest friend – how long have you known him or her?

Fran: Well, her name's Karen and we've known each other since we were at school. I didn't like her at first, but one day we sat together in class and we quickly became close friends.

Presenter: That's great. Do you still see each other a lot?

Fran: We do. We live quite near each other, so we meet up maybe two or three times a week for coffee – and we text a lot, too. We're always on our phones.

Presenter: And do you always get on?

Fran: Well, we're quite different people, so we disagree with each other about quite a few things. Actually, we argue quite a bit!

Presenter: Mm, so why are you friends then?

Fran: Well, that's a good question … When I've had a bad day, she'll always listen to me and make me smile. She's very funny and for me that's really important. Karen's not my only friend, of course, but she is my oldest and closest friend – she knows me better than anyone else.

Presenter: OK, great. So we've got someone who listens, who's funny and who's known for a long time. All important stuff, I'd say. Next up we've got Nick. Hi Nick, what about you?

Nick: Actually I have a whole group of close friends that I've known since I was at college. We used to meet up because we had similar interests, like sports. I've known Hannah the longest. She had an old car, so the five of us used to get in that at the weekends, drive to the beach and go surfing.

Presenter: And do you still do things like that today?

Nick: No, we haven't done that for a long time. We live in different places now and we all have families, too. We still keep in touch, but we don't meet up very often. I suppose we get together about three or four times a year, at one of our houses for a meal or something. But even if we don't see each other for months, nothing changes. I've made friends with lots of people over the years, but I think old friends are the best.

Presenter: Yes, that's often true. What do you think, Lewis? Does oldest mean best?

Lewis: Actually, I've only known Justin for about two years. We met at work and we got on really well from the start. We started going to football matches together because we both support the same team – Tottenham – and now we even live together.

Presenter: Really!?

Lewis: Yeah – when my old flatmate moved to another city, Justin moved in. We've lived together for about nine months now and no problems so far. Apart from Tottenham not winning …

Presenter: Ha! So, you live and work together. Is that a good thing?

Lewis: Well, except for football, we actually have very different interests, so we don't see each other all the time. I go out cycling a lot. Justin prefers to stay in. But I think we're good friends because he's really relaxed like me – we never argue with each other. In fact, we haven't argued once since we met.

3a Ss complete the extracts alone, then check in pairs. Don't give any answers yet.

Optional alternative activity

With **weaker classes**, you may want to go through the phrases first, checking understanding with questions, e.g. *Is an old friend someone who is old or someone you've known a long time? If I chat online with someone, do I write or speak? If I keep in touch with someone, how often do I speak or write to them?*

b Ss listen and check their answers. Check answers with the class and be prepared to give further explanations/examples where necessary. With **stronger classes**, you could go through the information in the Vocabulary checkpoint below.

Answers: 1 close friends 2 meet up 3 text
4 disagree with 5 keep in touch 6 see
7 made friends, old friends 8 got on 9 argue

Vocabulary checkpoint

Meet on its own usually means when you know someone for the first time, e.g. *I met a nice man at the party last night.*, or when you're arranging a time/place to meet, e.g. *Let's meet at the big clock at 7 p.m.* When we're referring to seeing friends, we use *meet up (with)*, e.g. *I met up with some old school friends last week.*

4a Ss complete the questions alone, then check in pairs. Check answers with the whole class.

Answers: 1 meet up 2 close friends 3 disagree with
4 text 5 keep in touch 6 old friends

Optional extra activity

Fast finishers can write another question or two using the phrases, depending on how much time is available.

b Ss work in pairs and discuss the questions. When they have finished, ask a few Ss to share anything interesting they found out about their partners with the class.

Further practice

Photocopiable activities: 9A Vocabulary, p215

Grammar

Present perfect with *for* and *since*

5a Write on the board: *Carla has known Tim since they were five.* Draw a timeline on the board to show the duration like this:

PAST ———————————————————→ NOW
we were 5

Point to the arrow above 'now' on the timeline and ask *Are they friends now?* (yes). Use the timeline to show that this means the action started when they were five and continues until now. Then delete *since they were five* from the sentence and write *for …* . Explain that they are both 20 now and elicit how to finish the sentence. (15 years)

Ss choose the correct alternatives in the Grammar box alone, then check in pairs. Encourage them to use the examples to help. Check answers with the whole class and be prepared to give further explanations/examples where necessary.

Answers: 1 continue 2 a period of time
3 when an action started

b Ss complete the table alone, then check in pairs. While they are working, draw the table on the board. In feedback, invite Ss to come to the board one by one and write their answers, then check with the whole class.

Answers:
for: a few minutes; a long time; years; over 20 years; three months
since: 2012; April; Monday; the 22nd; ten o'clock

Optional alternative activity

Write *for* and *since* on different sides of the board. Arrange Ss into two large teams (or more if you have a large class). Ask each team to think of a name and write their team names on the board somewhere. Each round, call out one of the phrases in Ex 4b. One person from one of the teams (a different person each time) comes to the board and touches the correct side: *for* or *since*. If they do it correctly, they get a point. Next round, the next team does the same. Teams take it in turns to do so until you've gone through all the phrases. The team with the most points at the end wins.

With **stronger classes**, extend the activity with the following phrases: For: *a while, ages, hours and hours*; Since: *this morning, last June, the summer*.

GRAMMAR BANK 9A   pp.132–133

Stronger classes could read the notes at home. Otherwise, check the notes with Ss, especially the time frame it refers to. In each exercise, elicit the first answer as an example. Ss work alone to complete the exercises, then check their answers in pairs. Then check answers with the whole class. Ss can refer to the notes to help them.

Answers: 9A

1 1 since   2 since   3 for   4 since   5 since   6 for
7 since   8 for   9 for   10 since
2 1 've/have known   2 lived   3 moved   4 met
5 've/have been   6 've not/haven't seen
7 's/has helped

6a 🔊 **9.2** Ss listen and answer the question alone, then check in pairs.

Answers: *For* is pronounced in its weak form /fə(r)/.

Pronunciation checkpoint

In some varieties of English, the /r/ sound isn't usually pronounced at the end of the word. So, *for her* sounds like /fəˈhɜː/. However, when it's followed by a vowel sound, as is the case in all five items in Ex 5a, it is pronounced, e.g. *for hours* /fəˈraʊwəz/.

b Ss listen again and repeat. Drill chorally and individually for further practice if necessary.

7a Read the example with the class. Ss make sentences alone, then check in pairs. Monitor and check they're forming the present perfect and using *for/since* correctly. In feedback, nominate a different student to come to the board and write each sentence. Check answers with the whole class.

Answers:

1 I've known my closest friend for 60 years.
2 We've lived next door to each other since 1990.
3 Ricky's worked at the post office for a long time.
4 Tania's been married to Paco since she was 21.
5 They've known each other since they were six.
6 My parents have lived here since last year.

b Read the example with the class and give a couple of examples, using *for* or *since* in sentences which are true for you. Ss write their sentences alone. Monitor and help with vocabulary where necessary, writing any new words/phrases on the board.

c Use one of your examples in Ex 6b and elaborate, in order to demonstrate giving more information. Ss share their sentences, giving more information where possible. When they have finished, nominate a few Ss to share any interesting information they found out from their partner with the class.

Further practice

Photocopiable activities: 9A Grammar 1, p213;
9A Grammar 2, p214

Speaking

Prepare

8 Give Ss a few minutes to answer the questions and make notes. Monitor and help with vocabulary, writing any new words/phrases on the board.

Optional extra activity

Fast finishers can write two more questions about friends.

Speak

9a Go through the Useful phrases with the class. Ss take turns to describe their friend to each other. Monitor and make notes on their use of language for later feedback.

b Ask a few Ss to share the information they found out with the class. Give Ss feedback on their language use on the board as a class.

Reflection on learning

Write the following questions on the board:
How does this use of the present perfect compare with the use you learnt in lesson 3c (to describe past experiences)? What's different and what's the same? In what other ways will you use this usage of the present perfect in the future?
Put Ss in pairs to discuss the questions. When they have finished, ask if anyone wants to share their ideas with the class, but don't force them to if they'd rather not.

Homework ideas

Grammar bank: 9A Ex 1–2, pp.132–133
Workbook: Ex 1–4, p52
App: grammar and vocabulary practice

Fast route: continue to Lesson 9B
Extended route: go to p110 for Develop your listening

9B What's on?

Introduction

The goal of this lesson is for Ss to describe films and TV shows that they want to watch. To help them achieve this, they will learn/revise the present perfect + *already, yet* and *just* and adjectives to describe films and TV shows.

Warm-up

Write the following types of films/TV shows on the board:
comedy, documentary, action, thriller, romance, horror.
Ask Ss to think of an example of a film or TV show for each category that they like. When they are ready, Ss compare their choices in pairs and find out if they have any answers in common. In feedback, elicit answers and have a brief class discussion about the films and TV shows.

Reading and vocabulary

VOCABULARY BANK 9B   p144
TV genres
This can be done before or after the suggested warmer, or for homework with Ex 1b done in the following class.

1 Ss match the pictures and words alone, then check in pairs. Check answers with the whole class and drill the words.

Answers: 1 C 2 I 3 E 4 A 5 G 6 H 7 J 8 D 9 B 10 F

2 Ss work in pairs and discuss the questions. When they have finished, elicit a few answers and have a brief class discussion.

1 Ss look at the photos and work in pairs to answer the questions. When they have finished, elicit some answers and have a brief class discussion.

2 Ss read the TV programme reviews and answer the questions alone, then check in pairs. Check answers with the whole class.

Answers: a 3 b 2 c 4 d 1

3a Ss work in pairs and discuss the adjectives. In feedback, draw three columns on the board and write positive, negative and neutral at the top of each one. Invite Ss to come to the board and write the adjectives in the right columns.

Answers:
positive: popular, funny, exciting, interesting, clever
negative: silly, sad, boring, scary
neutral: serious, true, long

Optional extra activities
You can do one or both of these activities, depending on how much time you have available.

1 Give Ss a few minutes to think of more adjectives to describe TV shows for each column. When they have finished, invite them to come to the board and write them up in the correct columns. Check understanding and spelling.

2 Ask Ss to work in pairs and think of other things (not TV shows) the adjectives can describe. In feedback, elicit their ideas and ask if the meaning changes, e.g. *long* can measure space and time.

b Ss choose the correct alternatives alone, then check in pairs. Check answers with the whole class.

Answers: 1 funny 2 boring 3 long 4 popular 5 scary 6 sad

c Ss discuss the sentences in pairs. Encourage them to think of examples of TV shows for each one. When they have finished, elicit a few Ss' ideas and find out if anyone had the same answers.

Further practice
Photocopiable activities: 9B Vocabulary, p218

Listening

4a 9.7 Refer Ss back to the photos in Ex 1, so they know which programmes Mark and Claire are discussing and go through the questions with the class. Ss listen and answer the questions alone, then check in pairs. Check answers with the whole class.

Answers:
1 Victoria
2 It shows her early years as queen and how she met Prince Albert.
3 eight
4 yes

b Ss listen again and note down who says each sentence. Check answers with the class.

Answers: 1 C 2 M 3 M

Audioscript 9.7

Mark: Have you seen anything good on TV lately, Claire?
Claire: Yes! I've just finished watching a really interesting drama.
Mark: Really? What was it about?
Claire: Well, it's about Queen Victoria, you know, the Queen of England in the nineteenth century. It shows her early years as queen and how she met her husband, Prince Albert. It's really interesting.
Mark: Oh yes, I think I heard about that. I haven't seen it yet though.
Claire: What about you?
Mark: Oh, I'm just watching *Game of Thrones* these days. Have you watched any episodes yet?
Claire: No! I still haven't seen that. I'd really like to though.
Mark: Oh really? You've got a lot to watch! They've already made eight series!
Claire: I know, I keep forgetting about it. What's it like?
Mark: It's amazing. The special effects are great and it's so exciting. You really should watch it.
Claire: OK then, I'll try it one of these days!

Grammar

Present perfect with *already*, *just* and *yet*

5 With **weaker classes**, you may want to review the information in the Grammar Checkpoint box below first.

Ss complete the Grammar box with the correct alternatives alone, then check in pairs. Encourage them to use the examples in the box to help. Check answers with the class. Check understanding by asking the following questions about each sentence in Ex 4b:
1 *Do we know exactly when this happened?* (no)
   Was it a long time ago? (no)
2 *Did this happen?* (no) *Does she plan to do it in the future?* (yes)
3 *Did they make it?* (yes).

Answers: 1 short 2 has 3 hasn't

Grammar checkpoint
Review what Ss have learnt so far about the present perfect by writing these two sentences on the board:
1 *I've lived here for ten years.*
2 *I've been to Kenya.*

Ask: *Which sentence describes something that happened in the past, but we don't know when?* (2) *Which sentence describes something which started in the past and continues to now?* (1) *Which two time periods does the present perfect connect?* (the past and now)

Explain that when we use the present perfect, it connects the past and now, this is either because the action started in the past and continues, or the action happened any time in the past (up to now), but we don't know exactly when.

GRAMMAR BANK 9B pp.132–133

Stronger classes could read the notes at home. Otherwise, check the notes with Ss, especially the word order. In each exercise, elicit the first answer as an example. Ss work alone to complete the exercises, then check their answers in pairs. Then check answers with the whole class. Ss can refer to the notes to help them.

Answers: 9B
1 1 I haven't had dinner yet.
   2 I haven't booked my flights yet.
   3 Our teacher has already given us homework for tonight.
   4 I've just bought a new phone.
   5 My parents haven't arrived yet.
   6 Has Yolanda done her homework yet?
   7 Nina has just woken up.
   8 I have already finished this exercise!
2 1 already 2 yet 3 yet 4 just 5 already 6 yet
   7 just 8 yet

6a 🔊 9.7 Play the recording for Ss to listen, then answer the question as a class.

Answer: They're stressed.

b Ss listen again and repeat. Drill chorally and individually for further practice if necessary.

7 Do the first sentence together as an example. Ss choose the correct alternatives alone, then check in pairs. Check answers with the whole class.

Answers: 1 yet 2 just 3 already 4 just 5 yet
6 already, yet

Optional alternative activity

Books closed. Read out each sentence, but instead of the options, say 'blank', e.g. *I haven't seen that new comedy BLANK*. Ss listen and write *already, just* or *yet*. When you've finished, don't give any answers, but ask Ss to open their books again and complete the exercise, comparing their answers. Check answers with the whole class.

8a Give Ss your answers first as an example. Ss complete the sentences alone. Monitor and help with vocabulary where necessary, writing any new words/phrases on the board. If you have a monolingual class, it may be easier for Ss to use the names of the films or TV shows in their own language. Otherwise, ask them to look up the films/TV shows online to find out the English names.

Optional extra activity

Fast finishers can write two extra sentences about films/TV shows using *already, just* or *yet*.

b In pairs Ss compare their sentences and find out if they have any films or TV shows in common. When they have finished, nominate a student from each group to share their ideas with the class.

Further practice

Photocopiable activities: 9B Grammar 1, p216; 9B Grammar 2, p217

Speaking

Prepare

9a 🔊 9.9 Ss listen and tick the programmes alone, then check in pairs. Check answers with the class. Ask if Ss ever plan their viewing at home like this.

Answers: We All Love Sally; Westfield, No Time to Escape

b Refer Ss back the adjectives in Ex 3a. Review their meaning by asking a few questions, e.g. *Which adjective is the opposite of exciting?* (boring) *Which adjective describes something which makes you laugh?* (funny). Ss listen again and note which adjectives they use. Check answers with the class.

Answers: boring, silly, serious, exciting, long

Audioscript 9.9

Steve: This documentary looks good. I've heard about that place, it sounds interesting.
Amy: Interesting – maybe, but not for me. Anyway, I want to watch that comedy series – *We All Love Sally*. I've heard a lot about it, but I haven't seen it yet.
Steve: Oh, I've already watched it. I finished it last night. Honestly it was a bit boring and very silly.
Amy: Really? But I haven't seen it yet and everyone at work is talking about it. How about this? Let's watch it, but then you can choose what to watch after that.
Steve: Umm … OK then. Let's have a look. *One Night in June* – oh that looks very serious. Anyway, we've just watched something similar. What about that crime drama, *Westfield*? It looks interesting and I haven't seen that yet. Should be exciting, too.
Amy: OK, deal. Then we can watch a film after that. Oh, look – *Galactic Empire*. I've already seen that but I don't mind watching it again.
Steve: Hmm, I haven't seen it yet, but it's very long, three hours in space Boring! What about *No Time To Escape*?
Amy: You know I don't like action films. I've watched lots of them and I've never seen one I like … but, I suppose you're right – I don't want to watch a three-hour long film. Let's try it and see what it's like.

c Give Ss plenty of time to prepare, choosing at least three films/TV programmes. If they have trouble thinking of ideas, they can go online to search recent films or best films and TV shows of this year. Monitor and help with vocabulary where necessary, writing any new words/phrases on the board.

Speak

10a Go through the Useful phrases. Ss work in pairs and share their ideas in pairs, then choose two programmes that they want to watch together. Monitor and make notes on Ss' language use for later feedback.

b Ss tell the class which programmes/films they chose. Give Ss feedback on their language use as a class.

Optional alternative activity

In Ex 9e, allocate A and B roles to each student within their pairs. When you clap your hands, all of the Bs move clockwise round the room to another student A. As tell Bs about their choices. When you clap your hands again, Bs move again, and so on until they reach their original partner. Bs then have a few minutes to tell their original partner as much as they can remember from talking to the other As.

Homework ideas

Grammar bank: 9B Ex 1–2, pp.132–133
Workbook: Ex 1–5, p53
App: grammar and vocabulary practice

Fast route: continue to Lesson 9C
Extended route: go to p111 for Develop your reading

9c School days

Introduction

The goal of this lesson is for Ss to talk about past activities and abilities. To help them achieve this, they will learn/revise *could/couldn't* and phrases related to education.

Warm-up

Put Ss in small groups and give them a few minutes to brainstorm a list of all the school subjects they can think of in English. When they have finished, invite Ss to the board to write the subjects. Check spelling and ask Ss which were their favourite/least favourite subjects and why.

Vocabulary and reading

Education

1 You could introduce the topic by telling Ss a little about your own school days, answering the questions. Ss discuss the questions in pairs. When they have finished, elicit answers from a few Ss and have a brief class discussion.

2 Focus attention on the quotes. Ss work in pairs and decide which of the quotes they agree with. Discuss as a class.

3a Do the first phrase in bold (*terrible at*) together as an example. Ss work in pairs to categorise the others. Encourage them to use dictionaries or their mobile devices if necessary. In feedback, go through each phrase, including the information in the Vocabulary checkpoint if necessary.

Answers:
positive: interested in, did (quite) well, got better at (it), passed my exams, good at, found (it) easy
negative: terrible at, found (it) boring, bad at, did badly, found (it) difficult
neutral: worked hard at, taking exams, studied for

Vocabulary checkpoint

Note that *found (it) easy* could be positive or negative, depending on the context, e.g. *I found it easy, so it was boring for me.* (negative) *I found sport easy because I was good at it and enjoyed it.* (positive)

Terrible at, interested in, bad at and *good at* are preceded by the verb *be. Find* + adjective is split with the object or a pronoun.

b Ss choose the correct alternatives alone, then check in pairs. Check answers with the whole class.

Answers: 1 at 2 in 3 hard 4 in 5 for, badly 6 found, better

c Ss discuss the sentences in pairs. For those that aren't true, encourage them to change the information so that they are, e.g. *I used to be terrible at sport.* When they have finished, elicit a few statements from Ss and find out if they have anything in common with other Ss in the class.

VOCABULARY BANK 9C p144
School subjects

1 Ss match the subjects and pictures alone and then check in pairs.

Answers: 1 E 2 A 3 D 4 F 5 G 6 C 7 H 8 B

Further practice

Photocopiable activities: 9C Vocabulary, p221

4a Make sure Ss only read the introduction to the article at this stage, then choose the best summary in pairs. Check answers with the whole class.

Answer: 3

b You may want to elicit/check: *CEO*, i.e. Chief Executive Officer, the director of a large company. Ss read the article and complete the sentences alone, then check in pairs. Check answers with the whole class.

Answers: 1 Scott 2 Clara 3 Nancy 4 Clara 5 Nancy 6 Scott

Optional alternative activity

Arrange Ss in groups of three. Each student within the group reads about a different person. They then share their information within the group and do Ex 4b together.

Vocabulary checkpoint

In British English, *programmes* are what you watch on the TV and *programs* are computer applications. In US English, *programs* is used for both.

Grammar

could/couldn't

5a Ss at this level shouldn't have too many problems with this grammar point, but be prepared to offer further examples if necessary. Ss complete the Grammar box alone, then check in pairs. Check answers with the whole class.

Answers: 1 knew 2 didn't know

GRAMMAR BANK 9C pp.132–133

Stronger classes could read the notes at home. Otherwise, check the notes with Ss. Elicit the first answer as an example. Ss work alone to complete the exercises, then check their answers in pairs. Then check answers with the whole class. Ss can refer to the notes to help them.

Answers: 9C
1 1 Could you 2 couldn't 3 drive 4 do 5 could
   6 couldn't 7 couldn't
2 1 ~~to~~ 2 ~~could~~ couldn't 3 ~~swimming~~ swim 4 Correct
   5 ~~not~~ 6 ~~not could~~ couldn't 7 Correct 8 ~~to~~

---

b Give Ss a few minutes to find more examples of could/couldn't in the article in Ex 4 then compare in pairs. Check answers with the whole class.

Answers: I just couldn't understand it; He couldn't read and write; The only thing I could do was use a computer; I could do it, but it took me a long time; she discovered she could write more easily

6a 🔊 9.10 Play the recording for Ss to listen and then answer the question in pairs. Check answers with the class.

Answer: couldn't

b Ss listen again and repeat. Drill chorally and individually for further practice if necessary.

7 Ss complete the text alone, then check in pairs. Check answers with the whole class and ask if any of the information is true for anyone in the class.

Answers: 1 could 2 couldn't 3 play 4 couldn't 5 could
6 couldn't

8a Read the examples with the class. Give Ss plenty of time to write their sentences. Monitor and help with vocabulary where necessary, writing any new words/phrases on the board. Make sure they write one false sentence.

Optional extra activity

Fast finishers can write two more sentences: one true and one false.

b Ss share their sentences in pairs and guess which one is false. In feedback, ask each pair if they guessed correctly.

Further practice

Photocopiable activities: 9C Grammar 1, p219;
9C Grammar 2, p220

Speaking

Prepare

9a 🔊 9.11 Go through the questions with the Ss so they know what to listen for. Ss listen and tick the questions he answers, then check in pairs. Check answers with the whole class.

Answers:
1 What did you like about your school?
2 Which subjects were you bad at?
3 Who was your favourite teacher?

b Ask Ss what they can remember about Kareem's answers. Play the recording again for Ss to listen and write the answers, then check in pairs. Check answers with the whole class.

Answers:
1 P.E. – they had a very good sports department.
2 Art
3 Mrs Henson, the maths teacher

c Give Ss plenty of time to think about their own answers to the questions in Ex 9a and make notes. Monitor and help with vocabulary where necessary, writing any news words/phrases on the board.

Audioscript 9.11

Erica: What did you like about your school, Kareem?
Kareem: Oh P.E., definitely – that was the best thing about it. We had a really good sports department, so we could play almost any sport we wanted to.
Erica: Wow, really?
Kareem: Yes, and we had lots of after-school clubs, too. I loved basketball and I was really good at it. We had a school team and we did quite well.
Erica: How lucky. I wasn't very good at sports. Which subjects were you bad at?
Kareem: Ha, I was terrible at art. I just couldn't draw anything. I still am! I remember once I painted a picture of a car, and my teacher thought it was a potato!
Erica: Who was your favourite teacher?
Kareem: Probably my maths teacher, Mrs. Henson. I was pretty bad at maths when I started her class. I couldn't understand much and I found it boring. But she spent a lot of time helping me. In the end I passed my exams with good grades. Yes, I'll always remember Mrs. Henson. What about you, Erica. What was the best thing about your school?

Speak

10 Arrange Ss in small groups to share their information from Ex 9a and ask questions. Monitor and make notes on their language use for later feedback.

Optional alternative activity

Ss do this as a mingling activity instead of in groups, i.e. walking around the class and discussing their school days with other Ss.

Reflection on learning

Write the following questions on the board:
What three phrases from today's lesson will you use most in the future?
How will you use them?
Put Ss in pairs to discuss the questions. When they have finished, ask if anyone wants to share their ideas with the class, but don't force them to if they'd rather not.

Homework ideas

Ex 10a: Ss record themselves talking about their school days and add it to their GSE portfolio.
Grammar bank: 9C Ex 1–2, pp. 132–133
Workbook: Ex 1–5, p54
App: grammar and vocabulary practice

Fast route: continue to Lesson 9D
Extended route: go to p112 for Develop your writing

 9D English in action

Introduction

The goal of this lesson is for students to practise asking for and giving information. To help them achieve this, they will learn a range of phrases for asking for and giving information.

Listening

1. Elicit some ideas for education as an example, e.g. *online, from a school/college, recommendations from friends*, etc. Ss work in pairs and discuss the other things. In feedback, ask a few Ss for their ideas and invite other Ss to add theirs.

2a 9.12 Ss listen and match/check their ideas, then check in pairs. Check answers with the whole class.

Answers: 1 hotels   2 public transport
3 education/courses   4 places to eat

b Ss listen again and choose the correct alternatives then check in pairs. Check answers with the whole class.

Answers: 1 Could   2 Sure   3 is   4 from   5 sure
6 course   7 Do   8 afraid   9 if   10 sorry

Audioscript 9.12

Receptionist: Hello, how can I help?
Hotel guest: I'd like to log onto the wifi. Could you tell me what the password is, please?
Receptionist: Sure. Are you a guest at the hotel?
Hotel guest: Yes, I am.
Receptionist: OK, well, your user name is your room number and the password is your surname.
Hotel guest: Oh right, thanks, great. And could you tell me when breakfast is? I have an early meeting tomorrow.
Receptionist: Yes, it's from six thirty until nine thirty, but you can order breakfast to your room if you need it before then.
Hotel guest: Hmm, yes I might do that. Thanks.

Passenger: Excuse me, do you know which platform the train to Leeds leaves from?
Guard: Yes, it's platform 14.
Passenger And where can I find it?
Guard: It's just over there.
Passenger: Thanks. And do you know what time it leaves?
Guard: Mm, I'm not sure. I think it leaves in six minutes.
Passenger: OK, thanks …

3
Receptionist: Debden College, how can I help you?
Student: Hi, yes, I'm interested in doing your photography course. Could you tell me how much it costs?
Receptionist: Yes, of course. It's £120 for twelve weeks.
Student: And when are the classes?
Receptionist: Let me check … er yes, they're every Tuesday between 6 and 9, starting next week. We have some places left, but you need to pay before Friday.
Student: OK. Do you know if I need to buy a camera?
Receptionist: I'm afraid I can't help you with that. You'll need to speak to the teacher. I'll give you her email address.
Student: Great, thanks.

4
Man: Excuse me, are you from around here?
Woman: Yes.
Man: Do you know if there's an Indian restaurant around here?
Woman: Er, yeah there are a couple. If you go down that road over there and then turn right at the end, you'll find one. It's probably the closest.
Man: Do you know if it's open now?
Woman: I'm sorry, I don't know. But it's not far, just five minutes away.

Grammar checkpoint

Do you know … ? and *Could you tell me … ?* introduce indirect questions. Show how the word order changes by writing on the board:
*Where **is** the **library**?*
*Could you tell me where the **library is**?*
Use arrows on the board to show how the subject and auxiliary change position in an indirect question.

3a 9.13 Ss listen and answer the question, then check in pairs. Check answers with the whole class.

Answer: It goes up.

b Ss listen again and repeat. Drill chorally and individually for further practice if necessary.

4a Ss work on their own to answer the questions. Check answers as a class.

Answers:
1 Could you tell me what the time is?
2 Do you know what time the lesson finishes?
3 Do you know if we have homework today?
4 Could you tell me when the next lesson is?
5 Do you know where the train station is?
6 Could you tell me what is the teacher's name?
7 Do you know if there is a bank near here?
8 Could you tell me the way to the nearest bus station?

b Ss work in pairs to answer the questions from Ex 4a. Ss use the Useful phrases to he/p them. Monitor and make notes on Ss' language use for later feedback.
5a Read the example with the class. Focus attention on the Useful phrases and elicit some other ideas for the first question stem (*Do you know … ?*) as an example. Ss write their own endings to the questions alone. Monitor and make sure Ss are forming indirect questions with the correct word order.
b Read the example with the class. Ask Ss to stand up and walk around asking their questions from Ex 5a to other Ss in the class. In feedback, ask different Ss to ask and answer their questions in open pairs.

Speaking

Prepare

6 Arrange Ss in pairs and assign them A or B roles. Ss read their information alone. Monitor and be on hand to help if necessary, checking Ss are forming the questions correctly.

Speak

7 Ss practise their conversations. Monitor and make notes on their language use for later feedback. When they have finished and if you have time, they can swap roles and practise the conversations again, but without preparing questions. In feedback, ask two Ss to perform the conversation in open pairs.

Reflection on learning

Write the following questions on the board:

Which phrases were most useful from this lesson?
How will you use them in the future?

Put Ss in pairs to discuss the questions. When they have finished, ask if anyone wants to share their ideas with the class, but don't force them to if they'd rather not.

---

9 Check and reflect

Introduction

Ss revise and practise the language of Unit 9. The notes below provide some ideas for exploiting the activities in class, but you may want to set exercises for homework, or use them as a diagnostic or progress test. For each grammar or vocabulary point, the first activity reviews the language and the second is more communicative, involving pairwork.

1 Remind Ss that we use the past simple for completed actions in the past when we know when they happened. Ss complete the description alone, then check in pairs. Check answers with the whole class.

Answers: 1 've known   2 moved   3 's lived   4 met
5 've become   6 have liked   7 were

2a Ss choose the correct words alone, then check in pairs. Check answers with the whole class.

Answers: 1 argue   2 close   3 see   4 on   5 old   6 touch

b Ss can do this as a speaking activity, using the phrases to speak about themselves and their friends. When they have finished, ask a few Ss to share any interesting information about their partner with the class.

3 Read the example with the class. Ss make sentences for the other activities alone, then check in pairs. Check answers with the whole class.

Answers: He's <u>already</u> been to the supermarket. He's <u>already</u> cleaned the house. He's <u>already</u> had a shower yet. He's <u>just</u> put the meat in the oven. He hasn't cooked the vegetables <u>yet</u>. He's <u>already</u> made a playlist. He hasn't done the washing up <u>yet</u>.

Optional extra activity

Write on the board: *a class party, a normal day at work, applying for university, organising an event* and *cooking a meal*. Put Ss in pairs and ask them to choose one of the activities and imagine they're organising it. Ss write sentences about what they've already and just done, and what they haven't done yet. When they have finished, each pair takes it in turns to read out their list to the class for them to guess what the activity is.

Optional extra activity

Before Ex 4a, do a backwards dictation. Put Ss in small teams. Each turn dictate the spelling of an adjective in the box backwards. The first team to call out the adjective wins a point. The team with the most points at the end wins.

4a Ss complete the sentences alone, then check in pairs. Check answers with the whole class.

Answers: 1 silly   2 popular   3 serious   4 true   5 clever
6 funny   7 long   8 sad

b Ss work in pairs and discuss films they've seen using the adjectives in Ex 4a. In feedback, ask a few Ss to share their ideas and have a brief class discussion.

5a Ss complete the sentences alone, then check in pairs. Check answers with the whole class.

Answers: 1 found   2 for, passed   3 did   4 at   5 hard, got

b Ss complete the prompts alone. Monitor and help with vocabulary, writing any new words/phrases on the board.

c Ss work in pairs and share their sentences. Encourage them to ask follow-up questions to find out more information.

6a Ss complete the sentences alone, then check in pairs. Check answers with the whole class.

Answers: 1 couldn't swim   2 could ride   3 could read
4 couldn't speak

b Ss work in pairs and discuss what they could and couldn't do, including if they could do any of the things described in the sentences in Ex 6a. In feedback, ask a few Ss to share any interesting information about their partners with the class.

Reflect

Ask Ss to rate each statement alone, then compare in pairs. Encourage them to ask any questions they still have about any of the areas covered in Unit 9.

9A Develop your listening

Introduction

Ss develop their listening skill of understanding a radio interview by learning how to identify examples.

Warm-up

If you have a pet (or have had one in the past), tell the class about it, including its name, age, what it likes/dislikes and any interesting quirks it has. You can also show the class a photo if you have one. Ss then discuss their own pets (past or present) in small groups.

1 Focus attention on the photos and elicit what Ss can see. Discuss the questions as a class.

Answers: elephant, giraffe, hen, goat, dog, cat; they are not the same type of animal in each photo.

2 🔊 **9.3** Ss listen to the interview and answer the questions alone, then check in pairs. Check answers with the whole class.

Answers:
1 At a local zoo. She's a vet.
2 No, because animals stay in groups only to stay safe.
3 They make friends with other monkeys who have the same character as them.

3 Give Ss a few minutes to read the focus box, or go through it together as a class. Answer the question as a class.

Answer: To help the listener understand the meaning of what they're saying and/or give more information about something.

4a *Stronger classes* can do the exercise from memory, then listen and check. Otherwise, Ss listen again and match the sentences, then check in pairs. Check answers with the whole class.

Answers: 1 b   2 a   3 c

b Play the recording again for Ss to listen and write the words which introduce each example. Check answers with the class.

Answers: a such as   b like   c For example

Audioscript 9.3

Interviewer: I have a special guest with me today. It's vet Dr Emily Carter. Emily works at the local zoo and has been there for ten years. She's worked with many different animals, such as bears, tigers and giraffes, and she's here today to talk about animal friendships.
So, Emily, can animals become friends with each other in the same way that humans do?

Emily: Yes, but only a very few of them.

Interviewer: Really? But a lot of animals live together in groups, like lions and penguins. Surely some of them make friends?

Emily: No, not really. The main reason that most of these animals live together is because it's safer for them, not because they're friends.

Interviewer: So, are there any animals that become real friends, like us humans?

Emily: Well we think that animals such as monkeys, elephants and horses make friends.

Interviewer: And are they the same as human friendships?

Emily: I think in some ways they are. For example, some scientists at a university in Vienna did some research on monkeys and found that monkeys choose friends with the same character as them. That's something humans also do sometimes.

Interviewer: Just amazing!

5a 🔊 **9.4** Go through the topics with the class, so they know what to listen for. Ss listen again and order the topics alone, then check in pairs. Check answers with the whole class.

Answers:
1 People like talking about animal friendships.
2 Animals sometimes become friends because of humans.
3 Animals become friends when one of them has no mother.
4 Dangerous animals make friends when they're on their own.
5 Animal friendship stories make us feel positive.

b Ss listen again and match the examples to the topics, then check in pairs You can tell Ss that there's no example for topic 1. Check answers with the whole class.

Answers: a e   b a   c b   d d, c

Audioscript 9.4

Interviewer: People love sharing videos and news stories about animal friendships online. They do it a lot. For example, yesterday someone sent me a video of a dog and a cat who are the best of friends. Did they choose each other because they have the same character, like monkeys?

Emily: Well, it's important to think about where these friendships happen. The animals don't live in the woods or the forest. They live in places made by humans, such as in a zoo or on a farm.

Interviewer: So, we make these friendships happen?

Emily: Sometimes. When a baby animal has lost its mother, we might ask another animal to look after it and they become friends. For example, last year we had a baby tiger without a mother, so we brought in a dog to look after it.

Interviewer: What about a dangerous animal that makes friends with an animal it normally eats? For example, the tiger in a Russian zoo that became friends with a goat.

Emily: Ah, yes, I remember seeing that in the news. I think that sometimes animals in zoos feel lonely when they're on their own. They decide that it's better to play with their food than eat it.

Interviewer: Why do you think people love reading about these kinds of animal friendships?

Emily: World news can be quite sad sometimes and the animal world can be difficult. I think that when we see a gorilla caring for a cat or a cat playing with a rabbit, we feel happy. We feel that the world is a better place.

Interviewer: Dr Emily Carter, thank you very much for coming today.

6a 🔊 **9.5** Play the first opinion and pause the recording. Elicit Ss' ideas and write them on the board. Play the rest of the recording for Ss to listen and write down their examples.

b Ss work in pairs and compare their ideas. Don't give any answers yet.

c 🔊 **9.6** Ss listen and check their ideas. Check answers with the whole class and ask if any Ss guessed correctly.

Answers: 1 fish   2 cats or rabbits   3 bears   4 tigers
5 spiders

Audioscript 9.6

1
I prefer pets that are easy to look after, such as fish.

2
The best pets are ones you can hug. For example, cats or rabbits.

3
Forests are scary because of animals, like bears.

4
Some wild animals make very bad pets. For example, tigers.

5
I don't like insects, such as spiders.

7 Ss work in pairs and discuss the questions. In feedback, elicit Ss' ideas and have a brief class discussion.

Homework ideas

Workbook: Ex 1–3, p55

9B ▶ Develop your reading

Introduction

Ss develop their reading skill of understanding a survey report by learning how to understand numbers in a text.

Warm-up

Tell the class about a recent TV programme you've watched or are currently watching. Include the type of programme, where/when it's set, the main actors and why you like it. Ss then discuss their own favourite programmes in small groups. In feedback, elicit Ss' programmes and find out if others know/like it, too.

1 Focus attention on the photo and elicit what Ss can see. Ss work in pairs and discuss the questions. In feedback, elicit Ss' ideas and have a brief class discussion.
2 Give Ss a few minutes to read the focus box or read it together as a class. Ss match the numbers and words alone, then check in pairs. Check answers with the whole class.

Answers: 1c 2e 3d 4a 5b

3a Give Ss a minute to read the introduction or read it together as a class. Ss work in pairs and answer the questions, then check answers with the whole class.

Answers: 1 last month 2 TV watching habits

b Ss read the report again and match the numbers and sentences alone, then check in pairs. Check answers with the whole class.

Answers: 1 19% 2 7% 3 37 4 ½ 5 over 55 6 40
7 50% 8 ¼

4 Ss read the report again and decide if the sentences are true or false alone, then check in pairs. Check answers with the whole class.

Answers: 1F 2T 3T 4F 5F

5 Ss work in pairs and discuss the questions. In feedback, ask a few Ss to share their ideas with the class.

Homework ideas

Workbook: Ex 1–4, p56

9C ▶ Develop your writing

Introduction

Ss develop their skill of writing an email of application by learning how to use formal phrases.

Warm-up

Bring/Download photos of a variety of different jobs to class. Show them to Ss and elicit the names of each job, writing them on the board. Describe one of the jobs by saying what the person does and asking Ss to guess the job, e.g. *They wear a uniform, work long hours and catch criminals.* (police officer) Give Ss a few minutes to choose one of the jobs and make notes on what the person does. Monitor and help with vocabulary where necessary, writing any new words/phrases on the board. When they have finished, arrange Ss in small groups to describe the job for other Ss to guess.

1 Give Ss a few minutes to read the job adverts. When they are ready, Ss work in pairs and discuss the questions. In feedback, elicit Ss' ideas and have a brief class discussion.
2a Ss read the email quickly and match it to the relevant job ad. Check the answer with the class.

Answer: A

b Ss read the email again and order the things alone, then check in pairs. Check answers with the whole class.

Answers: 1c 2a 3b

3 Give Ss a few minutes to read the Focus box or read it together as a class. Elicit the answer to the question.

Answer: They make the application sound polite and professional.

4 Ss match the phrases alone, then check in pairs. Check answers with the whole class.

Answers: 1c 2b 3g 4f 5h 6a 7d

Prepare

5 Give Ss plenty of time to choose a job and make notes, using the questions to help them. Monitor and help with vocabulary, writing any new words/phrases on the board.

Write

6 Ss write their emails alone. Monitor and check Ss' work while they write, and be on hand to offer help where necessary.

Homework ideas

Workbook: Ex 1–7, p57

10 ▶ OVERVIEW

10A Saving money

Introduction

The goal of this lesson is for Ss to give a short talk on money-saving tips. To help them achieve this, they will learn/revise the first conditional and vocabulary related to money.

Warm-up

Write on the board:
Money makes the world go around. and *Money is the root of all evil.*
If necessary, explain what they mean and which is positive and negative. Ss discuss which they agree with most and why. In feedback, elicit their ideas and have a brief class discussion.

Vocabulary

Money

1 Focus attention on the pictures and elicit what Ss can see and some vocabulary related to money, e.g. *coins, piggy bank*, etc. Ss work in pairs and discuss the questions. When they have finished, elicit a few answers and have a brief class discussion.

2a Read the survey with the class and briefly discuss how they think most people would answer the questions. Ss complete the survey alone. Encourage them to use dictionaries or mobile devices to check any new vocabulary, but be on hand to give further explanations and examples if necessary.

> **Vocabulary checkpoint**
> In some languages the verb for *earn* and *win* is the same. Check understanding by asking *Where do you earn money from?* (a job) *Where do you win money from?* (a competition)

b Ss complete the sentences alone, then check in pairs. Check answers with the whole class.

> **Answers:** 1 earn, save 2 spend, cost 3 lend 4 borrow
> 5 pay for, cash, credit 6 waste

> **Pronunciation checkpoint**
> Drill *earn* /ɜːn/, *borrow* /ˈbɒrəʊ/, *owe* /əʊ/ and *waste* /weɪst/ chorally and individually with the class.

c Ss work in pairs and compare their answers to the survey. When they have finished, find out how many answers they had in common.

129

VOCABULARY BANK 10A p145

Money and shopping

1 Ss label the photos with the words and phrases in the box alone. Then they check in pairs.

Answers: A 7 B 4 C 8 D 3 E 11 F 9 G 10 H 6
I 2 J 12 K 5 L 1

2 Ss answer each sentence with a word or phrase from Ex 1. Then check answers in pairs.

Answers: 1 voucher 2 coin 3 ATM 4 receipt
5 bank statement 6 counter

3 Ss complete each sentence with a word or phrase from Ex 1 in the correct form. Then check answers in pairs.

Answers: 1 wallet 2 coins 3 receipt 4 bank statement
5 notes 6 ATM

4 Ss work in pairs and discuss the questions. In feedback, find out which the most and least popular forms of payment are.

Further practice

Photocopiable activities: 10A Vocabulary, p224

Listening

First conditional

3a Read the example with the class. Ss discuss in pairs what they think will be said in the podcast about the topics listed. Check ideas with the class.

b 🔊 10.1 Ss work alone and listen for answers to the questions. Play the recording again for Ss to check their answers, then discuss as a class.

Answers:
1 Write a shopping list for the supermarket. Sell clothes you don't wear anymore. Make your own gifts for people. Wait before you buy something. Pay in cash, not credit card.
2 Ss check against their ideas.
3 Ss check against their ideas.

Optional alternative activity

With **weaker classes**, write the following gapped sentences on the board:

1 Write a ... for the supermarket.
2 Sell clothes that you don't ... .
3 Make your own ... for people.
4 Wait a month before you ... something.
5 Pay in ... , not ... .

Ss listen and write the missing words.

c Elicit the first answer as an example. Ss match the sentence halves alone, then check in pairs. Play the recording for Ss to check their answers.

Answers: 1 e 2 b 3 a 4 d 5 c

Audioscript 10.1

Presenter: Welcome to this week's edition of *Smart Money* where we help you to look after your cash. It's the start of the new year and many of you want to save money straight away. So, this week, we share our top five tips for spending less and saving more. First up we have food – I know I love spending money on food! What about you Luke, have you ever gone to the supermarket for one or two things and come back with ten?

Luke: Of course, especially when I'm hungry! Our first tip is to plan for your supermarket trip. Decide what meals you're going to cook first and then write a shopping list. If you make a list you'll only buy the food you need. And if you only buy what you need, you won't spend money on food you don't need.

Presenter: It'll also stop you buying special offers, too. We think these offers will save us money, but actually we spend more money because we buy things we don't need.

Luke: OK moving on. A quick tip from me next. If you have some great clothes that you don't wear any more, don't throw them away. If you sell your clothes, you can earn some extra money!

Presenter: Great idea! Now, buying gifts for people can be expensive so, if you haven't got much money, create your own gifts. If you make something, you'll spend more time on it, but less money.

Luke: Exactly. The person will really love it, too. Our fourth tip is about waiting before you buy something. We often feel like we need something as soon as we see it. But wait. If you still want it after a month, you'll know it's a good decision. If you don't want it any more, you won't waste your money.

Presenter: Our final tip is to use cash to pay for things because that way you'll pay more attention to the cost. You won't do that if you pay by card. So, those are our top five tips for saving money. Next week we're going to talk about getting around the city, so if you want to save money on transport, you should listen in. Bye for now!

Grammar

4 Ss complete the Grammar box alone, then check in pairs. Check answers with the class and explain that we don't use *will* in the *if*-clause. Use the first example to check understanding by asking *Is it possible that we'll bake something?* (yes) *Is 'you'll spend less money' a cause or result of baking something?* (result) *Does this refer to the past, present or future?* (future).

Answers: 1 future 2 present simple 3 infinitive 4 is

GRAMMAR BANK 10A pp.134–135

Stronger classes could read the notes at home. Otherwise, check the notes with Ss, especially the different modals we can use. In each exercise, elicit the first answer as an example. Ss work alone to complete the exercises, then check their answers in pairs. Then check answers with the whole class. Ss can refer to the notes to help them.

Answers: 10A
1 1 like, 'll organise 2 will cook, ask 3 will come, tell
4 visit, should see 5 try, 'll want 6 will come, don't
7 won't, don't 8 rains, can't have
2 1 I'll send you a message if I'm free tomorrow.
2 If we get home early, we'll make dinner.
3 If they don't get here soon, we should give them a call.
4 We'll go out tomorrow if the weather's nice.
5 I'll drive to the shop if we don't have any bread.
6 I won't see you tomorrow if you aren't at work.

5a 🔊 10.2 Ss listen to the sentences, paying attention to the pronunciation of *'ll*. Ask Ss to focus on the descending notation in each clause to help them. Elicit what happens.

Answers: When there's a comma, the speaker usually pauses. When there isn't a comma, there's no pause.

b Ss listen again and repeat. Drill chorally and individually for further practice if necessary.

5 Read the example with the class. Ss complete the sentences alone, then check in pairs. Check answers with the whole class.

Answers: 1 will/'ll find, look 2 eat, will/'ll get
3 lunch, 'll/will be 4 will not/won't save, drink 5 will be, share
6 have, 'll/will not

7a Use the example sentence to demonstrate the activity by telling Ss how you'd complete some of the sentences yourself. Ss then complete the sentences alone. Monitor and help with vocabulary, writing any new words/phrases on the board.

b Use your own examples from Ex 7a to give more information. Ss share their sentences with their partner, giving more information where possible. When they have finished, nominate a few Ss to share any interesting information they found out from their partners with the class.

Optional extra activity

Before class, write some sentence starters at the top of blank pieces of paper (a separate sentence starter for each page), e.g. *I won't go out tonight if …* , *If I go to the supermarket on the way home …* , etc. and stick them to the walls around the classroom. Ask Ss to walk around and complete each sentence however they wish by writing on the paper. When they have finished, collect the pieces of paper and organise the Ss into small groups – as many as there are pieces of paper. Give each group a piece of paper and ask them to check the sentences for correct verb forms. Monitor and help where necessary.

Further practice

Photocopiable activities: 10A Grammar 1, p222;
10A Grammar 2, p223

Speaking

Prepare

3a Read the activity with the class. Ss work in pairs and write their (five) tips. Monitor and help with new vocabulary, writing any new words/phrases on the board. Encourage Ss to use the topics in the box to help them.

b Read the example and go through the Useful phrases with the class. Give Ss (in their pairs) a few minutes to decide how to present their tips and practise doing so if they want to.

Speak

9a Put pairs together into groups to present their tips. Each pair takes turns to present their tips. Encourage the pair who's listening to make notes and ask questions. Monitor and make notes on their use of language, particularly the first conditional.

b Ask each group to share the best tip they heard.

Reflection on learning

Write the following questions on the board:
What were the three most useful phrases you learnt today?
How confident do you feel using the first conditional?
How can you improve?
In what other ways will you use the present perfect in the future?
Put Ss in pairs to discuss the questions. When they have finished, ask if anyone wants to share their ideas with the class, but don't force them to if they'd rather not.

Homework ideas

Grammar reference: 10A Ex 1–2, pp. 134–135
Workbook: Ex 1–5, p58
App: grammar and vocabulary practice

Fast route: continue to Lesson 10B
Extended route: go to p113 for Develop your reading

10B Everyday objects

Introduction

The goal of this lesson is for students to share information about everyday objects. To help them achieve this, they will learn/revise the present and past passive and time expressions.

Warm-up

Tell Ss that for some reason you have to leave your home immediately, but you have time to take three objects with you (the size doesn't matter). Tell the Ss which three items you'd take and why. Give Ss a few minutes to think of their own three objects to take in the same situation. When they're ready, arrange Ss in small groups to discuss their choices. In feedback, ask a few Ss to share their choices with the class.

Reading

Present and past passive

1 Introduce the activity by emptying your bag and/or pockets in front of the class and describing the objects there. Ss work in pairs and discuss the questions. (NB: Don't make Ss empty their bags/pockets unless they're comfortable with it.) In feedback, elicit Ss' answers and have a brief class discussion.

2a Give Ss one minute to read the introduction to the quiz and answer the question. Check answers with the class.

Answer: 3 things we use all the time

b Ask Ss complete the alternatives in the factfile. Ss then compare answers in pairs. Don't give any answers yet.

c Point Ss to p151 to check their answers, then work in pairs and discuss the questions. Check answers with the class and elicit how they feel about the facts.

Answers: 1 20 billion 2 minute
3 Jacob Davis (Levi Strauss was his business partner.) 4 2,500
5 3,500 6 a Danish king who helped people communicate better
7 Humphry Davy 8 more

Grammar

3 Write on the board: *2,500 pencils are made from one tree.* Ask: *Do we know who makes the pencils?* (No) *Is it important?* (No). Ss complete the Grammar box alone, then check in pairs. Check answers with the whole class.

Answers: 1 be 2 past participle 3 don't know

GRAMMAR BANK 10B   pp.134–135

Stronger classes could read the notes at home. Otherwise, check the notes with Ss, especially the additional uses of the passive described here. In each exercise, elicit the first answer as an example. Ss work alone to complete the exercises, then check their answers in pairs. Then check answers with the whole class. Ss can refer to the notes to help them.

Answers: 10B

1 1 were   2 made   3 designed   4 weren't   5 are
  6 are enjoyed   7 are sold   8 are worn
2 1 was/made   2 it wasn't used   3 was/used
  4 are made   5 are needed   6 were made

4a 🔊 **10.3** Play the recording for Ss to listen then answer the question as a class.

Answers: It is unstressed in each sentence. When we use the passive form, we don't stress the verb *be*.

b Ss listen again and repeat. Drill chorally and individually for further practice if necessary.

5 Before the activity, elicit what Ss know about chocolate, e.g. where it comes from, where it's made, how much is consumed in the world, etc. Ss complete the factfile alone, using the correct passive form, then check in pairs. Don't give any answers yet.

Answers: 1 was/made   2 was drunk   3 were used
4 was brought   5 is eaten   6 is added   7 are grown
8 aren't used

Audioscript 10.4

Presenter:	Today is World Chocolate Day, so here to tell us some interesting facts about chocolate is history professor Alice Barker. So, Alice, tell us about the history of chocolate.
Alice:	Well, it was first made over three thousand years ago in the Americas.
Ben:	Three thousand years ago?
Alice:	Yes, but it wasn't the same as the chocolate we have nowadays. It wasn't eaten, it was a drink.
Ben:	Like hot chocolate?
Alice:	Actually, no. For a long time it was drunk cold.
Ben:	Oh, right.
Alice:	People loved chocolate so much that cocoa beans were used as money.
Presenter:	Really? I didn't know that. Amazing. So, er … when did chocolate first come to Europe?
Alice:	It was in the sixteenth century. It was brought here by the Spanish.
Presenter:	Oh yes, of course.
Alice:	400 years later and half the world's chocolate is eaten each year here in Europe.
Presenter:	Really? Each year?
Alice:	Yes. I'm not sure that's a good thing though. These days lots of sugar is added to most of the chocolate we eat.
Presenter:	I see.
Alice:	Yes, but you know chocolate wasn't sweet until the 1500s.
Presenter:	OK.
Alice:	Then, during the 1800s, milk was added to chocolate, too.
Presenter:	Interesting! So, are cocoa beans still grown in the Americas then?
Alice:	Actually, over two-thirds are grown in West Africa each year.
Presenter:	Oh, right.
Alice:	That often surprises people. Another thing is white chocolate. Do you like white chocolate?
Presenter:	Yes, I do actually. It's possibly my favourite.
Alice:	Well cocoa beans aren't used to make white chocolate, so it's actually not really chocolate at all, I'm afraid.
Presenter:	Oh dear!

Listening and vocabulary

Time expressions

6 Ss choose the correct alternatives alone, then check in pairs. When they are ready, play the recording again for Ss to check their answers. Check answers with the whole class.

Answers: 1 ago   2 nowadays   3 For   4 century   5 These
6 until   7 During   8 each

Vocabulary checkpoint

Until here is used to emphasise the duration, coming after a negative verb, e.g. *Mariah didn't rest until she was sure all her employees knew what to do.*

7a Ss complete the sentences alone, then check in pairs. Check answers with the whole class.

Answers: 1 until   2 for   3 century   4 Each   5 Nowadays
6 These   7 ago   8 Until

b Read the example with the class and give one or two of your own. Ss complete the sentences for themselves. Monitor and help with vocabulary, writing any new words/phrases on the board.

c Read the example with the class. Ss work in pairs and compare their sentences, giving more information where possible. In feedback, ask a few Ss to tell the class about their partner.

Optional extra activity

If you have any *fast finishers*, tell them that you'll ask them to tel the class about their partners afterwards and give them time to prepare what they're going to say.

Speaking

Prepare

8a Write the names of the objects on the board, then put Ss in pairs to discuss what they know about them. When they have finished, elicit what Ss know, but don't give any further information about them.

b Divide Ss into A and B pairs. Refer As and Bs to p157. Give them time to read the information. Encourage them to use dictionaries or their mobile devices to check the meanings of new words, but also be on hand to help where necessary.

Speak

9a/b Arrange Ss in pairs so that they're facing each other. Ss share their information in pairs and make notes. Monitor and check they're using the passive forms correctly and make notes on their language use for later feedback.

c Ss work in pairs and discuss the question, then share their ideas with the class. Give Ss feedback on their language use as a class.

Write the following questions on the board:

How confident do you feel using the passive?
How can you improve?

Put Ss in pairs to discuss the questions. When they have finished, ask if anyone wants to share their ideas with the class, but don't force them to if they'd rather not.

Ex 8b: Ss write a description of one of the objects.
Grammar bank: 10B Ex 1–2, pp.134–135
Workbook: Ex 1–5, p59
App: grammar and vocabulary practice

Fast route: continue to Lesson 10C
Extended route: go to p114 for Develop your writing

10c Unusual hobbies

Introduction

The goal of this lesson is for Ss to describe their hobbies and interests. To help them achieve this, they will revise the tenses learnt on the course and learn phrases related to hobbies and interests.

Warm-up

Arrange Ss in small groups and give them a few minutes to brainstorm all the hobbies that they can think of. When they have finished, invite a student from each group to the board to write up their answers and check the spelling. Carry out a short class survey (by show of hands) to find out which of the hobbies students do.

Reading

1a Focus Ss attention on the photos and the questions. Elicit their ideas, but don't give any answers yet.

b Ss read the article to check their ideas. Check answers with the whole class.

Answers:
Photo A: visiting Comic-con and dressing up as superheroes
Photo B: living like people in a small English village in the seventeenth century
Photo C: living like people from 100 years ago

2 Ss read the text again and choose the correct alternatives. Check answers with the class.

Answers: 1 more 2 has a good time 3 they like it
4 use electricity 5 act 6 education

Grammar

Review of tenses

3 The aim here is to review the tenses Ss have studied throughout the course. Ss match the statements and underlined sentences alone, then check in pairs. Tell Ss that not all the statements will match sentences and that statements in the text match more than one sentence. Check answers with the class and ask if Ss would like you to review any of them in a bit more detail.

Answers: 1 G 2 E 3 D 4 B 5 H 6 F 7 A 8 C

GRAMMAR BANK 10C pp.134–135
Stronger classes could read the notes at home. Otherwise, check the notes with Ss. In each exercise, elicit the first answer as an example. Ss work alone to complete the exercises, then check their answers in pairs. Then check answers with the whole class. Ss can refer to the notes to help them.

Answers: 10C
1 1 've always liked 2 was 3 loved 4 came
   5 was sitting 6 fell 7 've had 8 'm looking after
   9 'm going to open 10 it'll 11 'm meeting
2 1 've lived 2 were playing 3 'll use 4 sent
   5 'm learning 6 don't like 7 has written 8 're staying

4a 🔊 **10.5** Play the recording for Ss to listen to the pronunciation of the contracted words.

b Ss listen again and repeat. Drill chorally and individually for further practice if necessary.

5a Read the example with the class. Ss write the questions alone, then check in pairs. In feedback, ask different Ss to come to the board and write the questions, then check answers.

Answers:
1 What games did you play when you were a child?
2 What were you doing yesterday at 8 p.m.?
3 How long have you lived in your house?
4 What are you doing/going to do this evening?
5 What are you going to do next weekend?
6 What do you think the weather will be like tomorrow?
7 What are you reading at the moment?
8 Where do you live at the moment?

b Ss work in pairs and discuss the questions. Monitor and check they're using the tenses correctly. In feedback, ask a few Ss to share any interesting information they found out about their partners.

Photocopiable activities: 10C Grammar 1, p228;
10C Grammar 2, p229

Vocabulary

Hobbies and interests

6a Tell Ss about a new hobby you've started recently if possible. Ss read the tips then work in pairs and discuss which they think is best. Elicit Ss answers in feedback.

b Show Ss where *learn about something* is in the text. Ss find the others and underline them alone, then check in pairs.

Optional alternative activity

Before class, write the phrases on cards and cut each one in half so that there's a word or words on each half. Shuffle them and distribute one card to each Ss. Ask Ss to stand up and find their partners, using the text to help them.

c Ss complete the sentences alone, then check in pairs. Check answers with the whole class and ask if any of the sentences are true for them.

Answers: 1 try, find   2 joined, for   3 time, about   4 try, start

7 Ss work in pairs and discuss the questions. Encourage them to ask follow-up questions to find out more information. In feedback, elicit Ss' answers.

Further practice

Photocopiable activities: 10C Vocabulary, p230

Speaking

Prepare

8a 🔊 10.6 Go through the hobbies and interests in the box and check Ss understand what they are. Ss listen and tick the ones they hear.

Answers: making model planes, football, gardening, running

b Go through the questions, so Ss know what to listen for.

Answers: 1 a magazine with parts and instructions
2 over fifty   3 football   4 gardening   5 She doesn't have time.

Audioscript 10.6

Rob: My son wants to try something new, but I can't think of any good ideas. Did you have any hobbies when you were young, Megan?

Megan: Oh, yes, when I was a little girl I was really interested in making model aeroplanes.

Rob: That sounds like great fun. When did you start doing that?

Megan: Well, one day my grandfather bought me a magazine all about model planes. It came with all the parts and instructions. I just loved it, so after that I bought it every week. I think I made over fifty!

Rob: Wow, that's brilliant. Did you join a club, or anything?

Megan: Oh no, I just did it for fun at home. What about you?

Rob: Oh, I really loved football. I used to spend every evening and weekend playing with my friends. I also joined the local team. These days I just spend a lot of time gardening – I like growing vegetables.

Megan: Oh really? That's nice. What are you growing at the moment?

Rob: Lots of tomatoes and potatoes. I love them! And you? Do you still have a hobby?

Megan: No, not really, and I don't have much free time because of work. But I'd like to try something new. Maybe I'll start doing a sport. But I've never been very good at sport.

Rob: What about running? It's quite simple and you can start slowly. And you get better at it quite quickly. I started running last year and next year I'm going to run a marathon!

Megan: Wow, really? You know that's a good idea. I might join the running club near me, too.

9 Give Ss plenty of time to prepare their answers. Monitor and help with vocabulary where necessary, writing any new words/ phrases on the board.

Speak

10a Read the examples and model the activity by talking about your own hobby. Ss work in pairs and discuss their hobbies and interests using the questions in Ex 10 to help them. Monitor and make notes on Ss' language use for later feedback.

b Give Ss a minute or two to decide what they'll share, then ask them to share them with the class. Give Ss feedback on their language use as a class

Teaching tip

It's generally not a good idea to go around the class when eliciting things from every student as in Ex 11b, as they might switch off when it's not their turn. It's better to nominate Ss randomly, or ask them to nominate each other. Some teachers like to use a ball, or soft toy to do this, and ask Ss to throw it to the student they nominate.

Reflection on learning

Write the following questions on the board:
Which tenses do you feel you need to work on further?
How can you do this?
Put Ss in pairs to discuss the questions. When they have finished, ask if anyone wants to share their ideas with the class, but don't force them to if they'd rather not.

Homework ideas

Ex 10: Ss write a description of their hobby for a blog.
Grammar bank: 10C Ex 1–2, pp.134–135
Workbook: Ex 1–6, p60
App: grammar and vocabulary practice

Fast route: continue to Lesson 10D
Extended route: go to p115 for Develop your listening

10D English in action

Introduction

The goal of this lesson is for Ss to practise asking for and giving clarification. To help them achieve this, they will learn a range of phrases for asking for more information, asking someone to repeat something, saying they don't understand and saying they understand.

Listening

1 Ss work in pairs and discuss the questions. In feedback, elicit answers and have a brief class discussion.

2a 🔊 10.10 Ss listen and answer the question alone, then check in pairs. Check answers with the whole class.

Answer: Not at first.

b Give Ss one minute to read the statements, so they know what to listen for. Ss listen and mark the sentences alone, then check in pairs. Check answers with the whole class.

Answers: 1 F 2 T 3 F 4 T 5 F

Ss listen again and number the phrases 1 or 2 alone, then check in pairs. Check answers with the class.

Answers:

1 What's a (potluck party)?; Sorry, can you say that again?; I'm not sure what you mean.; I see

2 What do you mean, exactly?; What was the first part, again?; I don't understand; OK, got it.

Audioscript 10.10

A: Hey Kim, what are you doing this weekend?

B: Not much, why?

A: I'm having a potluck party on Saturday evening. Would you like to come?

B: I'd love to, but what's a potluck party?

A: Oh, it's a party where we all bring our own dishes.

B: Um … I'm not sure what you mean.

A: So we all prepare a dish at home, then bring it to the party. At the party, we share our food together.

B: Ah, I see. Sounds great! What time shall I come round?

A: Make sure you're there by six.

B: Sorry, can you say that again?

A: Sure, try to be there before six if you can. That's when we're going to start eating.

B: I see. I know just what I'll bring, too, I'll …

A: No, don't tell me – it has to be a surprise!

A: Hey James, how do I send something to another country?

B: Hi Tania – you need a DX4518 form.

A: A form? What do you mean exactly?

B: You need to fill in a DX4518 form.

A: A … what? Sorry, I don't understand.

B: Sorry, I wasn't very clear. So, first, email Sally and ask her to send you the form. Then fill in the information (the address and things) and give it to the boss. She'll say if it's OK.

A: OK … Sorry … What was the first part again? The name of the form?

B: DX4518. Get it from Sally, do you know her? She works in Human Resources.

A: OK, got it! Thanks a million, James!

4a 10.11 Write the first phrase in the Useful phrases box on the board, say it a few times and elicit the stressed syllables. Ss listen to the rest of the phrases and underline the stress then check in pairs. Check answers with the class.

Answers: What's a potluck party?
What do you mean, exactly? Can you say that again?
What was the first bit? I'm not sure what you mean.
I don't understand. OK, got it. I see.

b Ss listen again and repeat. Drill the phrases chorally and individually if necessary.

5a Ss complete the conversation alone, then check in pairs. Don't give any answers yet.

b 10.12 Ss listen and check. Check answers with the class. If you have time, ask Ss to practice the conversation, then swap roles and practise it again.

Answers: 1 mean 2 what's 3 Got 4 last 5 see

Speaking

Prepare

6 Give Ss time to pick one of the topics and think about the details they'll need to explain. Monitor and help with vocabulary, writing any new words/phrases on the board.

Speak

7 Read the examples with the class and remind Ss to use the Useful phrases in Ex 3 to help. Monitor and make notes on Ss' language use for later feedback. When they have finished, ask a few Ss to share what they found out with the class. Give Ss feedback on their use of language as a class.

> **Reflection on learning**
>
> Write the following questions on the board:
> *Which phrases were most useful from this lesson?*
> *How will you use them in the future?*
> Put Ss in pairs to discuss the questions. When they have finished, ask if anyone wants to share their ideas with the class, but don't force them to if they'd rather not.

Homework ideas

Workbook: Ex 1–2, p61

10 Check and reflect

Introduction

Ss revise and practise the language of Unit 10. The notes below provide some ideas for exploiting the activities in class, but you may want to set the exercises for homework, or use them as a diagnostic or progress test. For each grammar or vocabulary point, the first activity reviews the language and the second is more communicative, involving pairwork.

1a Ss match the sentence halves alone, then check in pairs. Check answers with the whole class.

Answers: 1 b 2 d 3 a 4 c 5 e

b Elicit an ending for the first sentence half in Ex 1a as an example. Ss write their own endings for sentences 1–5 alone. Monitor and help with vocabulary and check Ss are forming the first conditional correctly. When they are ready, Ss read out their endings and guess the first halves in pairs. In feedback, ask different Ss to read out their endings and guess in open pairs.

2a Ss complete the sentences alone, then check in pairs. Check answers with the whole class.

Answers: 1 pay 2 lend 3 earn/ borrowing 4 save 5 cost

b Ss work in pairs and discuss the questions. In feedback, nominate a few Ss to share anything interesting they found out about their partner with the class.

3a Ss choose the correct alternatives alone, then check in pairs. Check answers with the whole class.

Answers: 1 was 2 grown 3 isn't 4 watched 5 are
6 was

b Ss complete the prompts alone. Monitor and help with vocabulary where necessary, writing any new words/phrases on the board.

4a Ss correct the mistakes alone, then check in pairs. Check answers with the whole class.

> **Answers:** 1 ~~about~~ **until** 2 ~~years~~ **century** 3 ~~during~~ **until** 4 ~~this~~ **these** 5 ~~before~~ **ago**

b Ss discuss the sentences in pairs. In feedback, nominate Ss to share any interesting information about their partner with the class.

5 Ss complete the text alone, then check in pairs. Check answers with the whole class.

> **Answers:** 1 is/'s 2 moved 3 have/'ve known 4 was having 5 helped 6 is/'s studying 7 am/'m staying 8 will/'ll be

6a Ss complete the sentences alone. Monitor and help with vocabulary, writing any new words/phrases on the board.

b Ss compare their sentences in pairs. Encourage them to ask follow-up questions to find out more information.

7 Ss complete the sentences alone, then check in pairs. Check answers with the whole class.

> **Answers:** 1 start 2 join 3 spent 4 do 5 find 6 been 7 tries

Reflect

Ask Ss to rate each statement alone, then compare in pairs. Encourage them to ask any questions they still have about any of the areas covered in Unit 10.

10 Talk about … (Units 9–10 review)

Introduction

Ss revise and practise the language of Units 9 and 10 in a communicative game. This can be done after the Check and reflect page as a fun way to revise the language of Units 9 and 10.

Arrange Ss into small groups. Write numbers 1–6 on pieces of paper and put them in a bag. Ss take turns to take a number and move along the squares. Talk about what's in the square and answer any questions from your group. The first person to reach FINISH wins.

10A Develop your reading

Introduction

Ss develop their reading skill of understanding a blog post by learning how to identify opinions.

Warm-up

Elicit and write on the board a list of typical everyday activities, e.g. *spend time with family, watch TV, study, work, go shopping, cook,* etc. Arrange Ss in small groups to discuss what activities would make up their ideal day and how long they'd spend doing each one.

1 Ss work in pairs and discuss the questions. In feedback, elicit Ss ideas and have a brief class discussion.

2 Ss read the first paragraph of the blog post, then work in pairs and answer the questions. Check answers with the whole class.

> **Answers:**
> 1 cleaning, travelling to work and queueing
> 2 whats he wants to do

3 Give Ss a few minutes to read the Focus box or read it together as a class. Answer the question as a class.

> **Answers:** An opinion is our own idea. A fact is something true.

4a Ss read the rest of the blog post alone and decide if the sentences are facts or opinions alone. Don't give any answers yet.

b Ss compare answers and say why they're opinions or facts. Check answers with the whole class.

> **Answers:**
> 1 F: We're all so busy these days …
> 2 F: … we spend 547 hours a year …
> 3 O: I don't think …
> 4 O: In my opinion …
> 5 F: The report says …
> 6 O: I think this …
> 7 O: For me, …
> 8 F: The average time …
> 9 F: I save …
> 10 O: I feel …

5 Ss read the post again and answer the questions alone, then check in pairs. Check answers with the whole class.

> **Answers:**
> 1 they plan their day
> 2 answers work emails and waits for the bus.
> 3 walk instead of catching the bus
> 4 cook a lot of meals at once and then freeze it
> 5 So she doesn't waste time on social media.
> 6 She reads a book, listens to music or practises the guitar.

6 Ss work in pairs and discuss the questions. They could refer back to their discussion in the warmer if you did it. In feedback, ask a few Ss to share their ideas with the class.

Homework ideas

Workbook: Ex 1–4, p62

10B ▶ Develop your writing

Introduction

Ss develop their writing skill of writing a description of an object by learning about the order of adjectives.

Warm-up

Tell Ss that you've lost your bag somewhere on the way to work today. Put Ss in pairs and ask them to discuss what you should do to try and find it. When they have finished, elicit their ideas and write them on the board.

1 Focus attention on the photo and elicit where it is (a lost property office). Ss work in pairs and discuss the question. In feedback, elicit their answers and have a brief class discussion.

2 Ss read the report alone, then work in pairs and answer the questions. Check answers with the whole class.

Answers:
1 A wallet
2 19 June around 5.30 p.m.
3 Between platform 5 and the exit
4 Money, cards, driving licence, a house key and a key ring.

3a Read the example with the class. Ss find more adjectives alone, then check in pairs. Check answers with the whole class.

Answers: 1 old, brown, leather 2 small, thin, silver 3 round, metal

b Ss order the categories alone, then check in pairs. Don't give any answers yet.

4 Ss read the Focus box and check their answers. Check answers with the whole class.

Answers: 1 age 2 size 3 shape

5 Elicit the first answer as an example. Tell Ss that in item 5, silver refers to the colour, not the material. Ss complete the sentences alone, then check in pairs. Check answers with the whole class.

Answers: 1 new, grey, cotton 2 thin, brown and plastic 3 old, black, leather 4 big, long, silver 5 thick, round, gold

Prepare

5a Give Ss plenty of time to make notes. Monitor and help with vocabulary, writing any new words/phrases on the board.

b Refer Ss back to the adjectives in Ex 4 for ideas. Ss complete the notes alone.

Write

7 Ss write their descriptions alone. Monitor and check Ss' work while they write, and be on hand to offer help where necessary.

Homework ideas

Workbook: Ex 1–6, p63

10C ▶ Develop your listening

Introduction

Ss develop their listening skill of understanding informal English by learning how to understand pauses.

Warm-up

Describe a reality TV show you've watched and invite Ss to ask you questions to find out more information. Ss discuss reality TV shows they've watched in their country/ies in small groups. In feedback, nominate a student from each group to tell you about them.

1 Ss work in pairs and discuss the questions. In feedback, elicit their ideas and have a brief class discussion.

2 Focus attention on the photo and elicit what people can see. Ss read the programme information, then work in pairs and answer the questions. Check answers with the whole class.

Answers:
1 They have to live like people did 150 years ago, in an old-fashioned house.
2 If they're the last person in the house.
3 £100,000

3a ◁》 10.7 Ss listen to the interview and answer the questions alone, then check in pairs. Check answers with the whole class.

Answers: Stacey is happy, Kenny is sad.

b Ss listen again and answer the questions for each speaker, then check in pairs. Check answers with the whole class.

Answers:
Stacey:
1 nothing 2 the food
Kenny:
1 The clothes and the friends he's made in the house.
2 the food

Audioscript 10.7

Linda Cox: Stacey! How do you feel? Are you sorry to be leaving the house?

Stacey: Actually ... I'm really happy to leave – I won't miss anything! I liked it at first but now I miss ... er ... I miss my family and ... um ... I miss my comfortable sofa and ... um ... my dog!

Linda Cox: Aw, what's your dog's name?

Stacey: Cookie, he's a little Yorkshire terrier and I love him to bits! He's always there for me and ... um ... well, I just miss him lots!

Linda Cox: Wow! OK. And what didn't you like in the house?

Stacey: Let me see ... oh the food in the house was terrible. I really didn't like it. I can't wait to get home and have a proper meal in front of the TV.

Linda Cox: Haha! OK Stacey, I'll let you go. Everybody ... Stacey!

Stacey: Thank you!

Linda Cox: And here's our second contestant to leave the house ... Kenny, everybody! Kenny! How does it feel to be leaving the house now?

Kenny: Well, I'm sad to be leaving the house, and ... er ... the new friends I made in there, you know?

Linda Cox: Aw, we're sad to see you go, too! What will you miss?

Kenny: Oh ... I think the thing I'll miss the most is the clothes, you know? I like wearing really smart clothes, like the ones we wore in the house. Basically, I've never had the chance to wear clothes like that. So yeah ... um ... I'm really sad to be leaving!

Linda Cox: And is there anything you won't miss?
Kenny: Actually, I won't miss the food. As Stacey said, it was terrible!
Linda Cox: Thanks Kenny. Kenny, everybody!!

4 Give Ss a few minutes to read the Focus box or read it together as a class. Elicit Ss answers to the question.

Answers: *um, er* and *oh*

5a 🔊 10.8 Give Ss a minute or two to read the extracts and decide if they're starters or fillers. Ss listen and complete the extracts alone. Don't give any answers yet.
b Ss compare answers in pairs. Check answers with the whole class.

Answers: 1 er   2 well   3 Let me see   4 Oh   5 um

6a 🔊 10.9 Go through the questions with the class, so they know what to listen for. Ss listen and tick the questions alone, then check in pairs. Check answers with the whole class.

Answers: 2, 3, 1

b **Stronger classes** can answer the questions from memory, then listen again and check. Otherwise, Ss listen again and answer the questions alone, then check in pairs. Check answers with the whole class.

Answers: 1 false   2 true   3 false   4 false   5 true   6 true

Audioscript 10.9

Linda Cox: How are you feeling right now, Jackie?
Jackie: Well, I have to say I'm feeling good. Um … I really enjoyed my time in the house, but I'm happy to be going home now. I … er … really miss, really miss my family.
Linda Cox: Yes, we understand, Jackie! What are you going to do when you get home?
Jackie: Um … I'm not sure, really! I mean there's so much that I've missed. I think … um … I'll have something nice to eat, maybe a pizza!
Linda Cox: That sounds great. Do you have anything to say to the people still in the house?
Jackie: Actually, yes. I love you all!
Linda Cox: Aw, Jackie, everybody!

7 Ss work in pairs and discuss the questions. In feedback, elicit Ss' ideas and have a brief class discussion.

Homework ideas

Workbook: Ex 1–3, p61

RESOURCE BANK

Photocopiable activities index

1A Grammar 1 Word order in questions

1 Complete the questions in the conversation using the words in brackets.

A: Hi Monika! ¹_____ (are / how / you)?

B: I'm great, thanks. I'm just really tired because I had a long day at work.

A: Oh, really? ²_____ (do / work / you / where)?

B: At a restaurant in the city centre. Sometimes I work very long hours.

A: ³_____ (many / how / work / hours / you / do) a day?

B: I normally work eight hours a day, but today I worked ten because someone was ill.

A: Oh, that's a long day! ⁴_____ (you / do / do / what) when you get home from work?

B: I watch TV and films. They help me relax.

A: Oh, me too. ⁵_____ (kind / of / films / do / what) you like?

B: I love comedies.

A: Yes, I do, too. Hey, let's go to the cinema together sometime.

B: That sounds great! ⁶_____ (cinema / what / favourite / 's / your)?

A: I usually go to the independent cinema in the city centre.

B: Oh, really? ⁷_____ (like / do / you / why) it?

A: They always have interesting films and they've got really good food. Here's their website.

B: Oh, look! There's a good comedy on this week.

A: Oh, I really want to see that one! ⁸_____ (is / the main actor / who)? I've forgotten.

B: I think it's Chris Pine.

A: And ⁹_____ (on / it / when / is)?

B: Saturday at 7 p.m. Is that OK for you?

A: I think so. ¹⁰_____ (the / film / how / long / is)? I'm working early on Sunday.

B: I think it's only 90 minutes.

A: Great, see you on Saturday, then!

2 Work in pairs and practise the conversation.

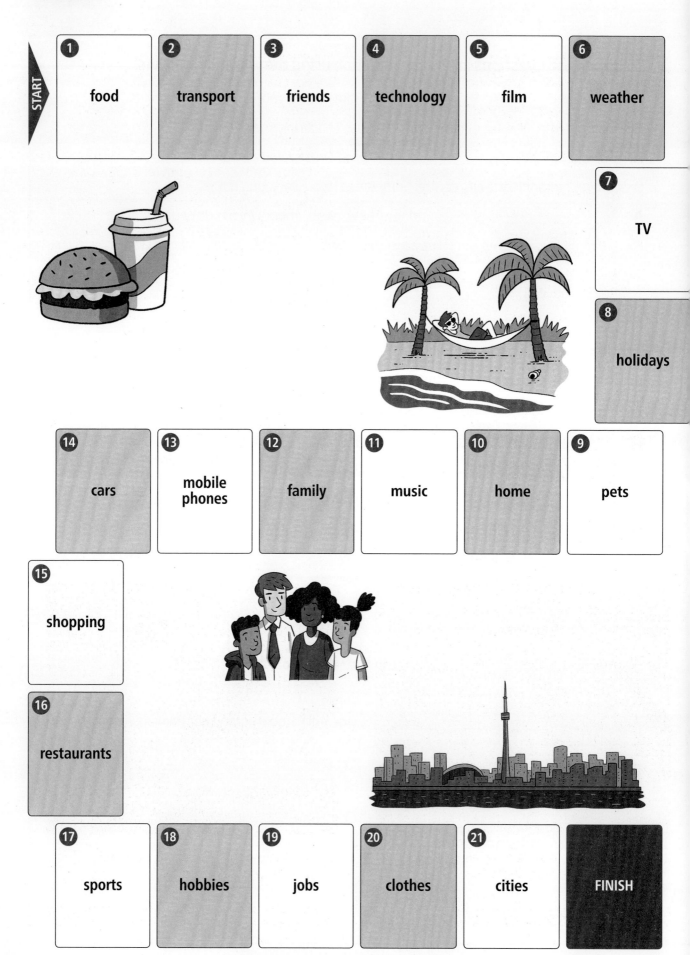

START

1. food
2. transport
3. friends
4. technology
5. film
6. weather
7. TV
8. holidays
9. pets
10. home
11. music
12. family
13. mobile phones
14. cars
15. shopping
16. restaurants
17. sports
18. hobbies
19. jobs
20. clothes
21. cities

FINISH

Quiz A

1 **Complete the questions with a suitable question word or phrase.**

1 _____ is a jaguar?
  a a big cat
  b a small horse
  c a fish

2 _____ is from Canada?
  a Arnold Schwarzenegger
  b Donald Trump
  c Ryan Gosling

3 _____ is Halloween?
  a 1st May
  b 14th February
  c 31st October

4 _____ of food is a tomato?
  a meat   **b** a fruit   **c** a vegetable

5 _____ is the Amazon River?
  a about 7,000 kilometres
  b about 4,000 kilometres
  c about 10,000 kilometres

6 _____ are the Pyramids?
  a in China   **b** in Egypt   **c** in Thailand

2 **Work in pairs. Take turns to ask and answer your quiz questions.**

Answers: 1a, 2c, 3c, 4b, 5a, 6b

Quiz B

1 **Complete the questions with a suitable question word or phrase.**

1 In _____ country do they eat haggis?
  a Turkey   **b** Scotland   **c** Germany

2 _____ hours is the flight from Beijing to Sydney?
  a about 11 hours 30 minutes
  b about 8 hours
  c about 20 hours 30 minutes

3 _____ is the capital of Morocco?
  a Marrakech
  b Rabat
  c Casablanca

4 _____ house is called The White House?
  a The President of the US
  b The Prime Minister of the UK
  c The President of Russia

5 _____ of drink is English Breakfast?
  a juice   **b** tea   **c** cola

6 _____ do penguins normally live?
  a The Arctic
  b The Antarctic
  c North America

2 **Work in pairs. Take turns to ask and answer your quiz questions.**

Answers: 1b, 2a, 3b, 4a, 5b, 6b

1 **Put the words in the correct order to make sentences.**

1 rarely / try / new / you / things _____

2 to / I / a / week / once / go / the gym _____

3 time / his / friends / sees / he / the / all _____

4 they / go / sometimes / together / to the cinema _____

5 we / ever / hardly / on holiday / go _____

6 before / reads / she / often / goes to bed / she _____

7 always / late / he / for / the train / is _____

8 doesn't / eat / breakfast / he / usually _____

9 am / in / the / often / bored / evenings / I _____

10 wears / she / a / watch / sometimes _____

11 a / month / once / my parents / I / see _____

12 twice / they / week / play / a / tennis _____

13 he / a nice person / is / always / not _____

14 clothes / he / comfortable / always / wears _____

15 three / times / she / year / visits a museum / a _____

16 hardly / up / they / wake / ever / early _____

17 usually / do the washing up / we / don't _____

18 I / on / look at photos / never / phone / my _____

2 **Choose five sentences from Exercise 1. Change them so three sentences are true for you and two sentences are false.**

3 **Work in pairs. Read your sentences to your partner. Guess which sentences are true and which are false.**

Find someone who ...	Name	Extra information
1 always does his/her homework. *How often do you do your homework?*		
2 goes to the cinema once a month or more.		
3 hardly ever eats breakfast.		
4 is usually on time.		
5 rarely goes shopping for clothes.		
6 tries new things all the time.		
7 never takes the bus.		
8 sometimes reads before bed.		
9 plays sport more than three times a week.		
10 eats in a restaurant twice a month or more.		

1 Complete the sentences with the verbs in the box. Then decide if you agree or disagree
   with each sentence.

ask	have	listen	plan	start	take (x2)	try

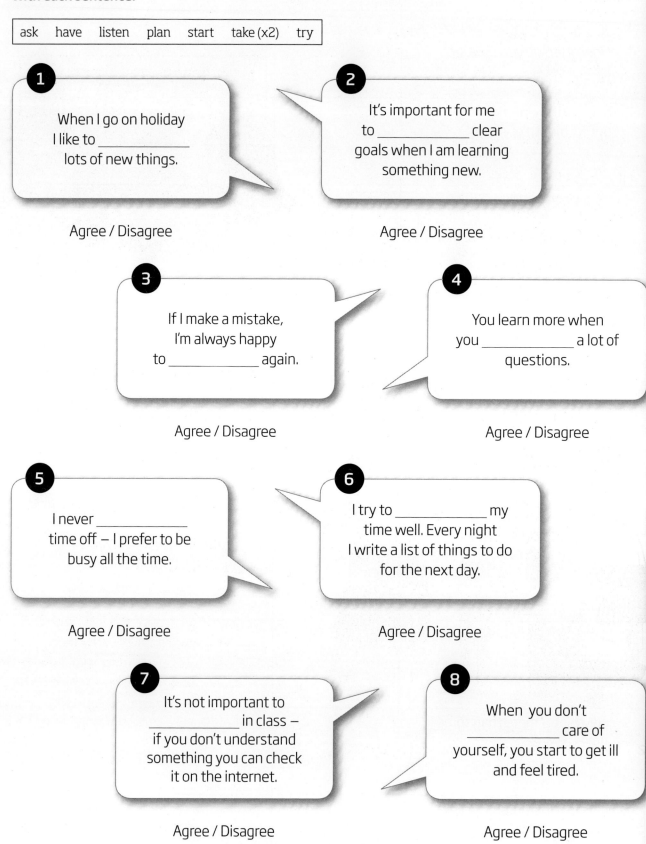

1
When I go on holiday
I like to _____
lots of new things.

Agree / Disagree

2
It's important for me
to _____ clear
goals when I am learning
something new.

Agree / Disagree

3
If I make a mistake,
I'm always happy
to _____ again.

Agree / Disagree

4
You learn more when
you _____ a lot of
questions.

Agree / Disagree

5
I never _____
time off – I prefer to be
busy all the time.

Agree / Disagree

6
I try to _____ my
time well. Every night
I write a list of things to do
for the next day.

Agree / Disagree

7
It's not important to
_____ in class –
if you don't understand
something you can check
it on the internet.

Agree / Disagree

8
When you don't
_____ care of
yourself, you start to get ill
and feel tired.

Agree / Disagree

2 Work in pairs. Compare your answers in Exercise 1 with your partner.

1C Grammar 1 Present simple and present continuous

1 Complete the conversations with the present simple or present continuous form of the verbs in brackets.

1 **A:** Hey Jess, what _____ you _____ (read)?

B: It's a book about film directors. I _____ (study) modern cinema this year at university, so it's really interesting!

A: Ah great, can I read it after you?

2 **A:** Would you like to meet for a drink later?

B: Sorry, I can't. I _____ (play) football every Tuesday with some friends.

A: Oh, that's OK. Don't worry about it.

3 **A:** Hey Mark! What _____ (do)?

B: I _____ (try) to fix my computer. It _____ (not work).

A: Can I help you at all?

4 **A:** Look! It _____ (rain) again.

B: Oh, no! My boots are outside and they _____ (get) wet.

A: Hurry up and bring them inside!

5 **A:** _____ you _____ (travel) a lot for your job?

B: Not really. I usually _____ (work) in our London office. But this week I _____ (help) in the Scottish office so I am in Glasgow all week.

A: That sounds great!

6 **A:** How often _____ you _____ (see) Paul?

B: Not very often unfortunately. He _____ (not live) near me and I never _____ (have) time to visit him.

A: What a shame!

2 Work in pairs and practise the conversations.

Card A

You are an actor.
You are making a film in London.
What is it called and who are you working with?

_____

Where are you from?   _____
Do you like London?   *yes/no*
Are you having a *fantastic/good/bad/terrible* time at the party?
Why?   _____

Card B

You are a writer.
You are writing a book in London.
What is it called and what is it about?

_____

Where are you from?   _____
Do you like London?   *yes/no*
Are you having a *fantastic/good/bad/terrible* time at the party?
Why?   _____

Card C

You are a singer.
You are making a new album in London.
What is it called and what type of music is it?

_____

Where are you from?   _____
Do you like London?   *yes/no*
Are you having a *fantastic/good/bad/terrible* time at the party?
Why?   _____

Card D

You are a film director.
You are making a film in London.
What is it called and who are you working with?

_____

Where are you from?   _____
Do you like London?   *yes/no*
Are you having a *fantastic/good/bad/terrible* time at the party?
Why?   _____

Card E

You are a famous sportsperson.
You are in London for a competition.
Which sport do you do and which competition are you in?

_____

Where are you from?   _____
Do you like London?   *yes/no*
Are you having a *fantastic/good/bad/terrible* time at the party?
Why?   _____

Card F

You are a TV presenter.
You are making a TV programme in London.
What is the programme about?

_____

Where are you from?   _____
Do you like London?   *yes/no*
Are you having a *fantastic/good/bad/terrible* time at the party?
Why?   _____

	actor	writer	singer	film director	sportsperson	TV presenter
Why is he/she in London?						
Where is he/she from?						
Does he/she like London?						
Is he/she enjoying the party?						

Student A

Joshua

Joshua is a secondary school student. He usually **1**_____ at 7 a.m., takes a shower and then eats breakfast. He **2**_____ at 8.15 a.m. and he usually walks there. He gets home around 4 p.m. and always **3**_____ for an hour and then does his homework. Joshua's mum often gets angry with him because he checks social media during dinner all the time.

Ali

Ali is a lawyer and **4**_____ very early. He doesn't like getting up early, but he has a lot to do at work each day. He **5**_____ in the afternoon and has a coffee – he really needs it! He always takes a taxi after work because he hates the bus and he doesn't have a car. When he gets home, he's tired, so he usually sits in his living room and **6**_____ .

Heather

Heather is a primary school teacher and she has a lot of hobbies. She enjoys **7**_____ and playing the piano. At the weekends, she never checks her emails. She thinks that is something you only do at work. She also **8**_____ every Saturday evening with her friends. They like to play cards together and they always have a **9**_____ !

Student B

Joshua

Joshua is a secondary school student. He usually gets up at 7 a.m., **1**_____ and then eats breakfast. He starts school at 8.15 a.m. and he usually walks there. He **2**_____ around 4 p.m. and always plays video games for an hour and then does his homework. Joshua's mum often gets angry with him because he **3**_____ during dinner all the time.

Ali

Ali is a lawyer and starts work very early. He doesn't like **4**_____ early, but he has a lot to do at work each day. He takes a break in the afternoon and has a coffee – he really needs it! He always **5**_____ after work because he hates the bus and he doesn't have a car. When he **6**_____ , he's tired, so he usually sits in his living room and and watches TV.

Heather

Heather is a primary school teacher and she has a lot of hobbies! She enjoys taking pictures of animals and **7**_____ . At the weekends, she never **8**_____ . She thinks that is something you only do at work. She also spends every Saturday evening with her friends. They like to **9**_____ together and they always have a good time!

2A Grammar 1 Past simple

1 Write sentences in the past simple using the prompts.

1 She / arrive / at the airport / at 9.15 a.m. _____

2 He / delete / a lot of emails / this morning. _____

3 The game / end / at 8 p.m. _____

4 They / be / excited / about the party. _____

5 Last week / we / play / ice hockey / in the street. _____

6 She / wake up / early / today. _____

7 Elliot / not be / at school / last week. _____

8 I / go / to / Thailand / and / try / pad thai. _____

9 She / travel / to China / last year. _____

10 They / watch / a film / at the cinema / last night. _____

11 Jason / get / a new bicycle / yesterday. _____

12 The rain / stop / at 10 a.m. / this morning. _____

13 Today / Chris and Amy / decide / to buy / a house. _____

14 Last week / I / have / a job interview. _____

15 Our first class / start / at 10 a.m. / this morning. _____

16 We / look / at photos / yesterday. _____

17 Jamie / miss / the bus / this afternoon. _____

18 I / talk / to Cheryl / last night. _____

19 They / not be / at home / two days ago. _____

20 She / take / the train / to New York. _____

2 Choose three sentences from Exercise 1 and change them so they are true for you.

3 Work in pairs and compare your sentences.

Grammar 2 Past simple

Card A

| arrive | be | decide | have | paint | start | travel | watch |

1 Almost 20 million people in the UK _____ the wedding of Prince Harry and Meghan Markle on TV.

2 Hastings Banda _____ President of Malawi until 1984.

3 The year 1752 _____ 354 days.

4 Justin Bieber _____ his singing career on Facebook.

5 In 1994, Canada _____ to make skiing their official winter sport.

6 Yuri Gargarin was the first man who _____ in space.

7 Van Gogh _____ more than 3,000 paintings in his lifetime.

8 Christopher Columbus first _____ in America in 1492.

Card B

| arrive | be | decide | have | paint | start | travel | watch |

1 Almost 10 million people in the UK _____ the wedding of Prince Harry and Meghan Markle on TV.

2 Hastings Banda _____ President of Malawi until 1994.

3 The year 1752 _____ 365 days.

4 Justin Bieber _____ his singing career at Disney World.

5 In 1994, Canada _____ to make hockey their official winter sport.

6 Neil Armstrong was the first man who _____ in space.

7 Van Gogh _____ more than 900 paintings in his lifetime.

8 Christopher Columbus first _____ in America in 1392.

Card C

| arrive | be | decide | have | paint | start | travel | watch |

1 Almost 30 million people in the UK _____ the wedding of Prince Harry and Meghan Markle on TV.

2 Hastings Banda _____ President of Malawi until 2004.

3 The year 1752 _____ 366 days.

4 Justin Bieber _____ his singing career on YouTube.

5 In 1994, Canada _____ to make ice skating their official winter sport.

6 Buzz Aldrin was the first man who _____ in space.

7 Van Gogh _____ more than 1,500 paintings in his lifetime.

8 Christopher Columbus first _____ in America in 1292.

Three things that make us feel afraid
1 _____
2 _____
3 _____

Three things that make us feel stressed
1 _____
2 _____
3 _____

Three things that make us feel surprised
1 _____
2 _____
3 _____

Three things that make us feel worried
1 _____
2 _____
3 _____

Three things that make us feel angry
1 _____
2 _____
3 _____

Three things that make us feel bored
1 _____
2 _____
3 _____

Three things that make us feel excited
1 _____
2 _____
3 _____

Three things that make us feel happy
1 _____
2 _____
3 _____

Three things that make us feel relaxed
1 _____
2 _____
3 _____

Three things that make us feel nervous
1 _____
2 _____
3 _____

2B Grammar 1 Past simple negative and questions

1 Put the words in the correct order to make questions.

1 you / do / what / yesterday / did / ?

_____

2 like / vegetables / did / you / young / you / were / when / ?

_____

3 you / at / last / were / home / night / ?

_____

4 at university / you / 2015 / were / in / ?

_____

5 did / you / travel / where / 2017 / in / ?

_____

6 where / you / did / go / night / last / ?

_____

7 your / do / did / you / English homework / ?

_____

8 was / who / best friend / your / when / a child / were / you / ?

_____

9 you / what / on / birthday / did / last / do / your / ?

_____

10 live / ago / you / five years / where / did / ?

_____

2 Complete the gaps with the negative form of a verb from the box. Then match each answer with a question from Exercise 1.

be (x2) celebrate come do eat enjoy live meet visit

a No, I _____ broccoli or carrots until I was ten years old. *2*

b I _____ my last birthday at all. I hate birthdays.

c I _____ in the same house as I do now. I was in another city five hours from here.

d No, I _____ to class last week.

e I went to Peru. I _____ Macchu Pichu, though.

f The cinema. The film I watched _____ very good.

g Well, I worked all day yesterday, so I _____ very much.

h Yes, but I _____ it as I found the work hard.

i No, I _____ . I went to my friend's house.

j Her name was Ashley. We _____ at school – she was in my dance class.

3 Work in pairs and practise asking and answering the questions in Exercise 1.

1 Look at the pictures and make negative sentences in the past simple using the prompts in brackets.

1 (hear/the alarm)

He didn't hear the alarm.

2 (be/happy)

_____

3 (know/the answer)

_____

4 (watch/the match)

_____

5 (rain)

_____

6 (be/angry)

_____

7 (tidy up)

_____

8 (close/the gate)

_____

9 (miss/the bus)

_____

2 Write two more negative sentences for each picture.

3 Work in pairs and compare your sentences.

Vocabulary Past time expressions

When did your partner last …	Guess	Your partner's answer
1 go to the cinema? *When did you last go to the cinema?*	*a month ago*	*last week*
2 celebrate his/her birthday?		
3 eat at a restaurant?		
4 check social media?		
5 go to the dentist?		
6 spend money?		
7 try something new?		
8 study maths?		
9 spend time with family?		
10 take the bus?		

1 Correct ten mistakes in the shopping list.

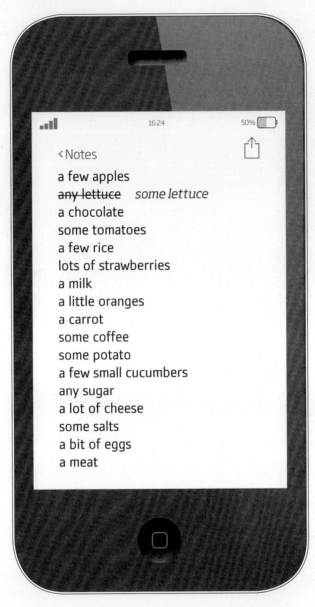

< Notes

a few apples
~~any lettuce~~ *some lettuce*
a chocolate
some tomatoes
a few rice
lots of strawberries
a milk
a little oranges
a carrot
some coffee
some potato
a few small cucumbers
any sugar
a lot of cheese
some salts
a bit of eggs
a meat

2 Complete the table with the items from the shopping list in Exercise 1.

Countable	Uncountable

3 Work in pairs and imagine you have the items on the shopping list in Exercise 1.
What are you going to make for dinner?

2C Grammar 2 Quantifiers

creamy	**creamy**	**creamy**	**creamy**
delicious	**delicious**	**delicious**	**delicious**
dry	**dry**	**dry**	**dry**
fresh	**fresh**	**fresh**	**fresh**
hot	**hot**	**hot**	**hot**
light	**light**	**light**	**light**
plain	**plain**	**plain**	**plain**
sour	**sour**	**sour**	**sour**
sweet	**sweet**	**sweet**	**sweet**

1 Complete the sentences with the comparative form of the adjectives in the box.

| beautiful | exciting | fast | hot | long | modern | peaceful | popular | sweet | tall |

Espresso Time is _____ than *Latte Central*.

2 Apples are _____ than lemons.

3 The woman is _____ than the man.

4 The beach is _____ than the mountains.

5 Crows are _____ than parrots.

6 Skydiving is _____ than hiking.

7 Cheetahs can run _____ than people.

8 The boy is _____ as the girl.

9 Jill has _____ hair than Natasha.

10 Alicia's house is _____ than Greg's.

Write other comparative sentences for the pictures in Exercise 1.

3A Grammar 2 Comparatives

START ➤	train / bus	?	you / your best friend	Canada / Spain
TV shows / films	running / walking	rock music / pop music	?	lion / elephant
London / Dubai	?	Saturday / Monday	English / your first language	?
horses / cats	football / ballet	computer / phone	pizza / sushi	town / countryside
?	museums / concerts	?	2018 / 1954 ➤	FINISH

good	tall	hot	beautiful	short
happy	boring	intelligent	small	cheap
crowded	lively	noisy	clean	easy

A

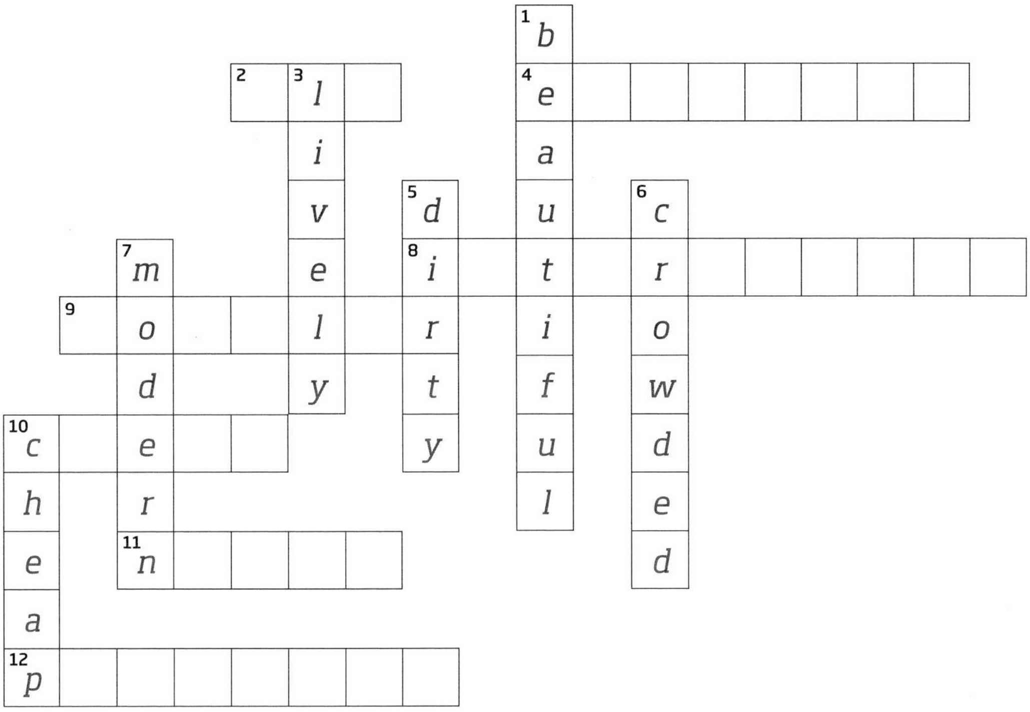

1 beautiful
3 lively
5 dirty
6 crowded
7 modern
10 cheap
4 e
8 i
9 o
11 n
12 p

B

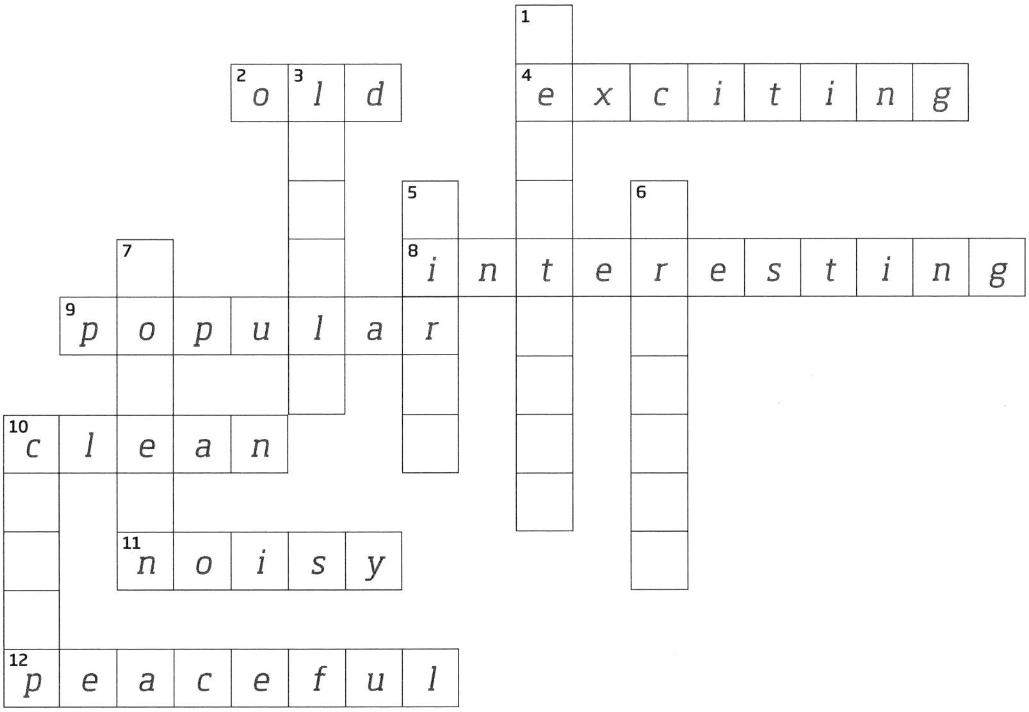

2 old
4 exciting
8 interesting
9 popular
10 clean
11 noisy
12 peaceful

1 Complete the sentences with the superlative form of the adjectives in brackets.

1 The _____ (long) rabbit ears in the world were …

2 The world's _____ (popular) tourist destination is France. The number of visitors to France is …

3 The Vatican, in Rome, is the world's _____ (small) country. Its area is …

4 The world's _____ (tall) building is …

5 The _____ (small) cinema in the world is in Germany and it has …

6 The world's _____ (large) stir-fry was cooked at the University of Massachusetts in the US. It weighed …

7 The world's _____ (heavy) apple was …

8 The _____ (fast) animal on land is the cheetah, which can run at …

9 The First World Hotel in Malaysia, is the world's _____ (big) hotel. It has …

10 The world's _____ (tall) man was an American called Robert Wadlow. He grew to …

2 Match the sentence beginnings in Exercise 1 with endings a–j.

a … 120 kilometres per hour. Some birds can fly even faster than this.   *8*

b … 0.44 square kilometres and fewer than 1,000 people live there.

c … 1,819 kilograms and was 4.27 metres wide.

d … 79 centimetres. The animal was a pet in the US.

e … 7,351 rooms. It has had over 35 million guests since 2006.

f … 828 metres tall. It is the Burj Khalifa in Dubai.

g … nine seats. It is owned by Johannes Gerhardt and opened in October 2006.

h … 1.849 kilograms. A farmer grew it in Japan in 2005.

i … around 83 million every year. The US is second, and Spain is third.

j … 2 metres 72 centimetres.

3 Work in pairs and discuss which is the most surprising fact.

3B Grammar 2 Superlatives

1 Complete the questions with the superlative form of the adjectives in brackets. The write your answers.

1 Who is ____________ (good) actor at the moment?

____

2 What is ____________ (dangerous) job?

____

3 Where is ____________ (relaxing) place in the world?

____

4 What is ____________ (beautiful) animal?

____

5 Who is ____________ (funny) person you know?

____

6 What is ____________ (old) building in your town?

____

7 Where is ____________ (interesting) place to visit in your country?

____

8 Who is ____________ (bad) singer in the world?

____

9 Which is ____________ (happy) country in the world?

____

10 What is ____________ (delicious) food you can cook?

____

2 Work in pairs. Ask and answer the questions in Exercise 1. Are your answers the same?

1 Complete texts A and B with the words in the box.

| airport transfers | breakfast included | check out | double rooms | four-star |
| free parking | organised tours | room service | sea view | 24-hour reception |

A

Majestic Hotel, Dubrovnik ★★★★

from
£80/night

Come and stay in our incredible
1_____ hotel in the
middle of Dubrovnik. The hotel has a
swimming pool and free wifi, and there's
2_____ with all
rooms – you can choose from fresh croissants,
omelettes, pancakes and more. Don't want to
get out of your pyjamas? Then just call for
3_____ ! We can bring
lots of delicious food to your room.

To see the city, we have
4_____ with a popular
local guide. Come and speak to us at our
5_____ for more information.

B

Mermaid Resort and Spa, Florida Keys ★★★★★

from
£200/night

Welcome to the fantastic Mermaid Resort and
Spa, a five-star hotel with a beautiful
6_____ from every room.
You can see the blue ocean from your window
when you open your curtains!

We have a variety of accommodation types,
including 7_____ , suites
and apartments. We also provide free
8_____ to and from the
hotel; or if you have a car with you there is
9_____ .

Do you enjoy a few extra hours in bed in the
morning? Ask us about our late
10_____ options. You can
stay until 12 noon or 2 p.m.

Come and join us here at the Mermaid and feel the beautiful Florida sun on your face.

2 Work in pairs. Which hotel would you like to stay in? Why?

3C Grammar 1 Present perfect with *ever* and *never*

Decide if each sentence is correct (✓) or incorrect (✗). Then correct the incorrect sentences.

	✓ / ✗	Correct sentence
1 Last year he's travelled to South America.	✗	*Last year he travelled to South America.*
2 I've never been on an aeroplane.		
3 Have you ever tried sushi?		
4 She has never meet a famous person.		
5 Did you ever see a film in an outdoor cinema?		
6 They haven't never driven in another country.		
7 We've never visited the Louvre in Paris.		
8 Has he ever taken an art course?		
9 She has never did yoga.		
10 I have never eaten pizza when I was in Italy.		
11 She has never been to the US.		
12 They have ever been to the theatre.		

2 Work in pairs. Have you done the things in Exercise 1? Tell your partner.

PHOTOCOPIABLE © Pearson Education Limited 2019

1

go abroad

Have you ever _____?

Which country did you like the most?

_____

2

receive a present you didn't like

Have you ever _____?

What was it?

_____

3

have room service

Have you ever _____?

What did you order?

_____

4

find money in the street

Have you ever _____?

What did you do?

_____

5

be on TV

Have you ever _____?

Did your family see you?

_____

6

study another language (not English)

Have you ever _____?

What did you study?

_____

7

break a bone

Have you ever _____?

Which bone did you break?

_____

8

live in a different town/city

Have you ever _____?

Where did you live?

_____

A

a bike	a bone	asleep
an art gallery	with chopsticks	to swim
a meal	a photo online	a sports car

B

a football match	a photo online	skiing
a meal	a bone	on TV
to swim	a bike	asleep

4A Grammar 1 *be going to, want* and *would like*

Put the words in the correct order to make sentences.

1 travel / I'd / to / country / next / like / a / year / to / different

_____

2 week / next / want / I / the cinema / go / to / to

_____

3 going / I'm / cake / to / make / a / tonight

_____

4 to / buy / I / a / I'm / want / when / sports car / 40

_____

5 play / after / football / to / like / work / I'd

_____

6 want / I / to / don't / chocolate / today / eat

_____

7 soon / I'm / to / going / house / move

_____

8 like / two / the beach / in / to / I'd / time / go / to / weeks'

_____

9 I'm / tomorrow / my / meet / going / to / lunch / for / friends

_____

10 I'm / to / the gym / tonight / go / going / to / not

_____

11 don't / work / I / go / to / on / Friday / want / to

_____

12 to / visit / gallery / like / I'd / today / an / later / art

_____

PHOTOCOPIABLE © **Pearson Education Limited 2019**

4A Grammar 2 *be going to, want* and *would like*

	Alex	Sam	Casey	Robin
Where / go?				
Why / go / there?				
Who / go / with?				
When / go?				

Alex

Use this information to answer the questions the other travellers ask you.

Where: The US

Why: the Grand Canyon; American food; Californian beaches

With: two friends

When: in the summer

Sam

Use this information to answer the questions the other travellers ask you.

Where: China

Why: Beijing; the Great Wall of China; love Chinese culture

With: your family

When: in the spring

Casey

Use this information to answer the questions the other travellers ask you.

Where: Switzerland

Why: skiing; delicious cheese

With: your husband/wife

When: in the winter

Robin

Use this information to answer the questions the other travellers ask you.

Where: Morocco

Why: busy markets; French and Arabic language; the sea

With: alone

When: in the autumn

1 **Match sentence beginnings 1–10 with the endings a–j.**

  1 Holi is a colourful Indian ...   *c*

  2 The 4th July is a public ...

  3 Hanbok is the traditional ...

  4 In Mexico they celebrate ...

  5 In Japan you give ...

  6 In Spain, they have dinner ...

  7 At Winterlude festival, Canadians have ...

  8 In some countries in Latin America, when you get ...

  9 At Christmas time, people often contact ...

10 For birthdays in the UK, it is common to go ...

  a ... clothing of South Korea. Koreans wear it for festivals.

  b ... parties with family and friends on New Year's Eve.

  c ... festival. It happens in March when spring arrives.

  d ... together with friends for a celebration, it is normal to arrive 15–20 minutes late.

  e ... old friends to share news with them and send good wishes.

  f ... Day of the Dead (El Día de los Muertos) on 2nd November.

  g ... out for a meal with close friends and family.

  h ... holiday in the US. It is called Independence Day.

  i ... fun ice skating on the Rideau Canal.

  j ... gifts with both hands. Gifts are a very important part of any celebration.

2 **Work in pairs. What things do you celebrate in your country? Tell your partner.**

1 Read the conversations and correct the mistake in each answer.

1 **A:** Chantelle's birthday is on Saturday.

 B: Oh, really? We'll ~~to~~ buy her a gift, then.
 Oh, really? We'll buy her a gift, then.

2 **A:** I've left a piece of cake in the fridge. It isn't for you!

 B: Don't worry, I won't not eat it.

 _____

3 **A:** I think I'm going to study French. There's a language course starting next month.

 B: I won't do it with you. I've always wanted to study French.

 _____

4 **A:** I need to eat something before I go to work.

 B: I'm making some toast – I'll makes some for you, too.

 _____

5 **A:** I can't find Dari's mobile number anywhere!

 B: I'll will give it to you.

 _____

6 **A:** I need to send a birthday card to my mum.

 B: I take it for you. I'm going to the post office this afternoon.

 _____

7 **A:** Dad, can you drive me to Lily's house tonight?

 B: Sorry, I can't. I'll asking your mum if she can drive you.

 _____

8 **A:** Do you have room service? I'd like to order some food.

 B: Of course, madam. We don't bring the menu to your room.

 _____

9 **A:** I'm really tired, I'm going to sleep now.

 B: OK, I will make any noise.

 _____

10 **A:** This pasta doesn't taste very nice.

 B: I'm sorry to hear that, sir. I will to ask the kitchen to make you some more.

 _____

2 Work in pairs and practise the corrected conversations.

1 Wow! This bag is so heavy!

2 I have to go to a party tonight. I don't really want to go alone.

3 Ugh! I just don't understand this grammar!

4 Excuse me, sir/madam, but my food is cold.

5 Oh no! I've missed my train. How will I get home?

6 After that party last night, my flat is so dirty.

7 Oops, I forgot to call the restaurant to change our booking for tonight.

8 I haven't eaten much today. I'm really hungry!

9 Uh oh! I forgot to make food to bring to our meeting tomorrow morning.

10 I don't have enough money for the concert tickets, but I really want to go!

11 Do you know where White Lane is? I think I'm lost.

12 I think I've broken my foot. It really hurts.

13 I have to go to work now, but there is an important letter coming for me this afternoon.

14 I'm going to miss you. When will I see you again?

1 Complete the sentences with the correct form of the verbs in the box.

bake	book	choose	make	plan	remind	send	set

1 When it's someone's birthday I always _____ a cake.

2 I've _____ the place where I'm going on holiday next year. I'm going to go to Yosemite National Park in the US.

3 I don't _____ invitations when I have a party. I just message my friends to tell them about it.

4 I need to _____ a date with my friends to celebrate our exam results – we are all very happy we passed!

5 I'd really like to _____ a singer for my birthday party.

6 My friend has asked me to _____ some food for her dinner party. I'm going to make a vegetable risotto and a fruit salad.

7 If I need to _____ people about a party, I always telephone them a week before so they don't forget about it!

8 I'm _____ lots of activities for our holiday. I want to try salsa dancing, go on a boat trip and visit the local caves.

2 Read the sentences in Exercise 1 again and change them so they are true for you. Then compare your sentences with a partner.

1 _____

2 _____

3 _____

4 _____

5 _____

6 _____

7 _____

8 _____

Choose the correct alternatives.

1   Smoking is very bad for you. You *have to/can't* stop doing it!

2   My birthday is next week and we still *can/have to* choose a place to have my party.

3   Dad said that we *can/don't have to* have ice cream today.

4   I'm sorry, you *can't/don't have to* use your credit card to pay for food here.

5   It's a very hot day today. You *can/don't have to* wear a jacket.

6   This is an exam. You *can't/can* use your mobile phone in here!

7   My computer is broken. I *have to/can* get a new one.

8   I'm not working today. Maybe we *can/don't have to* go for a coffee this afternoon?

9   The concert is free. You *can/don't have to* buy a ticket.

10   There are no trains from Euston train station today. We *can't/have to* take the bus.

11   You *can/can't* park here. This car park is only for the restaurant.

12   Tomorrow is a public holiday. I *don't have to/can't* go to bed early.

13   The business meeting tomorrow is very important. You *have to/can't* wear jeans.

14   When you go to university, you need to do a lot of work. You *don't have to/can't* be lazy!

15   I learned German in secondary school. I *have to/don't have to* speak it in my job in Berlin now.

16   Yes, miss. You *can/can't* get your money back for these headphones.

4C Grammar 2 *can* and *have to*

Student A

Imagine you are mayor of your town. You want your town to be very relaxed.
Complete the rules below.

RULES

1 People in _____ (*name of town*) _____.
2 People can't _____.
3 Everybody has to _____.
4 People can _____.
5 You don't have to _____.
6 You can't _____.
7 _____.

Student B

Imagine you are mayor of your town. You want your town to be very different, with rules that no other town has.
Complete the rules below.

RULES

1 People in _____ (*name of town*) _____.
2 People can't _____.
3 Everybody has to _____.
4 People can _____.
5 You don't have to _____.
6 You can't _____.
7 _____.

Student C

Imagine you are mayor of your town. You want the town to be very organised, with very clear rules.
Complete the rules below.

RULES

1 People in _____ (*name of town*) _____.
2 People can't _____.
3 Everybody has to _____.
4 People can _____.
5 You don't have to _____.
6 You can't _____.
7 _____.

4C Vocabulary -ed and -ing adjectives

A

Choose the correct alternatives. Then complete the sentences with names of students in the class.

1 _____ thinks shopping is *relaxed/relaxing*.

2 _____ is *excited/exciting* about the weekend.

3 _____ thinks adverts on TV are *bored/boring*.

4 _____ feels a bit *tired/tiring* at the moment.

5 _____ is *worried/worrying* about the environment.

B

Choose the correct alternatives. Then complete the sentences with names of students in the class.

1 _____ thinks that learning English is *tired/tiring*.

2 _____ doesn't like football because it's *boring/bored*.

3 _____ is *interested/interesting* in history.

4 _____ finds jazz music *relaxed/relaxing*.

5 _____ has read a lot of *excited/exciting* books.

C

Choose the correct alternatives. Then complete the sentences with names of students in the class.

1 _____ is *interested/interesting* in different cultures.

2 _____ thinks the news is often *surprised/surprising*.

3 _____ thinks cars are *excited/exciting*.

4 _____ sometimes feels *worried/worrying* about the future.

5 _____ gets *bored/boring* very easily.

Grammar 1 Relative clauses with *who, which* and *that*

1 Choose the correct alternatives. Then complete the sentences so they are true for you.

1 The place *who/that* I want to visit the most is _____ .

2 The actor *who/which* I like watching the most is _____ .

3 The person *which/who* has been my friend the longest is _____ .

4 The best book *who/that* I have ever read is _____ .

5 The person *which/who* has taught me the most in my life is _____ .

6 The nicest city *who/that* I have visited is _____ .

7 In my opinion, the job *who/which* is the most boring is _____ .

8 For me, the job *that/who* sounds the most exciting is _____ .

9 The food *who/which* I love the most is _____ .

10 It's important to me to be someone *who/which* _____ .

2 Work in pairs and compare your sentences in Exercise 1.

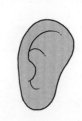
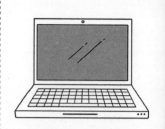
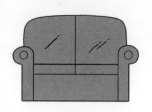

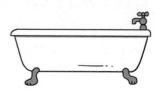

Card A

Job 1 I often work on my own. _____

Job 2 I have a job that is very creative and that is well-paid. _____

Job 3 I can work part-time, but I often work on Saturdays. _____

Job 4 I'm a good manager. _____

Job 5 I often wear interesting, colourful clothes. _____

Job 6 I have to remember a lot of information. _____

Card B

Job 1 I have to be very creative and have lots of new ideas. _____

Job 2 I use special programmes on a computer to do my work. _____

Job 3 There are a lot of different products where I work. _____

Job 4 I can make a lot of money. _____

Job 5 I work long hours and have to wait around a lot. _____

Job 6 I never work from home – I always work in the city streets.
_____

Card C

Job 1 Grammar, spelling and punctuation is very important. _____

Job 2 I need to know how to draw buildings very well. _____

Job 3 Good communication skills are important because I deal with customers
every day. _____

Job 4 I sometimes work long hours at my office in the city centre.

_____

Job 5 I sometimes meet famous actors. _____

Job 6 It's important to be interested in history to do my job. _____

5B Grammar 1 *look like, look* + adjective, *be like*

1 **Complete the conversations with the correct form of *look like, look* + adjective or *be like*.**

1 **A:** What does he _____?

   B: He's tall and blonde.

2 **A:** What is Suzy _____?

   B: She's really friendly.

3 **A:** How is David feeling?

   B: I'm not sure, but he _____ sad.

4 **A:** How old do you think those girls are?

   B: They _____ about 20.

5 **A:** What do you think she does?

   B: She _____ an artist.

6 **A:** How old is Louise's mum?

   B: I don't really know, but she _____ about 55.

7 **A:** Who does she _____?

   B: Her dad. She has the same eyes.

8 **A:** What is that actor _____?

   B: He's really good, actually. He can play any character.

9 **A:** What happened to her? She _____ angry.

   B: I don't know, but you're right.

10 **A:** What do they _____?

   B: They're both tall and have curly hair.

11 **A:** What does he do?

   B: He _____ a businessperson.

12 **A:** What city is in this photo?

   B: It _____ Dubai.

2 **Work in pairs. Practise asking and answering the questions in Exercise 1.**

A

B

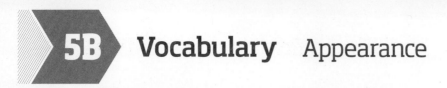

5B Vocabulary Appearance

Complete the sentences with the words in the box.

bald	beard	blonde	casual	curly	~~dark~~	long	moustache
slim	smart	straight	tall	tattoo			

Demi is nine years old. She has brown eyes and ¹____*dark*____ brown hair and looks like her dad, but her hair has always been ²_____ like her mum's.

Harry is ³_____ because he runs and plays sport a lot. At two metres, he's very ⁴_____ , too. He's the captain of his basketball team.

Camilla looks like her mother. She has always had light ⁵_____ hair and it's very ⁶_____ , not curly. Camilla's friends think she is a lot of fun.

Peter and Stefan are very ⁷_____ . They always wear a suit and tie to work. Peter is ⁸_____ but has a dark ⁹_____ . He usually wears expensive glasses. Stefan has fair hair and a ¹⁰_____ .

Peter   Stefan

Brianna exercises four days a week and always wears ¹¹_____ clothes. She has very ¹²_____ hair and has a small ¹³_____ of a rose above her ankle.

▷ **5C** ▷ **Grammar 1** *should, shouldn't* and imperatives

1 Find and correct the mistake in each sentence.

Money saving advice

1 Thinks before you buy something. Do you really need it?
Think before you buy something.

2 Finding a way to make more money. Can you do any extra work?

3 You should saving money to buy the big things you want. Don't spend money on little things you don't need.

4 You should to have money saved for an emergency.

5 You don't use your credit card every day. Only buy things you have the money for.

6 You should sell things that you don't need. Get you some extra cash!

7 Doesn't pay more than you have to for your phone. Do some research to get the lowest price.

8 You should planning your meals and grocery list. This will help you control your spending.

9 You should knew how much you have spent at the end of each month.

10 You look for a discount when you can.

11 Don't going shopping. This way, you won't want to buy things.

12 Using online supermarkets. You can see your total and you won't buy things you don't need.

13 Making dinner at home. This will be cheaper than going to a restaurant.

14 You shouldn't to buy your lunch from a shop every day. Take lunch with you from home.

15 Keep your extra coins somewhere and you use them when you need to.

2 Work in pairs. Do you agree with the advice in Exercise 1? What other advice would you give?

Student A

You are going travelling for six months alone. You have never travelled before.
Ask your friends for advice on:

* how to meet people

* how to stay safe

* what to do if you get lost

Student B

Your job is very stressful. You work long hours and your boss is extremely difficult to work for. Ask your friends for advice on:

* how to relax

* what to do about your boss

* how to change how you work

Student C

Your mum is angry at you because you missed her birthday. You have a bad memory and you forgot!
Ask your friends for advice on:

* what to say to your mum

* what gift to buy for your mum

* how to improve your memory so that you don't forget things

Student D

You live a very unhealthy lifestyle. You eat junk food a lot and you're tired all the time. You don't like going to the gym, but now you want to get healthy. Ask your friends for advice on:

* healthy food/drinks

* fun and healthy activities/sports to do

* other lifestyle changes to make

5C Vocabulary Shopping

1 Choose the correct alternatives.

1 I bought a mirror on sale online but I don't like it. You can usually *return things / compare prices* from a sale, but sometimes you have to pay to send them back.

2 I'm going to buy a new television soon, but I don't know which kind to get. I think I'll go online and *compare prices / keep the receipt* before I decide which one to buy.

8 I'm booking a big holiday and I'm a little worried about spending so much money. So I'm going to *buy the tickets on sale / pay by credit card*, so I can pay a little every month.

3 I want to do a language course, but they're expensive and I don't know if I'll like it. I think I'll *read reviews / pay by credit card* to see what other students say about this school.

7 I bought some shoes last week but they're really uncomfortable. I don't know why I didn't *try them on / read reviews* to see if they fitted me.

4 The mobile phone I bought last week has broken! Luckily, I've *asked for a discount / kept the receipt*, so I'll be able to get my money back.

6 I've found a dress I love in a sale, but there's a small hole at the bottom of it. I'm going to *compare prices / ask for a discount*, then fix it myself if I can.

5 Yesterday I was shopping online and I saw a coffee machine that I want to buy, but it's very expensive. I'm going to check other shops because I'd like to get it *on sale / by credit card* if I can.

2 Work in pairs. Have you had any similar experiences? What happened?

1 **Put the words in the correct order to make predictions.**

In 10 years

1 fast food / I / popular / will / think / less / be

_____

2 will / only / eat / chicken / beef / people / and / not

_____

3 farmers / the / will / world / need / more

_____

4 be / a lot / than / people / fatter / in the past / will

_____

5 teachers / be / there / won't / schools / in

_____

In 50 years

6 be / learn / easier / it / to / a language / will

_____

7 any / fruit / won't / or / there / be / vegetables

_____

8 of / Mandarin Chinese / the / 50% / speak / world / will

_____

9 have / we / heads / computers / in / will / our

_____

10 think / live / we'll / don't / I / houses / in / big

_____

In 100 years

11 will / no one / English / speak

_____

12 have / will / don't / people / think / pets / I

_____

13 won't / to / people / need / eat / real food

_____

14 more / I / will / there / think / cities / be

_____

15 there / won't / as many / languages / be

_____

2 **Work in pairs. Which predictions do you think will/won't happen? Why?**

Pescaville is a small fishing village. It's a very beautiful place by the sea. The local community is very close and everybody knows and helps each other. They have never had many visitors. However, Global Compass holiday company has made a proposal to the villagers. They want to make Pescaville into a new, modern tourist destination. They are planning to build hotels, restaurants, activity areas and souvenir shops. To do this they need to buy land from the residents and they are offering a lot of money. Tonight, there is a meeting in the village hall to discuss the village's options.

Resident A

You are the director of Global Compass.
You must convince people that your plan is a good idea. Think about the positive things that will happen, e.g. more businesses will come, there will be more choice for shopping and a more international atmosphere.

Resident B

You are the owner of a very small hotel.
You don't like the idea: you believe people come to your hotel because the place is very peaceful. Think about the negative things that will happen, e.g. you think you will lose business to big hotels, there will be higher prices and Global Compass will build ugly buildings.

Resident C

You are a mother/father of two small children.
You like Pescaville because you think it's a nice place to bring up children. Think about the negative things that will happen, e.g. more noise, more traffic and more crime. You think it will be a dangerous place for children.

Resident D

You are a young person who has just finished a tourism course. You love your village but you'd like it to change. Think about the good things that will happen, e.g. there will be more things to do and opportunities to meet people from different places. The atmosphere will be much better and there will also be more jobs.

6A   Vocabulary   Happiness

1. Is it important to earn a lot of money? Why/Why not?

2. Do you think you can have a good career and a happy family life? How?

3. Do you think it's important to eat well every day? Why/Why not?

4. Do you like to keep fit? How much exercise do you do each week?

5. How much free time do you have? Is it enough?

6. Do you have a lot of interests and hobbies? Why/Why not?

7. Do you have a busy social life? Are you happy with your social life?

8. What is a simple life to you? Do you want to live this type of life?

9. Do you think it's important to have a good sense of humour? Why/Why not?

Student A

You are a professional footballer who makes a lot of money. Your health is also very important for your job. Think about how you will answer the questions.

Student B

You are a relaxed parent of three children. You live in the countryside and have six chickens. Think about how you will answer the questions.

Student C

You are an important businessperson. You work for a very large company and you work around 60 hours a week. Think about how you will answer the questions.

Student D

You are a university student who is studying art. You share a flat with three of your best friends. Think about how you will answer the questions.

1 **Complete the conversations with the present continuous form of the verbs in the box.**

| do (x2)   go (x2)   make   meet   not start   play   study   take |

1 **A:** I _____ Jack tonight at 8 o'clock.

   B: Not him again! He wasn't very nice last time you met.

   A: Hey! I really like him! Anyway, we _____ to a great restaurant.

2 **A:** Jenny looks really worried. What's wrong with her?

   B: She _____ dinner for her parents tonight and she's really stressed about it.

   A: Oh, she's a great cook – I'm sure it will be delicious!

3 **A:** Hey, Mike! How are you?

   B: I'm good, thanks. Oh, I _____ to the cinema to see that new Spielberg film tonight. Want to come?

   A: No, thanks. I _____ tennis with my girlfriend.

4 **A:** Agnes, what _____ you _____ tonight?

   B: I _____ . I've got a big exam tomorrow.

   A: Oh, that's a shame. I wanted you to come to a party with me.

5 **A:** Marcus, guess what? I got that job I wanted!

   B: Wow, congratulations!

   A: Thanks, and I _____ until next month, so now I have two weeks off!

6 **A:** I'm really excited about tonight!

   B: Why, what _____ you _____ ?

   A: Jess and I _____ a Thai cooking class.

2 **Work in pairs and practise the conversations in Exercise 1.**

6B Grammar 2 Present continuous for future arrangements

You're going to a festival called Wild Thing. Complete the diary below with the activities you would like to attend.

WILD THING FESTIVAL

	FRIDAY	SATURDAY	SUNDAY
10.30 a.m.	∗ Yoga with Marta on Sunrise Beach ∗ Drawing class in the West tent ∗ Sea swimming competition	∗ Beginner guitar lessons in the West tent ∗ Salsa show on Stage two ∗ Aerobics class in the East tent	∗ Volleyball on Sunrise Beach ∗ Pilates class on Sunset Beach ∗ Beginner drums lessons in the East tent
3 p.m.	∗ Indian cooking class in the Wild Thing tent ∗ Intermediate Spanish lessons in the East tent ∗ The Wild Thing Choir: join the singers in the West tent	∗ French class in the West tent ∗ Zumba with Derek on Stage one ∗ Football match on Sunset Beach	∗ Classic Film Club 'Casablanca' in the East tent ∗ Gardening class in the West tent ∗ Romeo and Juliet on Stage one
9 p.m.	∗ Comedy Night in the East tent ∗ Ed Sheeran concert on Stage one ∗ DJ Kev G '80s night' on Sunset Beach	∗ Murder Mystery evening in the Wild Thing tent ∗ Rock concert on Stage one ∗ Classical music concert on Sunset Beach	∗ BBQ and closing fireworks

	Friday	Saturday	Sunday
morning			
afternoon			
evening			

190

PHOTOCOPIABLE © Pearson Education Limited 2019

cooking	exercise	a picnic	a haircut
an excuse	lunch	an excuse	shopping
a haircut	a meeting with someone	housework	a meeting
an appointment	a day off	lunch with someone	exercise
a barbecue	a picnic	shopping	a cake
cooking	a meal	an appointment with someone	work
a day off	housework	lunch	a meal

cooking	exercise	a picnic	a haircut
an excuse	lunch	an excuse	shopping
a haircut	a meeting with someone	housework	a meeting
an appointment	a day off	lunch with someone	exercise
a barbecue	a picnic	shopping	a cake
cooking	a meal	an appointment with someone	work
a day off	housework	lunch	a meal

6C Grammar 1 *may* and *might*

Complete the sentences with *may/might (not)* and a verb in the box.

be (x2)	buy (x2)	cook	fail	finish	get	go (x2)	have	look	meet	wake

1 There's a band playing tonight that I really like. I _____ a ticket to see them.

2 I don't feel very well today. I _____ to work tomorrow.

3 You shouldn't make so much noise, kids! Your mum's sleeping and you _____ her up.

4 Matt is having problems with his car. He _____ late to the meeting.

5 Julie wants to see the new Melissa McCarthy film. She and I _____ to the cinema this evening.

6 I haven't seen Sarah for ages! I _____ her for lunch tomorrow.

7 We are learning more and more about our health now. In the future, people _____ as unhealthy as they are now.

8 Rob hasn't studied for his exam and it's tomorrow! I think he _____ it.

9 We really love that house that we saw yesterday. We _____ it.

10 I don't like my boss! I _____ for a job in a different company.

11 I'm feeling very lazy today. I _____ dinner tonight.

12 You shouldn't drive so fast! You _____ an accident.

13 Helen said that she wants to travel. She _____ school!

14 The kids are playing very close to the road. They _____ hurt.

What are you doing tomorrow?

What are your plans for the summer?

What are you going to eat for dinner?

What TV series are you going to watch next?

Where would you like to go on your next holiday?

What do you want to do next year?

What do you think you will wear tomorrow?

Is there anything you want to change in your home?

What do you think the next thing you buy will be?

What new activities do you want to try in the future?

What are you doing this weekend?

Is there anything you want to learn how to cook?

Where do you think you will live in the future?

What do you think you will do on the next public holiday?

What do you think you will do on your next birthday?

A How many people do these things at the weekend?

1 do yoga   **2** go shopping   **3** play volleyball

Questions	Student(s)	Total
1		
2		
3		

B How many people do these things at the weekend?

1 play the guitar   **2** go running   **3** do lots of different activities

Questions	Student(s)	Total
1		
2		
3		

C How many people do these things at the weekend?

1 go dancing   **2** do homework   **3** play video games

Questions	Student(s)	Total
1		
2		
3		

D How many people do these things at the weekend?

1 go cycling   **2** do the gardening   **3** do nothing

Questions	Student(s)	Total
1		
2		
3		

Choose the correct options, a, b or c. Sometimes two options are correct.

1 a The child is too big for his favourite bicycle.
  b The child isn't small enough for his favourite bicycle.
  c The child is too much big for his favourite bicycle.

2 a Beth doesn't have enough money to buy a sports car.
  b Beth doesn't have money enough to buy a sports car.
  c Beth has not enough money to buy a sports car.

3 a I can't eat that cake – it's sweet too for me.
  b I can't eat that cake – it's too sweet for me.
  c I can't eat that cake – it's too enough sweet for me.

4 a There is much too traffic in the street – I hate it!
  b There is too many traffic in the street – I hate it!
  c There is too much traffic in the street – I hate it!

5 a The computer isn't fast enough – it's driving me crazy.
  b The computer is too slow – it's driving me crazy.
  c The computer is too much slow – it's driving me crazy.

6 a There are too people in the room, so let's go outside.
  b There are too many people in the room, so let's go outside.
  c The people are too many in the room, so let's go outside.

7 a I'm afraid your daughter is short too for this ride.
  b I'm afraid your daughter isn't short enough for this ride.
  c I'm afraid your daughter is too short for this ride.

8 a It's not hot enough outside to wear shorts.
  b It's not enough hot outside to wear shorts.
  c It's too cold outside to wear shorts.

You're eating in a restaurant.	You're having a picnic in the park.	You're at the gym.	You're at the airport.
You're skiing.	You're driving.	You're watching a football match.	You're looking at social media.
You're watching a film at the cinema.	You're cooking dinner.	You're working at the office.	You're on holiday.
You're visiting an art gallery.	You're in a supermarket.	You're in the city centre.	You're staying in a hotel.

7A Vocabulary Features of city life

1 Complete the paragraphs with the words and phrases in the box.

> area   cycle paths   flats   local (x2)   location   neighbours   night life
> pollution   public transport   traffic

Ellen

I live in the UK in an **1**_____ of Birmingham called Moseley. It's in a great **2**_____ because it's close to the city centre and the countryside. There are many delicious restaurants to eat at, and there are a lot of small, **3**_____ shops. You can buy so many interesting types of clothes there! One great thing about Birmingham is that there are a lot of parks. The bad thing about Birmingham is that there is a lot of **4**_____. Sometimes it takes an hour to drive two miles through the city centre!

Andrew

Where I live, we don't have much **5**_____ – the air is very clean because there are no factories and there is a lot of space. My house is in the countryside in Canada. There are no **6**_____ here because most people live in big houses on farms with animals. It's a great place to ride your bike, too. There are lots of **7**_____ and you can see some beautiful places on your bike. Another thing I love about where I live is that we know our **8**_____ very well. Everybody talks to each other here – it's the perfect place to live!

Olga

I live in the centre of the best city in Europe, Budapest! You can find everything here. There are great hospitals and schools, and the **9**_____ is amazing because we have buses, trams, a metro and trains. One of the best things about the city is the **10**_____. Lots of clubs, cafes and restaurants stay open until very late. My **11**_____ area has lots of activities for people to do: tennis, swimming, badminton. Budapest is a great place to live!

2 Work in pairs. Would you like to live in any of the places in Exercise 1? Why/Why not?

1   **Complete the sentences with the correct form of *used to* and the verbs in brackets.**

   1   I _____ (be) an actor, but now I'm studying to be a teacher.

   2   Sam _____ (eat) meat. He was a vegetarian.

   3   Laura told me she hasn't always been an architect. What _____ she _____ (do)?

   4   I only see Margot at Christmas now. We _____ (see) each other three times a year.

   5   She _____ (drive), but now she drives to work every day.

   6   _____ you _____ (play) video games when you were younger?

   7   I _____ (play) a lot of sport but now I play football, basketball and tennis.

   8   I always _____ (bake) at the weekend, but I don't anymore.

   9   We _____ (speak) English. We only started learning it two years ago.

   10   Charles _____ (smoke), but he stopped because he felt too unhealthy.

   11   Ken told me Amber and Ashley were in a band at university. _____ they _____ (sing) together?

   12   I don't live at home now, but I _____ (live) with my parents.

   13   I know you like rock music now. What _____ you _____ (listen) to when you were younger?

   14   I eat a lot of fruit and vegetables now, but I _____ (like) many of them when I was a child.

2   **Choose four of the sentences from Exercise 1 and change them so they are true for you.**

A

Work in groups and complete the sentences with your own ideas.

1 Before we had cars …
_____
_____

2 Before there were mobile phones …
_____
_____

3 Before English was an international language …
_____
_____

4 Before we used credit cards …
_____
_____

5 Before there were glasses …
_____
_____

B

Work in groups and complete the sentences with your own ideas.

1 Before there were TVs …
_____
_____

2 Before we had computers …
_____
_____

3 Before there was fast food …
_____
_____

4 Before we had fridges …
_____
_____

5 Before we had online shopping …
_____
_____

beach	mountain	lake
stream	forest	river
hill	wood	sea

Decide if the sentences are correct or incorrect. Then correct the incorrect sentences.

1 I don't usually like the chicken, but that was delicious!

 I don't usually like chicken, but that was delicious!

2 I used to have the cat called Bubbles. He was so cute!

3 Children often get very excited on their birthdays.

4 Next week I'm going to see film with my mum.

5 I need to buy the new t-shirts soon. Mine are old.

6 You left your mobile on top of the bookshelf.

7 Tonight I'm going to buy my dad a gift for his birthday.

8 Yesterday I ate the pasta for lunch. I love Italian food!

9 Can I borrow a book you had last week? It looked good.

10 The door at the back of the house is broken.

11 I'm watching TV show called *Utopia*. It's very exciting!

12 Can you please take a kids to the park tonight?

13 Did you like a film that you saw yesterday?

14 There's an armchair in the kitchen.

15 Shrewsbury is the town in the west of England.

a man	an accident	the problem	a question
in a band	a mistake	on the street	working long hours
a woman	a flower	the worst day	the shopping
in the evening	a banana	the money	an appointment
at the moment	a love song	housework	the moon
a fantastic day	the nicest thing	a knife	a public holiday
the name of	in the corner	a great time	the sky
a sign	a few days	on the TV	a river
a great idea	the police	a big surprise	the truth

Picture A

Picture B

8A Grammar 1 Past continuous

1 Complete the story with the past continuous or past simple form of the verbs in brackets.

In August last year, I ¹_____ (travelling) around Scotland with a friend of mine for a month. In Fort William we ²_____ (stay) with an old friend of ours from university and he ³_____ (talk) to us about Loch Ness, which is a lake that is famous because some people believe a monster called Nessie lives in it.

We ⁴_____ (decide) to go there the next day. While we ⁵_____ (drive), we ⁶_____ (see) a lot of beautiful trees and mountains. Finally, after an hour, we ⁷_____ (travel) beside Loch Ness. It ⁸_____ (look) like a big black mirror.

Soon we ⁹_____ (stop) at the Loch Ness Visitor Centre. It ¹⁰_____ (be) very busy, and lots of tourists ¹¹_____ (take) pictures in front of the lake. We ¹²_____ (buy) some lunch and we ate it outside while we ¹³_____ (wait) for an organised tour to start.

But then, while I ¹⁴_____ (look) at the water, I ¹⁵_____ (see) something moving. My friend ¹⁶_____ (stand) opposite me, so the lake was behind her, and she didn't see it.

I quickly ¹⁷_____ (run) to the water to see what it was, but when I ¹⁸_____ (get) closer, it was gone.

Was it Nessie? I will never know for sure.

2 Work in pairs and practise telling the story in Exercise 1.

Last Saturday at 7 p.m. someone stole an expensive necklace from a house in your neighbourhood. You are a police officer interviewing the neighbours. Ask questions to find out what people were doing at 7 p.m. on Saturday and complete the information below. The person who stole the necklace is lying. Who do you think it is?

1 _____ was watching a film.

2 _____ was playing a sport.

3 _____ was shopping.

4 _____ was taking a dance class.

5 _____ was having dinner.

6 _____ was driving somewhere.

7 _____ was studying French.

8 _____ was watching a film at the cinema.

9 _____ was staying in a hotel.

10 I think _____ was stealing the necklace.

A

You were watching a film. Think about:
1 where you were watching it
2 which film you were watching
3 who you were with

B

You were playing a sport. Think about:
1 where you were playing it
2 what sport you were playing
3 who you were with

C

You were shopping. Think about:
1 where you were shopping
2 what you were looking for
3 who you were with

D

You were taking a dance class. Think about:
1 where you were taking the class
2 what type of dancing you were doing
3 who you were with

E

You were having dinner. Think about:
1 where you were having dinner
2 what you ate
3 who you were with

F

You were driving somewhere. Think about:
1 where you were driving to
2 why you were going there
3 who you were with

G

You were studying French. Think about:
1 where you were
2 what you learnt
3 who you were with

H

You were watching a film at the cinema. Think about:
1 where you were
2 which film you were watching
3 who you were with

I

You were staying in a hotel. Think about:
1 where you were staying
2 why you were at a hotel
3 who you were with

J

You stole the necklace! Say you were doing something else. Think about:
1 where you were
2 what you were doing
3 who you were with

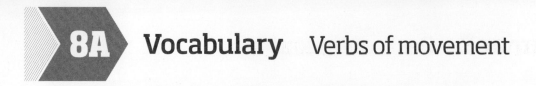

1 Choose the correct alternatives.

1 Zac ran out of the house and immediately fell *over/into* because he didn't see the step.

2 When I was younger I travelled *into/around* South East Asia – it was a fantastic experience.

3 She came *over/back* to the classroom because she had forgotten her bag.

4 Can you go *out/over* and get me a pint of milk, please?

5 They went *around/into* the shop to buy some cakes for the party.

6 She didn't want to get *over/up* because she went to bed very late.

7 I had to go and lie *down/around* – it was very hot and I was feeling unwell.

8 When Polly turned *around/out* she got a big shock – there was a mouse on her chair!

2 Work in pairs. Think of …

1 three reasons why you might have to get up.

_____

_____

_____

2 three things you can lie down on that are not a bed.

_____

_____

_____

3 three reasons why you might turn around.

_____

_____

_____

4 three reasons you might come back to the classroom after class.

_____

_____

_____

5 three reasons why you might go out of a room quickly

_____

_____

_____

6 three ways you can make a headache go away.

_____

_____

_____

8B Grammar 1 *because, so* and *to*

1 Match the sentence halves.

1 I love going to Jamaica on holiday ...   *d*

2 Last night it was raining, ...

3 I think we need to stop for lunch now ...

4 I want to go shopping ...

5 It was getting late, ...

6 He turned around ...

7 The baby was crying, ...

8 I used to walk in the forest ...

9 I'm excited to see Evan tonight ...

10 Every summer I go to Ireland for a month ...

11 We've been to Paris four times ...

12 There is too much pollution in cities ...

a ... because I'm really hungry!

b ... to visit the Louvre and other museums.

c ... so Mary gave her a toy.

d ... because it is usually hot and sunny.

e ... because he heard a strange noise.

f ... because I haven't seen him in a long time.

g ... to buy some new clothes for summer.

h ... to relax when I felt stressed.

i ... so we took a taxi to the restaurant.

j ... so we went to bed.

k ... so we should take public transport and drive less.

l ... to stay with my grandparents.

2 Write new endings for sentence beginnings 1–12 in Exercise 1.

3 Work in pairs and compare your new sentences with your partner.

rent a car	Vancouver	tired	lie down	do yoga
stay healthy	sea	boat	spend time with friends	traffic
pollution	neighbours	quiet	do gardening	exercise
money	a new shirt	a meal	interesting	relax
have a party	celebrate	oranges	Paris	flowers
watch	go on social media	a four-star hotel	stressed	afraid

D

You're going on holiday to South East Asia and are very excited. You p_____ your car at a friend's house and she drives you to the airport. First stop is Thailand!

K

You g_____ o_____ the plane and it's sunny and beautiful. But your bags are not in Thailand – oh dear! Without your bags, you take a b_____ to your hotel. Bangkok is amazing!

A

When you g_____ o_____ the bus, you don't have your money. You left it on the seat.

E

You get more money from the bank, and decide to r_____ a bike. It's a cheap way to move around the city.

C

The bike breaks. You g_____ i_____ a taxi but the roads are very busy so it takes two hours to go back to the hotel. You're tired and you sleep well.

I

The next day you decide to do a tour of the old city. You t_____ a train to go there. It's a very interesting place and Thai people are very friendly. Then you go back to the hotel to look at flights to Cambodia.

H

That evening, your bags arrive and you decide to fly to Angkor Wat in Cambodia the next day. But you arrive at the airport very late and you m_____ the flight! Luckily there is another one the day after tomorrow.

B

Two days later, you arrive in Cambodia and r_____ a small flat in a town near Angkor Wat. The local area is beautiful! A friend r_____ a car and offers to take you to Angkor Wat the next day.

G

After a week in Cambodia, you fly to Vietnam. You arrive safely in Hanoi and decide to take one of the city's trams that are more than 100 years old. There is a tram stop not far from your hotel. You g_____ o_____ and go for a short ride.

J

When you g_____ o_____ the tram you feel very tired from all your travel. It's time to relax for a few days before you go home.

F

You fly home and g_____ i_____ a taxi to go and pick up your car. You are annoyed when the driver p_____ the taxi at a shop for five minutes while he buys food. But finally you can g_____ o_____ o_____ the taxi at your friend's house and drive home. What a great trip it has been!

8C Grammar 1 Verb patterns

1 Complete the sentences with the correct form of the verbs in brackets.

1 I love ___*reading*___ (read) books.

2 My sister always wants _____ (spend) time with her friends after school.

3 My best friend likes _____ (drink) tea with biscuits.

4 I enjoy _____ (watch) football when I have time.

5 My cousin would like _____ (ride) her new bike this weekend.

6 Beth enjoys _____ (relax) in front of the television after work.

7 My dad hates _____ (eat) sweets because they're bad for his teeth.

8 I want _____ (become) a doctor so I have to study hard.

9 My sister enjoys _____ (swim) at the weekend.

10 We want _____ (travel) to Australia this summer.

11 My mum doesn't mind _____ (go) to the cinema, but she prefers watching films at home.

12 John would like _____ (go) to more sports games in his free time.

2 Choose the correct alternatives.

1 Frankie really *enjoys/would like* cooking because she thinks it's relaxing.

2 My sister *doesn't hate/doesn't mind* travelling by plane, but she prefers travelling by train.

3 Ben loves *play/playing* hockey. He plays with his team three times a week.

4 My parents want *going/to go* travelling next year. They are thinking about going to Mexico.

5 My mum doesn't like *watch/watching* funny films. She prefers dramas.

6 We *don't want/don't enjoy* to watch tomorrow's football match with our dad because he always shouts at the TV.

8C Grammar 2 Verb patterns

Student A

1 **Complete the questions with the correct form of the verbs in brackets.**

1 What jobs in the home don't you mind _____ (do)?

2 Do you love _____ (learn) English? Why/Why not?

3 Which place in the world would you really like _____ (visit)?

4 Which sports do you enjoy _____ (watch) on TV?

5 When do you want _____ (retire)?

2 **Work in pairs. Take turns to ask and answer the questions in Exercise 1. Then try to describe each person in the group.**

Student B

1 **Complete the questions with the correct form of the verbs in brackets.**

1 Do you love _____ (speak) to people you don't know?

2 What things don't you mind _____ (spend) money on?

3 Which sports do you enjoy _____ (play)?

4 Do you want _____ (earn) a lot of money in the future? Why/Why not?

5 Would you like _____ (live) in another country?

2 **Work in pairs. Take turns to ask and answer the questions in Exercise 1. Then try to describe each person in the group.**

Student C

1 **Complete the questions with the correct form of the verbs in brackets.**

1 Where do you want _____ (be) in ten years?

2 Would you like _____ (become) a famous pop star, sports star or film star?

3 What do you enjoy _____ (eat) for breakfast?

4 What type of music do you hate _____ (listen) to?

5 Do you love _____ (speak) in public? Why/Why not?

2 **Work in pairs. Take turns to ask and answer the questions in Exercise 1. Then try to describe each person in the group.**

1 **You are planning your next holiday.**
What kind of place would you like to visit?
a Somewhere hot where you can relax
b Somewhere with lots of mountains and activities
c Somewhere with an interesting culture

2 **You've decided where you want to go.**
You're going in two months. Now what do you do?
a Nothing yet. I have a lot of time to think about it!
b Book your flights and look at what adventure sports they have.
c Look at some places you can visit there.

3 **When you're there, you'll probably …**
a do things with the friends or family you are there with.
b look around alone.
c try to meet local people to talk to.

4 **When you pack your bags, you prefer to …**
a pack a big suitcase with everything you will need!
b travel light with just a backpack. You don't need a lot of things!
c pack things that will help you look like a local.

5 **When you are on your trip, you would like to …**
a go shopping. There's a lot you can buy!
b try new things, for example surfing.
c go sightseeing around the local area.

6 **While you are on holiday, you prefer to …**
a only take taxis or planes.
b rent a car and drive around the area on your own.
c take buses and trains so you can meet people on your journey.

7 **Your perfect holiday is …**
a to go on a cruise, where everything is in one place.
b to go on an adventure holiday. Show me the action!
c to go on a holiday where you can learn a lot about the area.

Results:

Mostly As: You enjoy easy holidays where you don't have to worry too much. You like things to be organised for you and don't want to feel stressed. You don't travel light because you like to have your things with you. A good holiday for you is a cruise, for example in the Caribbean or the Mediterranean.

Mostly Bs: You are an adventurer! When you're on holiday, you really want to be active and see what nature can show you. You don't want to sit down and relax – you want to play outside and enjoy all of your time in a new place. A great holiday for you is backpacking for a few months somewhere far from home that has a lot of activities to do outside.

Mostly Cs: You are very relaxed and want to talk to people when you travel. Understanding what life is like for people from a different country is a big reason why you like travelling. You only want to go shopping in local shops and eat in local restaurants. A perfect trip for you is to rent an apartment in one place that you can stay in for a while to get to know the local culture and people.

1   **Complete the questions with the correct form of the verbs in the box.**

be   have (x2)   know   live   own   study   work

1   How long _____ your house?

2   How long _____ your cat?

3   How long _____ at your job?

4   How long _____ English?

5   How long _____ your car?

6   How long _____ in California?

7   How long _____ Melania?

8   How long _____ married?

2   **Complete the sentences with *for* or *since*. Then match them to questions 1–8 in Exercise 1.**

a   I've had it _____ a few months.   *5*

b   I've worked at Blend _____ I was 25.

c   We've known each other _____ about ten years.

d   I've owned it _____ eight years.

e   I've been married _____ the 14th April 2014.

f   I've studied it _____ September last year.

g   I've had Snuffles _____ 2016.

h   I've lived here _____ a long time.

3   **Work in pairs. Practise asking and answering the questions in Exercise 1.**

Who ...	Student 1	Student 2	Student 3	Student 4
1 plays tennis? *Do you play tennis?* *How long have you played tennis?*	Sophie for six years			
2 has a pet?				
3 studies French?				
4 uses social media?				
5 lives in a flat?				
6 works in an office?				
7 live in the countryside?				
8 has a best friend?				

1 _____ has played tennis for the longest time.

2 _____ has had a pet for the longest time.

3 _____ has studied French for the longest time.

4 _____ has used social media for the longest time.

5 _____ has lived in a flat for the longest time.

6 _____ has worked in an office for the longest time.

7 _____ has lived in the countryside for the longest time.

8 _____ has known their best friend for the longest time.

1 Match the people 1–5 with their friends a–e. Write the name of each speaker.

1 I made friends with Lindsay when I went to South Africa last year. We don't live in the same country, but we email all the time now.

_____Marian_____

2 Gemma and I never argue. We met at a film night in university a few years ago and we get on so well.

_____

3 I don't see Gus very often, usually only twice a year. But we talk on social media almost every day.

_____

4 Stewart and I don't get on very well because we're very different. We argue a lot about things.

_____

5 Craig and I are old friends. We've known each other since we were in primary school.

_____

a I don't like to spend much time with Ann because I disagree with her on almost everything!

_____

b Scott and I often text. We can't meet up a lot because we live in different cities.

_____

c Marian and I met while we were travelling and we've kept in touch since then. We're going to meet up somewhere next year.

_____

d Ellie and I never disagree with each other. We both love cinema and enjoy watching the same movies.

_____

e Nicole and I first met when we were seven. Twenty years later, we're still really close friends.

_____

2 Work in pairs. Do you have any similar friendships to the people in Exercise 1?

9B Grammar 1 Present perfect with *already,* *just* and *yet*

Write sentences using the prompts and the words in brackets. Use the present perfect.

1 They / get married   (just)

_____

2 I / not buy anything   (yet)

_____

3 They / leave their house   (already)

_____

4 He / close his suitcase   (just)

_____

5 The boy / eat all of the chocolates   (just)

_____

6 The woman / not find a job   (yet)

_____

7 They / buy a new house   (just)

_____

8 The man / not learn to ski   (yet)

_____

9 She / finish university   (already)

_____

10 The man / turn on the water   (just)

_____

11 We / speak to the doctor   (already)

_____

12 They / not book a DJ for the party   (yet)

_____

13 You / finish your tea?   (yet)

_____

14 I / be on a trip to Italy   (just)

_____

15 He / not arrive home   (yet)

_____

16 We / pay for the TV   (already)

_____

9B **Grammar 2** Present perfect with *already, just* and *yet*

A Imagine you are a famous actor and complete the information.

Film star	
Name	
Years acting	
Married? How long?	
Cities/Countries you've worked in	
Somewhere you haven't worked yet, but you would like to (and why)	
Your past films	
Your most recent film	
What you're working on now	
Something you want to do in the future	
Advice for new actors	

B Imagine you work for a film magazine. Interview a famous actor and complete the interview notes.

Interviewer	
What's your name?	
How long have you been an actor?	
Are you married? How long?	
Where have you worked?	
Where haven't you worked yet but would like to? Why?	
What films have you been in?	
Which film have you just finished?	
What are you doing next?	
What haven't you done yet? What plans do you have for the future?	
What advice can you give to someone who has just decided to become an actor?	

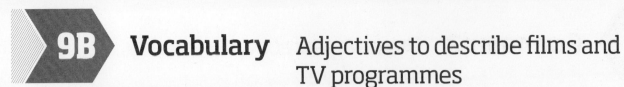

9B Vocabulary Adjectives to describe films and TV programmes

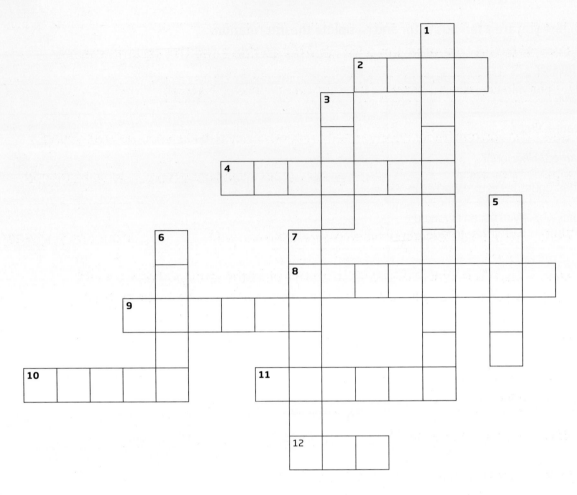

Across

2 *Titanic* is a _____ film – it's three hours!

4 Something a lot of people watch is _____ .

8 Action films are usually _____ .

9 Sherlock Holmes is a very _____ man – he's intelligent and he helps a lot of people.

10 Horror films need to be _____ .

11 When nothing happens, a show is _____ .

12 You might cry when you watch a _____ film.

Down

1 When a show is _____ , you don't want to stop watching it.

3 A film that is _____ shows something that happened in real life.

5 A comedy needs to be _____ .

6 Watching a _____ film is a good way to relax, laugh and forget about a bad day.

7 A drama is a _____ type of film. It isn't funny.

9C Grammar 1 *could/couldn't*

1 Complete the conversation with *could* or *couldn't* and the verbs in the box.

| communicate | dance | make | play | remember | ride | sing (x2) |

Ben: Do you remember how we used to spend all day outside when we were young?

Jack: Yeah, we ¹_____ in the garden for hours and not get bored. What happened to us?!

Ben: We got old! Remember when we were ten and we ²_____ in our own language?

Jack: Yes, I don't know how we did it! And we wore the same clothes, so mum ³_____ which one was you, and which one was me! I love having a twin brother!

Ben: That was really fun! Now it's easy, because we wear different clothes.

Jack: There was also that summer when I ⁴_____ a bike and you could. I was really angry with you!

Ben: Yeah, you were! But I ⁵_____ always _____ you laugh.

Jack: That's true. You were funny! You still are.

Ben: I remember that you ⁶_____ really beautifully. I always wanted to sing like you, but my voice was horrible.

Jack: No, you ⁷_____ , but you ⁸_____ – you were great at that!

Ben: Yeah, I was quite good then. But not now!

2 Work in pairs and practise the conversation in Exercise 1.

3 Was your childhood similar to Ben and Jack's? Why/Why not?

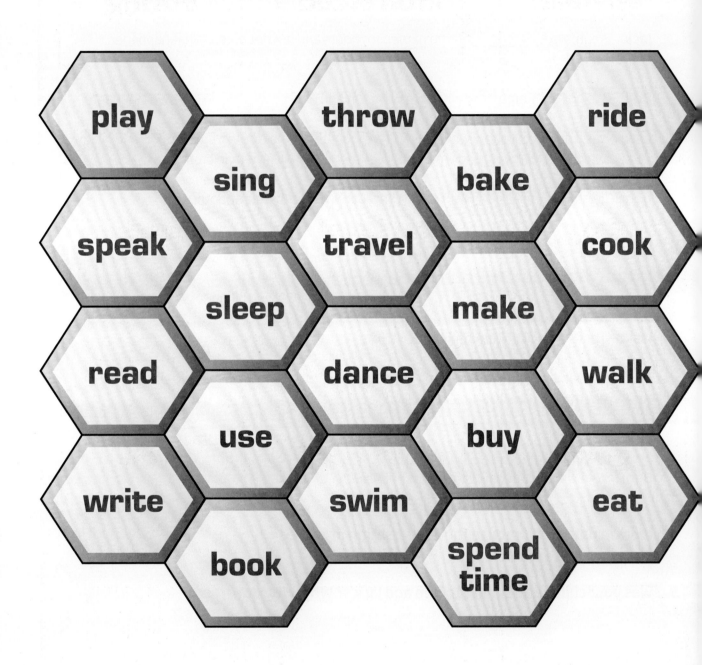

play

throw

ride

sing

bake

speak

travel

cook

sleep

make

read

dance

walk

use

buy

write

swim

eat

book

spend time

terrible	interested	boring
easy	difficult	bad
good	work hard	well
badly	exams	get better

Write sentences using the prompts. Use the first conditional.

1 he / go outside / he / get wet

_____

2 you / not eat / you / be hungry

_____

3 she / tired / she / stay up late

_____

4 you / work more hours / you / make more money

_____

5 you / buy lunch / I / buy dinner

_____

6 I / not see you as much / I / move to another city

_____

7 Leslie / have a baby / she / be very busy

_____

8 you / do yoga / you / feel healthier

_____

9 I / get better at English / I / speak it every day

_____

10 they / arrive late / they / not catch / their flight

_____

11 you / pass your exams / you / study hard

_____

12 Andrew / do exercise every day / he / get stronger

_____

13 you / need some help / I / help you

_____

14 I / not be able to sleep / I / watch a scary film

_____

15 Alison / not buy / her ticket today / she / not see the concert

_____

16 they / save money / they / be able to buy a house one day

_____

a

I don't really want to go to Eric's birthday party tonight.

b

I don't want to eat that. It doesn't look very nice.

c

My boss is always so angry. What should I do?

d

My ear hurts. Do you think I should go to the doctor?

e

I'm not sure if I should go to university next year.

f

Is it too late to start watching a film?

g

Do you think I should buy a car?

h

I'm so tired this morning. I just want to go back to sleep!

i

I think I want to start a new hobby.

j

I don't earn enough money.

k

I think I want to learn Italian.

l

Do you think we should go camping this weekend?

m

I don't want to go into work today.

n

I want to go shopping, but I don't have any time.

o

I think I want to take a holiday to another country.

p

I don't like saving money. I prefer to spend it.

borrow	cash	cost	credit	earn	lend
pay for	save	spend	waste		

borrow	cash	cost	credit	earn	lend
pay for	save	spend	waste		

borrow	cash	cost	credit	earn	lend
pay for	save	spend	waste		

borrow	cash	cost	credit	earn	lend
pay for	save	spend	waste		

borrow	cash	cost	credit	earn	lend
pay for	save	spend	waste		

borrow	cash	cost	credit	earn	lend
pay for	save	spend	waste		

Complete the texts using the present or past passive form of the verbs in brackets.

1

A man **1**_____ (find) in the mountains yesterday with a badly broken leg. He **2**_____ (help) down the mountain by the German tourists who found him and is now in hospital.

2

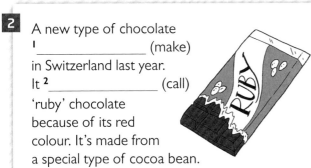

A new type of chocolate **1**_____ (make) in Switzerland last year. It **2**_____ (call) 'ruby' chocolate because of its red colour. It's made from a special type of cocoa bean.

3

Did you know that wife carrying is a real sport? It **1**_____ (invent) in Finland and the first Wife Carrying World Championships **2**_____ (hold) there in 1992.

4 An expensive necklace **1**_____ (take) from a museum in the UK last week. The police believe someone quickly sold the necklace but they don't know who it **2**_____ (buy) by. They think the money **3**_____ (use) to buy an island near the Bahamas.

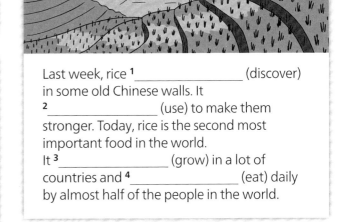

5

Last week, rice **1**_____ (discover) in some old Chinese walls. It **2**_____ (use) to make them stronger. Today, rice is the second most important food in the world. It **3**_____ (grow) in a lot of countries and **4**_____ (eat) daily by almost half of the people in the world.

6 Museums around the world can now share some of David Bowie's most interesting clothes and photographs. The travelling show **1**_____ (call) *David Bowie Is …*. There are clothes that **2**_____ (wear) by Bowie during his most famous interviews and videos, and many of the photographs **3**_____ (take) during his famous concerts.

2 Work in pairs and retell the news stories in Exercise 1. Try to use the passive.

Student A

| born | built | driven | grown | held | sent | stolen | used |

1 Barack Obama _____ in Nairobi, Kenya. (false)
2 Cars _____ on the left side of the road in Australia. (true)
3 In most places, rice _____ in water. (true)
4 Leonardo Da Vinci's painting *The Mona Lisa* _____ from the Louvre. (true)
5 About 200 million texts _____ each day around the world. (false)
6 The first modern Olympic Games _____ in Paris in 1896. (false)
7 The Eiffel Tower _____ in the 1700s. (false)
8 The London Underground _____ by 4.8 million passengers every day. (true)

Student B

| built | chosen | eaten | found | given | sold | taught | written |

1 The Titanic _____ at the bottom of the ocean in 1985. (true)
2 *The Great Gatsby* _____ by Stephen King. (false)
3 More pasta _____ in the US than in any other country in the world. (true)
4 In the UK, the queen or king _____ by the government. (false)
5 Around the world, more than 75 McDonald's hamburgers _____ every second. (true)
6 The Statue of Liberty _____ to the US by Germany. (false)
7 Most English-speaking children in Canada _____ French in school. (true)
8 The Taj Mahal _____ to be a museum. (false)

Student C

| called | drunk | eaten | invented | made | put | spoken | taken |

1 The telephone _____ by Alexander Graham Bell in 1876. (true)
2 *The Lord of the Rings* films _____ in Chile. (false)
3 More tea _____ in the UK than in any other country in the world. (false)
4 Elvis Presley _____ The King of Rock and Roll. (true)
5 Bunny Chow is a national dish that _____ in South Africa. (true)
6 The first photograph _____ in 1900 in France. (false)
7 English _____ by more than 700 million people as a first language. (false)
8 In the UK, it is bad luck if shoes _____ on a table. (true)

1 Choose the correct alternatives.

1 What did people do 100 years *ago/before* but we don't do now?

2 Which *century/nowadays* is the most interesting to you? Why?

3 What are some things all of the people in your group do *each day/each century*?

4 What did you not know *during/until* recently?

5 What are some activities that you do *these days/until now* that you didn't do when you were younger?

6 *During now/Nowadays,* what do you think is the biggest global problem? Why?

7 When do you think was the most difficult time *at/during* the 20th century? Why?

8 What is something your family has done *each year/this year* for as long as you can remember?

2 Work in groups and discuss the questions in Exercise 1.

10C Grammar 1 Review of tenses

1 Choose the correct alternatives.

1 A: I don't have enough money for my lunch.
   B: Don't worry, I *bought/ will buy/ buy* it for you.

2 A: Have you ever been to South Africa?
   B: Actually, yes. I *have visited/ was visiting/ visited* there in 2008.

3 A: What do you usually do at the weekend?
   B: Well, normally I *spend/ am spending/ am going to spend* time with my friends.

4 A: I'm going to see a film with Ali tonight. Do you want to come?
   B: Sorry, I can't. I *will meet/ meet/ am meeting* Josh for dinner.

5 A: I heard that you saw Lionel Messi! Where was that?
   B: Well, last night around 8 p.m. I *was going/ went/ have gone* home and he walked past me on the street!

6 A: There's so much to do around the house. Can you do the dishes, please?
   B: Don't worry, Dad, I *already do/ have already done/ will already do* them.

7 A: Next summer we're travelling to Peru for two weeks. What are your plans?
   B: We *are going to visit/ will visit/ visit* my family in Canada.

8 A: Hi! How are you? I haven't seen you in so long!
   B: I know! I've moved cities. I *am going to live/ have lived/ am living* in Chicago now.

9 A: Is Matt still here? I really need to talk to him.
   B: No, sorry. He *is just leaving/ just has left/ has just left*.

10 A: Mum's 60th birthday is this weekend. I haven't got her a gift yet.
    B: I haven't either. OK, tomorrow I *will get/ get/ was getting* her some jewellery from both of us.

2 Work in pairs. Practise the conversations in Exercise 1.

* What were you doing last night at 8 p.m.?
* What is the most exciting thing you have ever done?
* Name something you never do.
* Name something you are going to do next year.
* Name a place you haven't visited yet but would like to.
* Name one thing that you think will change in your life this year.
* Who are you seeing tonight?
* Name a course or project you are doing.
* Name somewhere you have just been.
* Name something you will buy this week.

My answers

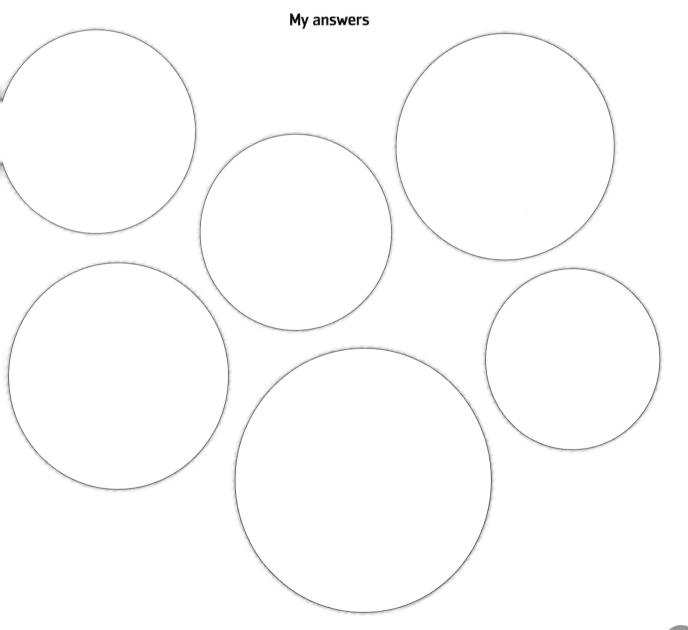

Goal A		START		Goal B

Student A

1 I recently gave <u>in</u> smoking. I don't do it anymore. ✗
   (up)
2 I really enjoy learning about different cultures. ✓
3 I think I'm going to start taking an art class. ✓
4 At the weekend, I often play chess <u>for funny</u> with my friends. ✗
   (for fun)
5 I <u>joined to</u> a new boat club last week. ✗
   (joined)
6 I am part <u>in</u> a football team. We play every week. ✗
   (of)
7 I really want to try something new this week. ✓
8 I spent time hiking during my last holiday. ✓

Student B

1 Last year, I gave up junk food. ✓
2 I've never <u>made</u> part of a volleyball team. ✗
   (been)
3 I don't need to cook every day, I do it for fun. ✓
4 I'm going to join a basketball team this year. ✓
5 I spend a lot of time <u>to sleep</u> at the weekend. ✗
   (sleeping)
6 I love learning about people on social media. ✓
7 Recently I found out <u>of</u> Comic-Con. ✗
   (about)
8 I started <u>play</u> the guitar when I was 12. ✗
   (playing)

Photocopiable notes and answer key

1A

Grammar 1 Word order in questions

Materials: One worksheet per student

Instructions:

Distribute the worksheets. Instruct Ss to make questions from the prompts to complete the conversation. Do the first one together if appropriate. Check answers as a class. Encourage peer correction and discuss any that Ss found problematic.

Then put Ss in pairs to roleplay the conversation (Ex 2). Remind Ss to focus on using the correct intonation for questions. With **stronger classes**, or in pairs, encourage Ss to invent their own answers to the questions to personalise the conversation. Then tell Ss to switch roles so that each student plays both parts.

Answer key:

1

1 How are you?
2 Where do you work?
3 How many hours do you work a day?
4 What do you do when you get home from work?
5 What kind of films do you like?
6 What's your favourite cinema?
7 Why do you like it?
8 Who is the main actor?
9 When is it on?
10 How long is the film?

Grammar 2 Word order in questions

Materials: One copy of the board and a dice (or a coin) per group of Ss

Instructions:

Put Ss in small groups and distribute a board and a dice (or a coin) to each group. The aim of the game is to move from the start square to the finish square by rolling the dice and forming questions. The winner is the first person to reach the finish.

Before Ss start playing the game, elicit some questions that could be asked about the first category, food (*What is your favourite food? When do you eat lunch? Where is your favourite restaurant? What meals can you cook? Do you like eating in restaurants? Why?*) and write them on the board. Ensure that Ss know that they can create any question related to the topic in the square as long as the word order is correct. Encourage them to use follow-up questions like '*Why?*' if they are asking *Yes/No* questions.

The first player rolls the dice and asks a question related to the topic written on the square they've landed on.

The group must decide whether the word order in the question is correct. If the group is happy with it, then the person to the player's left answers the question and then play passes to him/her. If the word order is incorrect, then the player who asked the question must move back to his/her original position before he/she moved. Allow groups to regulate their own games without getting too involved. Make notes of anything you would like to correct for feedback afterwards.

If you don't have a dice, Ss can play the game with a coin. They flip it and move two spaces for heads and one space for tails.

Vocabulary Question words

Materials: One copy of Quiz A and Quiz B per pair of Ss

Instructions:

Give each student either Quiz A or Quiz B and allow them a few minutes to complete the gaps in their respective quizzes. Make sure that they don't answer the questions at this point. Point Ss towards the pictures to highlight the meaning of *the pyramids* (Quiz A) and *penguin* (Quiz B) if necessary.

Next, pair each student with another person who has the same card and tell them to check their answers together. Monitor and help if necessary.

Re-arrange Ss into A/B pairs and tell them to ask each other their questions and to circle their partner's answers. When both Ss have finished, they check their partner's answers at the bottom of their sheet and give them a score.

At the end, check the missing question words, so that Ss all have the correct answers.

Answer key:

Quiz A 1 What **2** Who **3** When **4** What kind
5 How long **6** Where

Quiz B 1 which **2** How many **3** What **4** Whose
5 What kind **6** Where

1B

Grammar 1 Frequency expressions

Materials: One worksheet per student

Instructions:

Distribute the worksheets. Instruct Ss to write sentences from the prompts. Do the first one together if appropriate. Give Ss time to complete the rest of the sentences individually.

After you have corrected the answers together, get Ss to do Ex 2 individually. Then put Ss in pairs to complete Ex 3. When they have finished, ask some pairs to share their findings with the class.

Answer key:

1

1 You rarely try new things.
2 I go to the gym once a week.
3 He sees his friends all the time.
4 They sometimes go to the cinema together.
5 We hardly ever go on holiday.
6 She often reads before she goes to bed.
7 He is always late for the train.
8 He doesn't usually eat breakfast.
9 I am often bored in the evenings.
10 She sometimes wears a watch.
11 I see my parents once a month.
12 They play tennis twice a week.
13 He is not always a nice person.
14 He always wears comfortable clothes.
15 She visits a museum three times a year.
16 They hardly ever wake up early.
17 We don't usually do the washing up.
18 I never look at photos on my phone.

Grammar 2   Frequency expressions

Materials: One worksheet per student

Instructions:

Distribute the worksheets. Tell Ss that they are going to get to know their classmates better by asking questions about the information on the sheet.

Do the first question together, if appropriate, eliciting more than one way to find out the information from someone, e.g. *How often do you do your homework? / Do you do your homework every day? / Do you always do your homework?* Using these examples, ensure Ss understand that the grammar rules they learnt for statements also apply to questions, e.g. the frequency expression still goes after *be* but before other verbs.

Give Ss a few minutes to write questions for each row. With **stronger classes**, you could skip this step and begin the activity without Ss writing down their questions in advance. However, giving them thinking time is still advisable.

Check the questions with the whole class before beginning the activity. Then allow Ss a couple of minutes to think about what their own answers are to the questions, so that they will be ready when asked.

Tell Ss they must speak to as many different people in the class as they can, asking them questions from the sheet. When they find someone for whom a statement is true, they can write their classmate's name down next to it. If the statement is not true for that person, they should ask another question. Explain to Ss that they cannot write the same person's name twice (unless you have quite a small class). Point out the *Extra information* column. Explain that Ss must ask follow-up questions in order to complete this column. You may now want to model the activity with a strong student before starting.

Give Ss 10–15 minutes to complete the activity. When they have finished, ask for class feedback about what they have learnt.

Vocabulary   Success

Materials: One worksheet per student

Instructions:

Distribute the worksheets. Instruct Ss to complete the sentences with the correct verb in each gap. They then read the sentences again and decide if they agree or disagree with each sentence.

After they have done this individually, put the Ss in pairs so they can compare and discuss their answers.

Answer key:

1
1 try   2 have   3 start   4 ask   5 take   6 plan   7 listen
8 take

Grammar 1   Present simple and present continuous

Materials: One worksheet per student

Instructions:

Distribute the worksheets and ask Ss to read the instructions. Before Ss start the task, it might be a good idea to do a quick review of the key words associated with both the present simple (*always, every day* and other adverbs of frequency) and the present continuous (*right now, at the moment, this week*). Give Ss time to complete the activity individually.

When they have finished, put Ss in pairs to complete Ex 2, discussing if necessary where contractions can be used.

If you feel that your class is confident enough, you could get them to choose one of the mini-conversations and extend for as long as they can. Remind them that asking questions is a good way to prolong a conversation and tell them to think back to the first lesson where they focused on questions. Remind Ss to think about what tense they are using when they speak.

Answer key:

1
1 are (you) reading; am ('m) studying
2 play
3 are you doing; am ('m) trying; is not (isn't) working
4 is ('s) raining; are ('re) getting
5 Do (you) travel; work; am ('m) helping
6 do (you) see; does not (doesn't) live; have

Grammar 2   Present simple and present continuous

Materials: One card and one table per student

Instructions:

Tell Ss they are going to a VIP (very important person) party in London. Give each student a role card and tell them to read it and think of answers to their questions. Give them a time limit to fill in the information on their role card (e.g. three minutes).

Then give each student a copy of the table. If there are more than six Ss, tell them they have to find a person for each category (actor, singer, etc.) and complete the information. If there are fewer than six Ss, tell Ss to complete their own information in the table first, before looking for the other Ss. Check Ss know which questions to ask before they begin. Tell Ss to mingle and get as much information as possible from their classmates in order to complete the table.

When they have finished, get feedback from the class. Ask Ss to report back in the third person singular and to use both the present simple and the present continuous in their answers.

Vocabulary   Everyday activities

Materials: One A and B worksheet per pair of Ss

Instructions:

Tell Ss that they are going to find out about the lives of three different people. Put Ss in pairs and give one A and one B worksheet to each pair. Tell them to not show their sheets to their partners. Give the class time (e.g. five minutes) to read their worksheet individually and to think of what questions they could ask to elicit the missing information. For example, for worksheet A, gap 1, *What does he usually do at 7 a.m.?* For worksheet B, gap 1, *What does he do after he gets up?* You may wish to refer Ss back to the question forms from Lesson 1A, but grammatical accuracy in questions is not the main aim here.

Inform the class that they must now ask their partners questions to fill in the missing information on their sheets. Set a time limit (e.g. eight minutes) for them to do this. Give pairs the chance to compare their worksheets when they have finished and ask them to ensure that spelling and tenses are correct.

As an extension, ask pairs to work together to find as many similarities between the people in the texts as they can.

Answer key:
Student A
1 gets up **2** starts school **3** plays video games
4 starts work **5** takes a break **6** watches TV
7 taking pictures of animals **8** spends **9** good time
Student B
1 takes a shower **2** gets home **3** checks social media
4 getting up **5** takes a taxi **6** gets home **7** playing the piano
8 checks her emails **9** play cards
Possible similarities
Joshua and Heather both work/study in a school.
Joshua and Ali both get up early.
Joshua and Heather both enjoy playing games.

Grammar 1   Past simple

Materials: One worksheet per student and a copy of the answers per group of Ss

Instructions:

Distribute the worksheets. Tell Ss to write sentences, using the verb in the past simple and the prompts.

Rather than going through all the answers with the class, put Ss in groups of three or four and give them a copy of the answers to go through together. Tell them to ask you if there is something they don't understand. Ss then work individually to choose three sentences from Ex 1 and make them true for themselves.

Put Ss in pairs to compare their sentences. When they have finished, encourage Ss to tell the class about any interesting information they found out about their partners.

Answer key:

1
   1 She arrived at the airport at 9.15 a.m.
   2 He deleted a lot of emails this morning.
   3 The game ended at 8 p.m.
   4 They were excited about the party.
   5 Last week, we played ice hockey in the street.
   6 She woke up early today.
   7 Elliot wasn't at school last week.
   8 I went to Thailand and tried pad thai.
   9 She travelled to China last year.
   10 They watched a film at the cinema last night.
   11 Jason got a new bicycle yesterday.
   12 The rain stopped at 10 a.m. this morning.
   13 Today Chris and Amy decided to buy a house.
   14 Last week, I had a job interview.
   15 Our first class started at 10 a.m. this morning.
   16 We looked at photos yesterday.
   17 Jamie missed the bus this afternoon.
   18 I talked to Cheryl last night.
   19 They weren't at home two days ago.
   20 She took the train to New York.

Grammar 2   Past simple

Materials: One card per student

Instructions:

Divide the class into three equal groups and give the Ss in each group a different card (A, B or C). Tell Ss to work individually to complete the sentences with the verbs from the box in the correct tense (*past simple*). Each verb may only be used once.

Rearrange the class into groups of three so that there is an A, B and C student in each group. Explain that for each sentence, one student has the true information and the other two have false information. Tell the groups to discuss the sentences and decide which student has the correct information for each sentence. Then check answers with the class.

Answer key:
1A watched **2B** was **3A** had **4C** started **5B** decided
6A travelled **7B** painted **8A** arrived

Vocabulary   Feelings

Materials: One worksheet per group of Ss

Instructions:

Tell Ss that they are going to compete against each other in a game. Put Ss in groups of three or four. If you have a very strong class, or a few **stronger Ss**, you could put them in pairs.

Demonstrate the activity with the class. Write on the board *Three things that make us feel happy*, then ask the class to think of three possible answers (e.g. *A friend says something nice to you; You see a cute animal; It's sunny and warm outside*).

Tell them that they are going to do the same thing in their groups, but with different emotions. Give one worksheet to each group. Tell them they will have ten minutes to think of and write down three ideas for each category. They will get one point for each answer that none of the other groups have written. After ten minutes, or when all the groups have finished, ask each group to read out the answers to each category. If a group has an answer that no other group has written, they score a point. The group with the most points wins the game.

Grammar 1   Past simple negative and questions

Materials: One worksheet per student

Instructions:

Give each student a copy of the worksheet. Allow them time to complete the ordering activity alone, then check their answers as a class. Before starting Ex 2, explain that each sentence is a response to a question in Ex 1. This should help them when they complete the gaps and match the questions and answers. Ss work individually.

Then put Ss in pairs to practise asking and answering the questions from their worksheet. You could extend the task by instructing Ss to answer the questions in Ex 1 based on their own lives. If you do this, remind Ss to focus on the different question forms and negative forms used in the exercise.

Answer key:

1

1 What did you do yesterday?
2 Did you like vegetables when you were young?
3 Were you at home last night?
4 Were you at university in 2015?
5 Where did you travel in 2017?
6 Where did you go last night?
7 Did you do your English homework?
8 Who was your best friend when you were a child?
9 What did you do on your last birthday?
10 Where did you live five years ago?

2

a didn't eat (2)
b didn't celebrate (9)
c didn't live (10)
d didn't come (7)
e didn't visit (5)

f wasn't (6)
g didn't do (1)
h didn't enjoy (4)
i wasn't (3)
j didn't meet (8)

Grammar 2 Past simple negative and questions

Materials: One worksheet per student

Instructions:

Distribute the worksheets, either to individual Ss or to pairs. Explain the activity. Ask Ss to look at the first picture. Tell them that they need to write a negative sentence based on the picture in the past simple using the verb given, as in the example.

If Ss do the exercise individually, put them into pairs so they can compare their answers before you check them.

Tell Ss to write two more negative sentences for each picture. Put Ss in pairs to compare their sentences.

Answer key:

1

1 He didn't hear the alarm
2 He wasn't happy.
3 She didn't know the answer.
4 They didn't watch the match.
5 It didn't rain.

6 They weren't angry.
7 They didn't tidy up.
8 She didn't close the gate.
9 He didn't miss the bus.

Vocabulary Past time expressions

Materials: One worksheet per student

Instructions:

Tell Ss that they are going to see how well they know their partner by guessing their answers to some questions. Elicit and write the time expressions from the lesson on the board for Ss to refer to. Then ask one student to answer a question about another student, e.g. *Juan, guess: When did Carolina last go on holiday?* Elicit the meaning of *last* in this question (= *the most recent time*). Write the question and the student's answer on the board. Elicit how else the answer could be given, e.g. *six weeks ago; in May; last month.* Tell Ss that they need to try to use all of the expressions on the board at least once.

Put Ss in pairs and distribute the worksheets. Allow Ss time to complete the *Guess* column. Once they have finished, give the class a few minutes to think about their own answers to prepare them for their partner's questions.

Do the first question with one student if appropriate. Then give Ss a few minutes to ask each other the rest of the questions and to make notes in the *Your partner's answer* column. Encourage Ss to find out more information by asking follow-up questions, e.g. *When did you go? Who with? Where did you go?*

When they have finished, find out which Ss were good at guessing their partner's answers. Encourage Ss to tell the class about any interesting information they found out about their partners.

Grammar 1 Quantifiers

Materials: One worksheet per student

Instructions:

Distribute the worksheets and ask Ss to read the instructions for Ex 1. Instruct Ss to work individually for a few minutes to correct the mistakes in the list before putting them in pairs or small groups to compare their answers and complete any they haven't done. Go through the answers as a whole class and make sure the class can justify why they have made their corrections.

For Ex 2, refer Ss back to the first item on the list (*apples*). Ask them whether it is *countable* or *uncountable* and how they know. Then tell them to continue down the list doing the same for each of the items. For **fast finishers**, ask them to add as many other food items as they can to both columns.

Put Ss in pairs and allow them time to discuss their meal and then, if you have time, ask pairs to join up with another pair and tell them about their meal.

Answer key:

1

a few apples
some lettuce
some chocolate (*a little* and *a bit of chocolate* would work, too)
some tomatoes
some rice (*a little* and *a bit of rice* would work, too)
lots of strawberries
some milk
a few oranges
a carrot
some coffee
some potato**es**
a few small cucumbers
some sugar (*a little* and *a bit of sugar* would work, too)
a lot of cheese
some **salt**
a few eggs (*some* is also possible)
some meat

2

Countable apples tomatoes strawberries oranges carrots potatoes cucumbers eggs
Uncountable lettuce chocolate rice milk coffee sugar cheese salt meat

Grammar 2 Quantifiers

Materials: One copy of picture A and picture B per pair of Ss

Instructions:

Put Ss in pairs and tell them that you are going to give them each a picture. They must not show their picture to their partner.

Give each student a picture. Explain that there are ten differences between their images and that Ss must describe what they see to each other in order to find the differences using as many different quantifiers as possible. Tell them to circle any differences they find on their picture as they discover them. **Fast finishers** can write *There is/are* sentences about their partner's picture, using quantifiers.

When they have finished, ask pairs to tell you a difference they found between their images and write them on the board in a list. Encourage Ss to use the correct quantifiers when providing answers.

Answer key:
two women vs. a man and a woman
some grapes vs. a pineapple
some milk vs. some lemonade
an apple vs. some cheese
can of cola vs. a large bottle of water
a pizza vs. a bar of chocolate/some chocolate
orange juice vs. some pasta
a whole chicken vs. a fish
some/five strawberries vs. some/a bottle of shampoo
empty shelves in the middle vs. on the right / bread on the right
side of the shelves vs. in the middle

Vocabulary Adjectives to describe food

Materials: One set of cards per group of Ss

Instructions:

Put Ss in groups of three and tell them that they are going to play a game to practise describing foods using the adjectives from the lesson. Give each group a set of cards and put them face down in a pile. Explain that one student from each group turns over the top card. That student reads the adjective and names a food that it describes. If he/she can think of a type of food, they get one point. If he/she can't think of a word, they don't get a point and the card goes to the bottom of the pile. Then it is the turn of the student on his/her left.

If a student gets a card with an adjective that has already been used, they must say the name of a different food. If a student gets a *delicious* card, they can say whatever they like but it must be a food/dish they really enjoy. At the end of the game, the student with the most points wins.

Grammar 1 Comparatives

Materials: One worksheet per student

Instructions:

Distribute the worksheets and explain the task. Give Ss time to write the comparatives in each gap. Tell Ss they also need to use *less than* and *not as ... as*. When they have finished, they can discuss their answers with a partner and make any corrections.

Then put Ss in pairs for Ex 2 and give them time to think of other comparative sentences for the pictures. Suggest that they use opposite adjectives to the ones given, e.g. *3 The man is angrier than the woman; 8 The boy is shorter than the girl.* Tell them that they can also use other comparative adjectives to express the ideas, e.g. *1 Espresso Time is better than Latte Central.*

Answer key:

1

1 more popular **2** sweeter **3** more peaceful **4** hotter
5 less beautiful **6** more exciting **7** faster **8** not as tall
9 longer **10** less modern

2

Accept any comparative sentences that fit the images.

Grammar 2 Comparatives

Materials: One copy of the board, one dice (or alternative), one set of cards per group of Ss and one counter per student

Instructions:

Put Ss in groups of three or four. Give each group a board, a dice, a set of cards face down in a pile next to the board and give each student a counter.

Explain the rules of the game. Ss roll a dice (or see alternative below) and whoever has the highest number starts. The first student throws the dice, moves that number of circles and puts their counter on the circle. If the circle has words, then the student who threw the dice must make a comparative sentence about those two things. If the circle has a '?', then they should choose a card and make a comparative sentence with the adjective on the card. If a student makes an incorrect comparison, either grammatically or related to meaning, he/she must return to his/her previous circle. The student to reach the finish first wins.

If you do not have a dice, you can provide pieces of numbered paper (1–4 will do) for each pair. They can fold these up and pick one out of their partner's hand in order to see how many spaces to move.

Vocabulary Adjectives to describe places

Materials: One copy of puzzle A and puzzle B per pair of Ss

Instructions:

Put Ss in A/B pairs and give each of them an incomplete crossword. Make sure Ss are sitting face-to-face so they can't see each other's answers. Tell them that the object of the activity is to fill in the missing words in their crossword. They take turns to ask their partner to describe each word by asking for clues, e.g. A *What's 1 down?* Their partner then makes a sentence or gives a clue for the word (e.g. a definition, a synonym or an example). Use *old* as an example giving the following options:

a My grandmother is very _____ . (Explain that they can say *blank* in place of the gap.)

b Not young. / The opposite of young.

c When you are 90, you are _____ .

Give Ss a few minutes to think of what they could say to describe their words. If you think Ss will have difficulty thinking of clues, put two A and B pairs together to think of clues before they complete the crossword.

Ss work together in their pairs until they have completed their missing half of the puzzle. Remind them that if their partners do not get the missing words immediately, they can give more than one clue.

When they have finished, they can check their answers by looking at each other's crosswords.

Answer key:

				b						
o	l	d		e	x	c	i	t	i	n	g
	i			a						
	v		d	u		c				
m		e	i	n	t	e	r	e	s	t	i	n	g
p	o	p	u	l	a	r	i	o			
d		l	y	t	f	o	w				
c	l	e	a	n		y	u	d			
h		r			l	e					
e		n	o	i	s	y		d			
a											
p	e	a	c	e	f	u	l				

3B

Grammar 1   Superlatives

Materials: One worksheet per student

Instructions:

Distribute the worksheets and explain to the class what a *world record* is. Do the first item together if appropriate, ensuring that Ss understand what type of adjective needs to go into the gap (*a superlative form*). Ss then complete the task individually. Discuss the answers before moving on to Ex 2.

Ask Ss to look quickly through phrases a–j in Ex 2 and find the ending to the first sentence in Ex 1. Elicit why they think *d* is the correct ending (it includes the words *animal, pet, centimetres*) and then suggest they use the same technique to match the rest of the sentences.

Put Ss in pairs to discuss Ex 3, then ask a few Ss to share some of their opinions with the class. Share your own opinion, as well.

If appropriate, you could ask Ss to create their own world records afterwards. They could use the internet to find some real examples.

Answer key:

1

1 longest   **2** most popular   **3** smallest   **4** tallest   **5** smallest   **6** largest   **7** heaviest   **8** fastest   **9** biggest   **10** tallest

2

a 8   **b** 3   **c** 6   **d** 1   **e** 9   **f** 4   **g** 5   **h** 7   **i** 2   **j** 10

Grammar 2   Superlatives

Materials: One worksheet per student

Instructions:

Distribute the worksheets and instruct Ss to complete the gaps. Ss will probably use *most* with the long adjectives, but you can point out that *least* will sometimes also work. Write the answers on the board. Then ask Ss to write their answers to the questions.

Then put Ss in pairs. Tell the class that they are going to ask and answer the questions in their pairs and that they should give reasons for their choices. Do question one with a **stronger student**, e.g. *So, Carlos, in your opinion, who is the best actor at the moment? Oh, really? Why him/her? I think he/she was great in _____, but I prefer _____ because ...*. Remind Ss that they can put *I think* (or *I don't think*) in front of any sentence to make it into an opinion, e.g. *Apples are delicious → I think apples are delicious. / I don't think apples are delicious.*

While the class is speaking, monitor the pairs and, if appropriate, get involved yourself.

When they have finished, ask some Ss to say which question created the most discussion in their pairs.

Answer key:

1

1 the best   **2** the most dangerous   **3** the most relaxing   **4** the most beautiful   **5** the funniest   **6** the oldest   **7** the most interesting   **8** the worst   **9** the happiest   **10** the most delicious

Vocabulary   Hotels and places to stay

Materials: One worksheet per student

Instructions:

Distribute the worksheets. Do the first gapped sentence with a student if appropriate. Demonstrate how to complete the

sentences by looking for clues both before and after the gaps. Give Ss a few minutes to read the two texts and complete the gaps with the collocations in the box, then get them to check their answers in pairs. Encourage peer corrections and then check answers as a class.

Give Ss a few minutes to discuss the questions in Ex 2 in pairs or small groups, then choose a few individuals to explain which hotel they would like to stay in and why. Encourage them to use *I want to stay in ... because ...*.

Discuss which of the hotel services are important to each student and help them to explain why.

Answer key:

1

1 four-star   **2** breakfast included   **3** room service   **4** organised tours   **5** 24-hour reception   **6** sea view   **7** double rooms   **8** airport transfers   **9** free parking   **10** check out

3C

Grammar 1   Present perfect with *ever* and *never*

Materials: One worksheet per student

Instructions:

Distribute the worksheets and tell Ss that they must decide whether the sentences are correct or incorrect. They should put a tick or a cross in the ✓/✗ column and rewrite the incorrect sentences correctly in the third column. Point out that there is only one grammatical mistake in each incorrect sentence and that they should look carefully for places where the present perfect doesn't work because of a time phrase, e.g. question 1.

Set a time limit, e.g. ten minutes, for Ss to do this activity.

When the time limit is up, if they haven't finished, tell the class that there are seven incorrect sentences and that they should check back through their work carefully. If they have finished, tell Ss to check their answers with a partner.

You could make this activity into a game where you award points for correct answers, e.g. ten points per correct tick/cross in the 2nd column, and an extra ten points for the correction of any incorrect sentences.

Then put Ss in pairs or small groups and give them ten minutes to complete Ex 2. Encourage them to ask follow-up questions to discover more about their partner's experiences.

Answer key:

1

1 Incorrect – *Last year he travelled to South America.*
2 Correct
3 Correct
4 Incorrect – *She has never met a famous person.*
5 Incorrect – *Have you ever seen a film in an outdoor cinema?*
6 Incorrect – *They have never driven in another country.*
7 Correct
8 Correct
9 Incorrect – *She has never done yoga.*
10 Incorrect – *I didn't eat pizza when I was in Italy.* OR *I have never eaten pizza in Italy.*
11 Correct
12 Incorrect – *They have never been to the theatre.*

Grammar 2   Present perfect with *ever* and *never*

Materials: One card per student

Instructions:

Give each student a card and tell them to read the information. Explain that they have to find out how many people in the class have done the thing that is written on their card by asking the question: *Have you ever ... ?* If a student has done this thing, they should ask for more information, this time in the past simple. They use the question provided on their card and also their own questions.

When Ss have completed their question, tell Ss to mingle and ask other Ss their questions. They can either make a note of the answers or try to remember them.

When Ss have finished, get feedback from different members of the class. If there are more than ten Ss, you can put Ss with the same card together so that they can compare information before the feedback session.

Note that if you have a big class they may not be able to speak to everyone, so answers may vary, e.g. one student may say 12 people have been abroad, but another one will say only eight people have been abroad. If this is the case in your class, encourage Ss to start by saying *I spoke to X people, and Y have been abroad*. This will help with any discrepancies between Ss' results.

Answer key:

1 Have you ever been abroad?
2 Have you ever received a present you didn't like?
3 Have you ever had room service?
4 Have you ever found money in the street?
5 Have you ever been on TV?
6 Have you ever studied another language?
7 Have you ever broken a bone?
8 Have you ever lived in a different town or city?

Vocabulary   Verb phrases

Materials: One copy of worksheet A and worksheet B per pair of Ss

Instructions:

Explain to Ss that they are going to play noughts and crosses. If necessary, demonstrate how to play. On the board, draw 3x3 squares. Divide the class in half and tell one half to choose a square to put a nought (*O*) in. When they have chosen, ask the other half to choose a square to place a cross (*X*) in. This continues until one team has three squares in a row (vertically, horizontally or diagonally) or until there are no squares left (in this case, there is no winner). Teams should be encouraged to play tactically and to block one another from making a row.

Put Ss in pairs and give each pair a board A. If there are an uneven number of Ss, a third person in the group can act as a referee. Tell the class that they are going to play noughts and crosses, but to win a square they must produce a correct collocation from the lesson and use it in a sentence. Demonstrate by asking Ss to look at the top left square and elicit from Ss that the verb *ride* goes with *a bike* → *ride a bike*. Ss should only use the collocations they learnt in the lesson. Monitor and help settle any disputes if necessary. Ss can play another game with board B. If Ss use a pencil, the board can be reused multiple times.

You could extend the activity by having Ss make their own boards, mixing the language they learnt in the lesson in any way they choose. You could also encourage Ss to use different collocations from those they learnt in the lesson.

Answer key:

Board A
ride a bike; break a bone; fall asleep; visit an art gallery; eat with chopsticks; learn to swim; cook a meal; share a photo online; drive a sports car

Board B
watch a football match; share a photo online; go skiing; cook a meal; break a bone; be on TV; learn to swim; ride a bike; fall asleep

Grammar 1   *be going to*, *want* and *would like*

Materials: One worksheet per student

Instructions:

Distribute the worksheets and explain the task. If there are a lot of words to reorder, suggest that Ss find phrases that they recognise, e.g. a time phrase like *next year*, then the target grammar for this lesson, *I'd like to / I want to / I'm going to*. Also encourage Ss to cross out the words as they use them, so that they know which words they still have to use.

When they have finished, elicit answers from the class and correct if necessary.

Answer key:

1 I'd like to travel to a different country next year.
2 I want to go to the cinema next week.
3 I'm going to make a cake tonight.
4 I want to buy a sports car when I'm 40.
5 I'd like to play football after work.
6 I don't want to eat chocolate today.
7 I'm going to move house soon.
8 I'd like to go to the beach in two weeks' time.
9 I'm going to meet my friends for lunch tomorrow.
10 I'm not going to go to the gym tonight.
11 I don't want to go to work on Friday.
12 I'd like to visit an art gallery later today.

Grammar 2   *be going to*, *want* and *would like*

Materials: One copy of the table and one traveller card per student

Instructions:

Explain to Ss that they are all world travellers and are going to speak to three other travellers to find out where they'd like to go in the future. Give each student a copy of the table and tell them that they should first make questions with *be going to*, *want to* or *would like to* from the prompts in the first column of the table. Tell them that there is more than one way to ask the questions, but they must make at least one question with *going to*, one with *would like to* and one with *want to*. Write some possible questions on the board before moving on to the next stage, e.g. *Where are you going to travel to? Why do you want to go there?*

Divide the class into four equal groups and give each group a traveller card (Alex, Sam, Casey or Robin). (Alternatively, if you are short of time, put Ss in groups of four and give each student one traveller card from the set instead of the class mingle.)

Tell Ss to read the information on their role card and to think about how they will answer the questions on the board with it. Get them to think about which form (*be going to + infinitive*; *want to*; *would like to*) they will use for each answer. Then allow them a few minutes to complete the table with their own information.

Ss move around the class to find the three other travellers to complete their table. Remind them to use *be going to*, *want to* and *would like to* in their answers.

If they meet someone who has the same card as them, they can move on to speak to someone else. If they meet someone who has the same information as someone they have already spoken to, tell them to answer the other student's questions if necessary, then move on until they find the remaining missing people to complete their table.

For feedback, elicit information from a few Ss about the other travellers in their table by asking questions, e.g. *Where is Sam going to go?* Ensure that Ss provide a grammatically correct answer using *he/she is going to + infinitive/wants to/ would like to*.

Answer key:
1 Where **are you going to** go? / Where **do you want to** go? / Where **would you like to** go?
2 Why **are you going to** go there? / Why **do you want to** go there? / Why **would you like to** go there?
3 Who **are you going to** go with? / Who **do you want to** go with? / Who **would you like to** go with?
4 When **are you going to** go? / When **do you want to** go? / When **would you like to** go?

Vocabulary Celebrations

Materials: One worksheet per student

Instructions:

Distribute the worksheets and explain the activity. Match the first item together so that Ss understand what to do. Remind Ss to use a process of elimination, leaving any they aren't sure about until there are fewer options left to choose from.

When they are finished, elicit answers from the class and correct if necessary.

For Ex 2, put Ss in pairs or groups to discuss the questions. Monitor and ask questions where appropriate to encourage further discussion.

Answer key:
1
1 c 2 h 3 a 4 f 5 j 6 b 7 i 8 d 9 e 10 g

Grammar 1 *will, won't* for decisions and offers

Materials: One worksheet per student

Instructions:

Distribute the worksheets. Explain the task and give Ss time to read through the conversations and spot the errors. Tell them to cross out the mistakes and write the correct version below.

When correcting the mini-conversations, ensure that both the meaning and form of *will/won't* are understood.

Then in Ex 2 put Ss in pairs to practise the corrected conversations. Monitor and encourage them to use contractions where possible.

Answer key:
1
1 we'll buy (will buy) 2 won't eat (will not eat)
3 'll do (will do) 4 'll make (will make) 5 'll give (will give)
6 'll take (will take) 7 'll ask (will ask) 8 'll bring (will bring)
9 won't make (will not make) 10 'll ask (will ask)

Grammar 2 *will, won't* for decisions and offers

Materials: One slip of paper per student

Instructions:

Tell Ss you are going to give them a piece of paper with a different problem or situation on it. Give each student one slip of paper. If you have less than 14 Ss, choose the scenarios you think will generate the best responses. If you have more than 14 Ss, you can either put Ss in two different groups (there should be at least ten Ss per group) or give out the same slips to more than one student. Encourage Ss to ask for help if they do not understand something in their scenario.

If necessary, write some verbs on the board that will help your class respond to the scenarios (*carry, help, take, show, call, come,* etc.). Explain to Ss that it is fine to use the same verbs more than once.

Then allow Ss about eight to ten minutes to move around the class in a class mingle. Then Student A explains his/her problem and Student B responds with an *I'll* statement (offer or decision). Remind Student As to respond to Student B's offer or decision in an appropriate, natural manner, e.g. by saying *Thank you, How kind of you* or *Really? That's great.*

Ss then switch roles and repeat the process. They then swap slips of paper and move on to a new partner. Ss continue this process until time is up.

Ss can then work with a partner and try to remember the different scenarios and responses they encountered. Finally, invite some pairs to share their discussions with the class.

Vocabulary Organising events

Materials: One worksheet per student

Instructions:

Distribute the worksheets and explain the first task and then ask Ss to complete Ex 1 individually. Put Ss in pairs to check their answers. Be available to help them if there are any problems.

Tell Ss to work individually for Ex 2. They can change any part of the sentences, as long as they still use the target vocabulary from the lesson. When they have completed the sentences, ask Ss to work in their pairs again and compare their answers. When they have done this, invite Ss to tell the class about some of their answers.

Answer key:
1
1 bake 2 chosen 3 send 4 set 5 book 6 make
7 remind 8 planning

Grammar 1 *can, can't, have to, don't have to*

Materials: One worksheet per student

Instructions:

Remind Ss about the four different modal verbs that they have looked at in the lesson (*can/can't/have to/don't have to*) and then ask them to complete the exercise individually.

Put Ss in groups of three to check their work. Monitor and help if there are any problems. Note that *don't have to* will probably be the most difficult concept for Ss to understand, so be prepared to reinforce the idea that it means something is not necessary to do, and that there is a choice to do it if you want.

Answer key:
1 have to 2 have to 3 can 4 can't 5 don't have to 6 can't
7 have to 8 can 9 don't have to 10 have to 11 can't
12 don't have to 13 can't 14 can't 15 have to 16 can

Grammar 2   can, can't, have to, don't have to

Materials: One copy of worksheet A, worksheet B and worksheet C per group of Ss

Instructions:

Explain to Ss that they are going to be the mayor of their town and that they have to write some new laws for people who live there. Divide the class into three equal groups (or multiple groups with the same worksheet if you have a large class, e.g. 25+) and give each group a different worksheet (A, B or C).

Give groups about 15 minutes to write their laws, monitoring from time to time, but allow Ss to be creative and use their own ideas. Encourage them to go beyond what is on the card if they have more ideas to add, or if they have finished early.

When groups have finished, rearrange the class into new groups of three, so that there is an A, B and C student in each group. If there are extra Ss, there can be two As, Bs or Cs in any given group. Tell Ss they must now share the rules that they have made in their groups. Monitor and make notes of some good examples of the target language in use and any common errors to correct in the feedback stage.

Finally, rearrange Ss into new pairs and ask them to discuss which town they would like to live in the most, and why. Ask volunteers to feed back and encourage them to give reasons for their choice using can/can't/have to/don't have to examples they have heard.

Vocabulary   -ed, -ing adjectives

Materials: One copy of worksheet A, worksheet B and worksheet C per group of Ss

Instructions:

Divide the class into three equal groups and give each group a different worksheet (A, B or C). Ss choose the correct adjective form in each sentence.

Explain the activity. Tell Ss that they are going to mingle and ask questions to find out whether the person they are talking to agrees with each of the sentences they have on their card, e.g. for A1, ask the question *Do you think shopping is relaxing?* If the student answering doesn't agree with the question, they should move on to discuss the second sentence.

Ss take turns to ask and answer their questions until they have found a sentence that the student agrees with and written their name on the worksheet or they have worked through all five options.

Encourage Ss to ask follow-up questions, e.g. if someone tells them that they are excited about the weekend, they should ask why, or if they say they don't like football, they should give their own opinion too – *Neither do I!* or *Really? I love football!*

When Ss have finished, arrange them into groups of three with one A, B and C in each group. If your class is not divisible by three, make sure that there is at least one A, B and C in each group. Tell them to share their findings with their group and to report any interesting information they learnt about their classmates.

Answer key:

A
1 relaxing   2 excited   3 boring   4 tired   5 worried

B
1 tiring   2 boring   3 interested   4 relaxing   5 exciting

C
1 interested   2 surprising   3 exciting   4 worried   5 bored

5A

Grammar 1   Relative clauses with *who, which* and *that*

Materials: One worksheet per student

Instructions:

Distribute the worksheets and explain the first task. Tell Ss to ignore the gaps for the moment and to concentrate on choosing the correct option in italics. Monitor and check that they are looking for the clues in the sentence, e.g. *person, place,* to help them choose the correct word. Check the answer for each question as a whole class, then give Ss five to ten minutes to complete Ex 1 by writing something that is true for them in each gap.

Put Ss in pairs to compare their answers (Ex 2) and ask further follow-up questions about the information.

Invite some Ss to share the most interesting information they learnt about their partner.

Answer key:

1
1 that   **2** who   **3** who   **4** that   **5** who   **6** that   **7** which
8 that   **9** which   **10** who

Grammar 2   Relative clauses with *who, which* and *that*

Materials: One set of cards per group of Ss

Instructions:

Divide the class into groups of four (or five or six if the class is large). Divide each group into two teams, each consisting of at least two Ss. Give each group a set of cards and tell them to put them face down. Tell the teams to toss a coin or throw a dice to see who goes first. On their turn, each student picks up a card and describes it to the other members of his/her team, using a defining relative clause, e.g. *It's a person who ...* , *It's a thing which/that ...* . Tell Ss they have thirty seconds to describe what's on their card. If a team member guesses what is on the card correctly, the team keeps the card. If not, it is put on a separate 'used' pile. If they don't use a relative clause to describe the object, they lose their turn and the card is also put on the 'used' pile.

A member of the other team then takes a turn. This continues until all the cards have been used. Make sure that a different person does the describing each time.

The winners are the team which has the most cards at the end.

Vocabulary   Job skills and preferences

Materials: One copy of card A, card B and card C per group of Ss

Instructions:

Tell Ss that they are going to work together to guess some jobs using clues on their worksheets. Jobs 1–6 are the same across all three cards, but each card only provides one clue for each job.

Put Ss in groups of three and give the Ss a different card (A, B or C). If there is an odd number of Ss, you can give **weaker Ss** two cards and have them work in pairs with a **stronger student**.

Give Ss a few minutes to look at their card individually and think about what each job could be. Explain that some of the jobs are from this lesson, but some are not. Tell Ss not to worry if they can't guess what the jobs are at this stage as they will soon learn more information.

Groups must then decide what the jobs are by discussing their ideas and the information on their card, e.g. *I think job 1 is a _____ because my card says … .*

You could discuss phrases for agreeing and disagreeing before they start, e.g. *Yes, I agree because my card says … ; No, I don't think so because my card says … ; Yes, maybe; Or maybe it's … .*

Monitor the groups and check answers when they have finished.

As an extension, give each group of Ss two alternative jobs (try to give different jobs to different groups), making sure they are jobs all Ss will know. Don't reuse jobs from the first task. Suggested jobs include *film star, chef, mechanic, cleaner, actor.*

Then tell Ss that they should write three clues to describe each job, using as much language from the lesson as they can. Remind them that they can also use the phrases negatively, e.g. *I don't need good communication skills because I usually work alone.* When they are ready, put two groups together and tell them to read their clues to the other group. The other group should try to guess the job after each sentence.

Answer key:
1 writer   2 architect   3 shop assistant   4 businessperson
5 film extra   6 tour guide

 5B

Grammar 1   *look like, look* + adjective, *be like*

Materials: One worksheet per student

Instructions:

Distribute the worksheets and explain the task. Give Ss time to complete the gaps in the mini-conversations individually or in pairs if you prefer. Check the answers together as a class, paying particular attention to the form of the grammar as Ss are still likely to make errors with the 3rd person -*s*.

For Ex 2, put Ss in pairs to practise asking and answering the questions on the worksheet.

Answer key:

1
1 look like   2 like   3 looks   4 look   5 looks like   6 looks
7 look like   8 like   9 looks   10 look like   11 looks like
12 looks like

Grammar 2   *look like, look* + adjective, *be like*

Materials: One copy of worksheet A and worksheet B per pair of Ss

Instructions:

Put Ss in pairs and give each pair worksheet A and worksheet B. Tell them not to show their worksheet to their partner. Explain that each student has the same pictures as their partner, but that the pictures are arranged in a different order on the two worksheets.

Explain that Student A is going to describe one of the people on the sheet and that Student B must try to guess who he/she is describing. Write the following phrases on the board and tell Ss that they can only use these phrases when describing the people.

He/She looks like … (e.g. *He looks like a teacher.*)

He/She looks … (e.g. *She looks sad; He looks around 30/ young.*)

Remind them to use the feelings adjectives they learnt in Unit 2, review these with Ss if necessary.

To help Ss establish the gender of the person they're describing without having to say '*She's a woman*' which doesn't fit the rules of the game, encourage them to start the conversation like this:

Student A: *I've chosen a person.*
Student B: *What is he or she like? / What does he or she look like?*
Student A: *He/She looks/is/has … .*

Ss continue in this way, taking turns to describe and guess the correct person.

You could turn the game into a competition. Tell Ss that if they guess correctly after just one clue, they get three points. After two clues, they get two points. If they guess the correct person after that, they get one point. Ss could then be tactical when playing the game and give more difficult clues first, then give more obvious ones. The partner with the most points at the end wins.

Answer key:
Suggested answers:
Kevin: He looks around 25. He looks like a businessperson. He looks stressed.
Romesh: He looks about 45. He looks cool. He looks happy.
Melanie: She looks like a doctor. She looks tired. She looks about 30.
Sofia: She looks very happy. She looks like a student. She looks cool.
Michael: He looks around 35. He looks angry. He looks like a father.
Paul: He looks surprised. He looks around 60 to 70. He looks silly.
Laura: She looks about 20. She looks like a football fan. She looks excited.
Allison: She looks about 30. She looks worried. She looks like a businessperson.

Vocabulary   Appearance

Materials: One worksheet per student

Instructions:

Distribute the worksheets and explain the task. Give Ss enough time to do the task individually or in pairs. Remind them to cross out the words in the box as they use them, so they know what they still have to use.

When they have finished, go through the answers as a class and then ask Ss if they know anyone similar to the people in the descriptions.

As a follow-up, you could get Ss to write a similar description of someone in their family or a friend of theirs. If you feel that Ss in the class know each other well enough, you could even get them to write a description of a classmate.

Answer key:
1 dark   2 curly   3 slim   4 tall   5 blonde   6 straight   7 smart
8 bald   9 beard   10 moustache   11 casual   12 long   13 tattoo

 5C

Grammar 1   *should, shouldn't* and imperatives

Materials: One worksheet per student

Instructions:

Distribute the worksheets and explain the task. Give Ss time to read the advice and find the mistakes. Make it clear that the mistakes are only with *should* and *imperatives,* and that there is one error in each piece of advice.

Monitor and note down any common errors that occur for feedback later on. Check the answers as a class then put Ss in pairs to discuss the questions in Ex 2.

When Ss have finished, they can discuss their opinions about the advice and any other advice they would give with the whole class.

Answer key:

1

1 Think **2** Find **3** should save **4** should have **5** Don't use
6 Get some **7** Don't pay **8** should plan **9** should know
10 Look for **11** Don't go **12** Use **13** Make **14** shouldn't buy
15 and use them

Grammar 2   *should, shouldn't* and imperatives

Materials: One copy of worksheet A, worksheet B, worksheet C
and worksheet D per group of Ss

Instructions:

Put Ss in groups of four and tell them that they are a group of
close friends, and that each one of them in the group has a
problem they need advice about.

Give one card to each student in the group and tell Ss that they
should memorise their problem so that they can explain it to
their friends in their own words. They should also think of the
questions they can ask to get advice on the points listed on their
cards. Give Ss a few minutes to do this. They then do the activity
in their groups. While Ss are speaking, monitor and note good
uses of *should/shouldn't* and *imperatives* to feed back to the class
afterwards.

When groups have finished, elicit what the best advice was for
each of the problems they spoke about.

Vocabulary   Shopping

Materials: One worksheet per student

Instructions:

Distribute the worksheets and explain the first task. Give Ss time
to circle the correct option individually. Then check the answers
with the class.

Put Ss in pairs to discuss the questions in Ex 2 and encourage
them to use the vocabulary from Ex 1 to express the situations
they have been in. When they have finished, ask Ss to tell the class
about any interesting situations they have experienced.

Answer key:

1

1 return things **2** compare prices **3** read reviews
4 kept the receipt **5** on sale **6** ask for a discount
7 try them on **8** pay by credit card

Grammar 1   *will* for predictions

Materials: One worksheet per student

Instructions:

Distribute the worksheets and explain the task. Tell Ss that the
predictions are discussion points and not necessarily based on
fact. Do the first one together if appropriate, reminding Ss to look
for the subject of the sentence first. If you have a **weaker class**,
you may want to tell them what the first word of each prediction
is. Check the answers together with the class.

Ask Ss whether they have any questions about the meaning of
the sentences, then put them in pairs to discuss which predictions
they think will happen. Elicit some opinions from Ss as a way to
end the activity and provide feedback.

Answer key:

1

1 I think fast food will be less popular.
2 People will only eat chicken and not beef. (OR People will only eat beef and not chicken.)
3 The world will need more farmers.
4 People will be a lot fatter than in the past.
5 There won't be teachers in schools.
6 It will be easier to learn a language.
7 There won't be any fruit or vegetables. (OR There won't be any vegetables or fruit.)
8 50% of the world will speak Mandarin Chinese.
9 We will have computers in our heads.
10 I don't think we'll live in big houses.
11 No one will speak English.
12 I don't think people will have pets.
13 People won't need to eat real food.
14 I think there will be more cities.
15 There won't be as many languages.

Grammar 2   *will* for predictions

Materials: One information card per group and one resident card
per student

Instructions:

Divide the class into four equal groups. Give each group a copy of
the information card about Pescaville. If groups are larger than
five Ss, either give each group two copies of this card, or divide
each group in two. Read the text with the class and check that Ss
understand the situation.

Give Ss in each group the same resident's card (A, B, C or D). Allow
Ss time to read through the information and then tell them to
prepare what they will say at the meeting in their groups. Tell
them to make predictions using *will* and the ideas from the role
card, but suggest that they also think of some ideas of their own.

Rearrange the class into new groups of four so that each group
has a Resident A, B, C and D. If you don't have multiples of four,
double up the role cards of Resident C and/or D. Tell Ss to discuss
the future of Pescaville in their groups.

When Ss have finished, get feedback from the whole class.
Then tell Ss to forget their roles and have a class vote to see
whether the project should go ahead or not.

Vocabulary   Happiness

Materials: One copy of the question card and one copy of role
cards A–D per group of Ss

Instructions:

Put Ss in groups of four and give the Ss in each group a different
role card (A, B, C or D). If there is an odd number of Ss, there can
be an extra card in a group. Give each group a copy of the question
card. Tell Ss to read their role cards and to think about how they
would answer the questions on the question card.

Then tell Ss to discuss the questions in their groups. Remind Ss
that they must tell their group a bit about themselves to provide
the background to their choices and opinions. Encourage Ss to
challenge one another, e.g. *Why do you think it's important to earn
lots of money? You can live happily on much less than that.*

While they are talking, monitor and check Ss are using the correct
pronunciation of the target vocabulary and be on hand to help
with any vocabulary questions. Encourage debate by asking
questions yourself.

When they have finished, ask the class whether there were any
answers that Ss gave in their groups which were very different to
each other, and ask for reasons why.

241

6B

Grammar 1   Present continuous for future arrangements

Materials: One worksheet per student

Instructions:

Distribute the worksheets and allow Ss time to complete Ex 1 individually. Monitor and check Ss are using the present continuous in their answers. Then check the answers with the whole class.

Before putting Ss in pairs to practise the conversations (Ex 2), remind them that using contractions sounds more natural in spoken English. If you think your Ss might need more practise with this before working on their own, you could chorally drill each conversation.

As Ss are practising the conversations, monitor and listen for correct usage of contractions. When they have finished, invite various pairs to role play the conversations for the class.

Answer key:

1

1 'm (am) meeting; 're (are) going   **2** 's (is) making
3 'm (am) going; 'm (am) playing
4 are (you) doing; 'm (am) studying   **5** 'm (am) not starting
6 are (you) doing; are taking

Grammar 2   Present continuous for future arrangements

Materials: One worksheet per student

Instructions:

Start by asking Ss if they have ever been to a festival (music festival, literary festival, food festival, etc).

Distribute the worksheets. Ss work individually. They decide what they want to do and write the activity in the correct place in their diary. They should choose no more than five activities, so that they have some slots free. Give them a few minutes to complete this stage. Monitor and help if necessary.

Once they have finished tell them to mingle and discuss their plans with the rest of the class. They should try to fill the blank slots in their diary and also arrange to do events with other Ss, e.g. *A: What are you doing on Saturday afternoon? B: I haven't got any plans. A: I'm going to Zumba with Derek on Stage one, do you want to come?* They can also try to persuade Ss to come with them to events. Tell Ss they can change their minds if the other student makes a good argument!

Ss should write down their new and/or amended activities along with the student or Ss who are coming with them. They should only make one arrangement with a particular student and can also say no if they don't want to do the activity proposed. When they have finished, ask Ss what they have planned to do and when.

Vocabulary   *make, do, have*

Materials: One grid per pair of Ss

Instructions:

Put Ss in pairs and give each pair a copy of the grid. Tell them that they are going to play a game where they must connect three squares in a row; this can be vertically, horizontally or diagonally, but the squares must be touching. Each student should decide on a symbol to use to mark the squares they win.

The pairs take turns making a sentence using *do, have* or *make* with the word/phrase in a square of their choice. If the student uses the correct collocation in his/her sentence, he/she wins the square and can put his/her symbol in it. Some words are repeated in the grid, so tell Ss they must not say the same sentence twice. The winner is the first to win three squares in a row. Ss should try to block his/her partner's attempts to win. Suggest to the class that they use pencils, and that way they can play as many times as they like. Tell Ss that in repeat games they must make completely different sentences to those they made in other games.

6C

Grammar 1   *may* and *might*

Materials: One worksheet per student

Instructions:

Distribute the worksheets and explain the task. Look at the first sentence with the class and elicit what the answer should be. Point out that *may* and *might* are both possible with the target verbs.

Give Ss time to complete the rest of the sentences on their own. Put **fast finishers** in pairs to check their answers, and then write the answers up on the board once the majority of Ss have finished.

Answer key:

Note: *may (not)* is possible in each of the sentences as well.
1 might buy   **2** might not go   **3** might wake   **4** might be
5 might go   **6** might meet   **7** might not be   **8** might fail
9 might buy   **10** might look   **11** might not cook
12 might have   **13** might not finish   **14** might get

Grammar 2   *may* and *might*

Materials: One slip of paper per student

Instructions:

Tell the class that you are going to give each of them a slip of paper with a question on it. Note that you can remove any questions that you feel aren't relevant to your Ss, and if you have a small class just pick the ones you like best. If you have a class larger than 15, use the same questions more than once.

Distribute the questions and explain the task. Ss mingle and find a partner. One student starts by asking the question on his/her slip of paper. Their partner must then answer the question using *may/might (not)* at least once, but preferably more times. Tell Ss that they should try to use *may/might* as often as they can, especially if they don't have definite plans yet.

Once both Ss have asked their question, they swap questions and move on to find a new partner and repeat the process. Tell Ss not to worry if they get the same slip of paper again, or if they need to answer the same question more than once, as it will give them an opportunity to improve their answers.

Allow Ss time to ask and answer most, if not all, of the questions, but set an upper time limit in advance so that they don't get bored, e.g. 12 minutes.

Once everyone is seated again, ask Ss to tell the class about some of the interesting answers to their questions from the activity.

Vocabulary   Weekend activities

Materials: One set of cards per group of Ss

Instructions:

Tell Ss that they are going to do a short class survey and will have to ask three questions to as many people in the class as they can in seven minutes. If necessary, explain that you use surveys to ask a group of people the same questions and make notes of answers in order to learn about the things they think or do as a group.

Divide the class into four equal groups and give the Ss in each group a different worksheet (A, B, C or D).

Ss use the space in the table to write out the questions they will ask. Make sure that Ss understand that it is important that they record their answers using the spaces next to the questions.

While Ss are doing the survey, you could write on the board some useful sentence stems for reporting information, e.g. *No one ...; Everyone ...; Three people ...; Half of the class ...*.

Ss mingle as a class, writing the names of those who do the activities at the weekend on their sheets. When they have finished, ask Ss to sit down and to think about the information they learnt. Get them to write three sentences in their notebooks to describe the information they collected, using some of the sentence stems on the board. Put Ss in groups with one A, B, C and D in each group. If there are not multiples of four, make sure that there are no two Ss with the same card in a group (as they will have spoken to a different number of Ss so their answers may not be identical). Allow groups a few minutes to share their information. Encourage them to compare the results – are any of them surprising? Monitor and correct any errors while they do this.

Grammar 1   *too* and *enough*

Materials: One worksheet per student

Instructions:

Distribute the worksheets and explain the task. Do the first one together, find the two correct sentences and make sure that they realise that sometimes more than one answer can be correct. Tell Ss not to look for spelling mistakes or mistakes in meaning – the errors are grammatical or related to word order.

When correcting the answers, ask Ss to explain why the incorrect items are wrong to make sure they really understand the errors.

Answer key:

1 a, b   **2** a   **3** b   **4** c   **5** a, b   **6** b   **7** c   **8** a, c

Grammar 2   *too* and *enough*

Materials: One set of cards per pair of Ss

Instructions:

Tell Ss that they are going to play a guessing game. Put Ss in pairs and give each pair a set of cards, placed face down in a pile in front of them. One student picks up a card, reads it silently and then tries to get his/her partner to guess where he/she is going or what he/she is doing, by making sentences with *too/enough*. Ss must not use any of the words on their card.

Demonstrate by writing *You're at a party* on the board. Tell the class to imagine they are at a party and to tell the class about it, making sure that they are using the target language, e.g. *There are enough people; The music is too loud; There is not enough food.* Try to ensure that you have at least one of each of the target sentence structures on the board to act as a model during the activity.

Ss take turns picking a card and describing the situation on the card with *too* and *enough* sentences. Remind them that they must use *too/enough* in each sentence. Tell Ss that it is not necessary for their partner to say exactly what is on the card, but that the idea must be the same. Monitor and write down some good examples of different *too/enough* sentences to use for feedback later on.

Vocabulary   Features of city life

Materials: One worksheet per student

Instructions:

Distribute the worksheets and explain the task. Ask Ss to complete Ex 1 individually. Monitor and check for accuracy. Then check the answers with the whole class.

When Ss have completed the paragraphs, put them in pairs to discuss the questions in Ex 2. Monitor and correct pronunciation of the target vocabulary items if needed, e.g. *neighbours*. Encourage Ss to justify their decision about which place to live in, using the information in the paragraphs plus any general or local knowledge they happen to have.

Answer key:

1
1 area   **2** location   **3** local   **4** traffic   **5** pollution   **6** flats
7 cycle paths   **8** neighbours   **9** public transport
10 night life   **11** local

Grammar 1   *used to*

Materials: One worksheet per student

Instructions:

Explain the tasks to the class, then give Ss ten minutes to complete the gaps individually, using the verbs in brackets. Monitor closely and prompt Ss to use the correct form of the verbs when needed.

When they have finished, feed back with the class and make sure that Ss understand why *used to/didn't use to* has been used in each case.

Tell Ss to each choose four sentences from Ex 1 and make them true for themselves. Finish off by asking Ss to share some of their sentences with the class.

Answer key:

1
1 used to be   **2** didn't use to eat   **3** did (she) use to do
4 used to see   **5** didn't use to drive   **6** Did (you) use to play
7 didn't use to play   **8** used to bake   **9** didn't use to speak
10 used to smoke   **11** Did (they) use to sing   **12** used to live
13 did (you) use to listen   **14** didn't use to like

Grammar 2   *used to*

Materials: One copy of worksheet A and worksheet B per group of Ss

Instructions:

Put Ss in groups of three or four (or pairs for a greater challenge). Give half the groups Worksheet A and the other half of the groups Worksheet B. Make sure that everyone in each group looks at the same sheet.

Explain the activity. Write *Before there were aeroplanes ...* on the board and ask Ss to give you some examples of what life was like before aeroplanes, using *used to*, e.g. *people used to travel by boats more*; *people didn't use to travel as often*; *it used to take a long time to travel*; *there didn't use to be pilots*. Tell Ss that they should use both *used to* or *didn't use to* in their answers.

Tell Ss to work in their groups to complete the sentences, saying how things were different before the invention of each thing. Encourage them to write as many ideas as they can. Monitor and help with vocabulary.

Then put Ss in A/B pairs. Tell them to take turns to read their sentences to their partner without saying what the invention is, e.g. *Before (blank), people used to ... .* Their partner has to guess the invention from the clues. Alternatively, if your Ss were working in pairs earlier, you could now put two As and two Bs together to work in groups of four for this stage.

Vocabulary   Natural features

Materials: One set of cards per pair of Ss

Instructions:

Tell the class that they are going to play a memory game. Put Ss in pairs and give each pair a set of cards. Tell them to shuffle the cards then place them face down randomly on the desk.

Demonstrate the game by choosing and turning over any two cards. Show the cards to the class and if one of the cards shows a word and the other a picture, ask Ss whether the word matches the picture. If not, tell them that you must put them back on the table where you found them. If the word and picture do match, explain that Ss must then make a sentence using the word from the pair. If they do this without making a mistake, they keep the pair of cards and pick up another two cards. If the cards do not match, or if they can't make a sentence, it is their partner's turn. Play continues in this way until all of the cards have been matched and won.

Answer key:
1 beach   **2** mountain   **3** lake   **4** stream   **5** forest   **6** river   **7** hill   **8** wood   **9** sea

7C

Grammar 1   Articles

Materials: One worksheet per student

Instructions:

Distribute the worksheets and explain the task to Ss. Look at the first sentence with the whole class and read it aloud with them. Then focus their attention on the article in the sentence and elicit whether or not there is an error in it. Ask Ss to tell you why the article is incorrect.

Ss work individually to say whether the sentences are correct or incorrect, and to correct the ones which are wrong. Put Ss in pairs to check their answers. For ***fast finishers***, tell them that there are only five correct sentences so that they can double check their work.

When you correct the activity with the whole class, make sure that you ask Ss why the incorrect sentences are wrong.

Answer key:
1 Incorrect – I don't usually like (–) **chicken**, but that was delicious!
2 Incorrect – I used to have **a cat** called Bubbles. He was so cute!
3 Correct
4 Incorrect – Next week I'm going to see **a film** with my mum.
5 Incorrect – I need to buy (–) **new t-shirts** soon. Mine are old.
6 Correct
7 Correct
8 Incorrect – Yesterday I ate (–) **pasta** for lunch. I love Italian food!
9 Incorrect – Can I borrow **the book** you had last week? It looked good.
10 Correct
11 Incorrect – I'm watching **a TV show** called *Utopia*. It's very exciting!
12 Incorrect – Can you please take **the kids** to the park tonight?
13 Incorrect – Did you like **the film** that you saw yesterday?
14 Correct
15 Incorrect – Shrewsbury is **a town** in the west of England.

Grammar 2   Articles

Materials: One set of cards per group of Ss

Instructions:

Put Ss in groups of two or three. Give one set of cards to each group and tell them that they must make a story using as many of the phrases as possible. They should decide what kind of story to make, e.g. science fiction, love story, murder mystery, etc., and which phrases to use, but they must use exactly the same phrases with the same article as on the cards. Encourage Ss to arrange the cards they have used in order on the table, so that they can remember and retell the story. Emphasise that they will need to use other phrases as well, e.g. sometimes the same noun with a different article: *This story is about a woman ... the woman had the worst day of her life when ... .* Monitor and correct as necessary as they do the activity.

When Ss have made up their story, tell them to tell their story to Ss from other groups. Set a time limit of three minutes for them to practise their story in their groups.

Put Ss in new groups, so that each group member has created a different story. Allow the groups to move around the class, so that the storyteller can refer to their group's cards on the table, to make it easier. Alternatively, allow Ss to use their phones to take a picture of their cards, then they can move around without the cards.

As a follow-up, tell Ss to write up their story for homework.

Vocabulary   Prepositions

Materials: One copy of picture A and picture B per pair of Ss

Instructions:

Put Ss in pairs and distribute the two pictures to each pair. Tell them not to show their picture to each other.

Explain that their pictures are very similar, but that there are a lot of small differences between them. Tell them that they both need to ask each other questions to find these differences, e.g. *Is there a ... ? What is on the ... ? Where is the ... ?*

Allow Ss about ten minutes to find the differences in the pictures. Check the answers with the class, encouraging Ss to use prepositions, e.g. *In my picture, there are magazines on the coffee table, but in the other picture there are books on it.*

To give Ss additional writing practice, you could ask them to write sentences that describe the differences in the pictures.

Answer key:

The prepositions can be used in the following ways, but there may be more possibilities:

1 in the corner – lamp in the corner, clock in the corner
2 on – clock on wall, various things on tables/not on tables, TV on table, woman on sofa, plant on bookshelf, picture on bookshelf
3 in front of – coffee table in front of sofa
4 behind – dining table behind sofa, man behind sofa
5 opposite – armchairs opposite each other, TV opposite sofa
6 in the middle of – flowers in the middle of the dining table, clock in the middle of the wall
7 under – shoes under coffee table
8 between – bookshelf between two lamps, coffee table between two armchairs
9 next to – lamp next to bookshelf, side table next to sofa

Grammar 1   Past continuous

Materials: One worksheet per student

Instructions:

Before starting, remind Ss that the past continuous is used for actions in progress in the past and the past simple is used when this action in progress is interrupted by another single action or event.

Distribute the worksheets. Check the meaning of the word *monster* (*an imaginary or ancient creature that is large, ugly and frightening*) and ask if anyone has heard of *Loch Ness* or *Nessie*. Then give Ss time to complete the story, using the correct form of the verbs in brackets.

Check answers with the class and make sure that Ss understand why they have used each tense.

Put Ss in pairs to try and re-tell the story from memory. Monitor and check Ss are using the weak stress of *was/were*, and correct if necessary.

Answer key:

1

1 was travelling   **2** were staying (*stayed* is also possible. It depends whether this is thought of as temporary or not).
3 talked   **4** decided   **5** were driving   **6** saw   **7** were travelling
8 looked   **9** stopped   **10** was   **11** were taking   **12** bought
13 were waiting (*waited* is also possible)   **14** was looking
15 saw   **16** was standing   **17** ran   **18** got

Grammar 2   Past continuous

Materials: One copy of the instruction card per student, plus one role card per student

Instructions:

Give each student a copy of the instruction card and read through the instructions with the whole class. Then give each student a role card. If you have more than ten Ss, divide them into two groups or use some of the role cards twice. If you do this, tell Ss that some of the activities were being done by more than one person. Make sure you give the role of the thief (the final card) to a strong student, and only to one student.

Tell Ss to mingle and ask the other Ss questions to find out what they were doing, e.g. *What were you doing last Saturday at 7 o'clock?* Tell them to try to find out more information and decide if that person is telling the truth or not. Put examples on

the board if you think Ss need them, e.g. *Who were you with? What was it like?* Tell Ss to write a name next to each activity on the worksheet.

When they have finished, put Ss in pairs and tell them to discuss who they think the thief is, giving reasons. Get feedback from the class and then ask the thief to identify him/herself.

Vocabulary   Verbs of movement

Materials: One worksheet per student

Instructions:

Distribute the worksheets. Tell Ss to choose the correct preposition in each sentence individually, then check their answers in pairs.

Tell Ss that they are now going to have a competition in which they have to answer some questions, giving reasons why you might do something. You could get them to imagine that they are angry about something and ask them to give you three reasons why they could be angry, e.g. *Someone stole their money; They lost the tickets to a football match; They broke their favourite glass.*

Put Ss in pairs and tell them that in order to win, they must answer each question with three answers. They get one point for each answer they write that no one else has written. If they don't write three things, they don't get any points for that round, even if one or more of their answers is unique. Tell Ss that their English doesn't have to be grammatically correct, but they must be able to explain their idea to the class afterwards.

Set a time limit, e.g. ten minutes, for Ss to do the activity. When they have finished, go through their answers as a class, getting Ss to explain any answers that may not seem to fit. If there are any disputes, put it to a class vote. If any groups struggle to explain their idea, ask the class to help them give a suitable response, and do not penalise these mistakes.

The team with the most points at the end wins.

Answer key:

1
1 over   **2** around   **3** back   **4** out   **5** into   **6** up   **7** down
8 around

2

Suggested answers:
1 you have to go to work/school; you have to turn something off (e.g. a light); you have to answer the door or the phone; you have to give your seat to someone on the train; you want to dance; you want to make a cup of tea/coffee; the baby is crying; you have to go to the toilet
2 a sofa; the floor; a blanket; a rug/carpet; the grass
3 you hear a noise; you forgot something and have to go back to your house; someone is calling your name
4 you forgot your bag; you wanted to ask the teacher something; you can't find your mobile phone and think it might be in the class; it's raining a lot so you decide to leave later
5 you're late; you don't want to talk to someone in the room; your phone is ringing in another room; you see someone outside you need to speak to
6 drink some water; take some medicine; go to sleep for a while; move away from a loud noise

8B

Grammar 1 *because, so* and *to*

Materials: One worksheet per student

Instructions:

Distribute the worksheets and explain the task. While matching the sentence halves, monitor and prompt with questions if necessary, e.g. *Is this a cause or a result? Is it answering the question 'Why'?* Ask **fast finishers** to compare with a partner while they are waiting for others to finish, then check the answers as a whole class.

Ask Ss to write new endings for the sentence beginnings in Ex 1. Finally, put Ss in pairs to compare their new sentences.

Answer key:

1
1 d **2** i **3** a **4** g **5** j **6** e **7** c **8** h **9** f **10** l **11** b **12** k

Grammar 2 *because, so* and *to*

Materials: One set of cards per pair of Ss

Instructions:

Tell Ss that they are going to have a competition in pairs. Give each pair a set of cards. Instruct them to lay out all of the cards randomly, face up on one of their desks.

Ss choose two cards and say the words/phrases on the cards. They must then create a sentence connecting the two cards, and using either *because, so,* or *to + infinitive*. Tell them that they can change the tense of the verbs if necessary, but that the nouns and adjectives must stay as they are. If a student makes a correct sentence, he/she keeps the pair of cards. If a student is unable to make a correct sentence, they must put the cards back on the desk. For the first two cards on the sheet, some possible sentences are: *I rented a car because I wanted to see a lot of Vancouver; I want to drive to Vancouver, so I'm going to rent a car; I'm going to Vancouver to rent a car.*

Ss continue until they have used as many of the cards as possible. The winner is the player with the most pairs of cards at the end.

Alternatively, if you want to ensure that Ss do not use *because* every time, award points to each of the three words: *because* gets one point, *so* gets two points and *to* gets three points. In this case, the player with the most points wins.

When they have finished, Ss can play the game again, this time with cards facing down on the table, arranged neatly in rows. As before, they choose two cards, but this time they have a choice of whether to make a sentence or to pass, as it may be difficult to make a sentence with some card combinations (e.g. two emotions). Players must put cards back in their original position if they do not use them so that their partner has a chance to remember where they are and use them.

Vocabulary Transport

Materials: One set of slips of paper per pair of Ss

Instructions:

Put Ss in pairs and give each pair a shuffled set of the slips of paper. Tell the class that they need to complete the sentences in their pairs with the correct collocations from the lesson. They should try to do this from memory first, but can look back at their notes if they are having difficulty.

Once Ss have done this, tell them that the strips together make a story and that they must work with their partner to put it in the

correct order. Ask Ss what the story is about (*travelling in South East Asia*).

If necessary, tell Ss what the first line is, or ask the class to work together to find it. Then encourage Ss to find connections between sentences using place names, other nouns and time expressions.

When pairs have finished, check the order of their stories. If there are parts that are out of sequence, tell them how many are incorrect before pointing out what they are. If there are **fast finishers**, ask them to try to retell the story from memory, using as many of the collocations as possible.

Answer key:

1 D park **2 K** get off; bus **3 A** get off **4 E** rent **5 C** get in
6 I take **7 H** miss **8 B** rent; rents **9 G** get on **10 J** get off
11 F get in; parks; get out of

8C

Grammar 1 Verb patterns

Materials: One worksheet per student

Instructions:

Distribute the worksheets and explain the first task. Ss complete the sentences using the correct form of the verbs in brackets. They then choose the correct options in the sentences in Ex 2. Check answers for both activities as a class.

Answer key:

1
1 reading **2** to spend **3** drinking **4** watching **5** to ride
6 relaxing **7** eating **8** to become **9** swimming
10 to travel **11** going **12** to go
2
1 enjoys **2** doesn't mind **3** playing **4** to go **5** watching
6 don't want

Grammar 2 Verb patterns

Materials: One copy of worksheet A, worksheet B or worksheet C per student

Instructions:

Divide the class into three groups. Give one group the Student A worksheets, one group the Student B worksheets and one group the Student C worksheets.

Tell Ss to complete the questions with the correct form of the verb in brackets and then to check their answers with the other Ss in their group. Monitor to check that all Ss have completed the questions correctly.

Then rearrange the class into groups of three, so that there is a Student A, a Student B and a Student C. If necessary, make extra groups of four rather than two. Tell Ss to ask and answer each other the questions and encourage them to ask more follow-up questions.

Ask Ss to think of adjectives to describe the other Ss in their group, based on the answers they gave to the worksheet questions. Write an example on the board, e.g. *My partner is a bit shy, because she doesn't like talking to people she doesn't know.*

Then rearrange the class into new pairs and ask Ss to tell each other about their original partners.

Finally, get feedback from different members of the class.

Answer key:

Student A

1 doing **2** learning **3** to visit **4** watching **5** to retire

Student B

1 speaking **2** spending **3** playing **4** to earn **5** to live

Student C

1 to be **2** to become **3** eating **4** listening **5** speaking

Vocabulary Travel

Materials: One quiz per student and one results sheet per pair of Ss

Instructions:

Distribute a quiz to each student and explain that they must read through the questions very quickly to find out what the quiz is about. Give Ss a minute or less to do this and then elicit the topic (*holiday preferences/what type of holidays people like*).

Tell Ss that you are going to give them a few minutes to read back through the quiz again to find and underline as many travel collocations as they can from the main lesson. Ask Ss to tell you the collocations they have found before continuing.

Next tell Ss that they are going to find out their partner's answers to the quiz questions. Ensure that they do not answer any of the questions themselves – they should only write the answers to what their partner says on their worksheets. Put Ss in pairs and tell them to choose one person to start asking the quiz questions and the other to answer them and then it is their partner's turn to ask the questions.

Once a pair has finished, give them one copy of the results sheet and let them read results about their travel styles in their pairs. Get some feedback from the class once everyone is finished about what their travel styles are. Ask whether pairs were similar or different, and which answers were the most different for them and why.

Grammar 1 Present perfect with *for* and *since*

Materials: One worksheet per student

Instructions:

Distribute the worksheets and explain the task. Tell Ss to complete the questions using the present perfect simple. Check answers with the whole class, then give Ss time to match the questions to the answers and complete the gaps in Ex 2. When correcting these, ask Ss to say why they have chosen *for/since* for each item. Then put Ss in pairs to practise asking and answering the questions.

Answer key:

1

1 have you owned **2** have you had **3** have you worked
4 have you studied **5** have you had **6** have you lived
7 have you known **8** have you been

2

a 5 – for **b** 3 – since **c** 7 – for **d** 1 – for **e** 8 – since
f 4 – since **g** 2 – since **h** 6 – for

Grammar 2 Present perfect with *for* and *since*

Materials: One worksheet per student

Instructions:

Put Ss in groups of five. Tell them they are going to interview each other in order to get to know the members of their group better. Distribute the worksheets and go through the example answer with the class. Then ask which tense the questions use (*present simple* and *present perfect*). Tell Ss to look at the example answers and point out the use of *for* and *since*.

Tell Ss to work in their group and write questions for each piece of information. Monitor the groups and check their answers.

Then give Ss a moment to think of their own answers to each question, but encourage them not to write them down.

Next, tell Ss to take turns to ask each other the questions and record the answers in the table. Encourage them to ask for and give further information about each answer.

When Ss have asked each member of their group all the questions, they should then fill in statements 1–8 at the bottom of the worksheet with the name of a person from the group.

If the class is large enough, rearrange the groups so that members of different groups work together. Tell them to exchange information about the people they have interviewed. Finally, get feedback from each group.

Answer key:

1 Do you play tennis? How long have you played tennis?
2 Do you have a pet? How long have you had a pet?
3 Do you study French? How long have you studied French?
4 Do you use social media? How long have you used social media?
5 Do you live in a flat? How long have you lived in a flat?
6 Do you work in an office? How long have you worked in an office?
7 Do you live in the countryside? How long have you lived in the countryside?
8 Do you have a best friend? How long have you known your best friend?

Vocabulary Describing a relationship

Materials: One worksheet per student

Instructions:

Distribute the worksheets and explain that speech bubbles 1–5 need to be matched to speech bubbles a–e. Ss do this by reading through the texts in the speech bubbles and using the vocabulary from the lesson and other contextual clues to decide which people are talking about one another.

For example, speech bubble 1 is positive overall and talks about travelling abroad (*to South Africa*) and using email to stay in touch. Speech bubble c also talks about meeting someone while travelling and keeping in touch with a person they met there. These two are therefore a match as they can only be referring to each other.

Tell Ss to match the pairs of speech bubbles by drawing lines on the worksheet and to write the name of the speaker under each speech bubble. Conduct class feedback, asking volunteers to tell you what clues led them to match a pair.

Finally, put Ss in pairs and allow them time for the discussion in Ex 2. Encourage them to discuss how their friendships are different to the people in Ex 1 as well as how they are similar.

Answer key:

1
1 Marian – **c** Lindsay **2** Ellie – **d** Gemma **3** Scott – **b** Gus
4 Ann – **a** Stewart **5** Nicole – **e** Craig

9B

Grammar 1   Present perfect with *already, just* and *yet*

Materials: One worksheet per student

Instructions:

Distribute the worksheets and explain the task. Do the first sentence together and elicit what the whole sentence should be (*They have just got married*). Set a time limit, e.g. eight minutes, for Ss to complete the rest of the worksheet individually. Once the time is up, check the answers with the whole class.

Answer key:
1 They have just got married.
2 I haven't bought anything yet.
3 They have already left their house.
4 He has just closed his suitcase.
5 The boy has just eaten all of the chocolates.
6 The woman hasn't found a job yet.
7 They have just bought a new house.
8 The man hasn't learnt to ski yet.
9 She has already finished university.
10 The man has just turned on the water.
11 We have already spoken to the doctor.
12 They haven't booked a DJ for the party yet.
13 Have you finished your tea yet?
14 I have just been on a trip to Italy.
15 He hasn't arrived home yet.
16 We have already paid for the TV.

Grammar 2   Present perfect with *already, just* and *yet*

Materials: One worksheet per student

Instructions:

Distribute the worksheets. Tell Ss that they are each going to imagine they are a famous actor and that they must complete the first table with information about their life before they are interviewed for a magazine. Tell them that they should try to make this interesting because their fans will read the interview later and will want to know some fun details about their lives. Give Ss a time limit to do this, e.g. eight minutes. Write *already, just* and *yet* on the board and tell the class that they must use each one at least twice during their interview. Encourage them to think about how they will use them in their answers, giving them a few minutes to do this.

When they have had time to think about this, tell them that they are also going to act as an interviewer. Give Ss a few minutes to read through the interview questions in the second table and answer any questions they may have about meaning.

Put Ss in pairs to do the interviews and check that they are making notes of their partner's answers. Get pairs to change roles so that they both have a turn as interviewer and actor. Monitor and make notes of any good examples of present perfect with *just, already* and *yet* to feed back afterwards.

When the interviews have finished, put Ss in new pairs to tell each other about the information they learnt from their previous partner. Finally, ask the class who had the most interesting partner and why.

Vocabulary   Adjectives to describe films and TV programmes

Materials: One worksheet per student

Instructions:

Distribute the worksheets. Tell Ss that they must use the clues to find the missing words for each of the gaps in the crossword. Encourage them to do the easier ones first and not to look back at their class notes unless they are stuck. If there are **fast finishers**, get them to think of some examples of shows or films that could be described using the words in the crossword (except for numbers 2 and 9). Put Ss in pairs to check their answers.

Answer key:

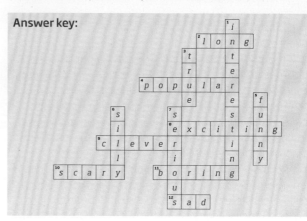

9C

Grammar 1   *could, couldn't*

Materials: One worksheet per student

Instructions:

Distribute the worksheets. Ss complete the conversation individually. Monitor and help them if necessary. Choose two **stronger Ss**, whose work you have checked for accuracy, to read out the completed conversation to the class. Put Ss in pairs to practise the conversation. Monitor to ensure *could* is not stressed in the pronunciation.

Finally, give Ss some time to discuss their own childhood experiences in relation to the text.

Answer key:

1
1 could play   2 could communicate   3 couldn't remember
4 couldn't ride   5 could (always) make   6 could sing
7 couldn't sing   8 could dance

Grammar 2   *could, couldn't*

Materials: One board per group of Ss

Instructions:

Put Ss in groups of four with two A/B groups. If the class does not divide into four, you can have some groups of five instead. Team A's objective is to get across the board from left to right; Team B's objective is to get across the board from right to left. Team A starts on any square on the left edge and Team B starts on any square on the right edge. Afterwards, they can choose any square they wish as long as it hasn't already been used correctly (see below).

When a player chooses a square, he/she must make a sentence using *could/couldn't* and the word on the square, e.g. *I could read when I was three.* If the sentence is formed correctly, the team wins the square and crosses it out. Encourage Ss to make interesting and complex sentences if possible. Sentences can be personal, but if this is challenging or too sensitive, Ss could invent sentences that are untrue or that are about other people they know.

If a team wins a square, then that square cannot be used again, so the other team will need to go around that square. Make sure that Ss understand the idea of 'blocking' their opponents' path by choosing squares that they think their opponents will use.

If there are any disputes, you should act as the referee. Try not to get involved except for refereeing purposes. Monitor and note down good examples of *could/couldn't* for past ability and discuss these with the class after the game has finished.

Vocabulary   Education

Materials: One set of cards per group of Ss

Instructions:

Put Ss in groups of two or three. Give one set of cards to each group. Tell them to put the cards face down in a pile. One student then takes a card from the top of the pack. He/she must then say a sentence about themselves using the word on the card and the correct preposition/verb from the vocabulary set in the lesson. The sentence must be correct, but doesn't have to be true. The student scores one point for a correct sentence. Another student in the group/pair can score a point if they guess correctly whether the sentence is true or false. If they are incorrect the student who said the sentence also scores a bonus point.

Before starting the activity, pick one card and demonstrate with one student how the activity works.

e.g. 'boring'

A: *I find football really boring.*

B: *That's false – you love football!*

A: *Yes, correct!*

Monitor and correct Ss as necessary.

10A

Grammar 1   First conditional

Materials: One worksheet per student

Instructions:

Distribute the worksheets. Explain the task to the class and then do sentence 1 together. Check that Ss can correctly identify the conditional part of the sentence, and remind them that sometimes the *if* clause comes first and sometimes it comes in the second part of the sentence. Also point out that they need to turn some of the sentences into negative statements. Encourage Ss to use contractions where possible. Ss complete the worksheet individually, then check answers as a class.

Answer key:
1 If he goes outside, he'll get wet.
2 If you don't eat, you'll be hungry.
3 She'll be tired if she stays up late.
4 If you work more hours, you'll make more money.
5 If you buy lunch, I'll buy dinner.
6 I won't see you as much if I move to another city.
7 If Leslie has a baby, she'll be very busy.
8 If you do yoga, you'll feel healthier.
9 I'll get better at English if I speak it every day.
10 If they arrive late, they won't catch their flight.
11 You'll pass your exams if you study hard.
12 If Andrew does exercise every day, he'll get stronger.
13 If you need some help, I'll help you.
14 I won't be able to sleep if I watch a scary film.
15 If Alison doesn't buy her ticket today, she won't see the concert.
16 If they save money, they'll be able to buy a house one day.

Grammar 2   First conditional

Materials: One card per student

Instructions:

Explain that Ss are each going to get a card with a problem or question on it. Give each student one card. If you have more than 16 Ss, you can give cards to more than one student.

Tell Ss to mingle and find a partner. Ss read out the problem or question on their card. Their partner must then reply using a first conditional to tell the speaker what they should do, and why. If you think it is necessary, write this example on the board:

A: *I might go to Anna's for dinner tonight.*

B: *That's great! If you go, you'll meet Peter, her new boyfriend.*

Ss can make any first conditional sentence they like, but it must be relevant to the problem/question. If a student meets someone with the same card, they must give different responses.

Set a time limit of about ten minutes, or until Ss have discussed most of the problems on the worksheet.

For feedback, ask the class what the best advice they received was.

An alternative way to do the activity is by telling Ss that after they speak to someone, they swap their cards, then find a new partner. Doing this, allows Ss to act the part of the person with the problem and the person giving advice.

Answer key:
Suggested answers:

a If you go, you'll spend time with your friends; If you go, you'll make Eric happy.

b If you eat it, you'll be healthy; I'll pay you ten pounds if you eat it!; If you don't eat it, mum will be angry.

c If you ask him/her what's wrong, maybe he'll/she'll talk to you about it; Maybe you'll be happier if you find another job.

d If you go to the doctor, he/she will give you some medicine; If you wait until tomorrow, maybe it will go away; I'll drive you to the doctor's if you want.

e If you go, you'll probably be able to make more money; If you go to university, you'll make a lot of friends.

f If we start watching a film now, we'll be tired in the morning; If we don't start watching the film right now, it'll be too late.

g If you buy one, you'll be able to drive to work; If you buy a car, you'll create more pollution; You'll be able to take weekend trips if you get one.

h If you go to bed early tonight, you won't feel tired tomorrow; If you sleep a little in the afternoon, you'll feel better.

i If you join a sports team, you'll meet new people; If you learn to paint, you'll be able to make gifts for your friends and family.

j If you take a course and learn new skills, you'll be able to make more money; If you find a new job, you'll be able to make more money.

k If you learn Italian, you'll be able to go on holiday to Italy and speak to local people; If you study a language, you'll learn more about a new culture.

l If we go camping this weekend, we'll get wet; If we go camping, I'll bring my new tent.

m I'll bring you some cake if you come to work today!; If you come, we'll be able to finish that project we started; If you don't go, we can go shopping!

n If you shop online, you won't need as much time; If you go in your lunch break, you'll have time.

o If you go to another country, you'll be able to practise speaking English; If you stay in your own country, you won't learn about a new culture.

p If you spend all your money, you won't have any when you're older; If you don't save some money, you won't be able to buy big things like a house or a car.

Vocabulary   Money

Materials: One bingo board per student (Remember to prepare more than one per student if you wish to play several rounds.)

Instructions:
Distribute one empty board to each student and ask the class if anyone knows how to play bingo. If they don't, tell them that they must write nine words in each of the squares. You will call out one word at a time. If they hear a word that is on their board, they cross out that word. The first person to cross out three words in a row, either horizontally, vertically or diagonally, and shout bingo!, is the winner. Tell Ss that instead of just reading out words, you are going to read out sentences with gaps in them. Explain that these gaps represent money verbs that come from the lesson. You can either say *blank* where the gaps are, or replace each gap with a silly word (e.g. *banana*) to make it fun.

Give each student one empty board and ask Ss to choose nine of the ten verbs at the top of the worksheet.

Once Ss have filled in their boards with the verbs, start the game by reading out one of the gapped sentences below. Ss cross out that word if they have it on their board. Continue reading the gapped sentences and make sure you keep track of which words

have already been covered as you go along. When someone shouts *bingo*, ask them to read the words in their winning line back to you to check they have crossed out the correct items.

To make the game more challenging, tell Ss that they need to have two lines to win, or even a T-shape. Alternatively, play more than one game.

You can use these example sentences, or you can invent your own

borrow – I've forgotten my wallet! Can I _____ some money to buy a coffee?

cash – Are you going to pay by _____ or card?

cost – Oh, this dress is beautiful! How much does it _____ ?

credit – I'm only going to use my _____ card for online shopping.

earn – Some business people get a lot of money for their work. They _____ a lot.

lend – Do you have enough money to buy your lunch? I can _____ you some.

pay for – How would you like to _____ your meal? By cash or by card?

save – I want to buy a new phone, so I really need to _____ money

spend – I love clothes, so I _____ a lot of money on shopping online every month.

waste – I think very carefully about how I spend my money. I don't like to _____ it.

10B

Grammar 1   Present and past passive

Materials: One worksheet per student

Instructions:
Distribute the worksheets and explain the task. When Ss are completing the gaps, monitor and help individuals who are having difficulty. About half of the verbs are irregular, most of which appear in the main lesson, e.g. *worn, grown, made, eaten.*
For *found* and *taken,* you could tell Ss to think back to when they were studying the present perfect if you think that will help. If necessary, provide these past participles.

Put Ss in pairs to compare answers and ask them to say whether they used the past or present passive in each case and to explain why. Then put the answers on the board for the class to check.

Ss then work with their partner to practise telling the stories themselves. Remind them that they should try to use the passives given in the story.

Answer key:
1
1 1 was found   2 was helped
2 1 was made   2 is called
3 1 was invented   2 was held
4 1 was taken   2 was bought   3 was used
5 1 was discovered   2 was used   3 is grown   4 is eaten
6 1 is called   2 were worn   3 were taken

Grammar 2   Present and past passive

Materials: One copy of worksheet A, worksheet B and worksheet C per group of Ss

Instructions:

Put Ss in groups of three and give the Ss in each group a different card (A, B or C). Allow Ss time to read through their own cards and complete the gaps with a passive form of the verb provided in the box.

Arrange Ss in new groups of three or four with other Ss who have the same worksheet. Tell them to check their answers together and to ask you for help if there are any issues.

Put Ss back in their groups of three (so that there is an A, B and C student in each group). If there are extra Ss, put weaker learners in the same group as a stronger learner with the same card.

Tell the class that they are going to test their partners. Ask them to read out their sentences and write down whether each group member thinks the answer is true or false. Tell Ss to make a note of the answers given. When they have completed all three cards, the Ss check answers as a group and the student with the most correct answers is the winner.

Answer key:

Student A
1 was born (false – in Hawaii)
2 are driven (true)
3 is grown (true)
4 was stolen (true – in 1911, but it was returned two years later)
5 are sent (false – about 18.6 billion as of 2014)
6 was held (false – It was held in Athens in 1896.)
7 was built (false – 1887–1889)
8 is used (true)

Student B
1 was found (true)
2 was written (false – by F. Scott Fitzgerald)
3 is eaten (true – Italy is 2nd)
4 is chosen (false – It is passed down through the royal family)
5 are sold (true)
6 was given (false – It was a gift from France to the US)
7 are taught (true)
8 was built (false – It was built as a mausoleum for the emperor's favourite wife)

Student C
1 was invented (true)
2 were made (false – in New Zealand)
3 is drunk (false – the most tea is drunk in China)
4 was called (true)
5 is eaten (true)
6 was taken (false – in 1826/1827 in France)
7 is spoken (false – over 360 million people)
8 are put (true)

Vocabulary   Time expressions

Materials: One worksheet per student

Instructions:

Distribute the worksheets. Tell Ss to work individually to choose the correct option in each question. Check answers as a class. Then put Ss in groups of four and tell them to discuss their options and their answers to the questions one by one. Encourage them to give as much detail as they can in their answers and to ask each other questions to lengthen and deepen the discussion.

While the groups talk, you can monitor and ask questions to show interest and prompt further discussion, and help with vocabulary if necessary.

When they have finished, ask groups to decide which question generated the most discussion in their group and briefly tell the class what they discussed.

Answer key:
1
1 ago   2 century   3 each day   4 until   5 these days
6 Nowadays   7 during   8 each year

10C

Grammar 1   Review of tenses

Materials: One worksheet per student

Instructions:

Distribute the worksheets and explain the task. Encourage Ss to think carefully about the key words in both the A and B lines so that they can work out why they need to use a particular tense.

When they have finished, put Ss in groups of three or four to check their answers together. Tell them only to ask you for help if there is an issue that they can't resolve. As this is a review and not new material, Ss should have enough knowledge to work out the correct answers together. Finally, check answers as a class.

Then put Ss in pairs to practise the mini-conversations, focusing on using contractions wherever possible.

Answer key:
1
1 will buy   2 visited   3 spend   4 am meeting   5 was going
6 have already done   7 are going to visit   8 am living
9 has just left   10 will get

Grammar 2   Review of tenses

Materials: One worksheet per student

Instructions:

Distribute the worksheets and demonstrate the activity. Write your own answer to one of the talking points in one of the circles on the worksheet, e.g. *cooking*. Ask Ss to guess which talking point it is referring to (*What were you doing last night at 8 p.m.*). Once they have guessed, tell them to ask you questions to find out more information about what you were doing, e.g.*What were you cooking? What time did you eat? Who did you eat with?* Tell the class that at the end of the activity they will report back to the class what they have learnt about their partner.

Tell the class that they should choose any six of the talking points and write corresponding answers in the circles, in a random order. They should only write a maximum of three words in each circle, preferably less. Set a time limit for this stage, e.g. four minutes. Put Ss in pairs and tell them to take turns to ask and answer questions so that they can find out what the words in the circles refer to.

When the majority of Ss have finished, put them in new pairs and ask them to tell each other what they learnt about their former partner. They should try to include as many details as they can remember.

Vocabulary   Hobbies and interests

Materials: One worksheet A and worksheet B, one 'Goal!' worksheet and one coin (or similar marker) per pair of Ss

Instructions:

Put Ss in A/B pairs and give each pair a copy of their worksheet. Tell them not to show it to each other. Write a sentence with a collocation from the lesson on the board, but include a mistake in it, e.g. *I love spending time to repair old cars*. First ask the class to point out where the collocation is in the sentence, and then ask whether it is used correctly or not (no, it should be *repairing* old cars). Tell Ss that for this task they will need to identify whether other collocations are correct or incorrect.

Demonstrate the activity and explain the rules. The object of the game is to score goals. Someone places the coin on the *Start* square. Student B reads his/her first sentence to Student A, who must identify whether the collocation in it is correct or incorrect. Answers have been provided on each player's sheet. If it is incorrect, he/she must correct it. If Student A successfully corrects the sentence, he/she moves the coin one square towards his/her goal. If not, the coin stays where it is. On Student B's turn, if he/she answers correctly, the coin is moved back towards his/her goal. When a goal is scored, the coin returns to the *Start* square.

If there are **fast finishers**, they can continue playing the game and try to make their own sentences, or they can use some other sentences from the lesson. They can read them as they are, or change a word in the collocation that their partner must try to correct. Play continues like this until all the sentences have been read out, and hopefully at least one player has been able to score a goal.

Answer key:

Student A
1 incorrect – gave up   2 correct   3 correct
4 incorrect – for fun   5 incorrect – joined
6 incorrect – part of   7 correct   8 correct

Student B
1 correct   2 incorrect – been part   3 correct   4 correct
5 incorrect – sleeping   6 correct
7 incorrect – found out about   8 incorrect – started playing